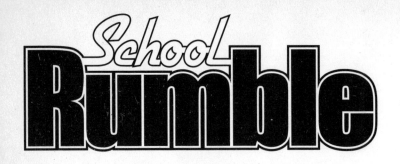

School Rumble

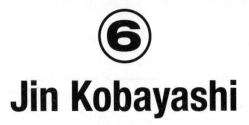

6

Jin Kobayashi

TRANSLATED AND ADAPTED BY
William Flanagan

LETTERED BY
Michaelis/Carpelis Design

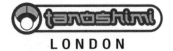

LONDON

Published in the United Kingdom by Tanoshimi in 2007

1 3 5 7 9 10 8 6 4 2

School Rumble, Volume 6 is a work of fiction. Names, characters, places and incidents are the products of the author's imagination or are used fictitiously. Any resemblance to actual events, locales, or persons, living or dead, is entirely coincidental.

First published in Japan by Kodansha Ltd., Tokyo in 2004

Published by arrangement with Kodansha Ltd., Tokyo and with Del Rey, an imprint of Random House Inc., New York

Tanoshimi
The Random House Group Limited
20 Vauxhall Bridge Road, London, SW1V 2SA

www.tanoshimi.tv
www.rbooks.co.uk

Addresses for companies within The Random House Group Limited can be found at: www.randomhouse.co.uk

Random House Group Limited Reg. No. 954009

A CIP catalogue record for this book is available from the British Library

ISBN 9780099506652

The Random House Group Limited makes every effort to ensure that the papers used in its books are made from trees that have been legally sourced from well-managed and credibly certified forests. Our paper procurement policy can be found at: www.randomhouse.co.uk/paper.htm

Printed and bound in Germany by GGP Media GmbH, Pößneck

Translator and adaptor – William Flanagan
Lettering – Michaelis/Carpelis Design

Honorifics Explained

Throughout the Tanoshimi Manga books, you will find Japanese honorifics left intact in the translations. For those not familiar with how the Japanese use honorifics and, more important, how they differ from English honorifics, we present this brief overview.

Politeness has always been a critical facet of Japanese culture. Ever since the feudal era, when Japan was a highly stratified society, use of honorifics—which can be defined as polite speech that indicates relationship or status—has played an essential role in the Japanese language. When addressing someone in Japanese, an honorific usually takes the form of a suffix attached to one's name (example: "Asuna-san"), or as a title at the end of one's name, or in place of the name itself (example: "Negi-sensei," or simply "Sensei!").

Honorifics can be expressions of respect or endearment. In the context of manga and anime, honorifics give insight into the nature of the relationship between characters. Many English translations leave out these important honorifics, and therefore distort the feel of the original Japanese. Because Japanese honorifics contain nuances that English honorifics lack, it is our policy at Tanoshimi not to translate them. Here, instead, is a guide to some of the honorifics you may encounter in Tanoshimi Manga.

-san: This is the most common honorific, and is equivalent to Mr., Miss, Ms., or Mrs. It is the all-purpose honorific and can be used in any situation where politeness is required.

-sama: This is one level higher than "-san" and is used to confer great respect.

-dono: This comes from the word "tono" which means "lord." It is an even higher level than "-sama" and confers utmost respect.

-kun: This suffix is used at the end of boys' names to express familiarity or endearment. It is also sometimes used by men among friends, or when addressing someone younger or of a lower station.

-chan: This is used to express endearment, mostly toward girls. It is also used for little boys, pets, and even among lovers. It gives a sense of childish cuteness.

-Bozu: This is an informal way to refer to a boy, similar to the English terms "kid".

-Sempai/Senpai: This title suggests that the addressee is one's senior in a group or organization. It is most often used in a school setting, where underclassmen refer to their upperclassmen as "sempai." It can also be used in the workplace, such as when a newer employee addresses an employee who has seniority in the company.

Kohai: This is the opposite of "-sempai" and is used toward underclassmen in school or newcomers in the workplace. It connotes that the addressee is of a lower station.

Sensei: Literally meaning "one who has come before," this title is used for teachers, doctors, or masters of any profession or art.

[blank]: This is usually forgotten in these lists, but it is perhaps the most significant difference between Japanese and English. The lack of honorific means that the speaker has permission to address the person in a very intimate way. Usually, only family, spouses, or very close friends have this kind of permission. Known as yobisute, it can be gratifying when someone who has earned the intimacy starts to call one by one's name without an honorific. But when that intimacy hasn't been earned, it can be very insulting.

Cultural Note

To preserve some of the humor found in *School Rumble*, we have elected to keep Japanese names in their original Japanese order—that is to say, with the family name first, followed by the personal name. So when you hear the name Tsukamoto Tenma, Tenma is just one member of the Tsukamoto family.

School Rumble 6

Jin Kobayashi

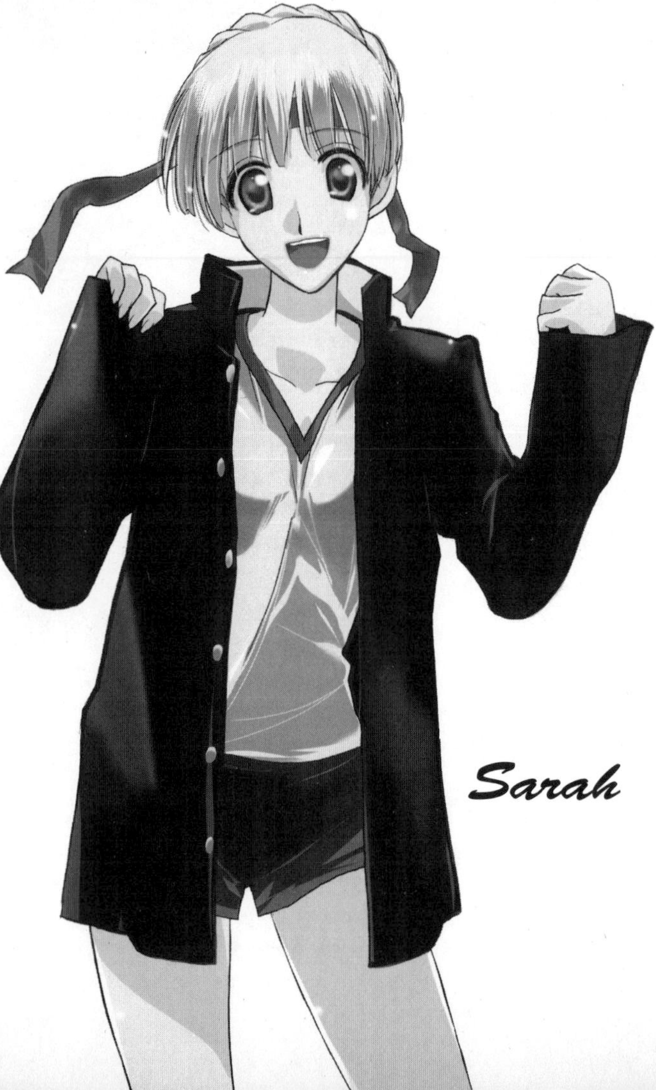
Sarah

Contents

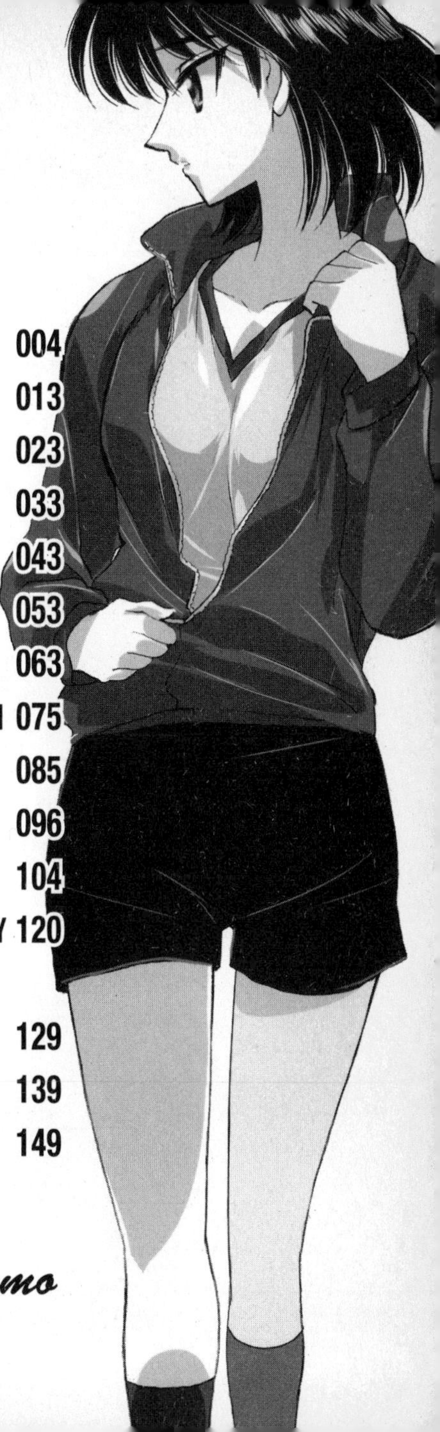

Yakumo

あらすじ *Story*

Tsukamoto Tenma is in her second year of high school. She is our heroine, and like many, many girls her age, she is in love. However, she can't seem to make her feelings known to Karasuma Ôji, her classmate and the man she loves. And that's pretty much the setup. Tenma did dropkicks, and Harima's beard went away, but with everything going on, Karasuma didn't even appear in Volume 5! Yeah, I can get all angry over it, but we're here in Volume 6. Well, don't forget that this is a romantic comedy, and just hang on to your hat and come along for the ride. Yo!

登場人物 *Characters*

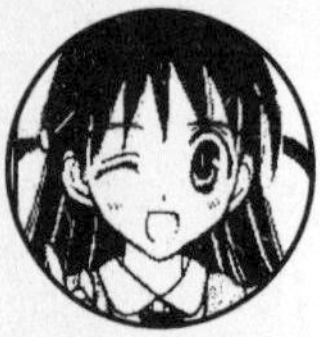

Tsukamoto Tenma

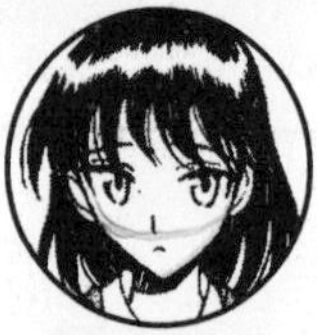

Tsukamoto Yakumo

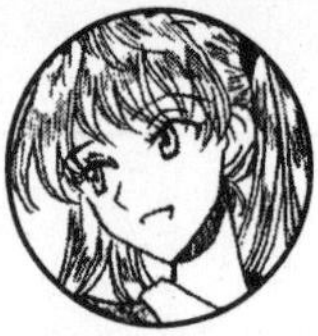

Sawachika Eri

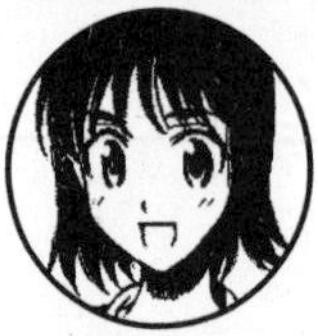

Suô Mikoto

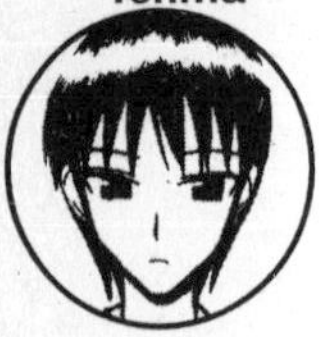

Takano Akira

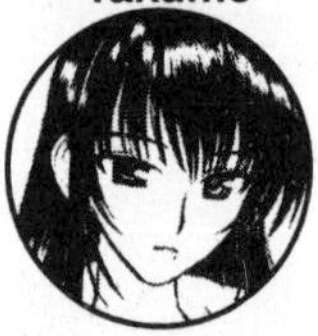

Osakabe Itoko

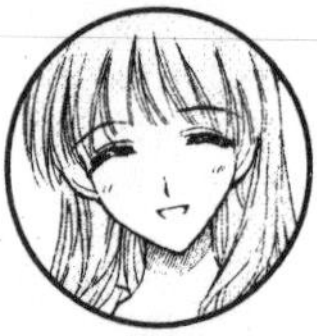

Anegasaki Tae

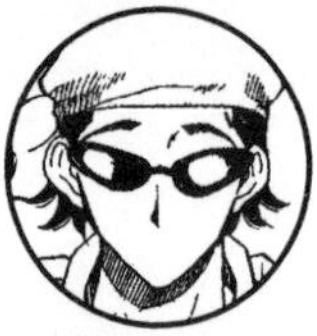

Harima Kenji

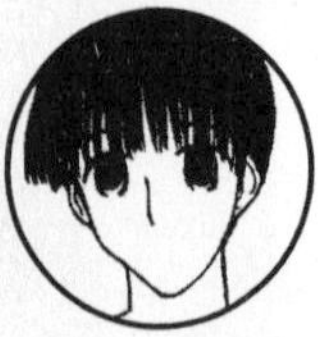

Karasuma Ôji

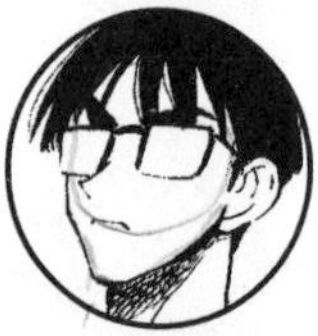

Hanai Haruki

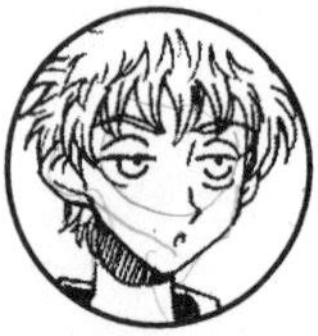

Imadori Kyô-suke

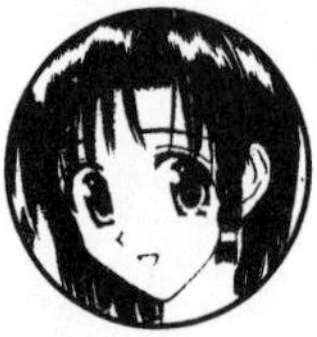

Ichijô Karen

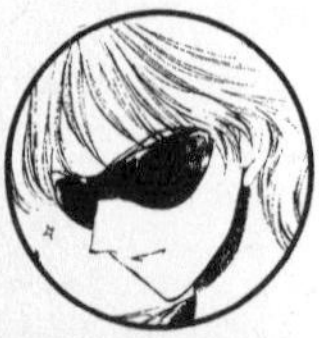

Harry McKenzie

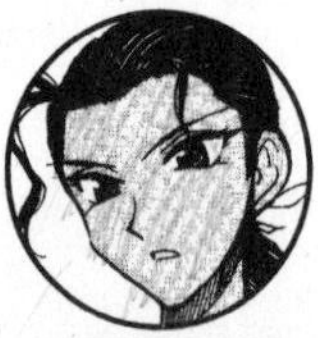

Lala Gonzalez

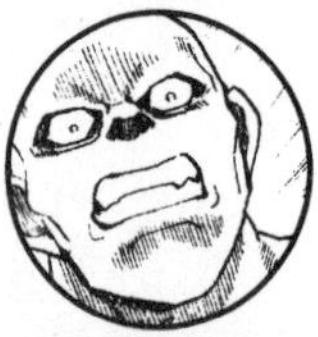

Tennôji Noboru

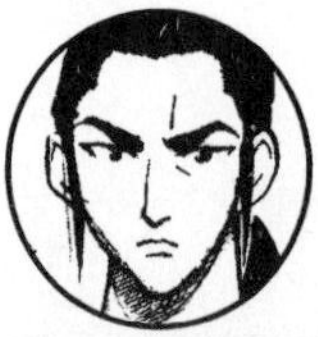

Tôgô Masakazu

73 COOKIE'S FORTUNE

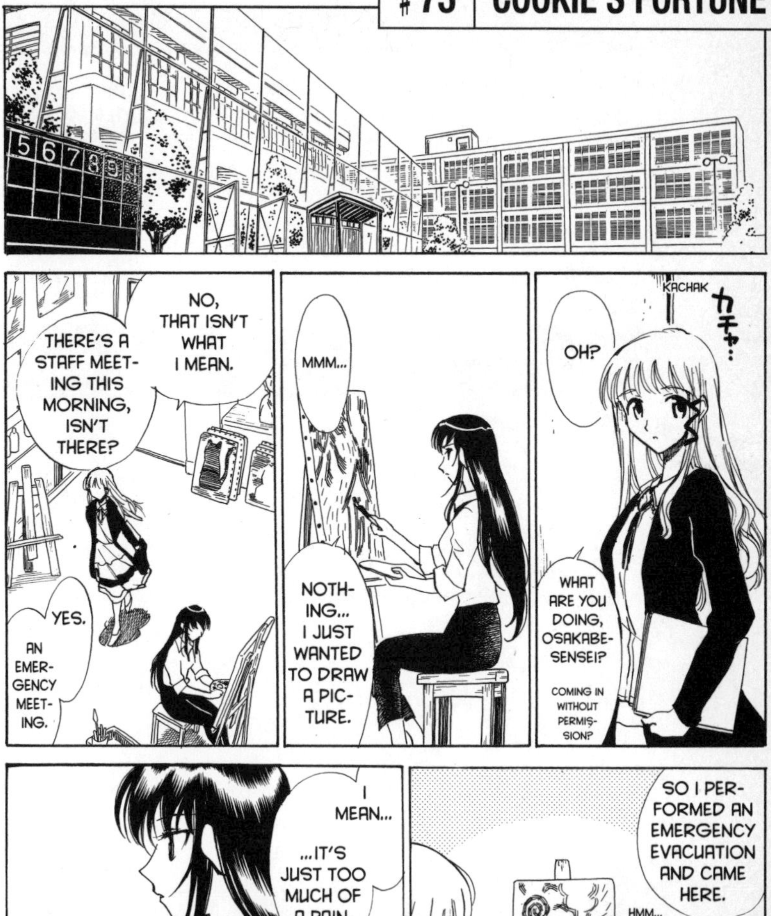

5 6 7 8 9
KACHAK
カチャ…
OH?
WHAT ARE YOU DOING, OSAKABE-SENSEI?
COMING IN WITHOUT PERMISSION?
MMM...
NOTHING... I JUST WANTED TO DRAW A PICTURE.
NO, THAT ISN'T WHAT I MEAN.
THERE'S A STAFF MEETING THIS MORNING, ISN'T THERE?
YES.
AN EMERGENCY MEETING.
SO I PERFORMED AN EMERGENCY EVACUATION AND CAME HERE.
HMM...
AHH! THIS IS TOO HARD!
I'M SURPRISED YOU DRAW SO MUCH.
..... THAT WAS MY PAINTING.
I MEAN...
...IT'S JUST TOO MUCH OF A PAIN.
?

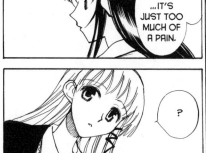

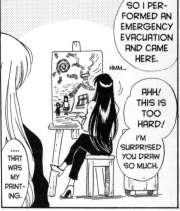

Harima: The Victim, but Treated as the Perpetrator.

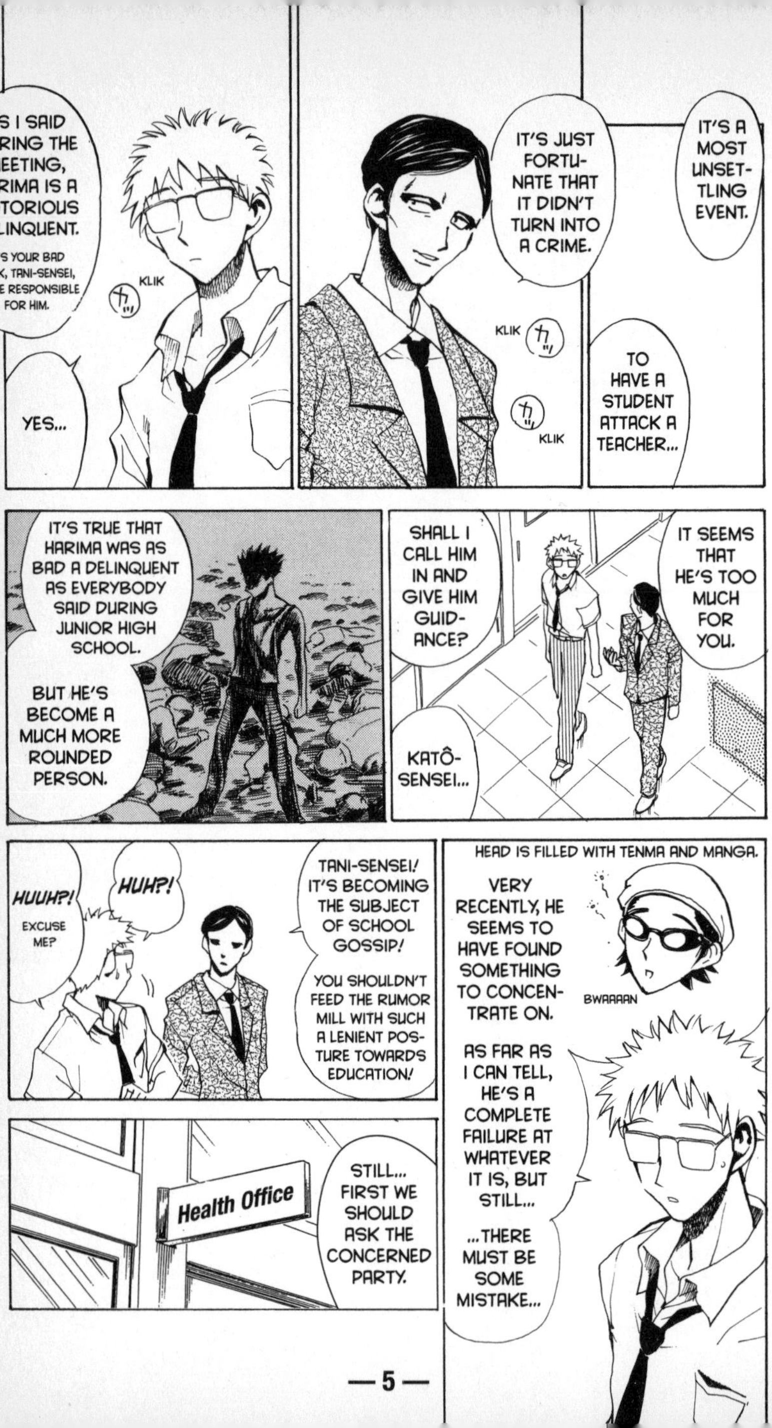
IT'S A MOST UNSETTLING EVENT.
TO HAVE A STUDENT ATTACK A TEACHER...
IT'S JUST FORTUNATE THAT IT DIDN'T TURN INTO A CRIME.
KLIK
KLIK
AS I SAID DURING THE MEETING, HARIMA IS A NOTORIOUS DELINQUENT.
IT'S YOUR BAD LUCK, TANI-SENSEI, TO BE RESPONSIBLE FOR HIM.
KLIK
YES...
IT SEEMS THAT HE'S TOO MUCH FOR YOU.
SHALL I CALL HIM IN AND GIVE HIM GUIDANCE?
KATÔ-SENSEI...
IT'S TRUE THAT HARIMA WAS AS BAD A DELINQUENT AS EVERYBODY SAID DURING JUNIOR HIGH SCHOOL.
BUT HE'S BECOME A MUCH MORE ROUNDED PERSON.
HEAD IS FILLED WITH TENMA AND MANGA.
VERY RECENTLY, HE SEEMS TO HAVE FOUND SOMETHING TO CONCENTRATE ON.
BWAAAAN
AS FAR AS I CAN TELL, HE'S A COMPLETE FAILURE AT WHATEVER IT IS, BUT STILL...
...THERE MUST BE SOME MISTAKE...
TANI-SENSEI! IT'S BECOMING THE SUBJECT OF SCHOOL GOSSIP!
YOU SHOULDN'T FEED THE RUMOR MILL WITH SUCH A LENIENT POSTURE TOWARDS EDUCATION!
HUH?!
HUUH?!
EXCUSE ME?
STILL... FIRST WE SHOULD ASK THE CONCERNED PARTY.
Health Office

The Woman: Taking a Nap.

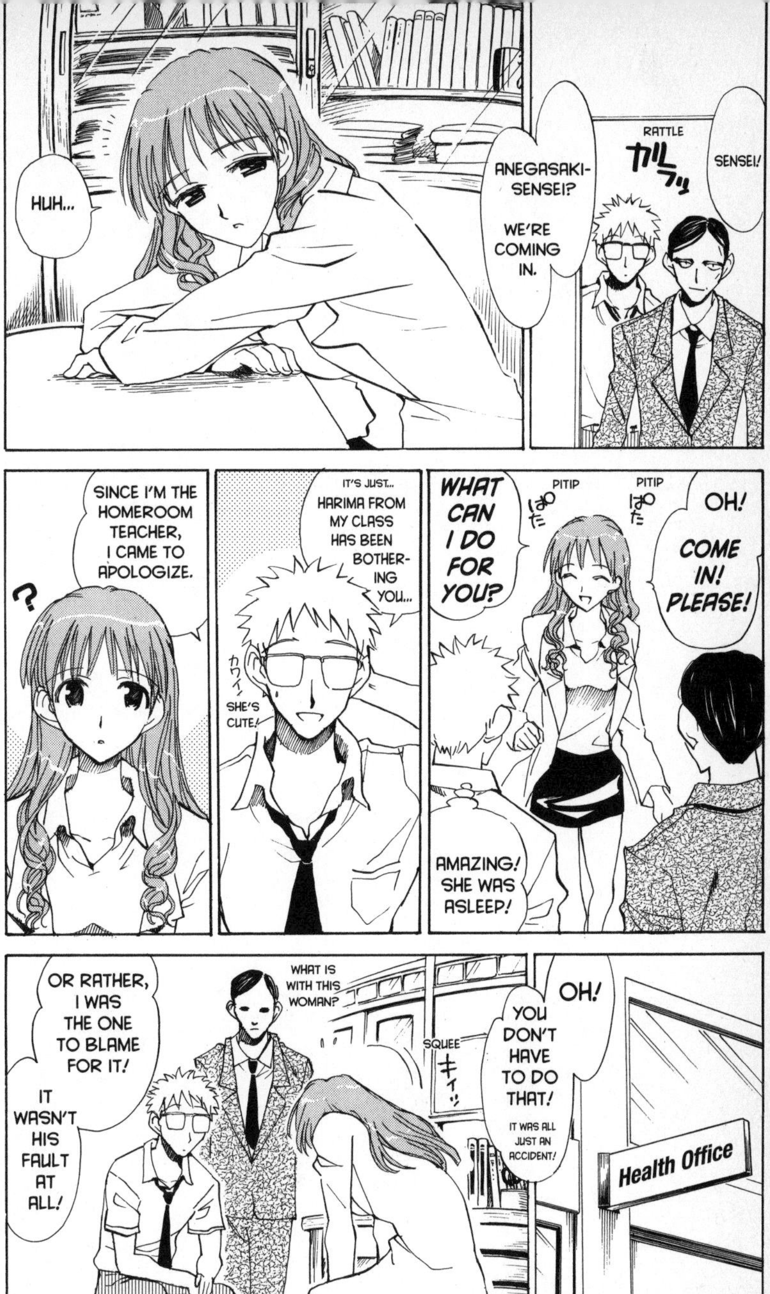
SENSEI!
RATTLE
ANEGASAKI-SENSEI?
WE'RE COMING IN.
HUH...
OH!
COME IN! PLEASE!
PITIP
PITIP
WHAT CAN I DO FOR YOU?
AMAZING! SHE WAS ASLEEP!
IT'S JUST... HARIMA FROM MY CLASS HAS BEEN BOTHERING YOU...
SHE'S CUTE!
SINCE I'M THE HOMEROOM TEACHER, I CAME TO APOLOGIZE.
?
OH!
YOU DON'T HAVE TO DO THAT!
IT WAS ALL JUST AN ACCIDENT!
Health Office
SQUEE
WHAT IS WITH THIS WOMAN?
OR RATHER, I WAS THE ONE TO BLAME FOR IT!
IT WASN'T HIS FAULT AT ALL!

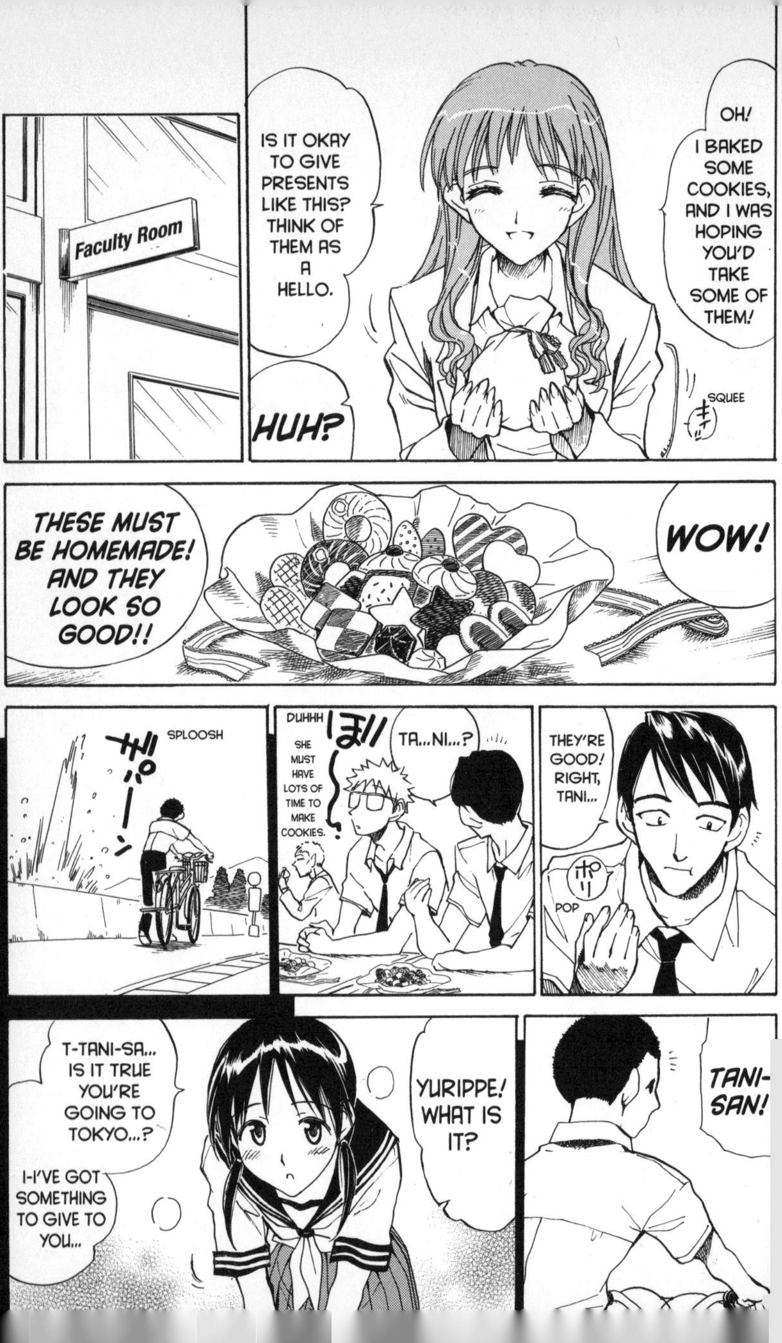
OH! I BAKED SOME COOKIES, AND I WAS HOPING YOU'D TAKE SOME OF THEM!
SQUEE
IS IT OKAY TO GIVE PRESENTS LIKE THIS? THINK OF THEM AS A HELLO.
HUH?
Faculty Room
WOW!
THESE MUST BE HOMEMADE! AND THEY LOOK SO GOOD!!
THEY'RE GOOD! RIGHT, TANI...
POP
TA...NI...?
DUHHH
SHE MUST HAVE LOTS OF TIME TO MAKE COOKIES.
SPLOOSH
TANI-SAN!
YURIPPE! WHAT IS IT?
T-TANI-SA... IS IT TRUE YOU'RE GOING TO TOKYO...?
I-I'VE GOT SOMETHING TO GIVE TO YOU...

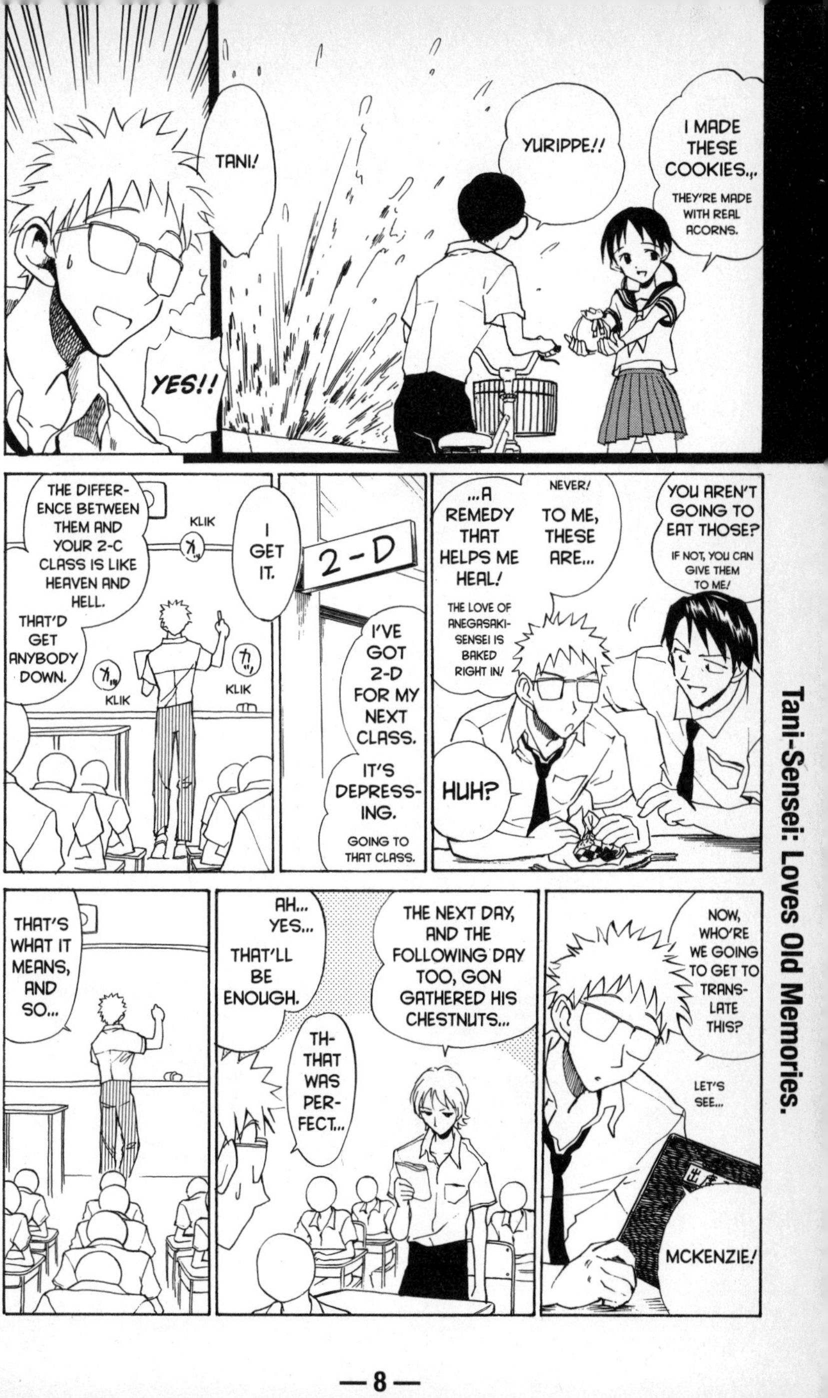
I MADE THESE COOKIES...
THEY'RE MADE WITH REAL ACORNS.
YURIPPE!!
TANI!
YES!!
YOU AREN'T GOING TO EAT THOSE?
IF NOT, YOU CAN GIVE THEM TO ME!
NEVER!
TO ME, THESE ARE...
...A REMEDY THAT HELPS ME HEAL!
THE LOVE OF ANEGASAKI-SENSEI IS BAKED RIGHT IN!
HUH?
2-D
I'VE GOT 2-D FOR MY NEXT CLASS.
IT'S DEPRESS-ING.
GOING TO THAT CLASS.
I GET IT.
THE DIFFER-ENCE BETWEEN THEM AND YOUR 2-C CLASS IS LIKE HEAVEN AND HELL.
KLIK
THAT'D GET ANYBODY DOWN.
KLIK
KLIK
NOW, WHO'RE WE GOING TO GET TO TRANS-LATE THIS?
LET'S SEE...
MCKENZIE!
THE NEXT DAY, AND THE FOLLOWING DAY TOO, GON GATHERED HIS CHESTNUTS...
AH... YES... THAT'LL BE ENOUGH.
TH-THAT WAS PER-FECT...
THAT'S WHAT IT MEANS, AND SO...

Tôgô Masakazu: Speaks a Little Like an Old Man.

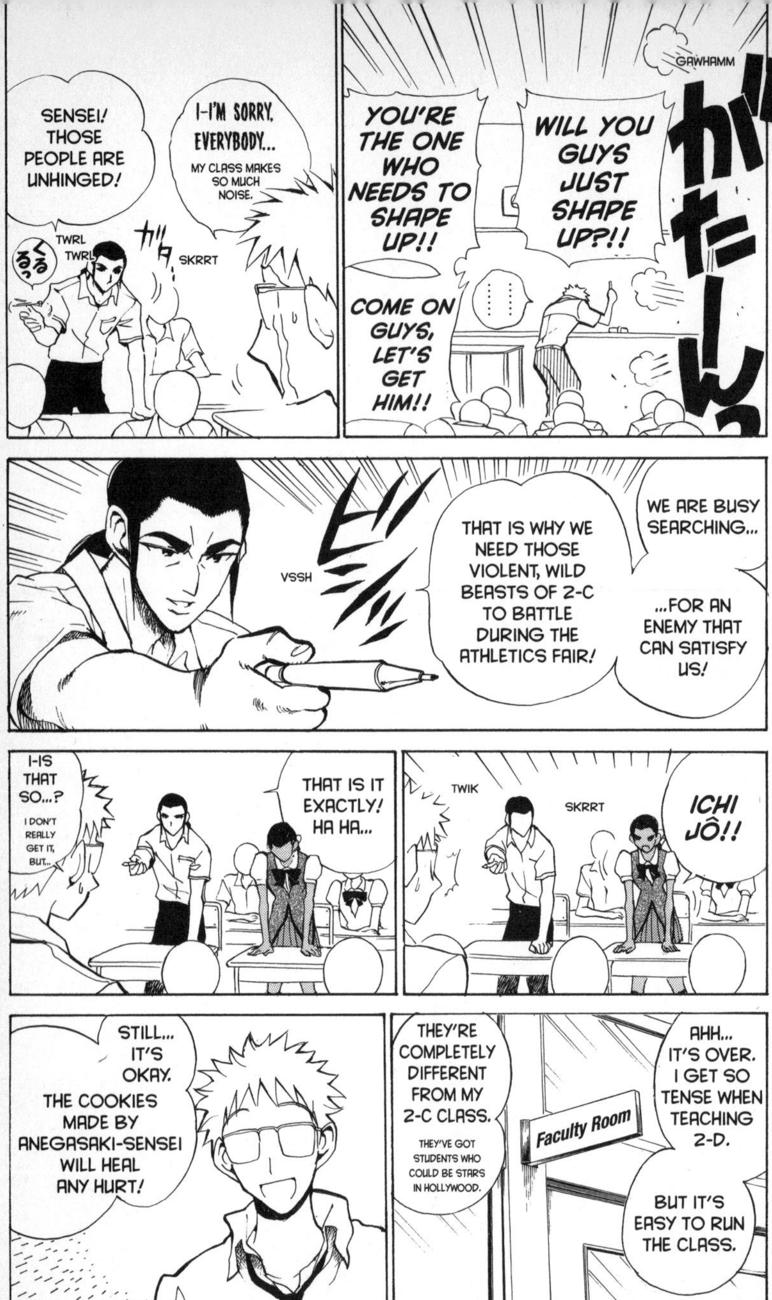
がたーんっ
GAWHAMM
WILL YOU GUYS JUST SHAPE UP?!!
YOU'RE THE ONE WHO NEEDS TO SHAPE UP!!
COME ON GUYS, LET'S GET HIM!!
I-I'M SORRY, EVERYBODY... MY CLASS MAKES SO MUCH NOISE.
SENSEI! THOSE PEOPLE ARE UNHINGED!
ガタ
SKRRT
くるっ
TWRL TWRL
WE ARE BUSY SEARCHING...
...FOR AN ENEMY THAT CAN SATISFY US!
THAT IS WHY WE NEED THOSE VIOLENT, WILD BEASTS OF 2-C TO BATTLE DURING THE ATHLETICS FAIR!
VSSH
ICHI JÔ!!
SKRRT
TWIK
THAT IS IT EXACTLY! HA HA...
I-IS THAT SO...? I DON'T REALLY GET IT, BUT...
AHH... IT'S OVER. I GET SO TENSE WHEN TEACHING 2-D.
BUT IT'S EASY TO RUN THE CLASS.
Faculty Room
THEY'RE COMPLETELY DIFFERENT FROM MY 2-C CLASS. THEY'VE GOT STUDENTS WHO COULD BE STARS IN HOLLYWOOD.
STILL... IT'S OKAY. THE COOKIES MADE BY ANEGASAKI-SENSEI WILL HEAL ANY HURT!

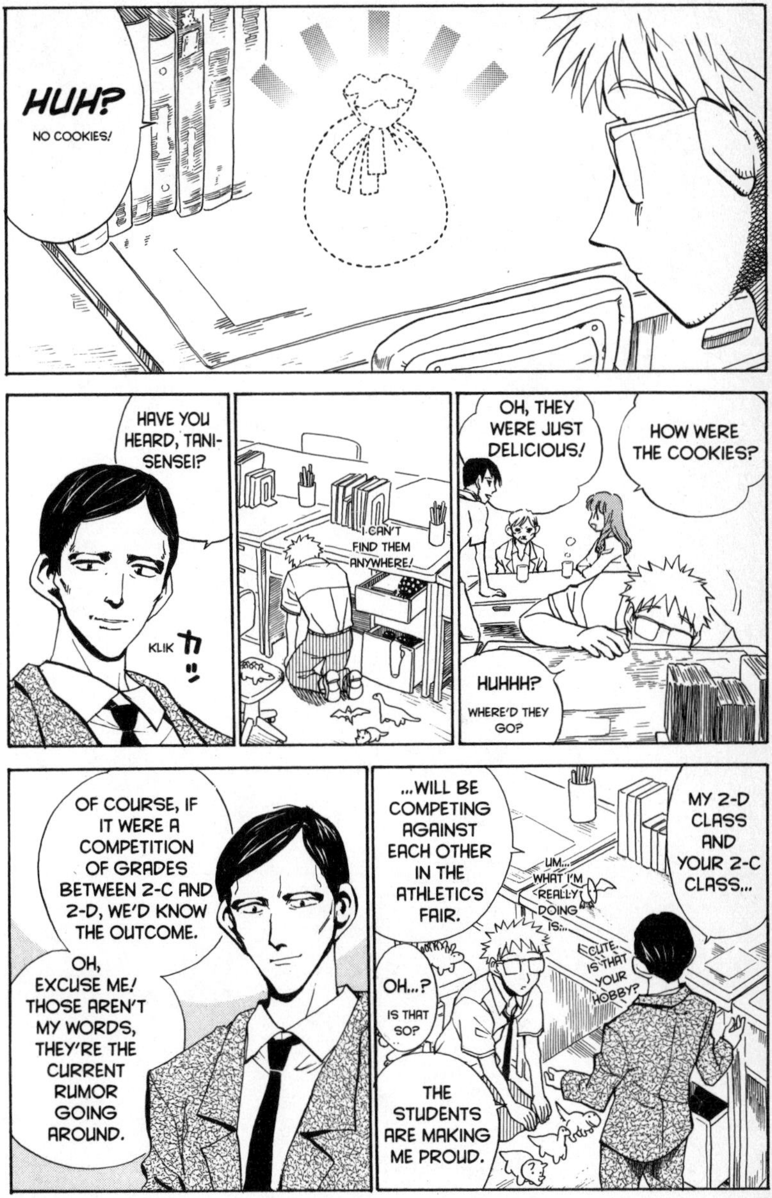
HUH?
NO COOKIES!
HOW WERE THE COOKIES?
OH, THEY WERE JUST DELICIOUS!
HUHHH?
WHERE'D THEY GO?
I CAN'T FIND THEM ANYWHERE!
HAVE YOU HEARD, TANI-SENSEI?
KLIK
カッ
MY 2-D CLASS AND YOUR 2-C CLASS...
...WILL BE COMPETING AGAINST EACH OTHER IN THE ATHLETICS FAIR.
UM... WHAT I'M REALLY DOING IS...
CUTE. IS THAT YOUR HOBBY?
OH...?
IS THAT SO?
THE STUDENTS ARE MAKING ME PROUD.
OF COURSE, IF IT WERE A COMPETITION OF GRADES BETWEEN 2-C AND 2-D, WE'D KNOW THE OUTCOME.
OH, EXCUSE ME! THOSE AREN'T MY WORDS, THEY'RE THE CURRENT RUMOR GOING AROUND.

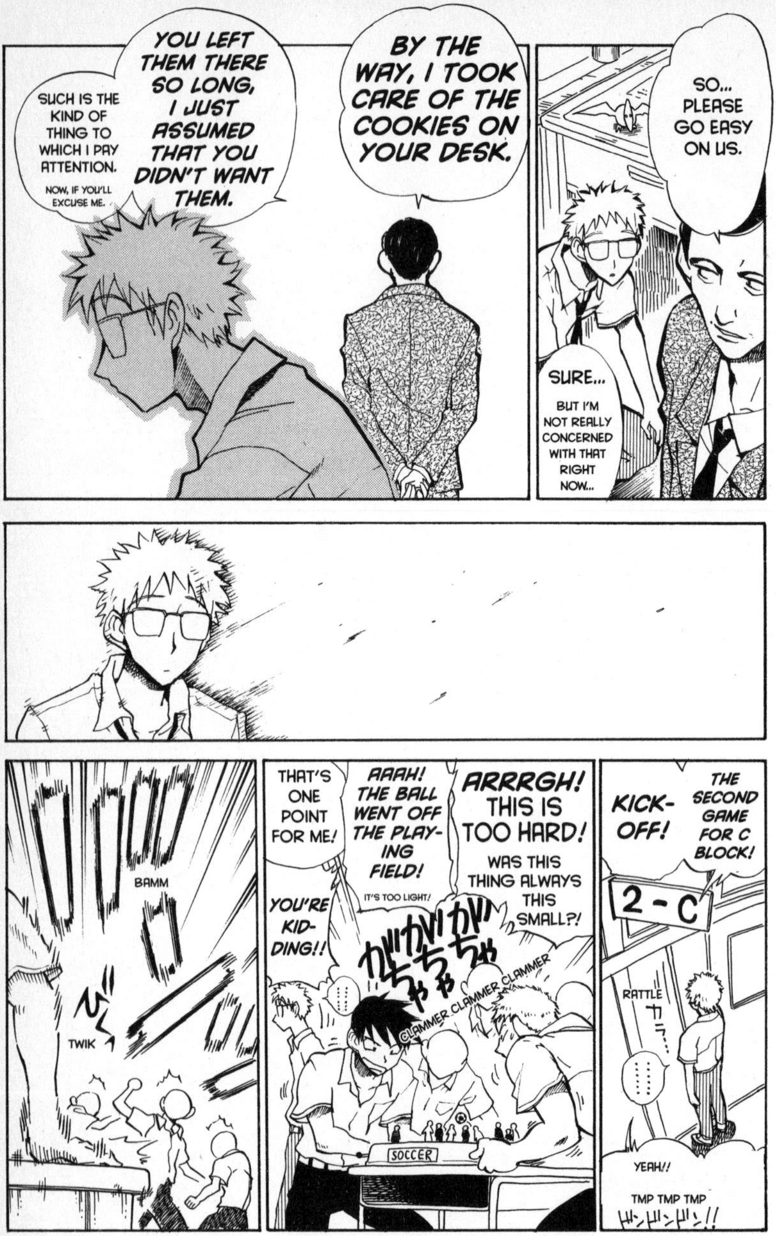
SO... PLEASE GO EASY ON US.
SURE...
BUT I'M NOT REALLY CONCERNED WITH THAT RIGHT NOW...
BY THE WAY, I TOOK CARE OF THE COOKIES ON YOUR DESK.
YOU LEFT THEM THERE SO LONG, I JUST ASSUMED THAT YOU DIDN'T WANT THEM.
SUCH IS THE KIND OF THING TO WHICH I PAY ATTENTION.
NOW, IF YOU'LL EXCUSE ME.
THE SECOND GAME FOR C BLOCK!
KICK-OFF!
2 - C
RATTLE
......
YEAH!!
TMP TMP TMP
ARRRGH! THIS IS TOO HARD!
WAS THIS THING ALWAYS THIS SMALL?!
AAAH! THE BALL WENT OFF THE PLAY-ING FIELD!
IT'S TOO LIGHT!
THAT'S ONE POINT FOR ME!
YOU'RE KID-DING!!
CLAMMER CLAMMER CLAMMER
......
SOCCER
BAMM
TWIK

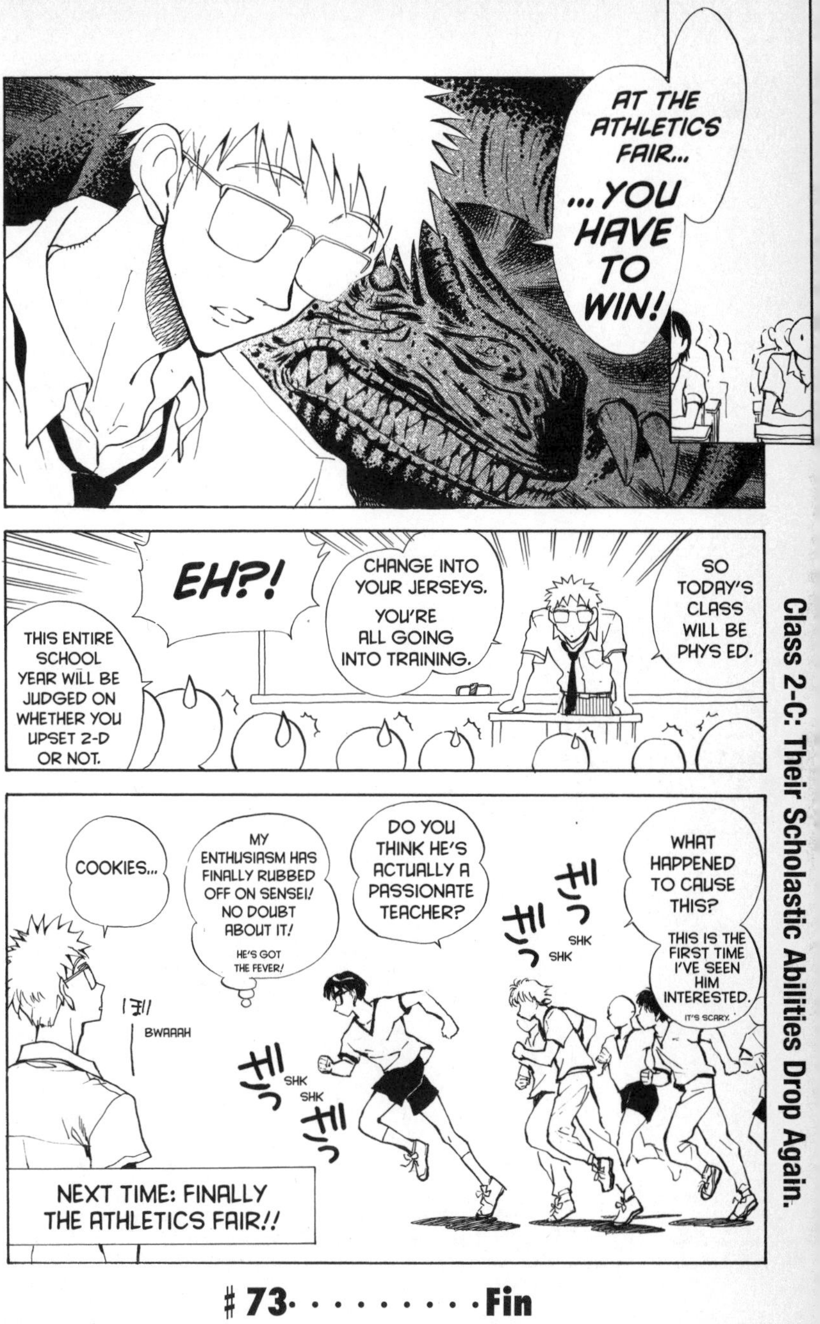
AT THE ATHLETICS FAIR...
...YOU HAVE TO WIN!
SO TODAY'S CLASS WILL BE PHYS ED.
CHANGE INTO YOUR JERSEYS.
YOU'RE ALL GOING INTO TRAINING.
EH?!
THIS ENTIRE SCHOOL YEAR WILL BE JUDGED ON WHETHER YOU UPSET 2-D OR NOT.
WHAT HAPPENED TO CAUSE THIS?
THIS IS THE FIRST TIME I'VE SEEN HIM INTERESTED.
IT'S SCARY.
SHK
SHK
DO YOU THINK HE'S ACTUALLY A PASSIONATE TEACHER?
MY ENTHUSIASM HAS FINALLY RUBBED OFF ON SENSEI! NO DOUBT ABOUT IT!
HE'S GOT THE FEVER!
COOKIES...
BWAAAH
SHK
SHK
NEXT TIME: FINALLY THE ATHLETICS FAIR!!

Class 2-C: Their Scholastic Abilities Drop Again.

 # 73· · · · · · · · · ·Fin

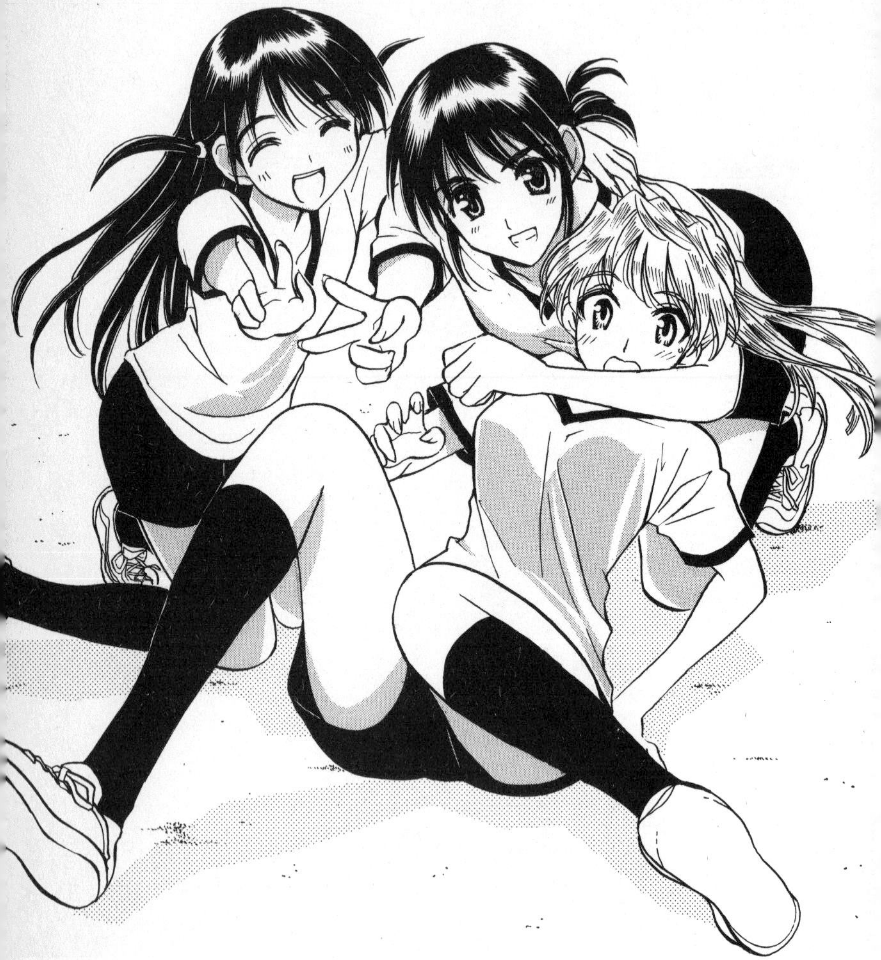

#74 WINNING

<Opening Ceremonies>

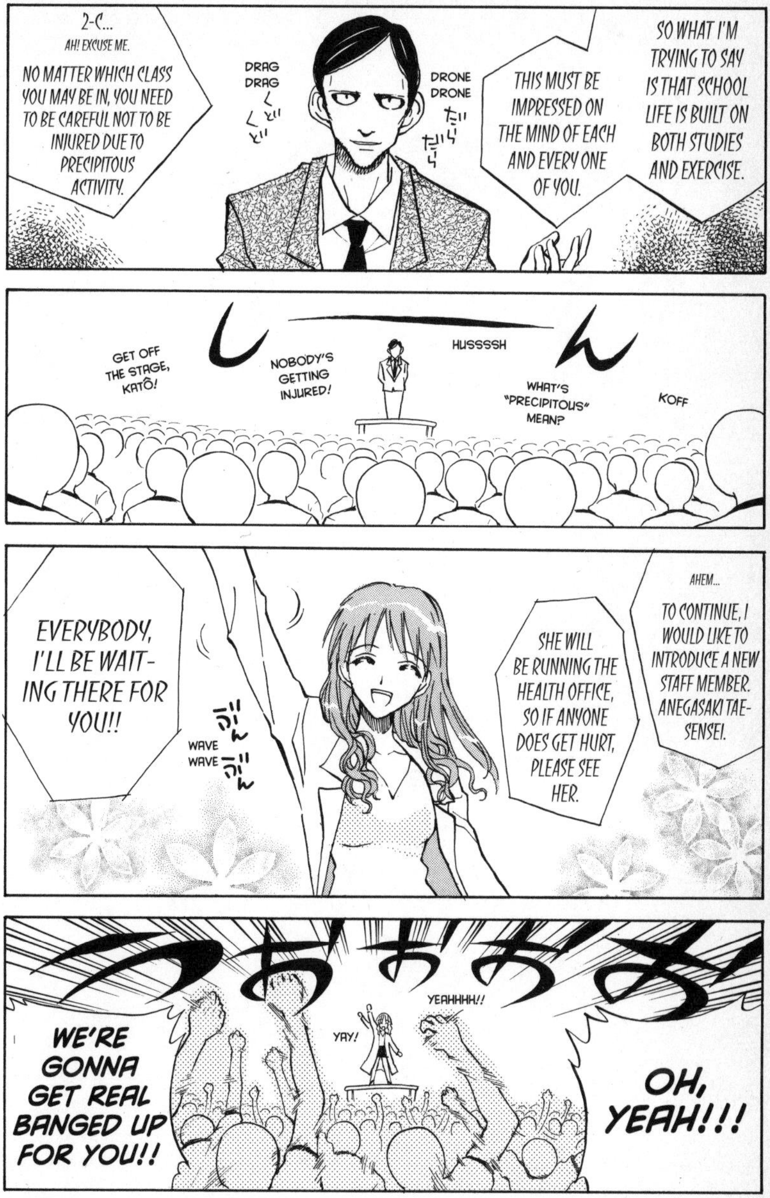
SO WHAT I'M TRYING TO SAY IS THAT SCHOOL LIFE IS BUILT ON BOTH STUDIES AND EXERCISE.
THIS MUST BE IMPRESSED ON THE MIND OF EACH AND EVERY ONE OF YOU.
DRONE DRONE
DRAG DRAG
2-C...
AH! EXCUSE ME.
NO MATTER WHICH CLASS YOU MAY BE IN, YOU NEED TO BE CAREFUL NOT TO BE INJURED DUE TO PRECIPITOUS ACTIVITY.
KOFF
WHAT'S "PRECIPITOUS" MEAN?
HUSSSSH
NOBODY'S GETTING INJURED!
GET OFF THE STAGE, KATÔ!
AHEM...
TO CONTINUE, I WOULD LIKE TO INTRODUCE A NEW STAFF MEMBER. ANEGASAKI TAE-SENSEI.
SHE WILL BE RUNNING THE HEALTH OFFICE, SO IF ANYONE DOES GET HURT, PLEASE SEE HER.
WAVE WAVE
EVERYBODY, I'LL BE WAITING THERE FOR YOU!!
YEAHHHH!!
OH, YEAH!!!
YAY!
WE'RE GONNA GET REAL BANGED UP FOR YOU!!

Woman: Figures that She'd Be an Airhead.

<Grudge Matches Abound>

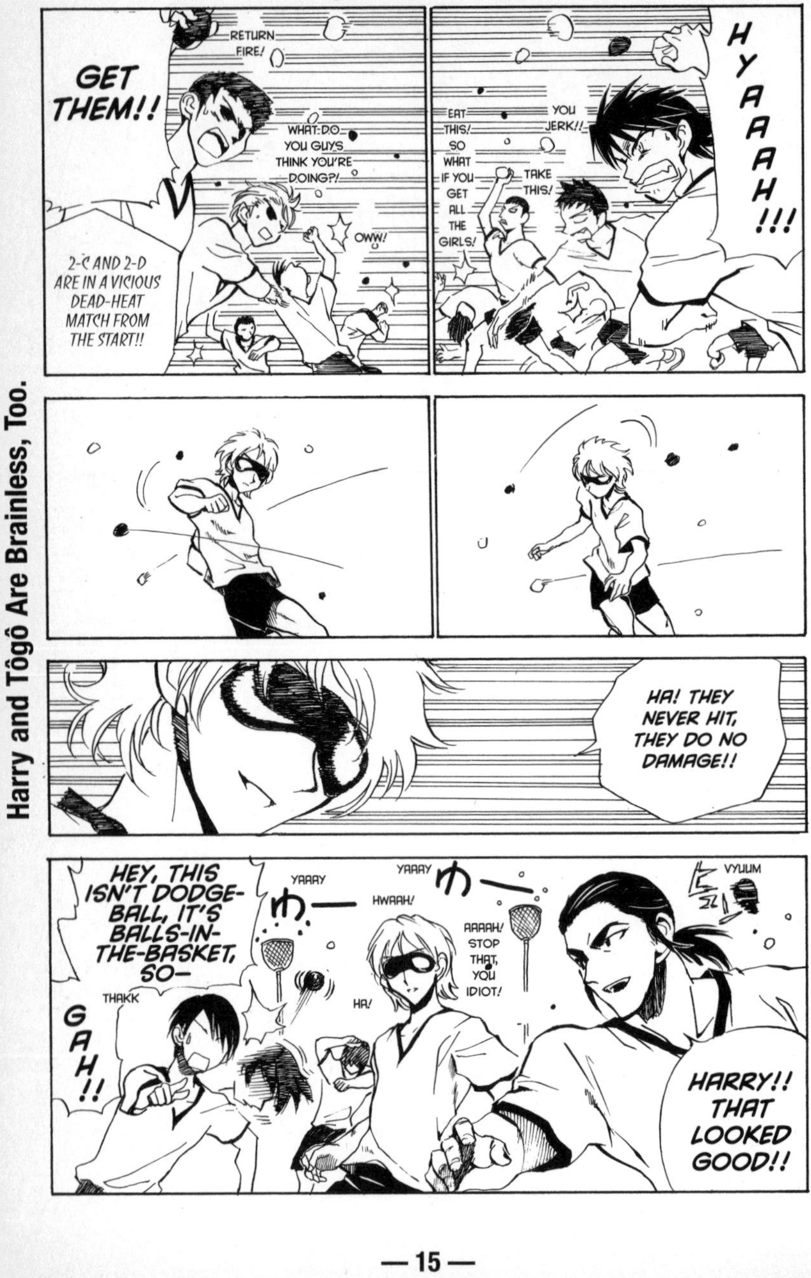

HYAAAH!!!
YOU JERK!!
EAT THIS! SO WHAT IF YOU GET ALL THE GIRLS!
TAKE THIS!
RETURN FIRE!
GET THEM!!
WHAT DO YOU GUYS THINK YOU'RE DOING?!
OWW!
2-C AND 2-D ARE IN A VICIOUS DEAD-HEAT MATCH FROM THE START!!
HA! THEY NEVER HIT, THEY DO NO DAMAGE!!
VYUUM
HARRY!! THAT LOOKED GOOD!!
ゆー
YAAAY
AAAAH! STOP THAT, YOU IDIOT!
HWAAH!
YAAAY
ゆー
HA!
HEY, THIS ISN'T DODGE-BALL, IT'S BALLS-IN-THE-BASKET, SO—
THAKK
GAH!!

Harry and Tôgô Are Brainless, Too.

<Nara-kun's Ambition>

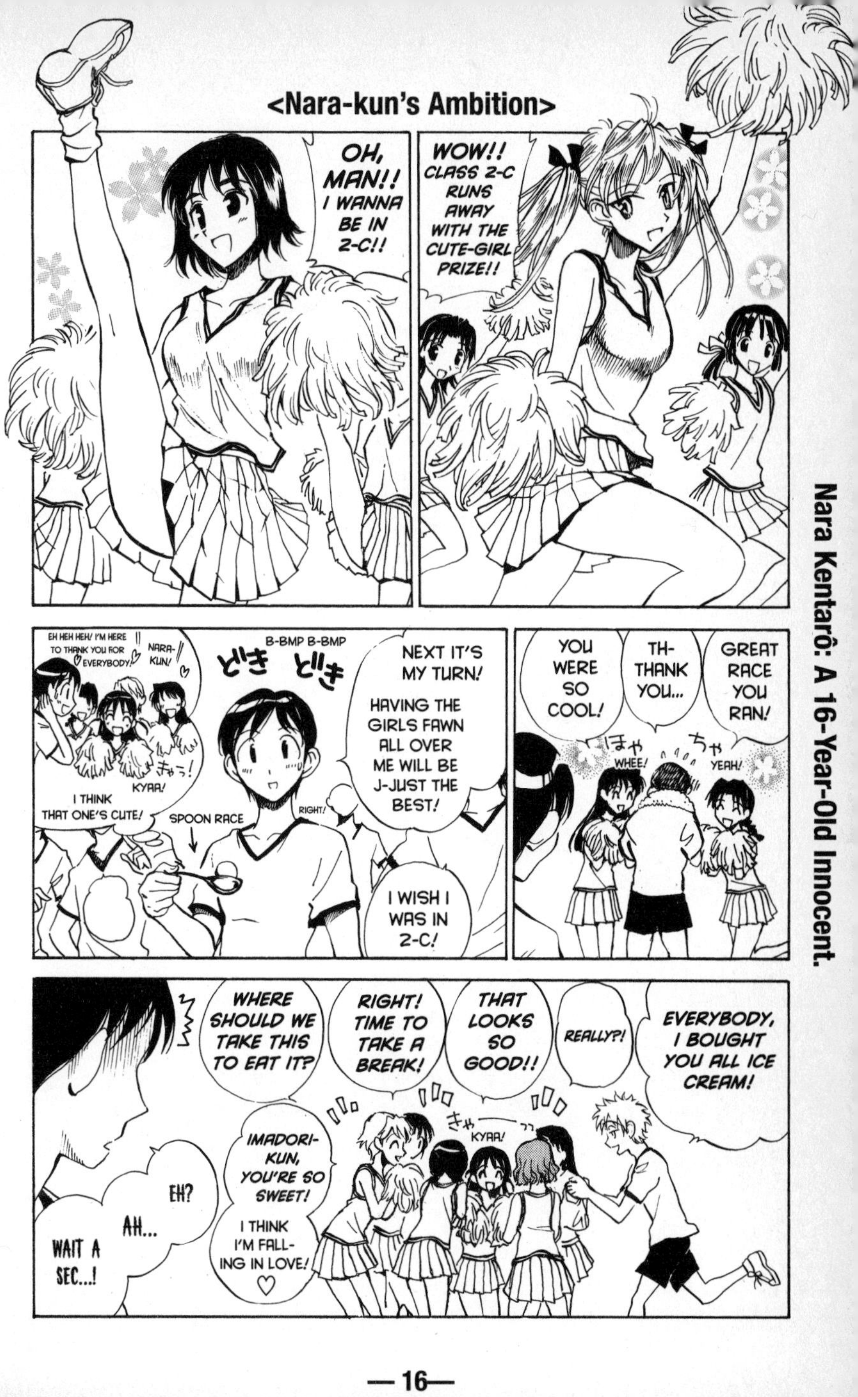
WOW!! CLASS 2-C RUNS AWAY WITH THE CUTE-GIRL PRIZE!!
OH, MAN!! I WANNA BE IN 2-C!!
GREAT RACE YOU RAN!
TH-THANK YOU...
YOU WERE SO COOL!
ちゃ
YEAH!
ほゃ
WHEE!
NEXT IT'S MY TURN!
HAVING THE GIRLS FAWN ALL OVER ME WILL BE J-JUST THE BEST!
I WISH I WAS IN 2-C!
どき どき
B-BMP B-BMP
RIGHT!
SPOON RACE
NARA-KUN!
EH HEH HEH! I'M HERE TO THANK YOU FOR EVERYBODY!
きゃっ!
KYAA!
I THINK THAT ONE'S CUTE!
EVERYBODY, I BOUGHT YOU ALL ICE CREAM!
REALLY?!
THAT LOOKS SO GOOD!!
RIGHT! TIME TO TAKE A BREAK!
WHERE SHOULD WE TAKE THIS TO EAT IT?
きゃー
KYAA!
IMADORI-KUN, YOU'RE SO SWEET!
I THINK I'M FALL-ING IN LOVE! ♡
EH?
AH...
WAIT A SEC...!

Nara Kentarô: A 16-Year-Old Innocent.

<Lala, Making the Effort>

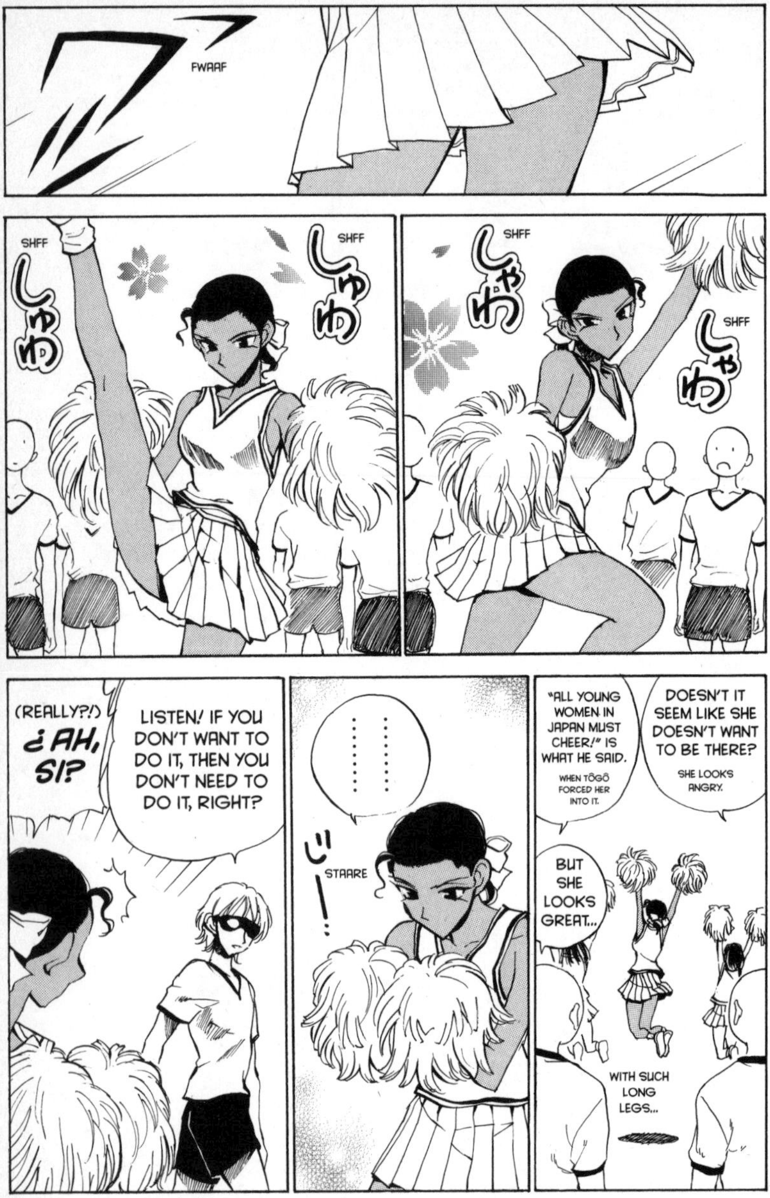
FWAAF
SHFF
SHFF
SHFF
SHFF
DOESN'T IT SEEM LIKE SHE DOESN'T WANT TO BE THERE?
SHE LOOKS ANGRY.
"ALL YOUNG WOMEN IN JAPAN MUST CHEER!" IS WHAT HE SAID.
WHEN TŌGŌ FORCED HER INTO IT.
BUT SHE LOOKS GREAT...
WITH SUCH LONG LEGS...
......
STAARE
LISTEN! IF YOU DON'T WANT TO DO IT, THEN YOU DON'T NEED TO DO IT, RIGHT?
¿AH, SÍ?
(REALLY?!)

Lala: Unusually Obedient.

<Harima, Currently Working on a Manga.>

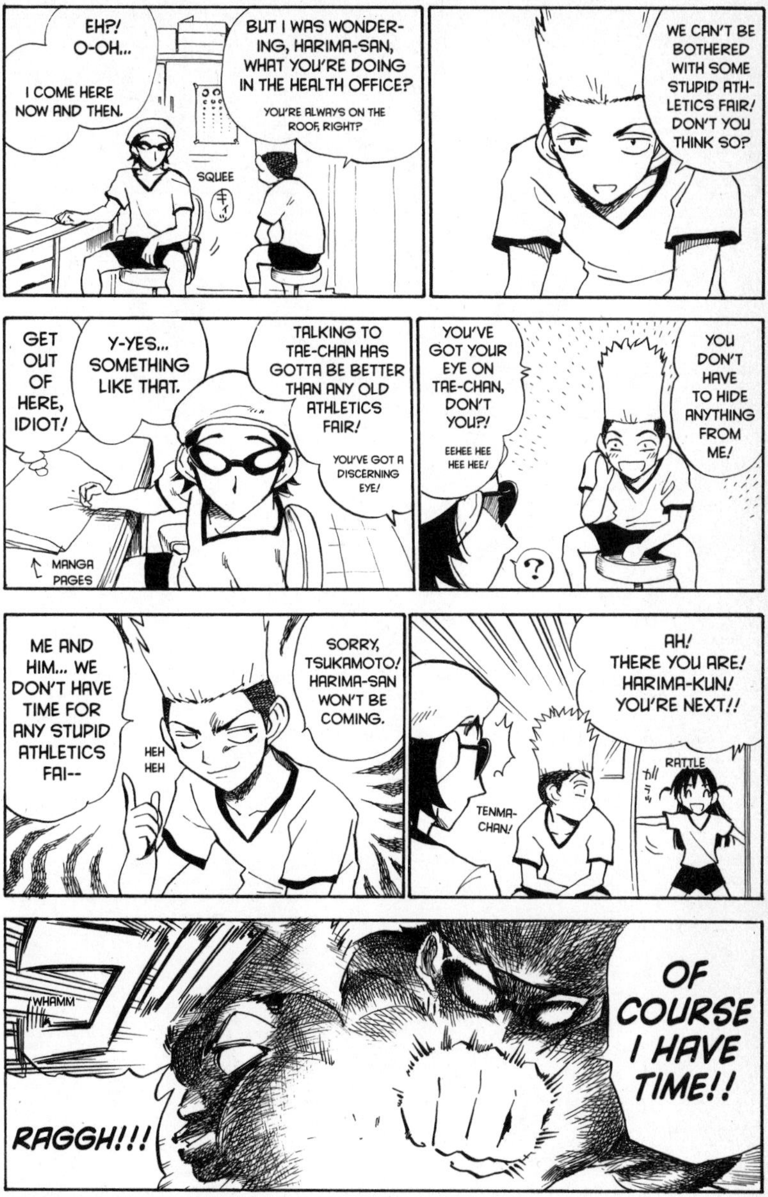
WE CAN'T BE BOTHERED WITH SOME STUPID ATHLETICS FAIR! DON'T YOU THINK SO?
BUT I WAS WONDERING, HARIMA-SAN, WHAT YOU'RE DOING IN THE HEALTH OFFICE?
YOU'RE ALWAYS ON THE ROOF, RIGHT?
EH?! O-OH...
I COME HERE NOW AND THEN.
SQUEE
YOU DON'T HAVE TO HIDE ANYTHING FROM ME!
YOU'VE GOT YOUR EYE ON TAE-CHAN, DON'T YOU?!
EEHEE HEE HEE HEE!
?
TALKING TO TAE-CHAN HAS GOTTA BE BETTER THAN ANY OLD ATHLETICS FAIR!
YOU'VE GOT A DISCERNING EYE!
Y-YES... SOMETHING LIKE THAT.
GET OUT OF HERE, IDIOT!
MANGA PAGES
AH! THERE YOU ARE! HARIMA-KUN! YOU'RE NEXT!!
RATTLE
TENMA-CHAN!
SORRY, TSUKAMOTO! HARIMA-SAN WON'T BE COMING.
HEH HEH
ME AND HIM... WE DON'T HAVE TIME FOR ANY STUPID ATHLETICS FAI--
OF COURSE I HAVE TIME!!
WHAMM
RAGGH!!!

This Guy's Name: Yoshidayama Jirô.

Tsukamoto Tenma: Her "Muscle" Hurts.

<High Speed: Tenma.>

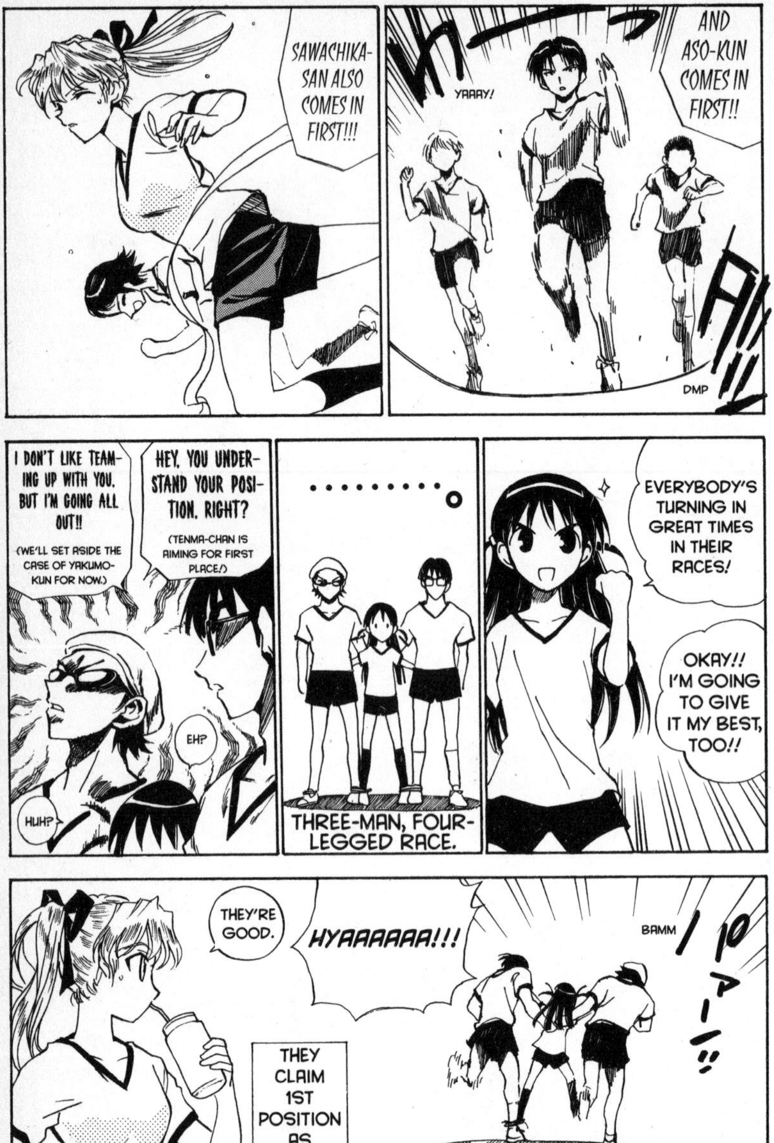
AND ASO-KUN COMES IN FIRST!!
YAAAY!
DMP
SAWACHIKA-SAN ALSO COMES IN FIRST!!!
EVERYBODY'S TURNING IN GREAT TIMES IN THEIR RACES!
OKAY!! I'M GOING TO GIVE IT MY BEST, TOO!!
..........o
THREE-MAN, FOUR-LEGGED RACE.
HEY, YOU UNDERSTAND YOUR POSITION, RIGHT?
(TENMA-CHAN IS AIMING FOR FIRST PLACE!)
I DON'T LIKE TEAMING UP WITH YOU. BUT I'M GOING ALL OUT!!
(WE'LL SET ASIDE THE CASE OF YAKUMO-KUN FOR NOW.)
EH?
HUH?
BAMM
HYAAAAAAA!!!
THEY'RE GOOD.
THEY CLAIM 1ST POSITION AS WELL.
BEING CARRIED.

<The Ultimate Deciding Battle.>

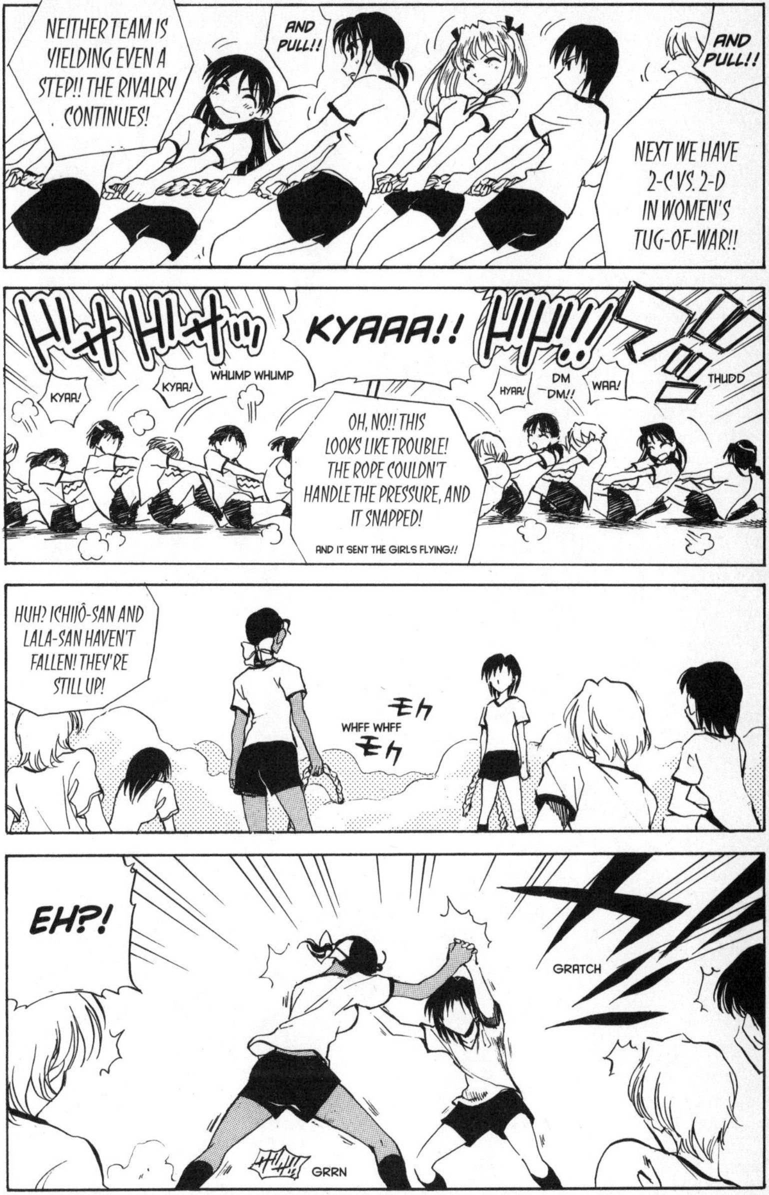
AND PULL!!
NEXT WE HAVE 2-C VS. 2-D IN WOMEN'S TUG-OF-WAR!!
AND PULL!!
NEITHER TEAM IS YIELDING EVEN A STEP!! THE RIVALRY CONTINUES!
THUDD
WAA!
DM DM!!
HYAA!
OH, NO!! THIS LOOKS LIKE TROUBLE! THE ROPE COULDN'T HANDLE THE PRESSURE, AND IT SNAPPED!
AND IT SENT THE GIRLS FLYING!!
KYAAA!!
WHUMP WHUMP
KYAA!
KYAA!
WHFF WHFF
HUH? ICHIJÔ-SAN AND LALA-SAN HAVEN'T FALLEN! THEY'RE STILL UP!
GRATCH
GRRN
EH?!

Ichijô and Lala: Entered the Amateur Wrestling Club at the Same Time.

<Lala: Again Making Every Effort!!>

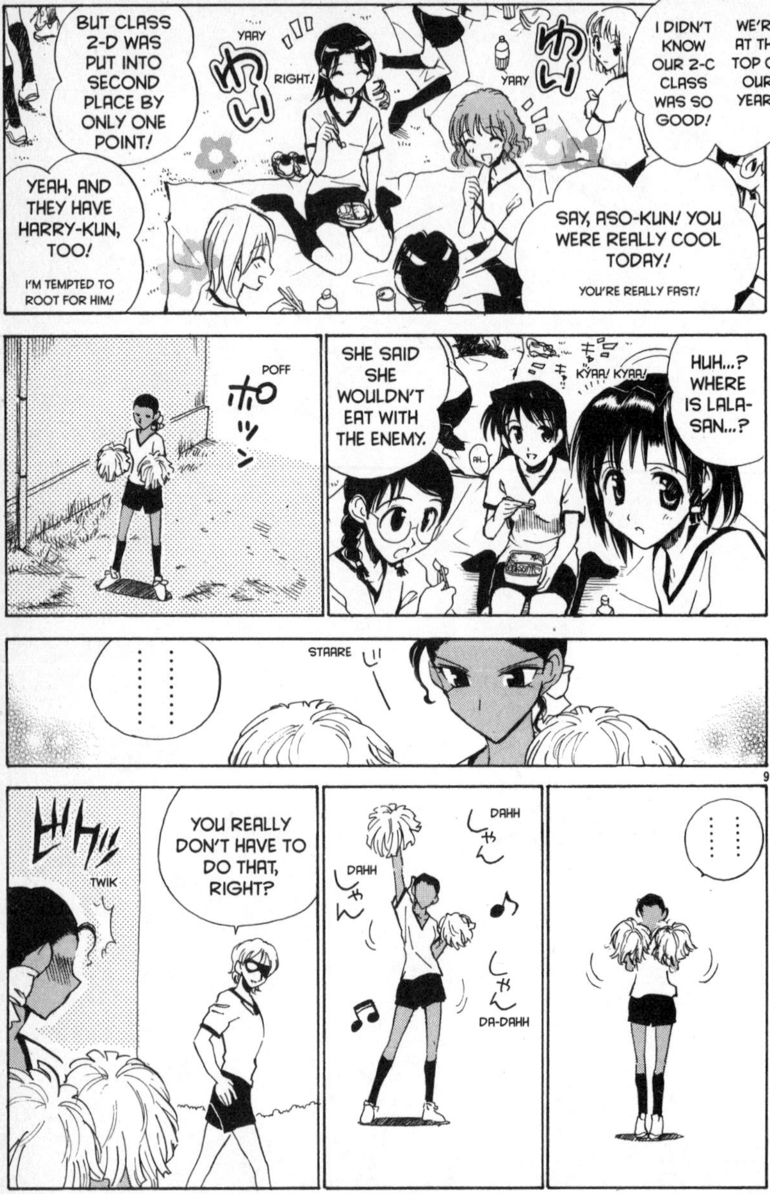
WE'RE AT THE TOP OF OUR YEAR!
I DIDN'T KNOW OUR 2-C CLASS WAS SO GOOD!
YAAY
RIGHT!
YAAY
BUT CLASS 2-D WAS PUT INTO SECOND PLACE BY ONLY ONE POINT!
SAY, ASO-KUN! YOU WERE REALLY COOL TODAY!
YOU'RE REALLY FAST!
YEAH, AND THEY HAVE HARRY-KUN, TOO!
I'M TEMPTED TO ROOT FOR HIM!
HUH...? WHERE IS LALA-SAN...?
KYAA! KYAA!
SHE SAID SHE WOULDN'T EAT WITH THE ENEMY.
AH...
POFF
STARRE
......
9
......
DAHH
DAHH
DA-DAHH
YOU REALLY DON'T HAVE TO DO THAT, RIGHT?
TWIK

<Hanai: 2nd Defeat.>

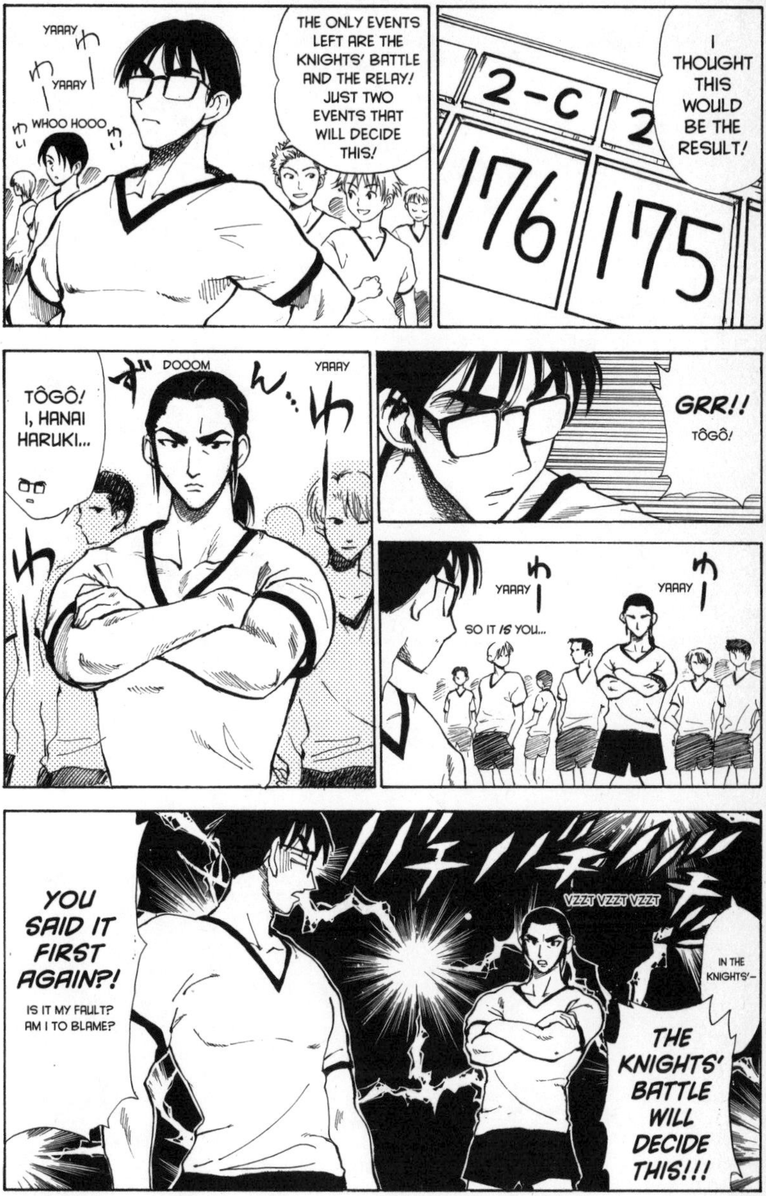
I THOUGHT THIS WOULD BE THE RESULT!
2-C
2
176
175
THE ONLY EVENTS LEFT ARE THE KNIGHTS' BATTLE AND THE RELAY! JUST TWO EVENTS THAT WILL DECIDE THIS!
YAAAY
YAAAY
WHOO HOOO
GRR!!
TÔGÔ!
YAAAY
YAAAY
SO IT *IS* YOU...
YAAAY
DOOOM
TÔGÔ! I, HANAI HARUKI...
IN THE KNIGHTS'–
THE KNIGHTS' BATTLE WILL DECIDE THIS!!!
VZZT VZZT VZZT
YOU SAID IT FIRST AGAIN?!
IS IT MY FAULT? AM I TO BLAME?

School Rumble: Enters the Warring States Period!!

 # 74 . . . . Fin

#75 BATTLEGROUND

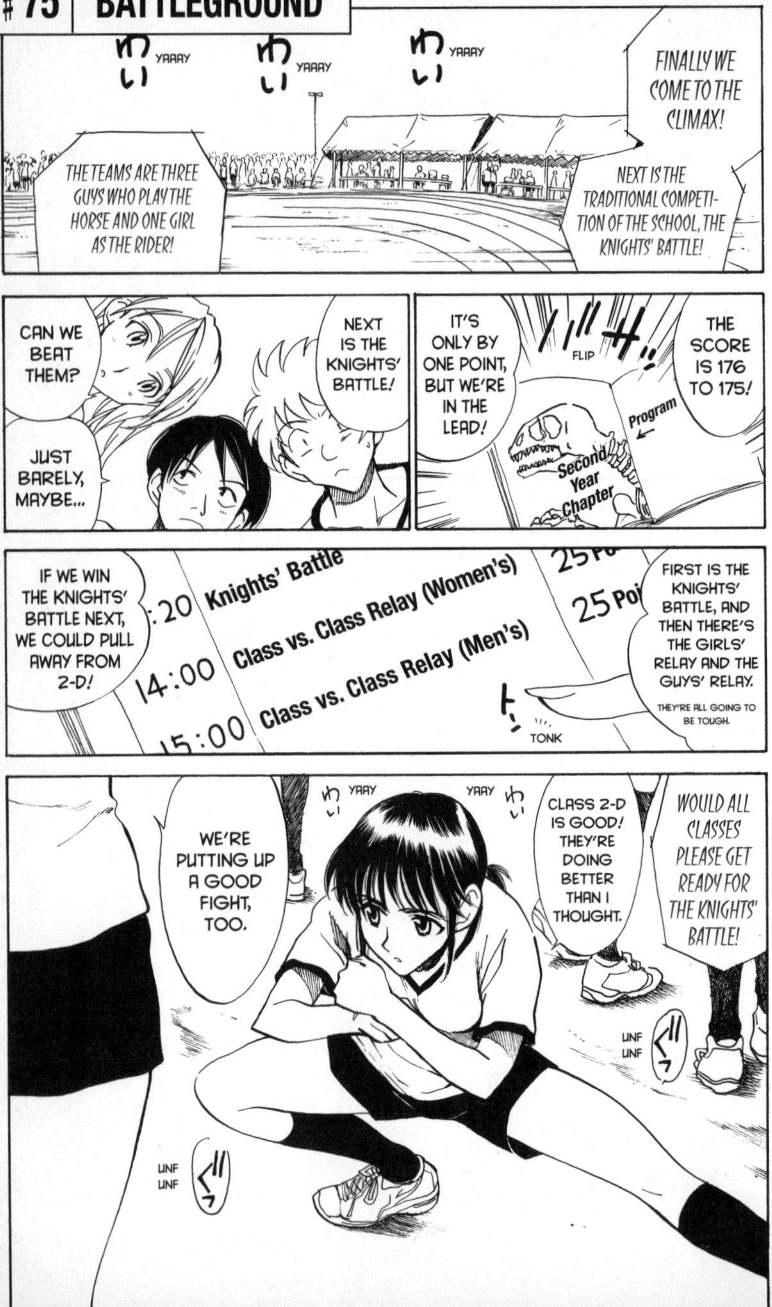

FINALLY WE COME TO THE CLIMAX!
NEXT IS THE TRADITIONAL COMPETITION OF THE SCHOOL, THE KNIGHTS' BATTLE!
わい YAAAY
わい YAAAY
わい YAAAY
THE TEAMS ARE THREE GUYS WHO PLAY THE HORSE AND ONE GIRL AS THE RIDER!
THE SCORE IS 176 TO 175!
Program
FLIP
Second Year Chapter
IT'S ONLY BY ONE POINT, BUT WE'RE IN THE LEAD!
NEXT IS THE KNIGHTS' BATTLE!
CAN WE BEAT THEM?
JUST BARELY, MAYBE...
FIRST IS THE KNIGHTS' BATTLE, AND THEN THERE'S THE GIRLS' RELAY AND THE GUYS' RELAY.
THEY'RE ALL GOING TO BE TOUGH.
TONK
:20 Knights' Battle
Class vs. Class Relay (Women's)
25 Poi
14:00 Class vs. Class Relay (Men's)
15:00
IF WE WIN THE KNIGHTS' BATTLE NEXT, WE COULD PULL AWAY FROM 2-D!
WOULD ALL CLASSES PLEASE GET READY FOR THE KNIGHTS' BATTLE!
CLASS 2-D IS GOOD! THEY'RE DOING BETTER THAN I THOUGHT.
わい YAAY
わい YAAY
WE'RE PUTTING UP A GOOD FIGHT, TOO.
UNF UNF
UNF UNF

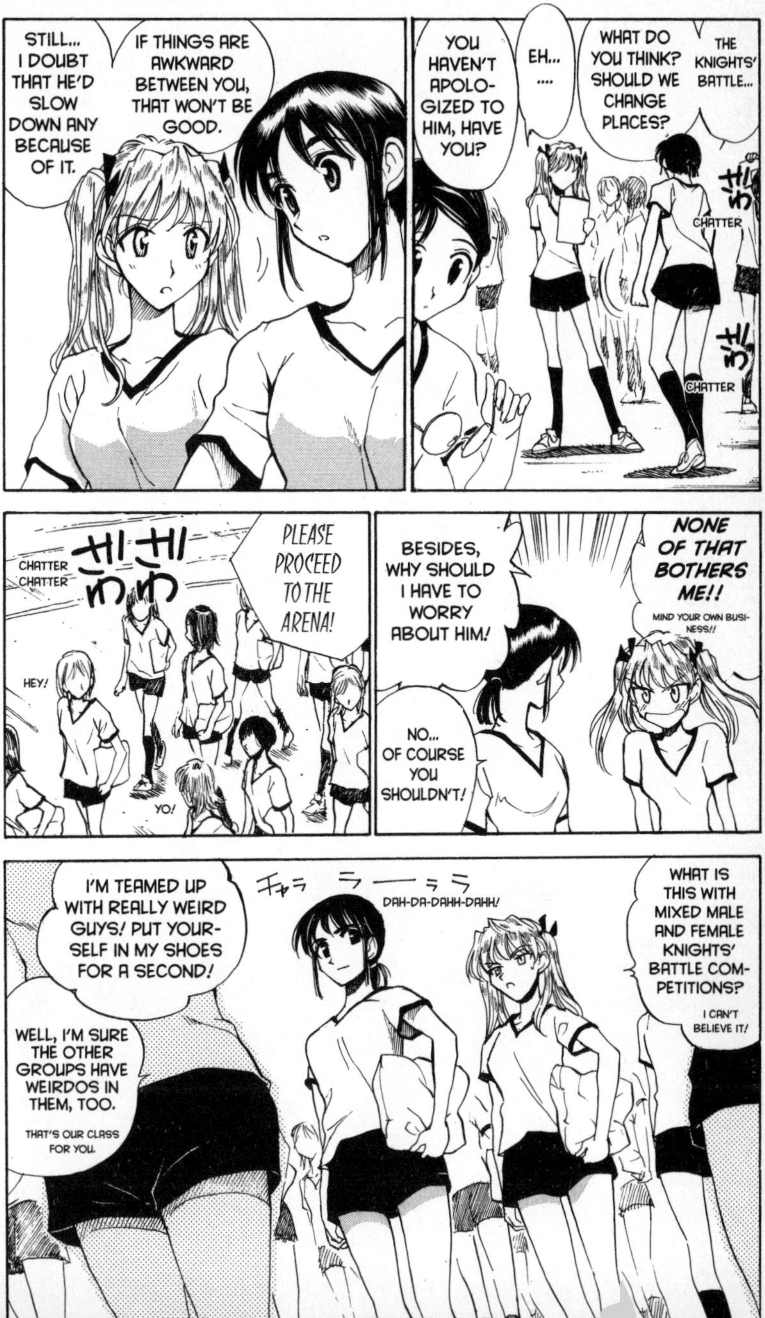
THE KNIGHTS' BATTLE...
WHAT DO YOU THINK? SHOULD WE CHANGE PLACES?
EH... ....
YOU HAVEN'T APOLOGIZED TO HIM, HAVE YOU?
CHATTER
CHATTER
IF THINGS ARE AWKWARD BETWEEN YOU, THAT WON'T BE GOOD.
STILL... I DOUBT THAT HE'D SLOW DOWN ANY BECAUSE OF IT.
NONE OF THAT BOTHERS ME!!
MIND YOUR OWN BUSINESS!!
BESIDES, WHY SHOULD I HAVE TO WORRY ABOUT HIM!
NO... OF COURSE YOU SHOULDN'T!
PLEASE PROCEED TO THE ARENA!
CHATTER CHATTER
HEY!
YO!
WHAT IS THIS WITH MIXED MALE AND FEMALE KNIGHTS' BATTLE COMPETITIONS?
I CAN'T BELIEVE IT!
DAH-DA-DAHH-DAHH!
I'M TEAMED UP WITH REALLY WEIRD GUYS! PUT YOURSELF IN MY SHOES FOR A SECOND!
WELL, I'M SURE THE OTHER GROUPS HAVE WEIRDOS IN THEM, TOO.
THAT'S OUR CLASS FOR YOU.

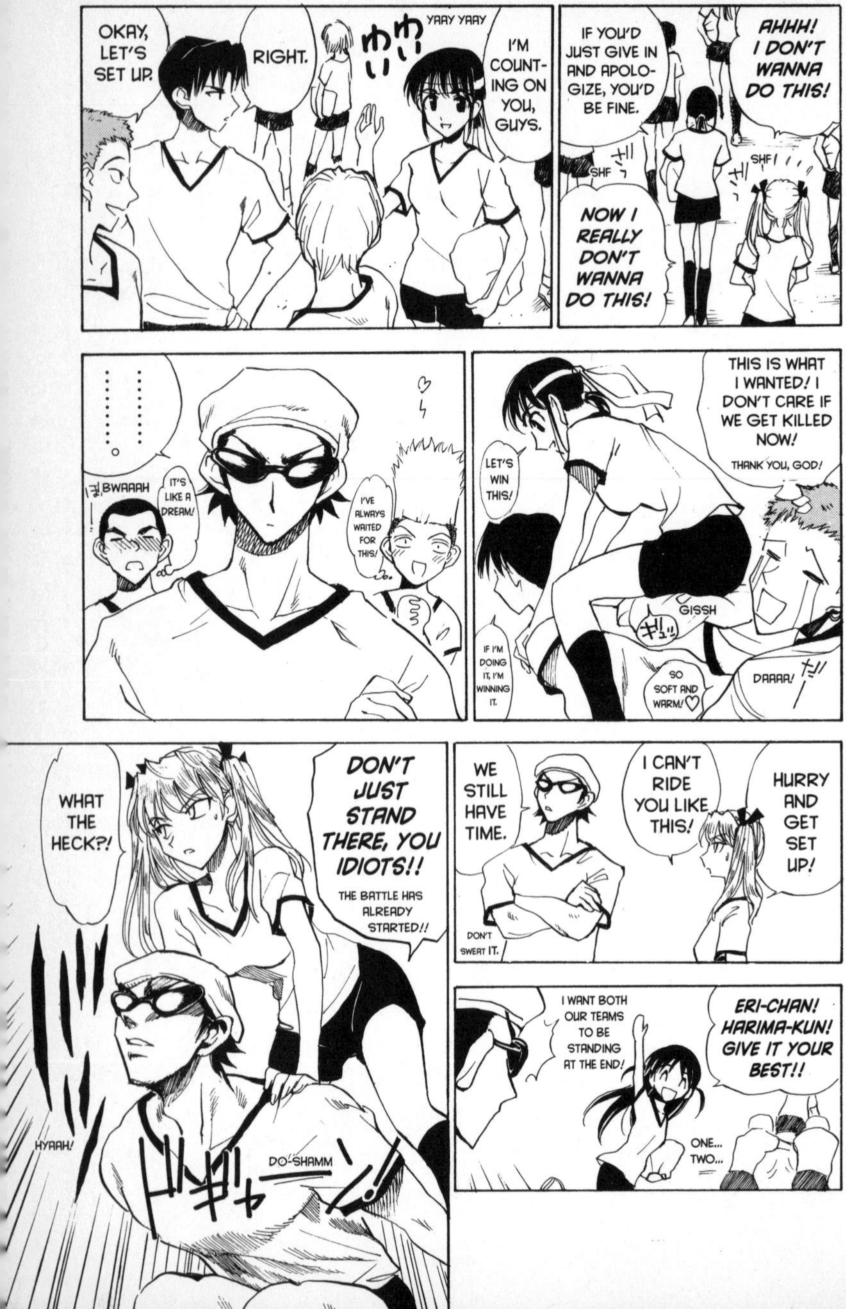
AHHH! I DON'T WANNA DO THIS!
IF YOU'D JUST GIVE IN AND APOLOGIZE, YOU'D BE FINE.
SHF
SHF
NOW I REALLY DON'T WANNA DO THIS!
YAAY YAAY
I'M COUNTING ON YOU, GUYS.
RIGHT.
OKAY, LET'S SET UP.
THIS IS WHAT I WANTED! I DON'T CARE IF WE GET KILLED NOW!
THANK YOU, GOD!
LET'S WIN THIS!
GISSH
DAAAA!
SO SOFT AND WARM!♡
IF I'M DOING IT, I'M WINNING IT.
I'VE ALWAYS WAITED FOR THIS!
......
IT'S LIKE A DREAM!
BWAAAH
HURRY AND GET SET UP!
I CAN'T RIDE YOU LIKE THIS!
WE STILL HAVE TIME.
DON'T SWEAT IT.
ERI-CHAN! HARIMA-KUN! GIVE IT YOUR BEST!!
I WANT BOTH OUR TEAMS TO BE STANDING AT THE END!
ONE... TWO...
DON'T JUST STAND THERE, YOU IDIOTS!!
THE BATTLE HAS ALREADY STARTED!!
WHAT THE HECK?!
HYAAH!
DO-SHAMM

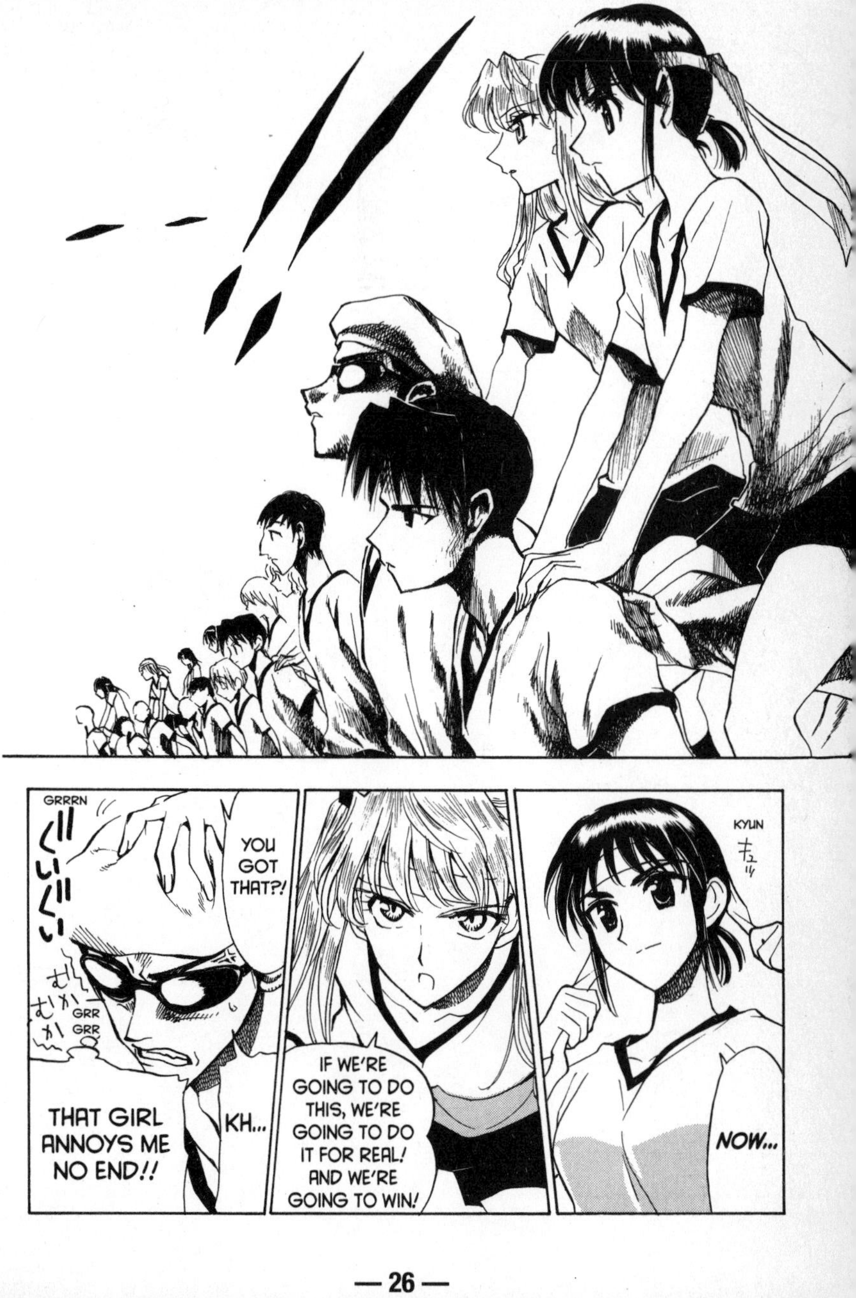
KYUN
キュ
NOW...
IF WE'RE GOING TO DO THIS, WE'RE GOING TO DO IT FOR REAL! AND WE'RE GOING TO WIN!
YOU GOT THAT?!
GRRRN
ぐいぐい
KH...
むかむか
GRR GRR
THAT GIRL ANNOYS ME NO END!!

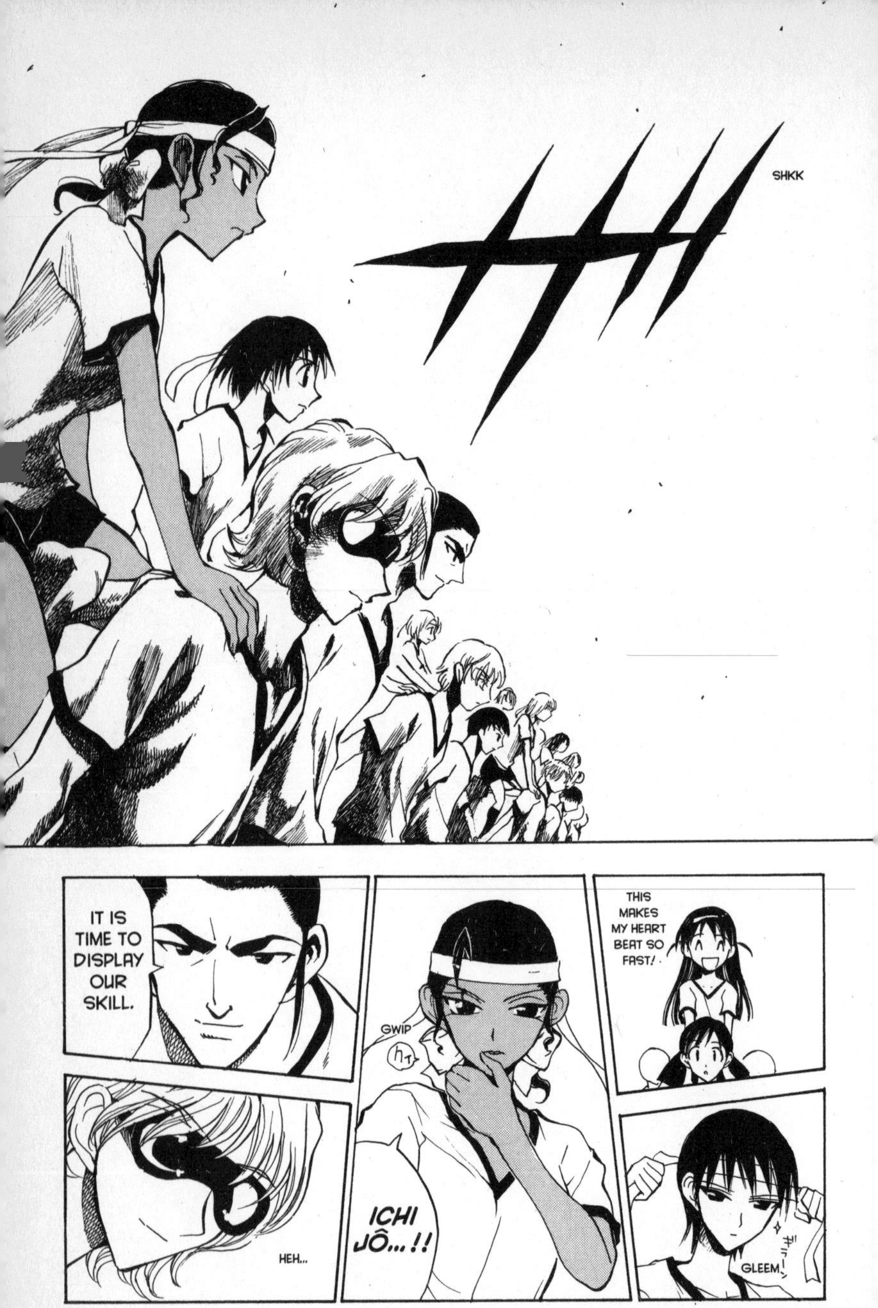
SHKK
THIS MAKES MY HEART BEAT SO FAST!
GLEEM
GWIP
ICHI JÔ...!!
IT IS TIME TO DISPLAY OUR SKILL.
HEH...

It Looks like One Team Isn't Quite Knight-Level.

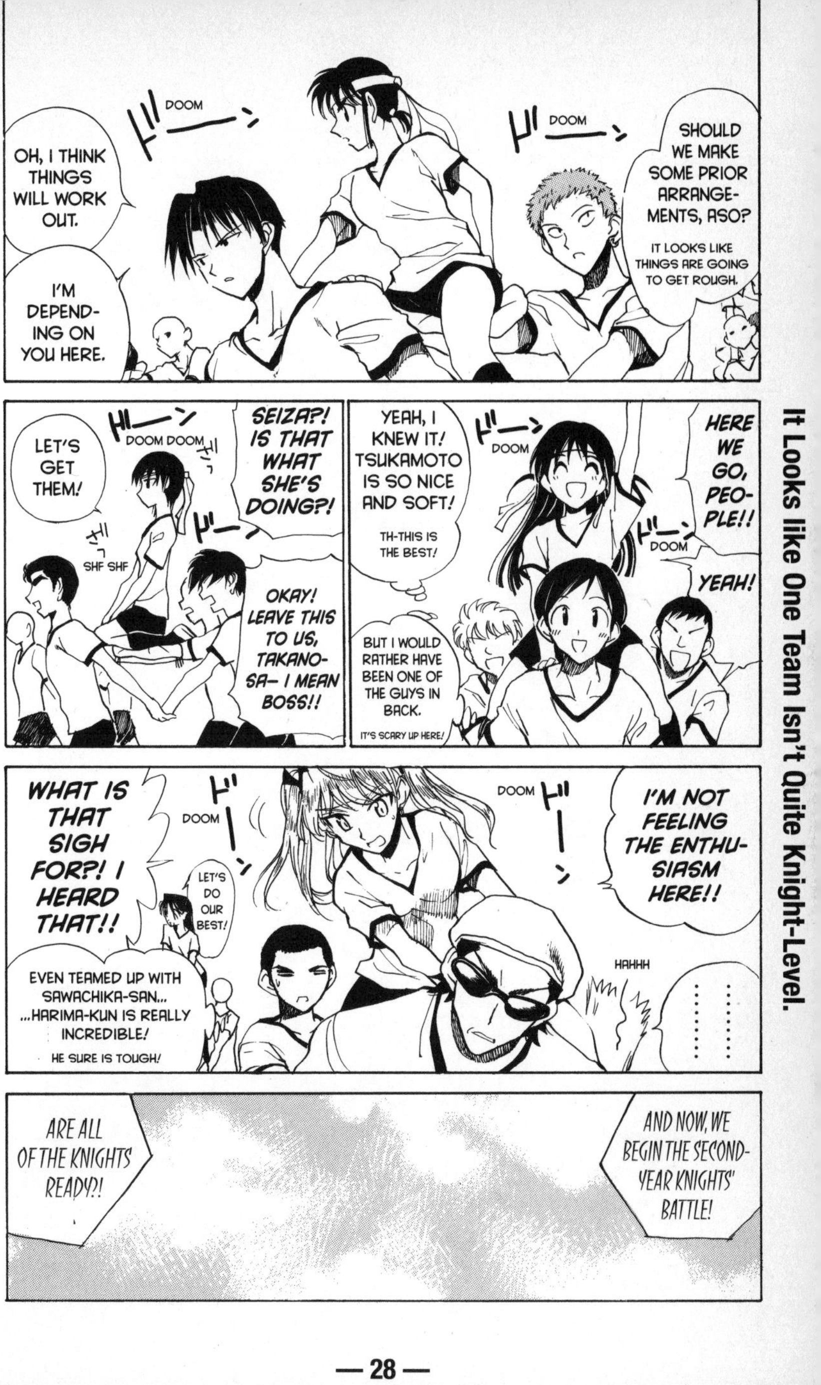
SHOULD WE MAKE SOME PRIOR ARRANGEMENTS, ASO?
IT LOOKS LIKE THINGS ARE GOING TO GET ROUGH.
DOOM
DOOM
OH, I THINK THINGS WILL WORK OUT.
I'M DEPENDING ON YOU HERE.
HERE WE GO, PEOPLE!!
DOOM
DOOM
YEAH!
YEAH, I KNEW IT! TSUKAMOTO IS SO NICE AND SOFT!
TH-THIS IS THE BEST!
BUT I WOULD RATHER HAVE BEEN ONE OF THE GUYS IN BACK.
IT'S SCARY UP HERE!
SEIZA?! IS THAT WHAT SHE'S DOING?!
OKAY! LEAVE THIS TO US, TAKANO-SA— I MEAN BOSS!!
DOOM DOOM
LET'S GET THEM!
SHF SHF
I'M NOT FEELING THE ENTHUSIASM HERE!!
DOOM
......
HAHHH
DOOM
WHAT IS THAT SIGH FOR?! I HEARD THAT!!
LET'S DO OUR BEST!
EVEN TEAMED UP WITH SAWACHIKA-SAN... ...HARIMA-KUN IS REALLY INCREDIBLE!
HE SURE IS TOUGH!
AND NOW, WE BEGIN THE SECOND-YEAR KNIGHTS' BATTLE!
ARE ALL OF THE KNIGHTS READY?!

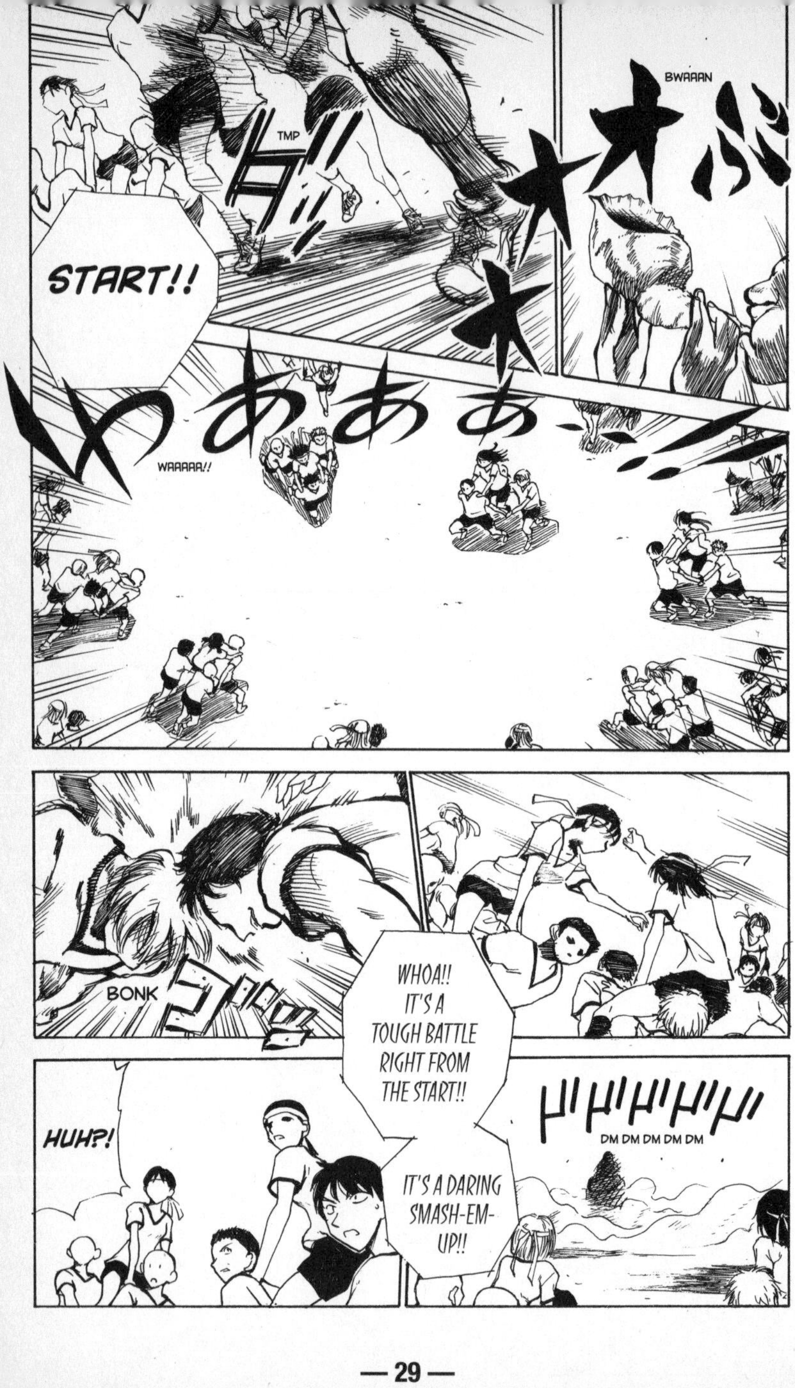
BWAAAN
TMP
START!!
WAAAAA!!
WHOA!! IT'S A TOUGH BATTLE RIGHT FROM THE START!!
BONK
DM DM DM DM DM
IT'S A DARING SMASH-EM-UP!!
HUH?!

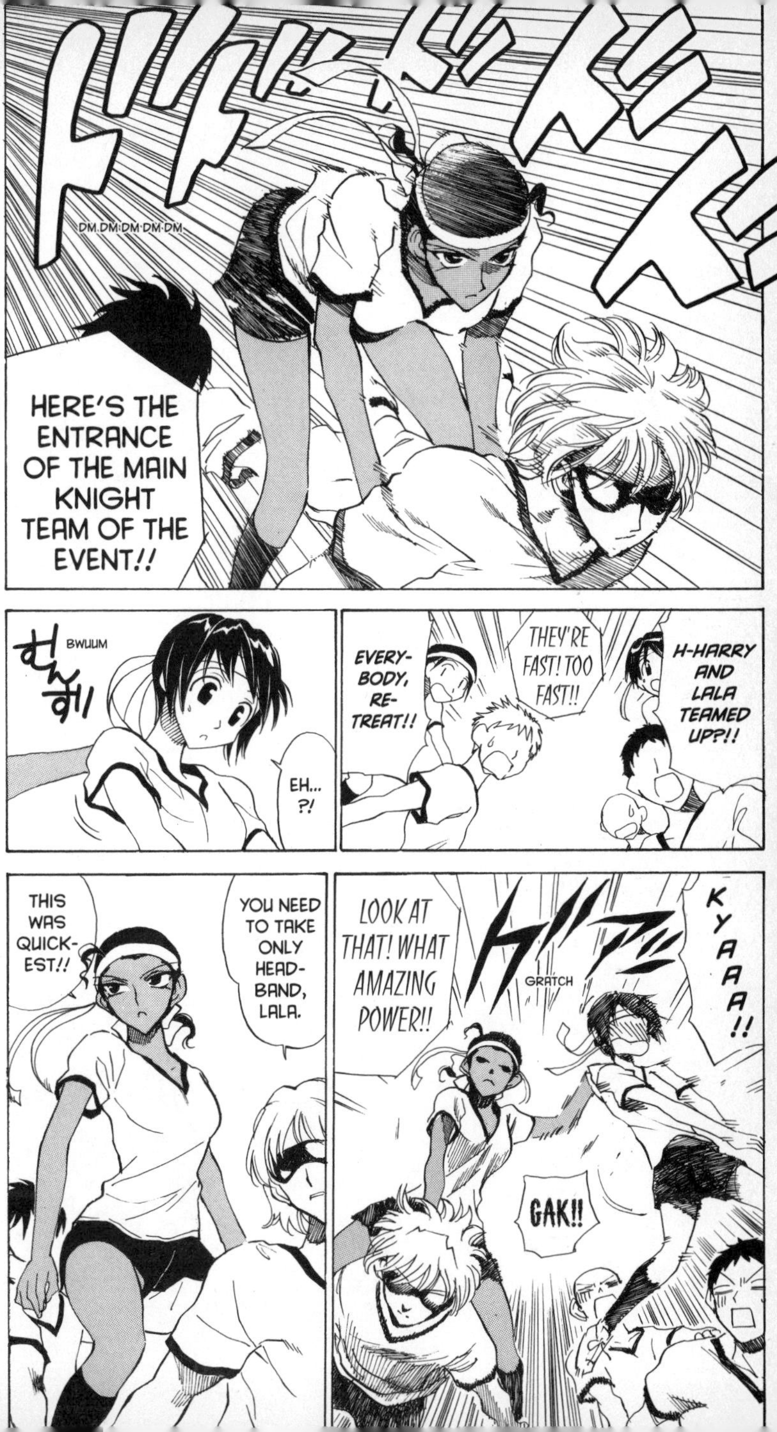
DM.DM.DM.DM.DM
HERE'S THE ENTRANCE OF THE MAIN KNIGHT TEAM OF THE EVENT!!
H-HARRY AND LALA TEAMED UP?!!
THEY'RE FAST! TOO FAST!!
EVERY-BODY, RE-TREAT!!
BWUUM
EH... ?!
KYAAAA!!
GRATCH
LOOK AT THAT! WHAT AMAZING POWER!!
GAK!!
YOU NEED TO TAKE ONLY HEAD-BAND, LALA.
THIS WAS QUICK-EST!!

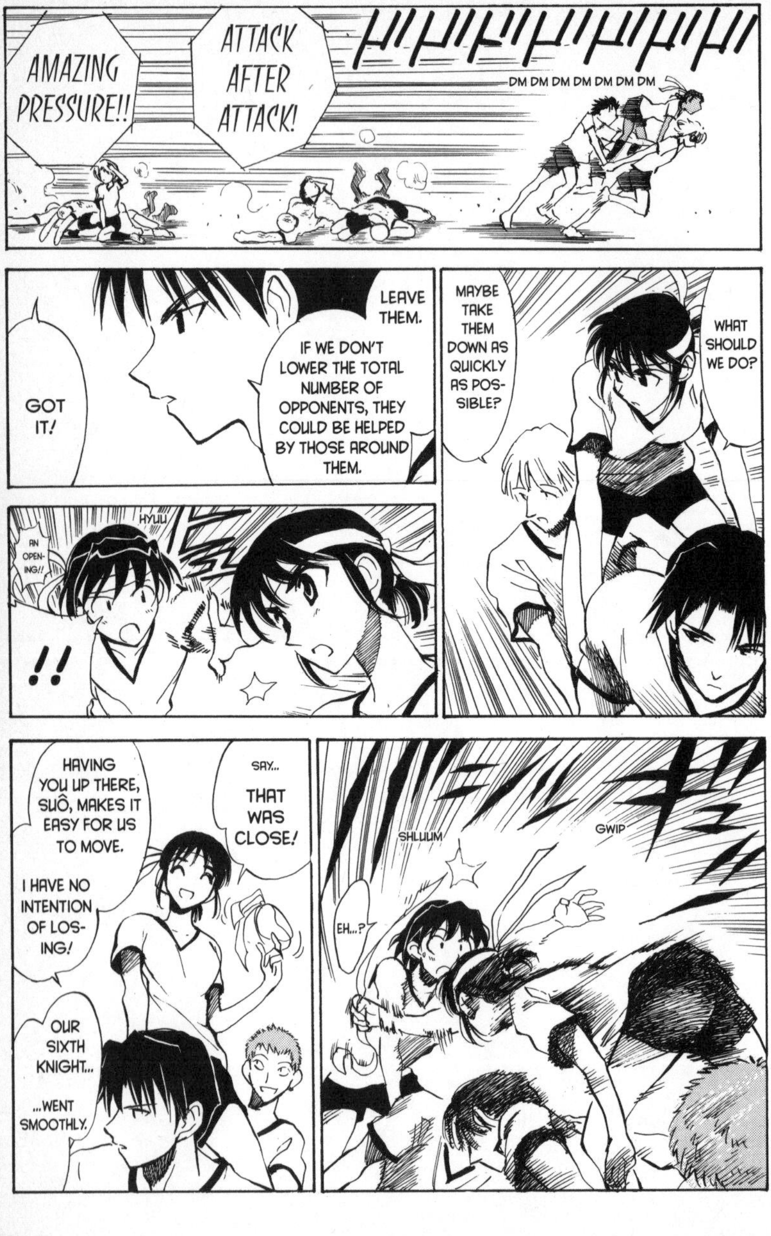
DM DM DM DM DM DM DM
ATTACK AFTER ATTACK!
AMAZING PRESSURE!!
WHAT SHOULD WE DO?
MAYBE TAKE THEM DOWN AS QUICKLY AS POS-SIBLE?
LEAVE THEM.
IF WE DON'T LOWER THE TOTAL NUMBER OF OPPONENTS, THEY COULD BE HELPED BY THOSE AROUND THEM.
GOT IT!
HYUU
AN OPEN-ING!!
!!
GWIP
SHLUUM
EH...?
SAY...
THAT WAS CLOSE!
HAVING YOU UP THERE, SUÔ, MAKES IT EASY FOR US TO MOVE.
I HAVE NO INTENTION OF LOS-ING!
OUR SIXTH KNIGHT...
...WENT SMOOTHLY.

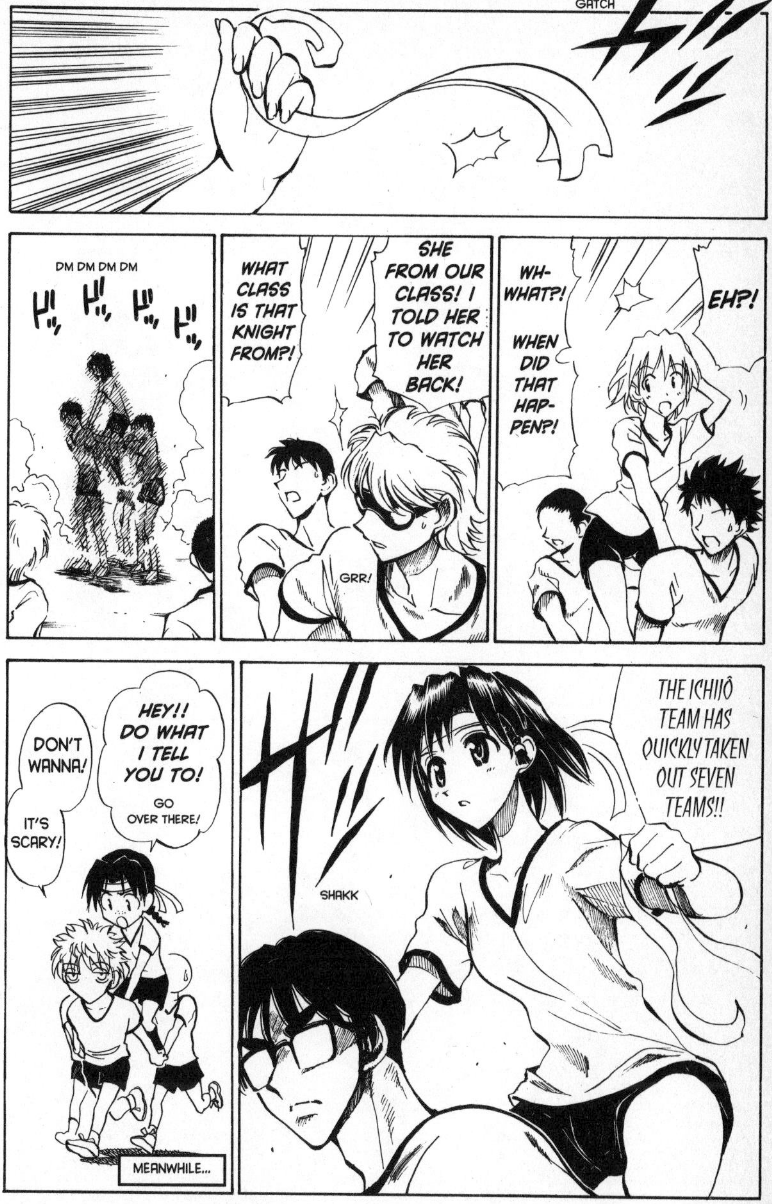
GATCH
EH?!
WH- WHAT?!
WHEN DID THAT HAP- PEN?!
SHE FROM OUR CLASS! I TOLD HER TO WATCH HER BACK!
WHAT CLASS IS THAT KNIGHT FROM?!
GRR!
DM DM DM DM
THE ICHIJÔ TEAM HAS QUICKLY TAKEN OUT SEVEN TEAMS!!
SHAKK
HEY!! DO WHAT I TELL YOU TO!
GO OVER THERE!
DON'T WANNA!
IT'S SCARY!
MEANWHILE...

Another Descent to Earth...Okay, That's Too Much!

 # 75· · · · · · · · · ·Fin

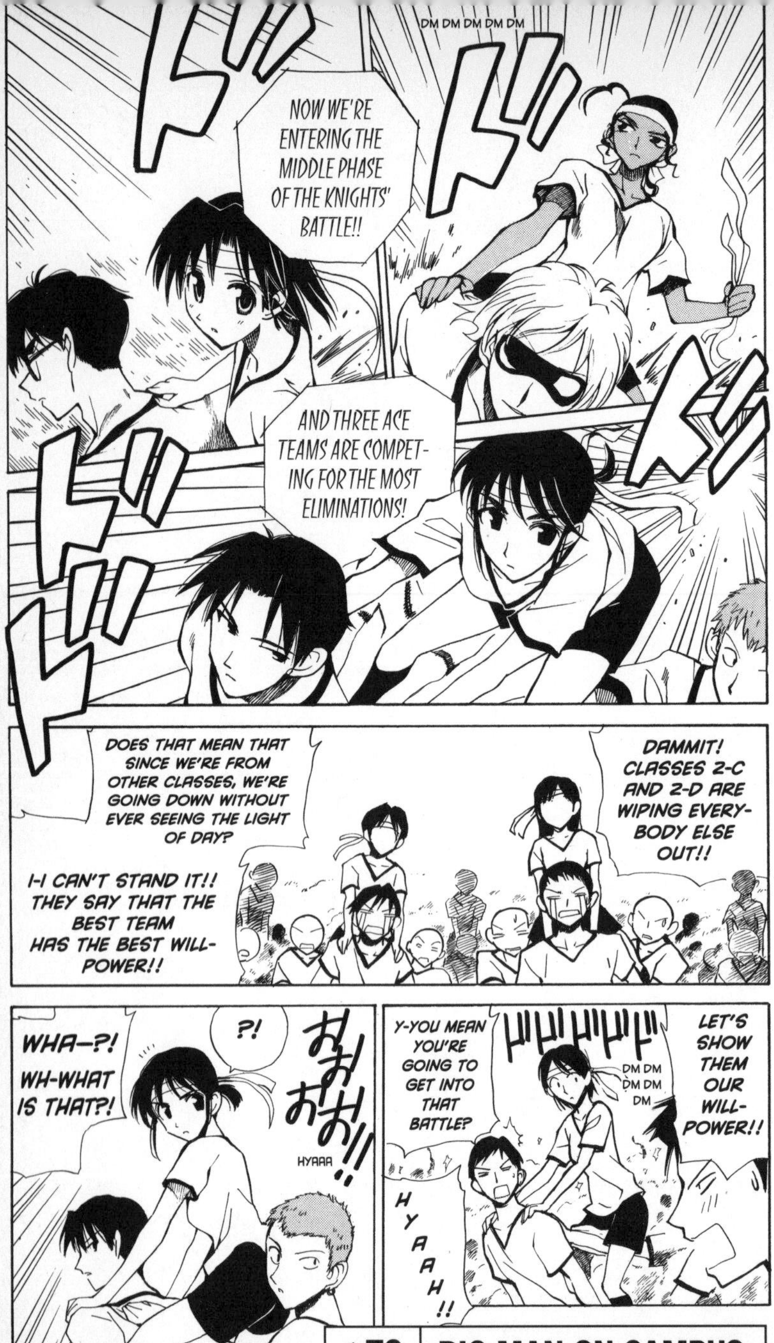
DM DM DM DM DM
NOW WE'RE ENTERING THE MIDDLE PHASE OF THE KNIGHTS' BATTLE!!
AND THREE ACE TEAMS ARE COMPET-ING FOR THE MOST ELIMINATIONS!
DAMMIT! CLASSES 2-C AND 2-D ARE WIPING EVERY-BODY ELSE OUT!!
DOES THAT MEAN THAT SINCE WE'RE FROM OTHER CLASSES, WE'RE GOING DOWN WITHOUT EVER SEEING THE LIGHT OF DAY?
I-I CAN'T STAND IT!! THEY SAY THAT THE BEST TEAM HAS THE BEST WILL-POWER!!
LET'S SHOW THEM OUR WILL-POWER!!
DM DM DM DM DM
Y-YOU MEAN YOU'RE GOING TO GET INTO THAT BATTLE?
HYAAH!!
?!
HYAAA
WHA—?! WH-WHAT IS THAT?!

#76 BIG MAN ON CAMPUS

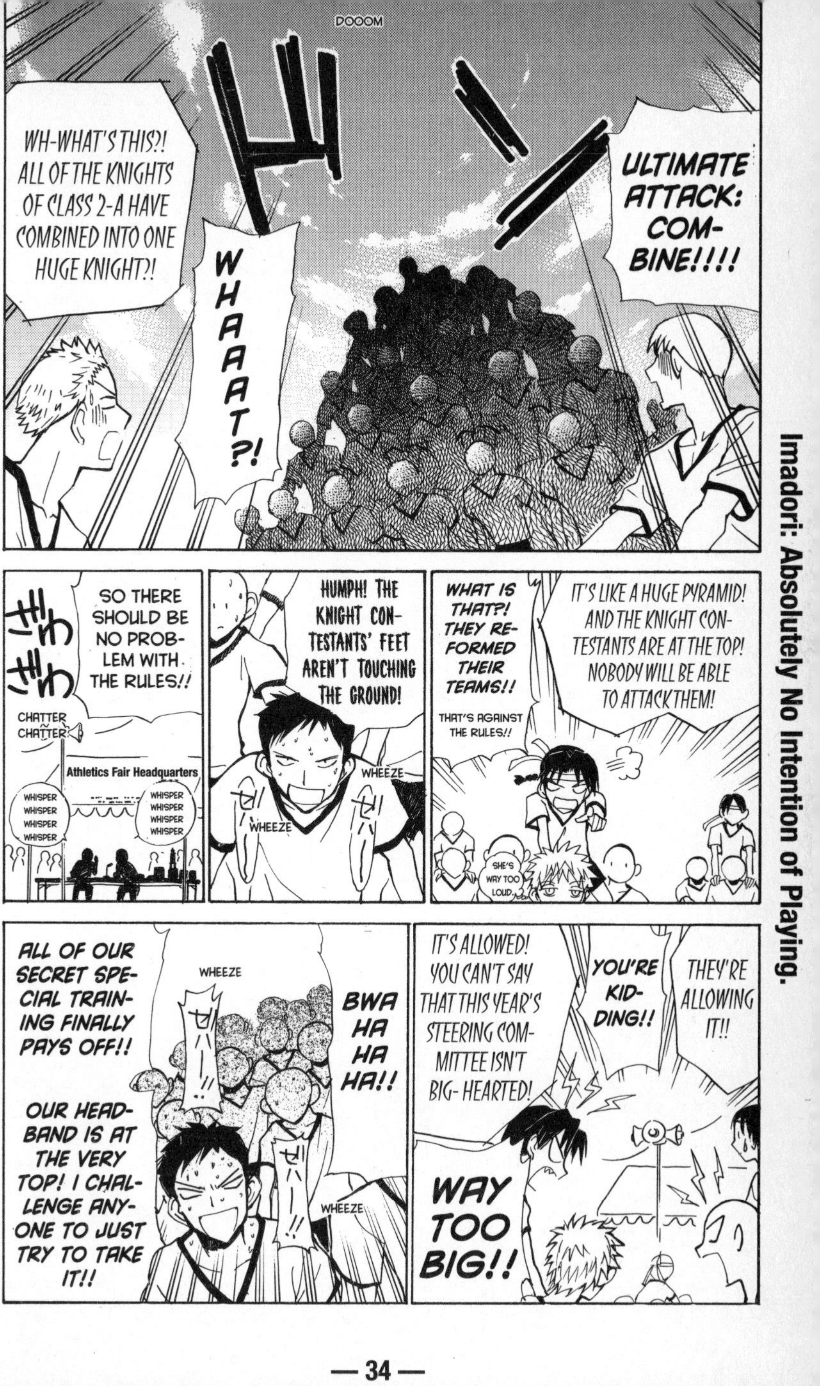
ULTIMATE ATTACK: COM-BINE!!!!
DOOOM
WHAAAAT?!
WH-WHAT'S THIS?! ALL OF THE KNIGHTS OF CLASS 2-A HAVE COMBINED INTO ONE HUGE KNIGHT?!
IT'S LIKE A HUGE PYRAMID! AND THE KNIGHT CON-TESTANTS ARE AT THE TOP! NOBODY WILL BE ABLE TO ATTACK THEM!
WHAT IS THAT?! THEY RE-FORMED THEIR TEAMS!!
THAT'S AGAINST THE RULES!!
SHE'S WAY TOO LOUD.
HUMPH! THE KNIGHT CON-TESTANTS' FEET AREN'T TOUCHING THE GROUND!
WHEEZE
WHEEZE
SO THERE SHOULD BE NO PROB-LEM WITH THE RULES!!
ざわ ざわ
CHATTER CHATTER
Athletics Fair Headquarters
WHISPER WHISPER WHISPER WHISPER
WHISPER WHISPER WHISPER WHISPER
THEY'RE ALLOWING IT!!
YOU'RE KID-DING!!
IT'S ALLOWED! YOU CAN'T SAY THAT THIS YEAR'S STEERING COM-MITTEE ISN'T BIG-HEARTED!
WAY TOO BIG!!
BWA HA HA HA!!
WHEEZE
ALL OF OUR SECRET SPE-CIAL TRAIN-ING FINALLY PAYS OFF!!
OUR HEAD-BAND IS AT THE VERY TOP! I CHAL-LENGE ANY-ONE TO JUST TRY TO TAKE IT!!
WHEEZE

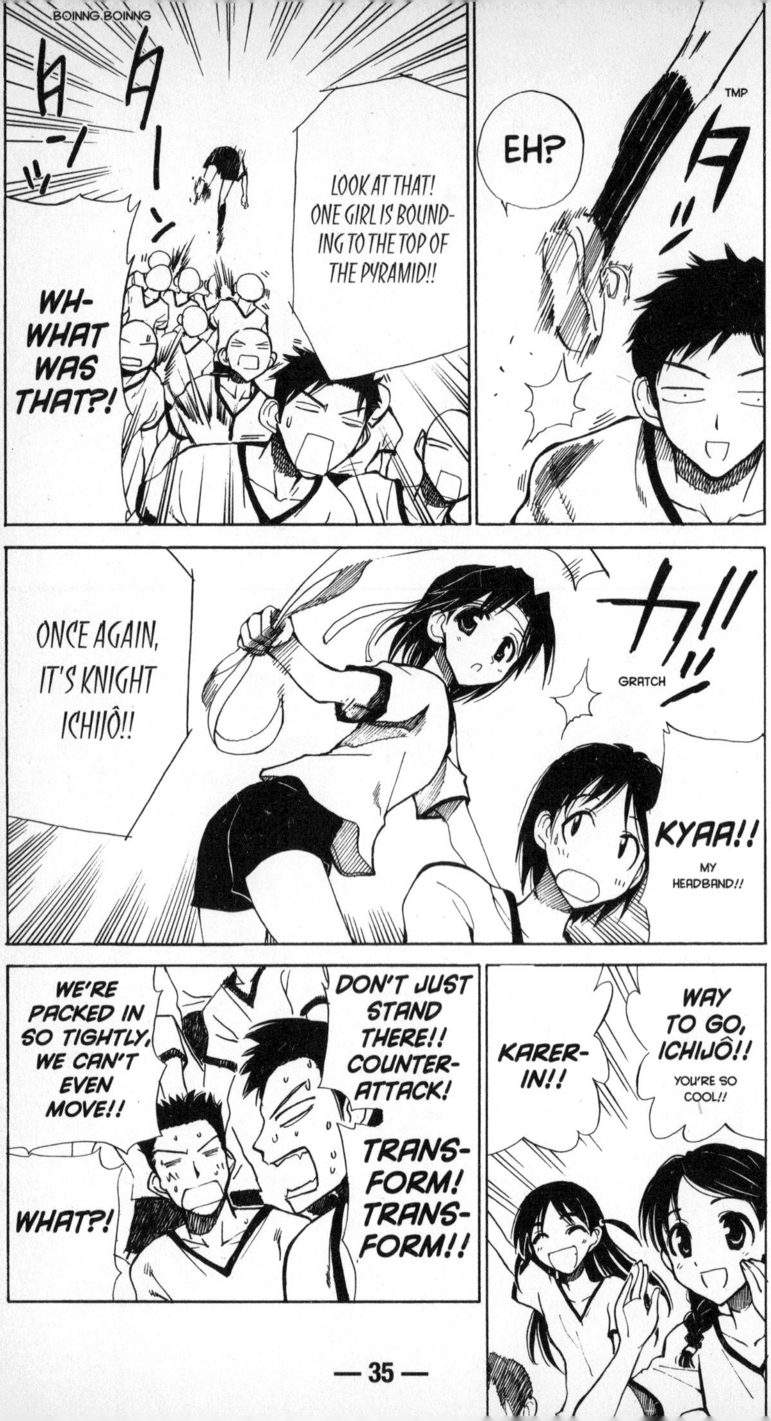
TMP
EH?
BOINNG BOINNG
LOOK AT THAT! ONE GIRL IS BOUNDING TO THE TOP OF THE PYRAMID!!
WH-WHAT WAS THAT?!
GRATCH
ONCE AGAIN, IT'S KNIGHT ICHIJÔ!!
KYAA!!
MY HEADBAND!!
WAY TO GO, ICHIJÔ!!
YOU'RE SO COOL!!
KARER-IN!!
DON'T JUST STAND THERE!! COUNTER-ATTACK!
WE'RE PACKED IN SO TIGHTLY, WE CAN'T EVEN MOVE!!
TRANS-FORM! TRANS-FORM!!
WHAT?!

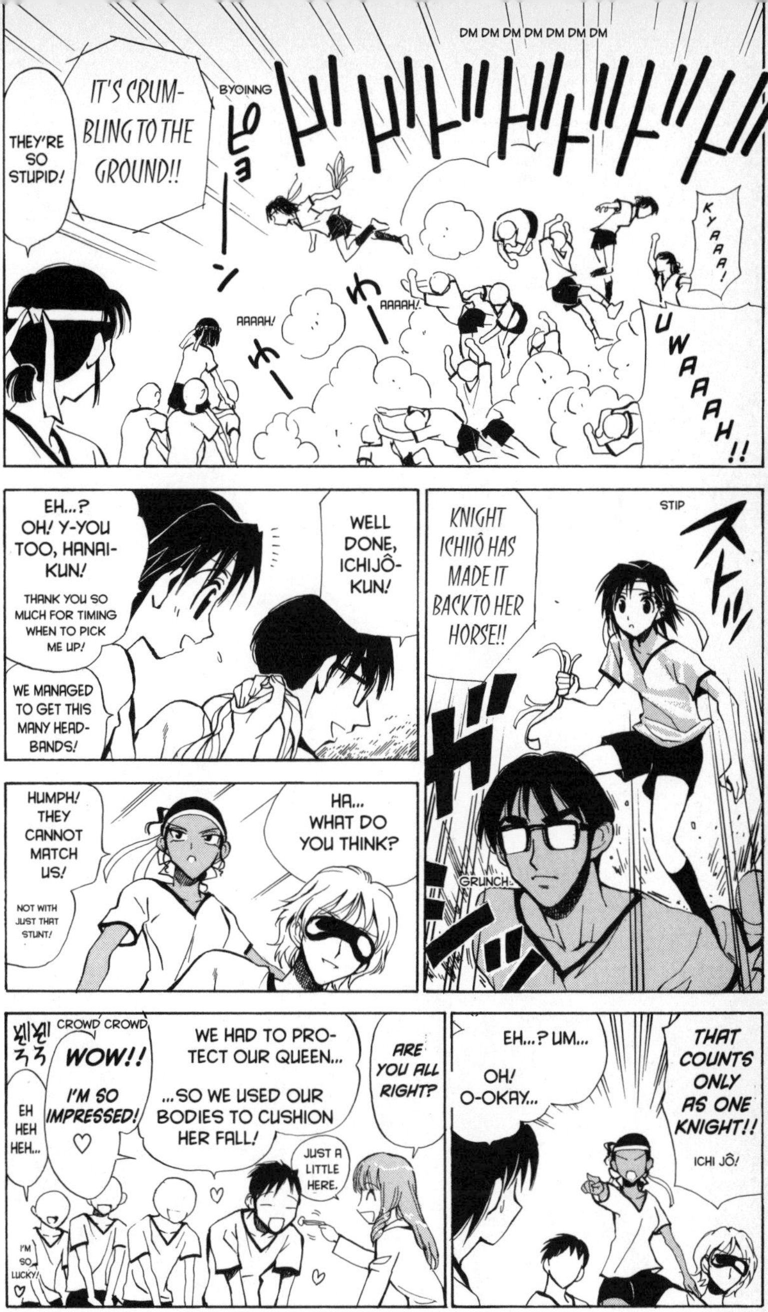
DM DM DM DM DM DM DM
KYAAA!
UWAAAAH!!
BYOINNG
AAAAH!
AAAAH!
IT'S CRUMBLING TO THE GROUND!!
THEY'RE SO STUPID!
STIP
KNIGHT ICHIJÔ HAS MADE IT BACK TO HER HORSE!!
GRUNCH
WELL DONE, ICHIJÔ-KUN!
EH...? OH! Y-YOU TOO, HANAI-KUN!
THANK YOU SO MUCH FOR TIMING WHEN TO PICK ME UP!
WE MANAGED TO GET THIS MANY HEADBANDS!
HA... WHAT DO YOU THINK?
HUMPH! THEY CANNOT MATCH US!
NOT WITH JUST THAT STUNT!
THAT COUNTS ONLY AS ONE KNIGHT!!
ICHI JÔ!
EH...? UM...
OH! O-OKAY...
ARE YOU ALL RIGHT?
JUST A LITTLE HERE.
WE HAD TO PROTECT OUR QUEEN...
...SO WE USED OUR BODIES TO CUSHION HER FALL!
CROWD CROWD
WOW!!
I'M SO IMPRESSED! ♡
EH HEH HEH...
I'M SO LUCKY! ♡

Hanai: Already Being Treated as a Horse.

Them, Too.

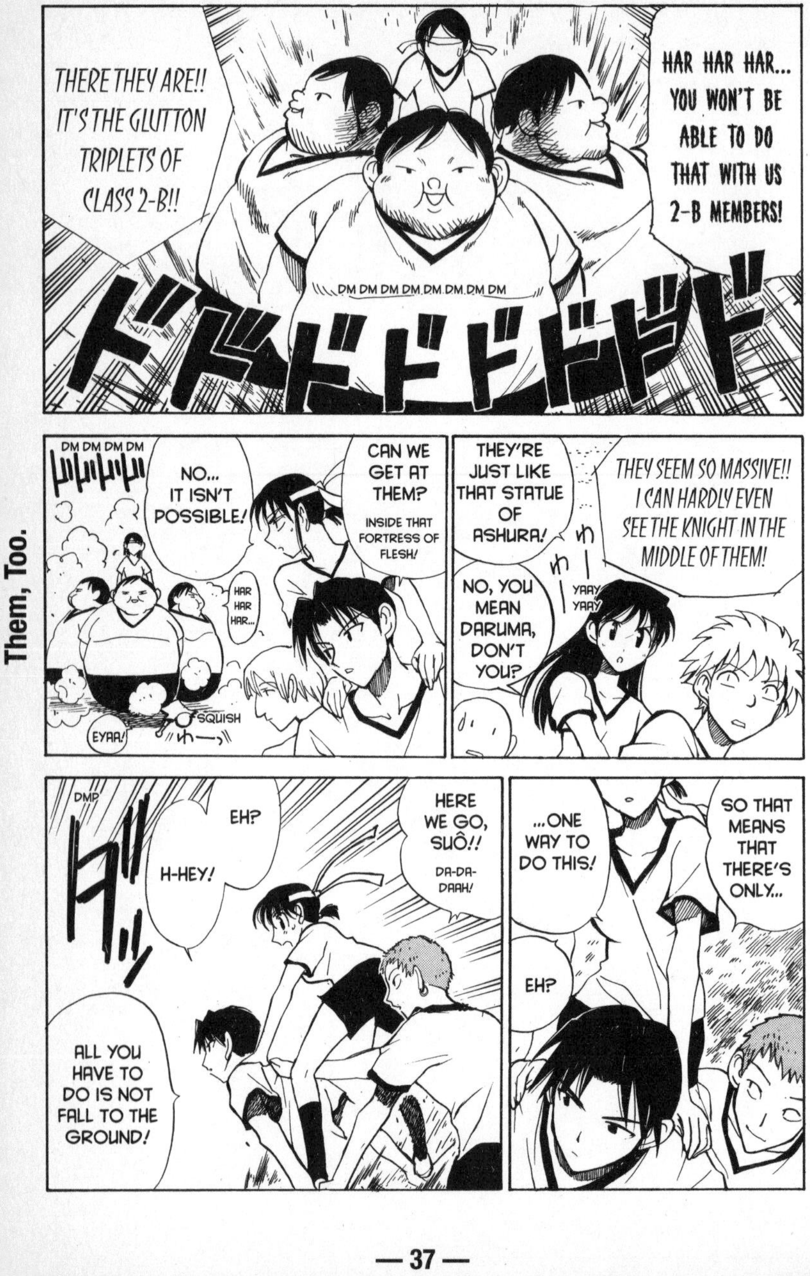
HAR HAR HAR... YOU WON'T BE ABLE TO DO THAT WITH US 2-B MEMBERS!
THERE THEY ARE!! IT'S THE GLUTTON TRIPLETS OF CLASS 2-B!!
DM DM DM DM DM DM DM DM
THEY SEEM SO MASSIVE!! I CAN HARDLY EVEN SEE THE KNIGHT IN THE MIDDLE OF THEM!
THEY'RE JUST LIKE THAT STATUE OF ASHURA!
YAAY YAAY
NO, YOU MEAN DARUMA, DON'T YOU?
CAN WE GET AT THEM?
INSIDE THAT FORTRESS OF FLESH!
NO... IT ISN'T POSSIBLE!
DM DM DM DM
HAR HAR HAR...
SQUISH
EYAA!
SO THAT MEANS THAT THERE'S ONLY...
...ONE WAY TO DO THIS!
EH?
HERE WE GO, SUÔ!!
DA-DA-DAAH!
EH?
H-HEY!
DMP
ALL YOU HAVE TO DO IS NOT FALL TO THE GROUND!

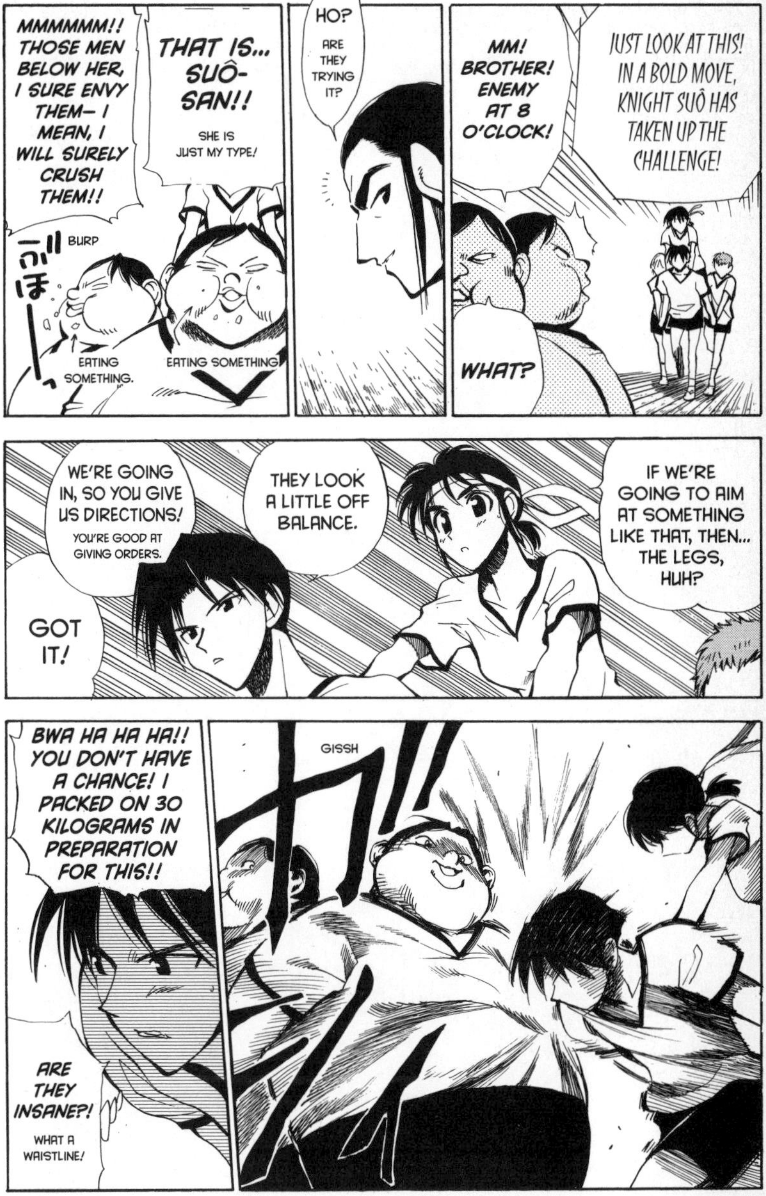
JUST LOOK AT THIS! IN A BOLD MOVE, KNIGHT SUÔ HAS TAKEN UP THE CHALLENGE!
MM! BROTHER! ENEMY AT 8 O'CLOCK!
WHAT?
HO? ARE THEY TRYING IT?
THAT IS... SUÔ-SAN!!
SHE IS JUST MY TYPE!
MMMMMM!! THOSE MEN BELOW HER, I SURE ENVY THEM– I MEAN, I WILL SURELY CRUSH THEM!!
BURP
EATING SOMETHING
EATING SOMETHING.
IF WE'RE GOING TO AIM AT SOMETHING LIKE THAT, THEN... THE LEGS, HUH?
THEY LOOK A LITTLE OFF BALANCE.
WE'RE GOING IN, SO YOU GIVE US DIRECTIONS!
YOU'RE GOOD AT GIVING ORDERS.
GOT IT!
GISSH
BWA HA HA HA!! YOU DON'T HAVE A CHANCE! I PACKED ON 30 KILOGRAMS IN PREPARATION FOR THIS!!
ARE THEY INSANE?!
WHAT A WAISTLINE!

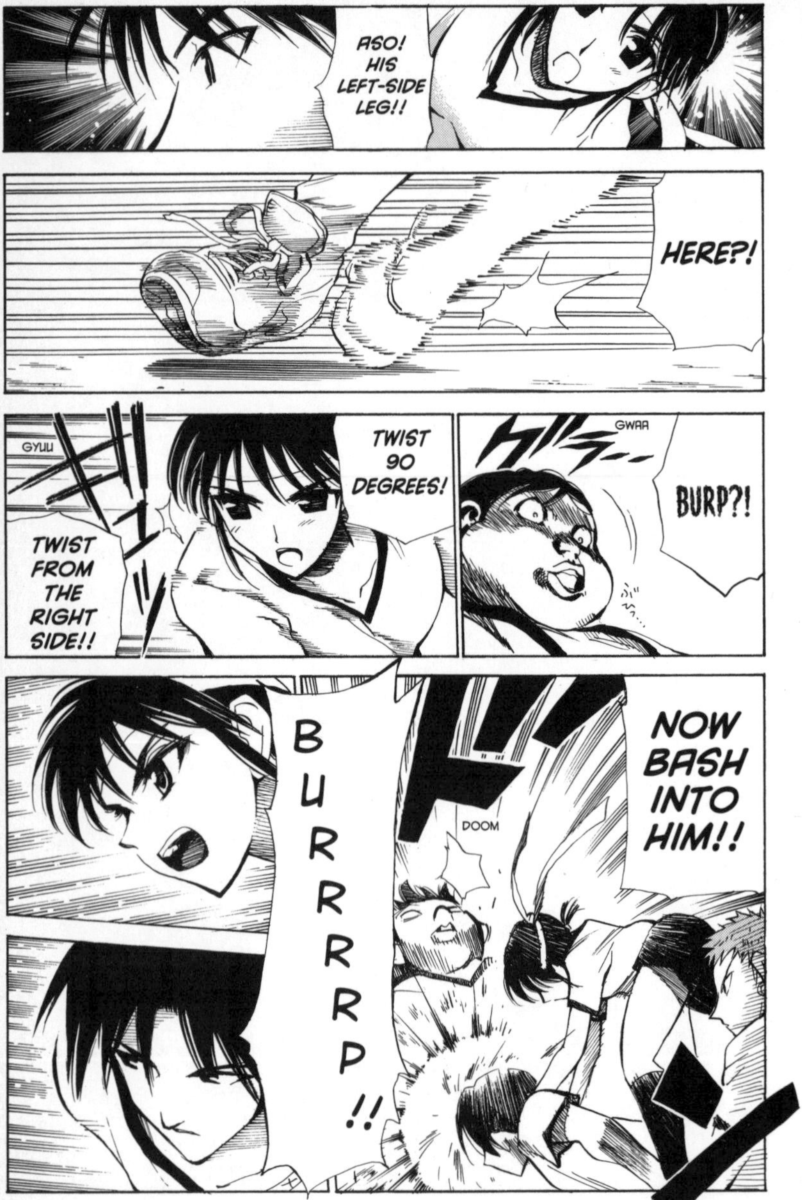
ASO! HIS LEFT-SIDE LEG!!
HERE?!
GWAA
BURP?!
TWIST 90 DEGREES!
GYUU
TWIST FROM THE RIGHT SIDE!!
NOW BASH INTO HIM!!
DOOM
BURRRP!!

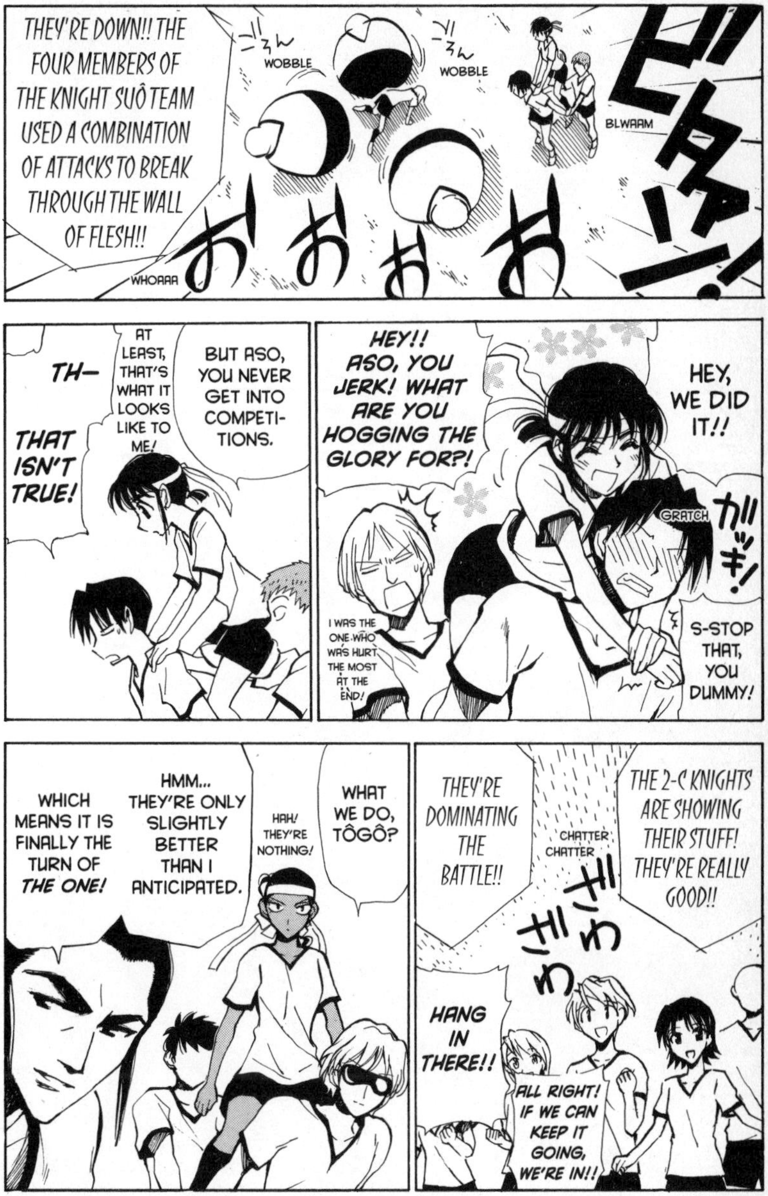
ビタン!
BLWAAM
ごろん
WOBBLE
ごろん
WOBBLE
おおぉお
WHOAAA
THEY'RE DOWN!! THE FOUR MEMBERS OF THE KNIGHT SUÔ TEAM USED A COMBINATION OF ATTACKS TO BREAK THROUGH THE WALL OF FLESH!!
HEY, WE DID IT!!
HEY!! ASO, YOU JERK! WHAT ARE YOU HOGGING THE GLORY FOR?!
ガッキ!
GRATCH
S-STOP THAT, YOU DUMMY!
I WAS THE ONE WHO WAS HURT THE MOST AT THE END!
BUT ASO, YOU NEVER GET INTO COMPETITIONS.
AT LEAST, THAT'S WHAT IT LOOKS LIKE TO ME!
TH—
THAT ISN'T TRUE!
THE 2-C KNIGHTS ARE SHOWING THEIR STUFF! THEY'RE REALLY GOOD!!
CHATTER CHATTER
THEY'RE DOMINATING THE BATTLE!!
ざわざわ
HANG IN THERE!!
ALL RIGHT! IF WE CAN KEEP IT GOING, WE'RE IN!!
WHAT WE DO, TÔGÔ?
HAH! THEY'RE NOTHING!
HMM... THEY'RE ONLY SLIGHTLY BETTER THAN I ANTICIPATED.
WHICH MEANS IT IS FINALLY THE TURN OF THE ONE!

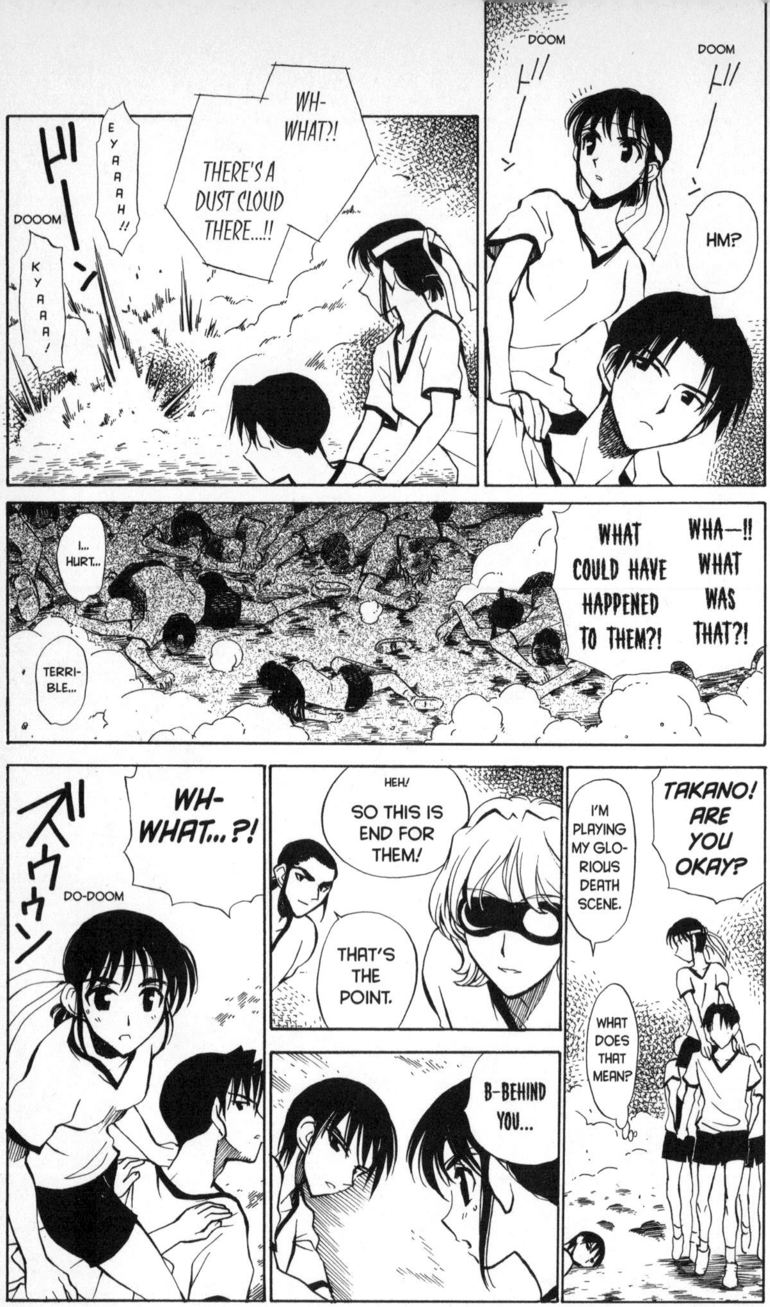
DOOM
DOOM
HM?
WH-WHAT?!
THERE'S A DUST CLOUD THERE...!!
EYAAAAH!!
DOOOM
KYAAAA!
WHA—!! WHAT WAS THAT?!
WHAT COULD HAVE HAPPENED TO THEM?!
I... HURT...
TERRIBLE...
TAKANO! ARE YOU OKAY?
I'M PLAYING MY GLORIOUS DEATH SCENE.
WHAT DOES THAT MEAN?
HEH!
SO THIS IS END FOR THEM!
THAT'S THE POINT.
B-BEHIND YOU...
WH-WHAT...?!
DO-DOOM

You Mean He Was in the Same School?

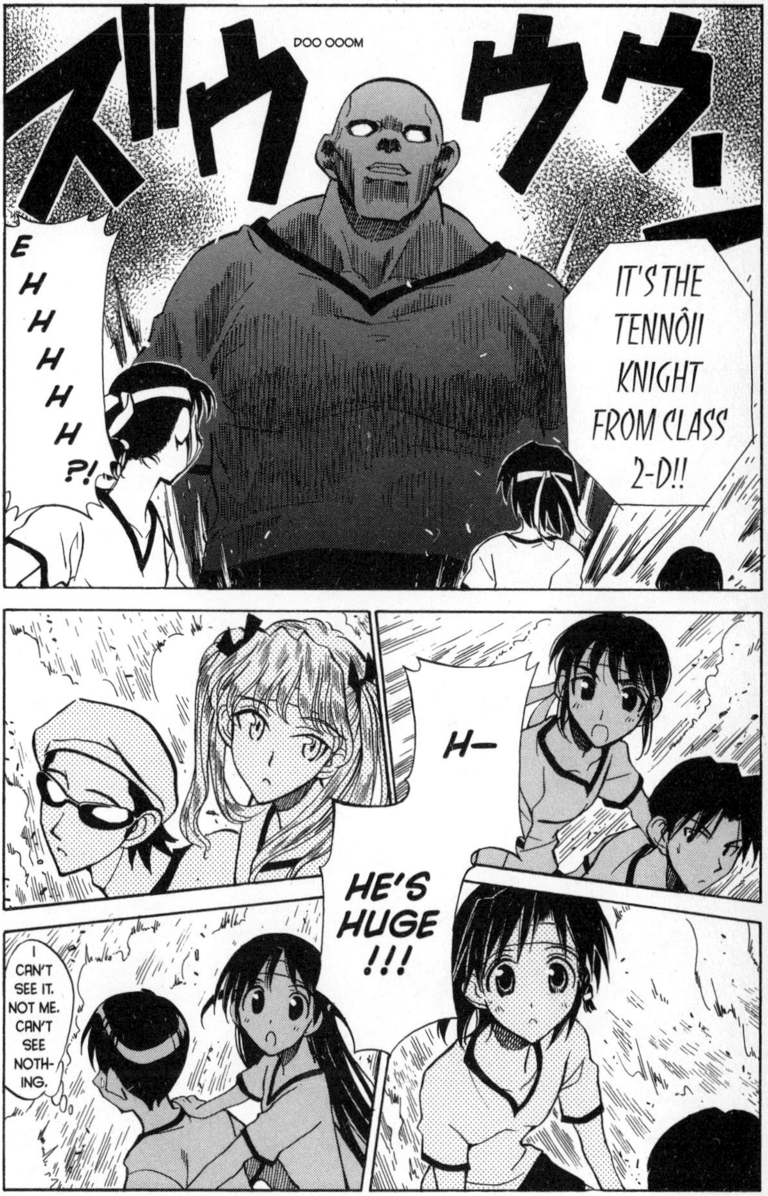
DOO OOOM
IT'S THE TENNÔJI KNIGHT FROM CLASS 2-D!!
EHHHHHH?!
H—
HE'S HUGE!!!
I CAN'T SEE IT. NOT ME. CAN'T SEE NOTHING.

76· · · · · · · · ·Fin

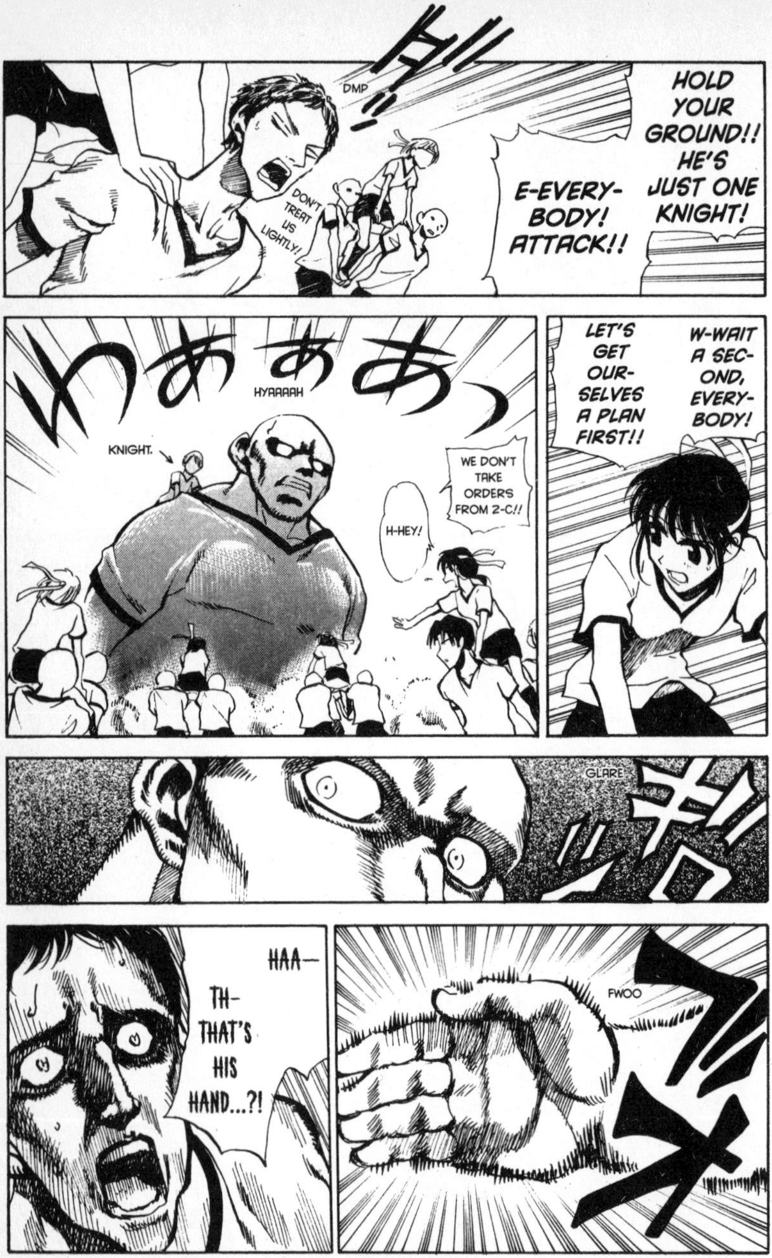
HOLD YOUR GROUND!! HE'S JUST ONE KNIGHT!
E-EVERY-BODY! ATTACK!!
DMP
DON'T TREAT US LIGHTLY!
W-WAIT A SEC-OND, EVERY-BODY!
LET'S GET OUR-SELVES A PLAN FIRST!!
わあああっ
HYAAAAH
WE DON'T TAKE ORDERS FROM 2-C!!
H-HEY!
KNIGHT.
GLARE
FWOO
HAA—
TH-THAT'S HIS HAND...?!

77 FAREWELL TO THE KINGS

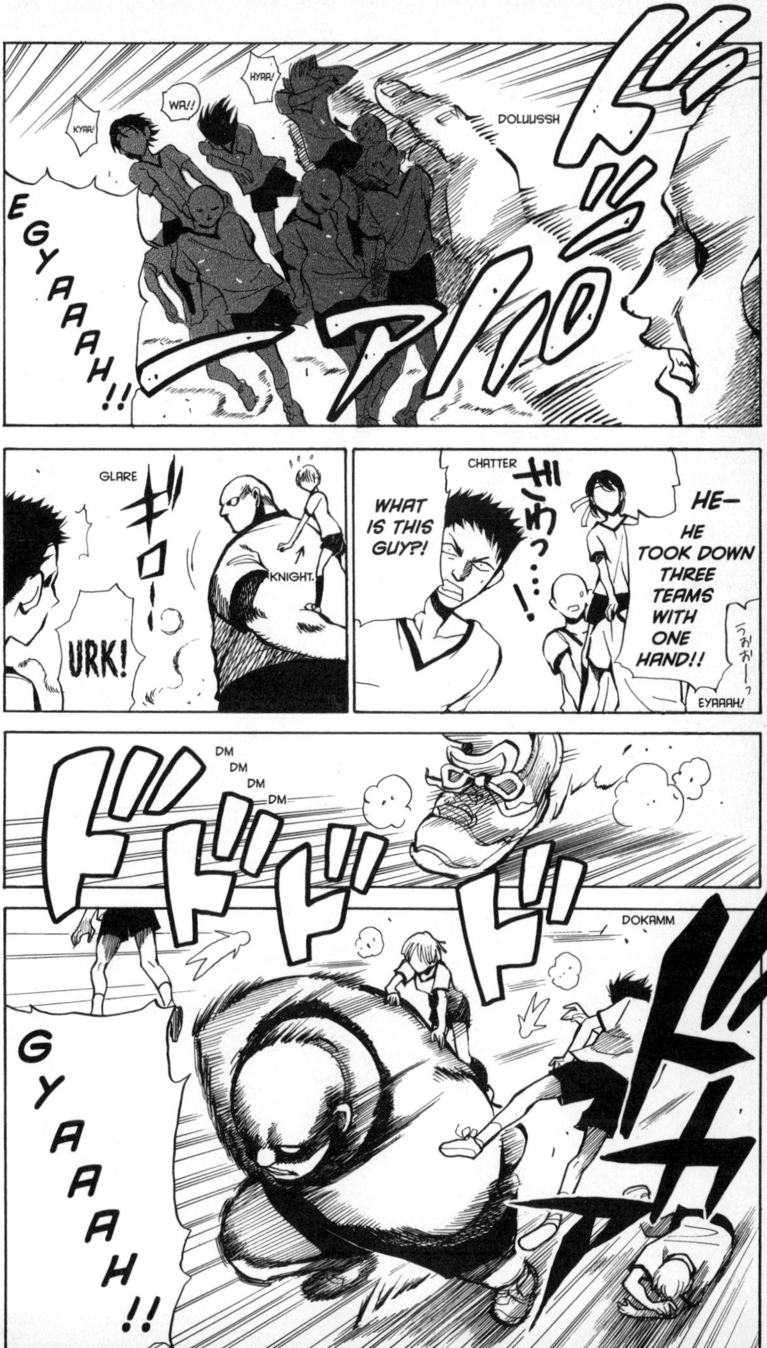
DOLUUSSH
HYAA!
WA!!
KYAA!
EGYAAAAH!!
CHATTER
HE— HE TOOK DOWN THREE TEAMS WITH ONE HAND!!
うおおーっ
EYAAAH!
WHAT IS THIS GUY?!
GLARE
KNIGHT.
URK!
DM DM DM DM
DOKAMM
GYAAAAH!!

Tennôji Noboru: A Still-Growing 2nd-Year Student.

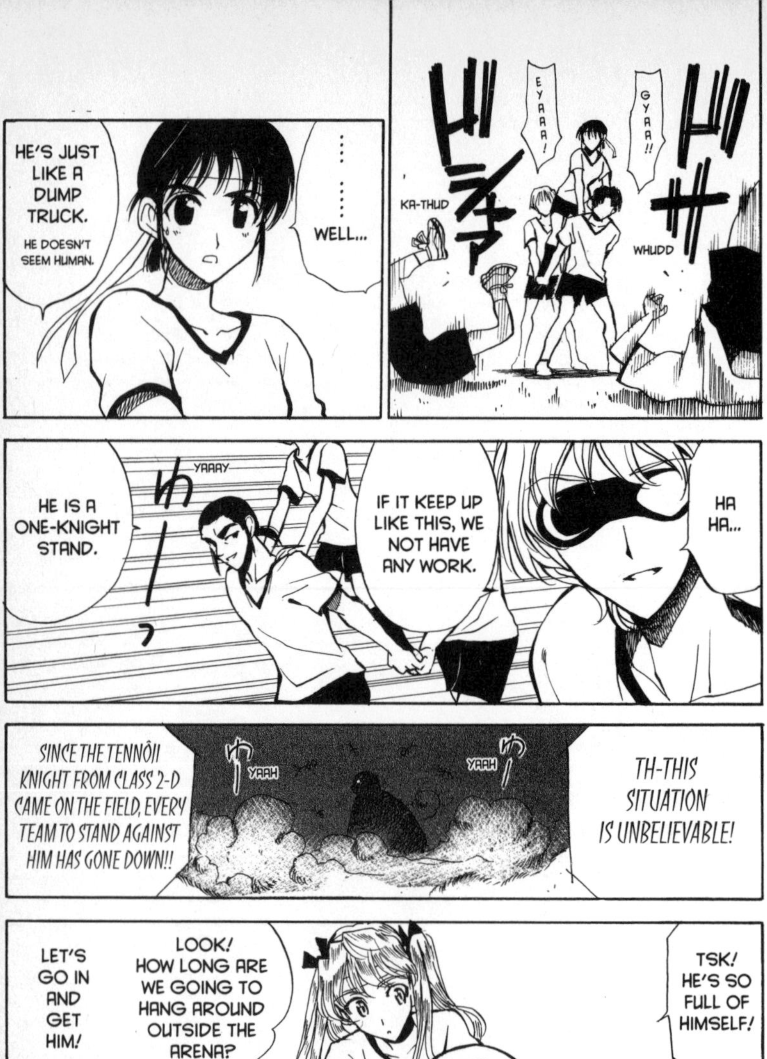
GYAAA!!
EYAAA!
WHUDD
KA-THUD
WELL...
HE'S JUST LIKE A DUMP TRUCK.
HE DOESN'T SEEM HUMAN.
HA HA...
IF IT KEEP UP LIKE THIS, WE NOT HAVE ANY WORK.
YAAAY
HE IS A ONE-KNIGHT STAND.
TH-THIS SITUATION IS UNBELIEVABLE!
YAAH
YAAH
SINCE THE TENNÔJII KNIGHT FROM CLASS 2-D CAME ON THE FIELD, EVERY TEAM TO STAND AGAINST HIM HAS GONE DOWN!!
TSK! HE'S SO FULL OF HIMSELF!
LOOK! HOW LONG ARE WE GOING TO HANG AROUND OUTSIDE THE ARENA?
LET'S GO IN AND GET HIM!
WHAT ARE YOU ACTING SO COOL ABOUT?
IT'S TOO MUCH OF A PAIN. IF YOU WANT TO GO, THEN GO BY YOURSELF!
HUH?!

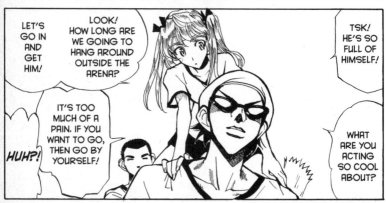

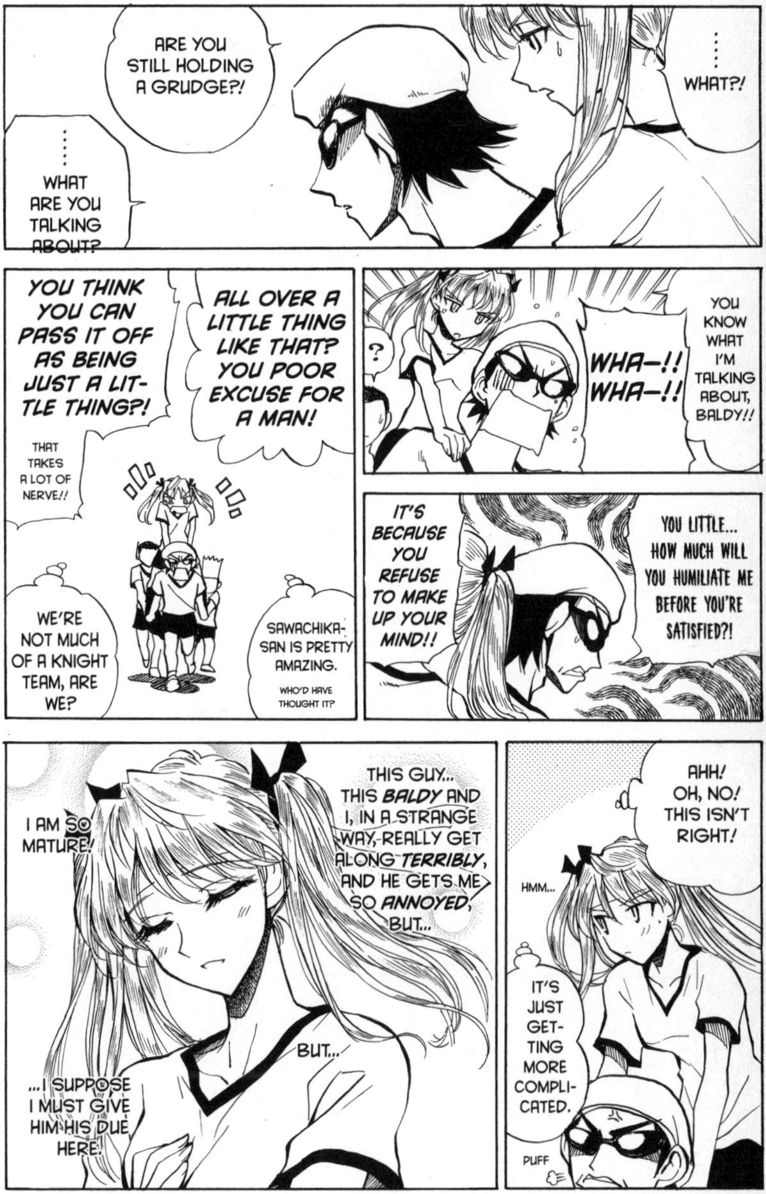
......
WHAT?!
ARE YOU STILL HOLDING A GRUDGE?!
......
WHAT ARE YOU TALKING ABOUT?
YOU KNOW WHAT I'M TALKING ABOUT, BALDY!!
WHA-!! WHA-!!
?
YOU LITTLE... HOW MUCH WILL YOU HUMILIATE ME BEFORE YOU'RE SATISFIED?!
IT'S BECAUSE YOU REFUSE TO MAKE UP YOUR MIND!!
ALL OVER A LITTLE THING LIKE THAT? YOU POOR EXCUSE FOR A MAN!
YOU THINK YOU CAN PASS IT OFF AS BEING JUST A LIT-TLE THING?!
THAT TAKES A LOT OF NERVE!!
SAWACHIKA-SAN IS PRETTY AMAZING.
WHO'D HAVE THOUGHT IT?
WE'RE NOT MUCH OF A KNIGHT TEAM, ARE WE?
AHH! OH, NO! THIS ISN'T RIGHT!
HMM...
IT'S JUST GET-TING MORE COMPLI-CATED.
PUFF
THIS GUY... THIS *BALDY* AND I, IN A STRANGE WAY, REALLY GET ALONG *TERRIBLY*, AND HE GETS ME SO *ANNOYED*, BUT...
I AM SO MATURE!
BUT...
...I SUPPOSE I MUST GIVE HIM HIS DUE HERE.

Sawachika Eri: Slowly Heading Toward Being an Adult.

...Or Not.

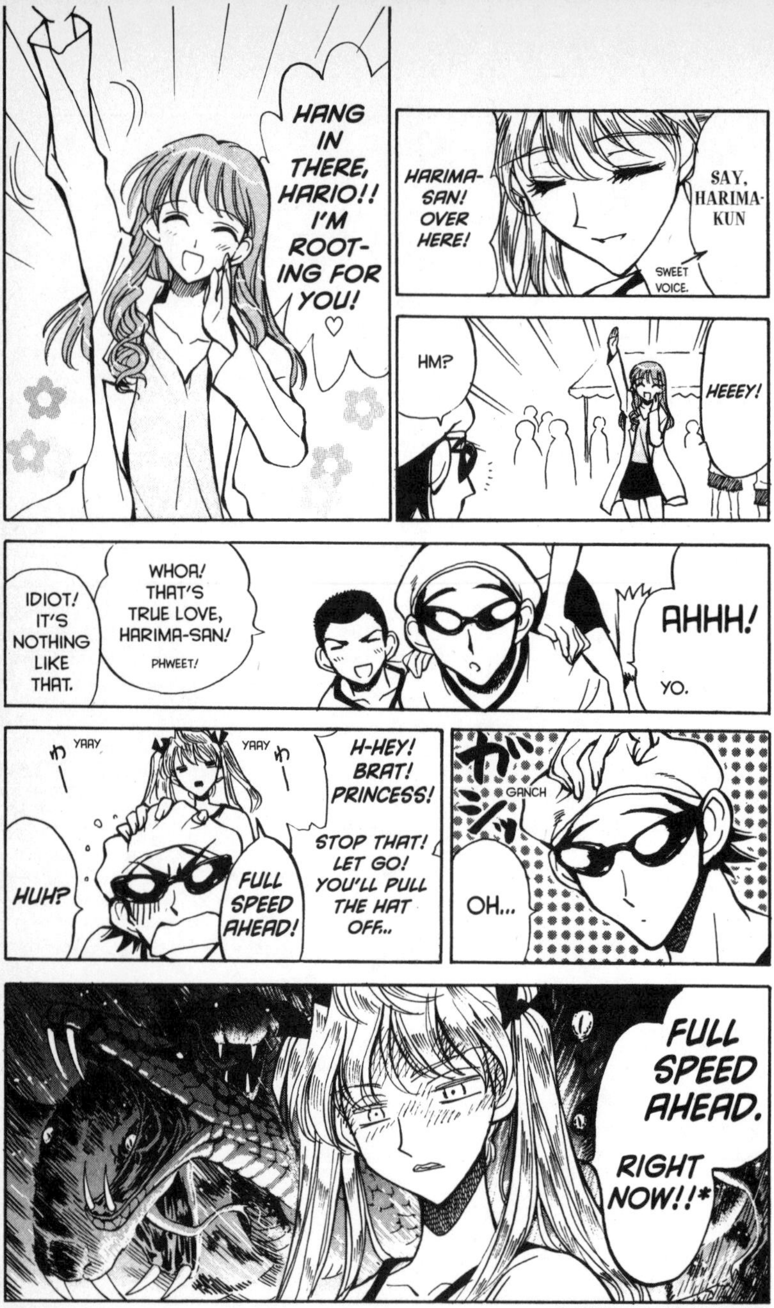

SAY, HARIMA-KUN
SWEET VOICE.
HARIMA-SAN! OVER HERE!
HEEEY!
HM?
HANG IN THERE, HARIO!! I'M ROOTING FOR YOU! ♡
AHHH!
YO.
WHOA! THAT'S TRUE LOVE, HARIMA-SAN!
PHWEET!
IDIOT! IT'S NOTHING LIKE THAT.
ガシッ
GANCH
OH...
H-HEY! BRAT! PRINCESS!
STOP THAT! LET GO! YOU'LL PULL THE HAT OFF..
FULL SPEED AHEAD!
わー
YAAY
わー
YAAY
HUH?
FULL SPEED AHEAD.
RIGHT NOW!!*

*SCARY COMMAND IN ENGLISH

Sawachika: For Some Reason Is Very Annoyed.

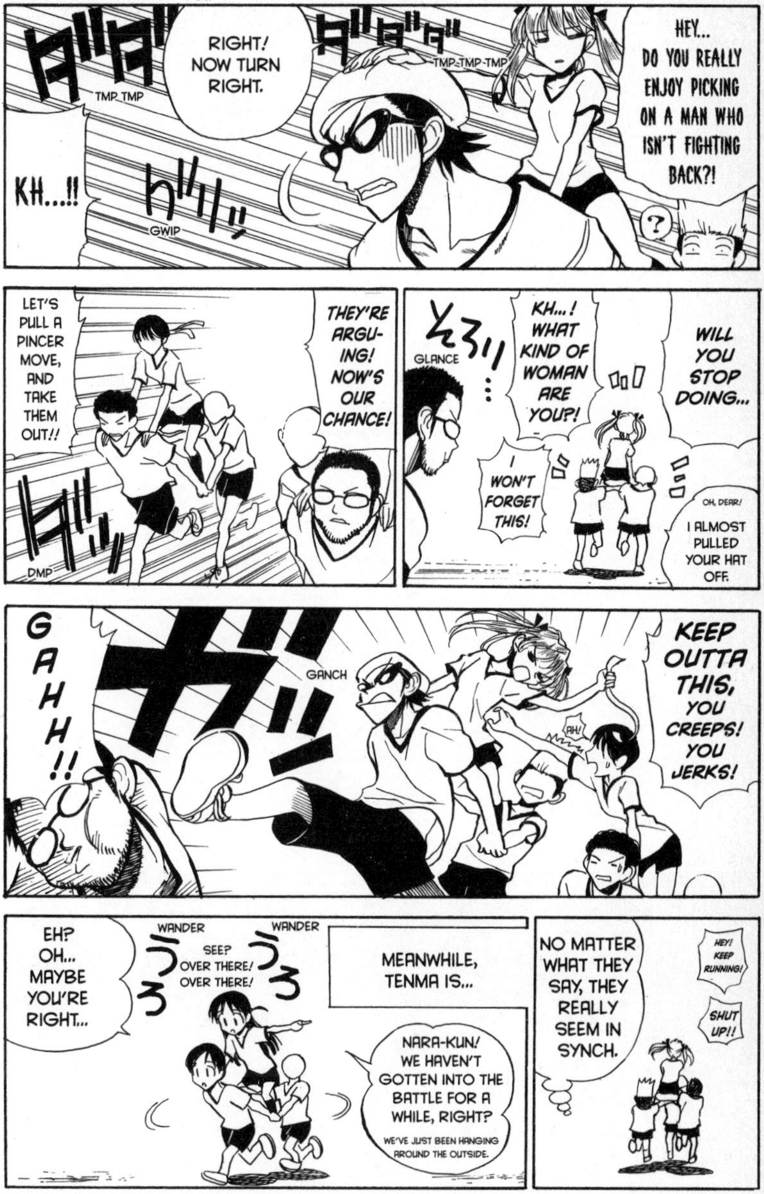
HEY... DO YOU REALLY ENJOY PICKING ON A MAN WHO ISN'T FIGHTING BACK?!
?
TMP-TMP-TMP
RIGHT! NOW TURN RIGHT.
TMP TMP
KH...!!
GWIP
WILL YOU STOP DOING...
OH, DEAR! I ALMOST PULLED YOUR HAT OFF.
KH...! WHAT KIND OF WOMAN ARE YOU?!
I WON'T FORGET THIS!
GLANCE
THEY'RE ARGU-ING! NOW'S OUR CHANCE!
LET'S PULL A PINCER MOVE, AND TAKE THEM OUT!!
DMP
KEEP OUTTA THIS, YOU CREEPS! YOU JERKS!
AH!
GANCH
GAHH!!
HEY! KEEP RUNNING!
SHUT UP!!
NO MATTER WHAT THEY SAY, THEY REALLY SEEM IN SYNCH.
MEANWHILE, TENMA IS...
NARA-KUN! WE HAVEN'T GOTTEN INTO THE BATTLE FOR A WHILE, RIGHT?
WE'VE JUST BEEN HANGING AROUND THE OUTSIDE.
WANDER
WANDER
SEE? OVER THERE! OVER THERE!
EH? OH... MAYBE YOU'RE RIGHT...

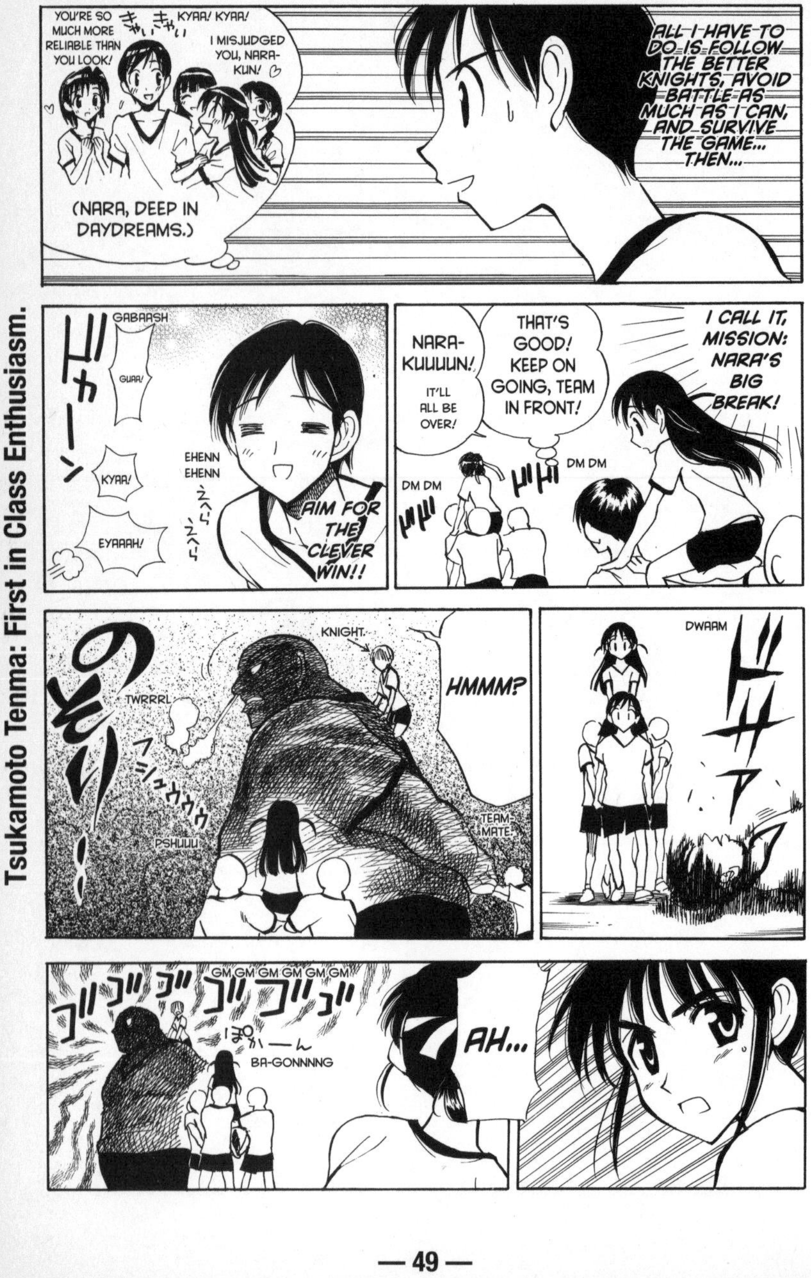
ALL I HAVE TO DO IS FOLLOW THE BETTER KNIGHTS, AVOID BATTLE AS MUCH AS I CAN, AND SURVIVE THE GAME... THEN...
I MISJUDGED YOU, NARA-KUN! ♡
KYAA! KYAA!
きゃいきゃい
YOU'RE SO MUCH MORE RELIABLE THAN YOU LOOK!
(NARA, DEEP IN DAYDREAMS.)
I CALL IT, MISSION: NARA'S BIG BREAK!
THAT'S GOOD! KEEP ON GOING, TEAM IN FRONT!
NARA-KUUUUN!
IT'LL ALL BE OVER!
DM DM
DM DM
AIM FOR THE CLEVER WIN!!
EHENN EHENN
えへらえへら
GABAASH
ジャーン
GUAA!
KYAA!
EYAAAH!
DWAAM
ドサァ
HMMM?
KNIGHT.
TEAM-MATE.
TWRRRL
フシュウウウ
PSHUUU
のそり…
AH...
GM GM GM GM GM GM
ゴゴゴゴゴゴ
ぽかーん
BA-GONNNNG

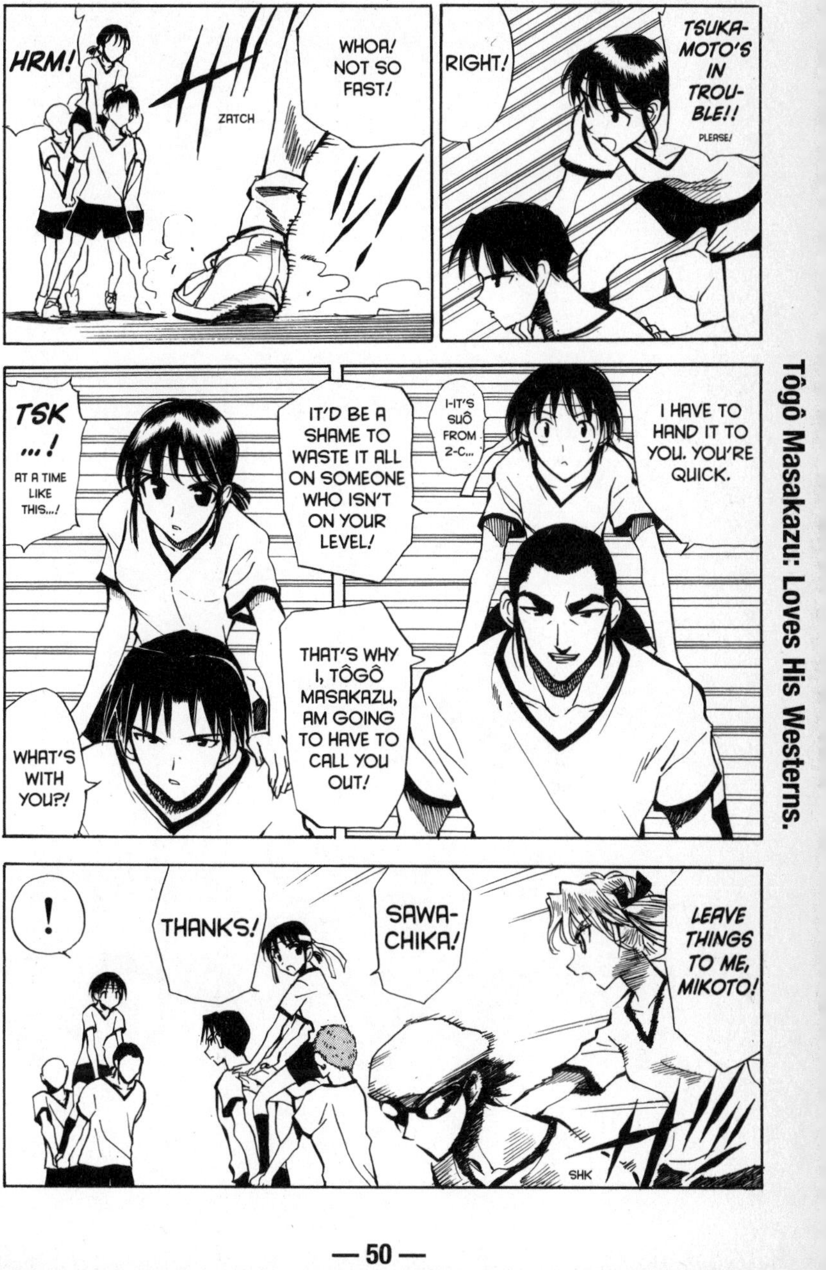
TSUKA-MOTO'S IN TROU-BLE!!
PLEASE!
RIGHT!
WHOA! NOT SO FAST!
ZATCH
HRM!
I HAVE TO HAND IT TO YOU. YOU'RE QUICK.
I-IT'S SUÔ FROM 2-C...
IT'D BE A SHAME TO WASTE IT ALL ON SOMEONE WHO ISN'T ON YOUR LEVEL!
THAT'S WHY I, TÔGÔ MASAKAZU, AM GOING TO HAVE TO CALL YOU OUT!
TSK ...!
AT A TIME LIKE THIS...!
WHAT'S WITH YOU?!
LEAVE THINGS TO ME, MIKOTO!
SHK
SAWA-CHIKA!
THANKS!
!

Tôgô Masakazu: Loves His Westerns.

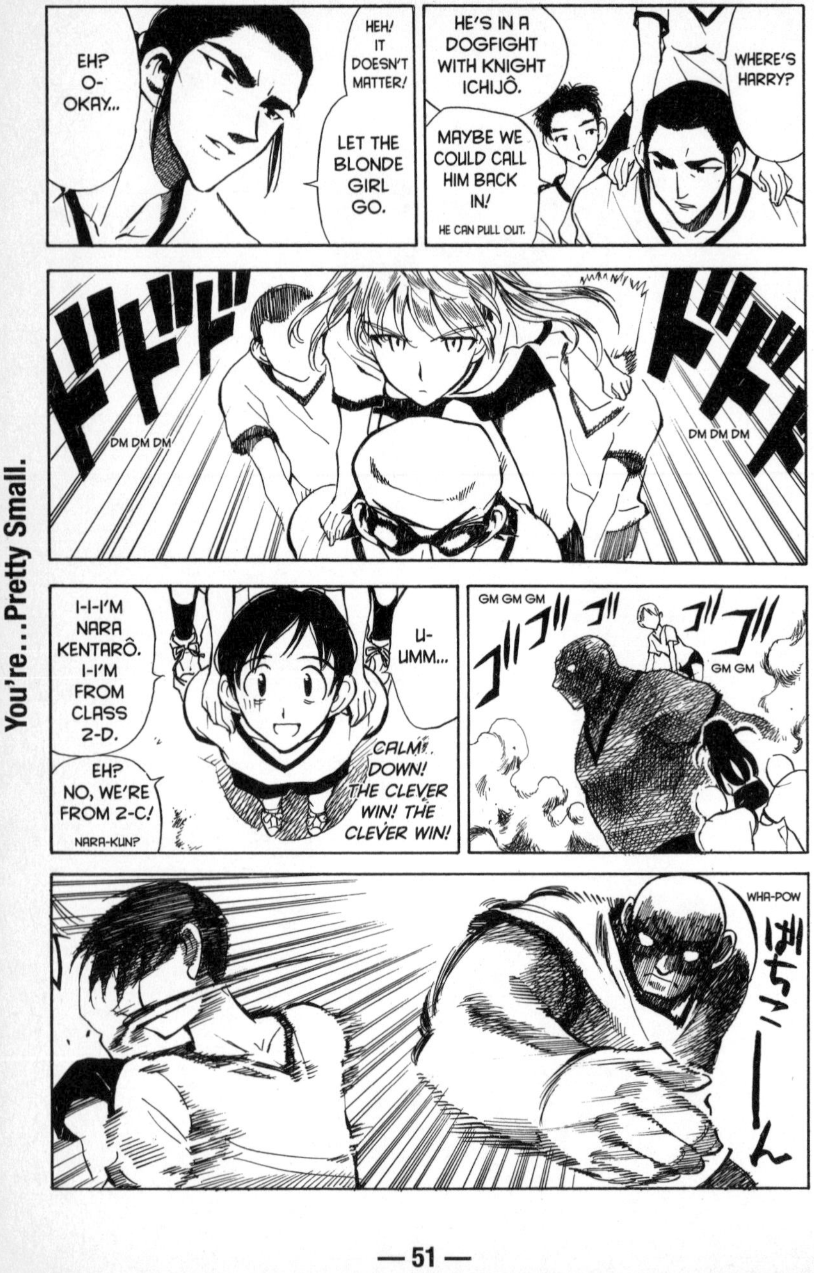
WHERE'S HARRY?
HE'S IN A DOGFIGHT WITH KNIGHT ICHIJÔ.
MAYBE WE COULD CALL HIM BACK IN!
HE CAN PULL OUT.
HEH! IT DOESN'T MATTER!
LET THE BLONDE GIRL GO.
EH? O-OKAY...
DM DM DM
DM DM DM
GM GM GM
GM GM
U-UMM...
I-I-I'M NARA KENTARÔ. I-I'M FROM CLASS 2-D.
CALM DOWN! THE CLEVER WIN! THE CLEVER WIN!
EH? NO, WE'RE FROM 2-C!
NARA-KUN?
WHA-POW

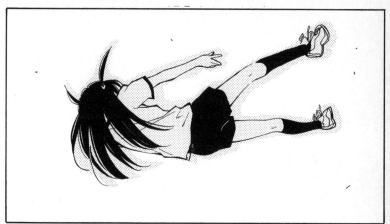

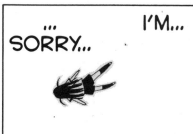

...
SORRY...

I'M...

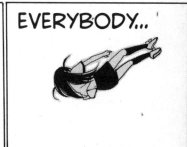

EVERYBODY...

10

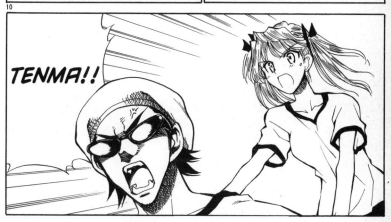

TENMA!!

77 ········ Fin

78 DEAD OR ALIVE

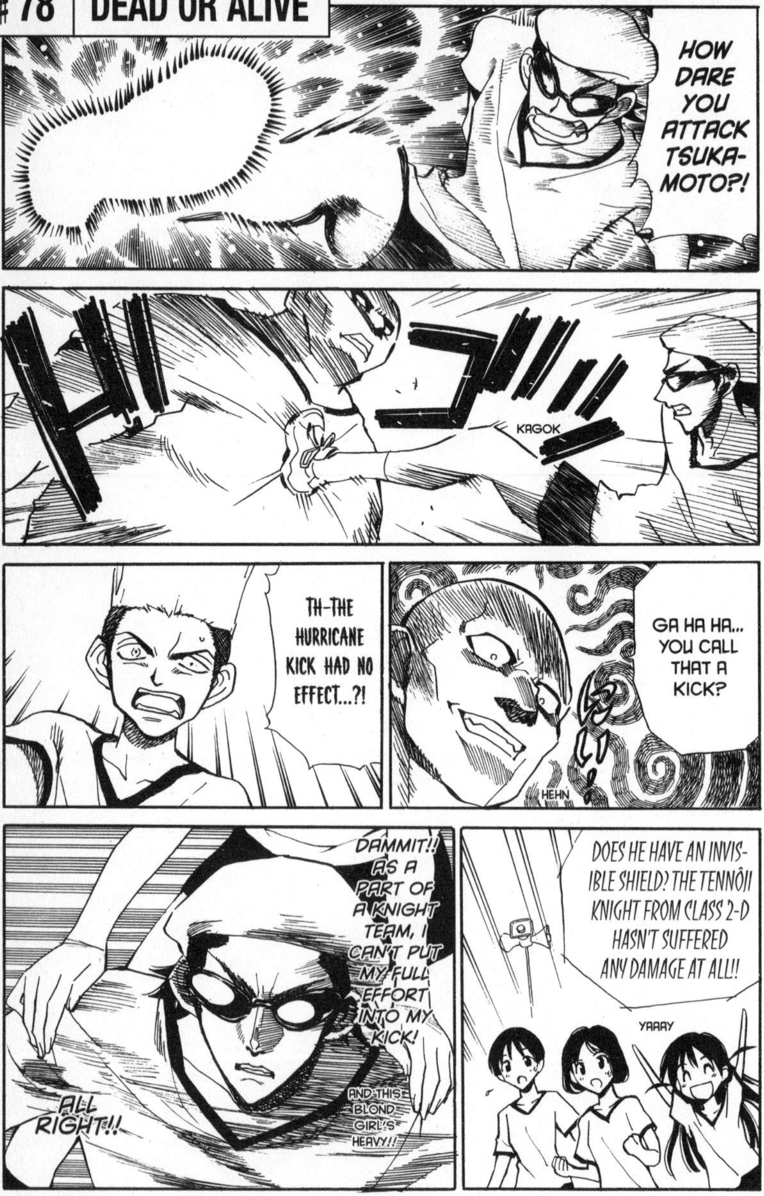
HOW DARE YOU ATTACK TSUKA-MOTO?!
KAGOK
GA HA HA... YOU CALL THAT A KICK?
HEHN
TH-THE HURRICANE KICK HAD NO EFFECT...?!
DOES HE HAVE AN INVIS-IBLE SHIELD? THE TENNÔJI KNIGHT FROM CLASS 2-D HASN'T SUFFERED ANY DAMAGE AT ALL!!
YAAAY
DAMMIT!! AS A PART OF A KNIGHT TEAM, I CAN'T PUT MY FULL EFFORT INTO MY KICK!
AND THIS BLOND GIRL'S HEAVY!!
ALL RIGHT!!

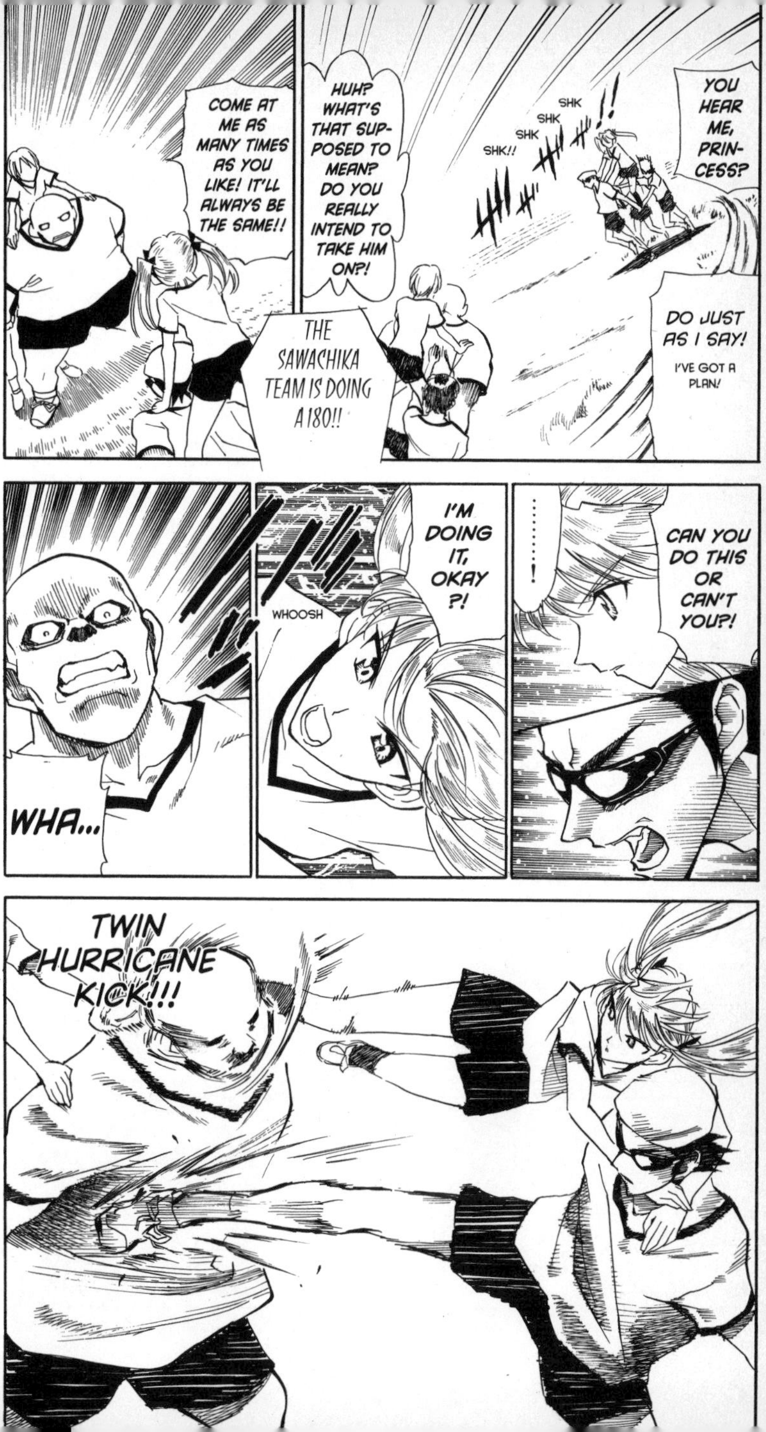
YOU HEAR ME, PRIN-CESS?
SHK!! SHK SHK SHK
DO JUST AS I SAY!
I'VE GOT A PLAN!
HUH? WHAT'S THAT SUP-POSED TO MEAN? DO YOU REALLY INTEND TO TAKE HIM ON?!
THE SAWACHIKA TEAM IS DOING A 180!!
COME AT ME AS MANY TIMES AS YOU LIKE! IT'LL ALWAYS BE THE SAME!!
CAN YOU DO THIS OR CAN'T YOU?!
......!
I'M DOING IT, OKAY?!
WHOOSH
WHA...
TWIN HURRICANE KICK!!!

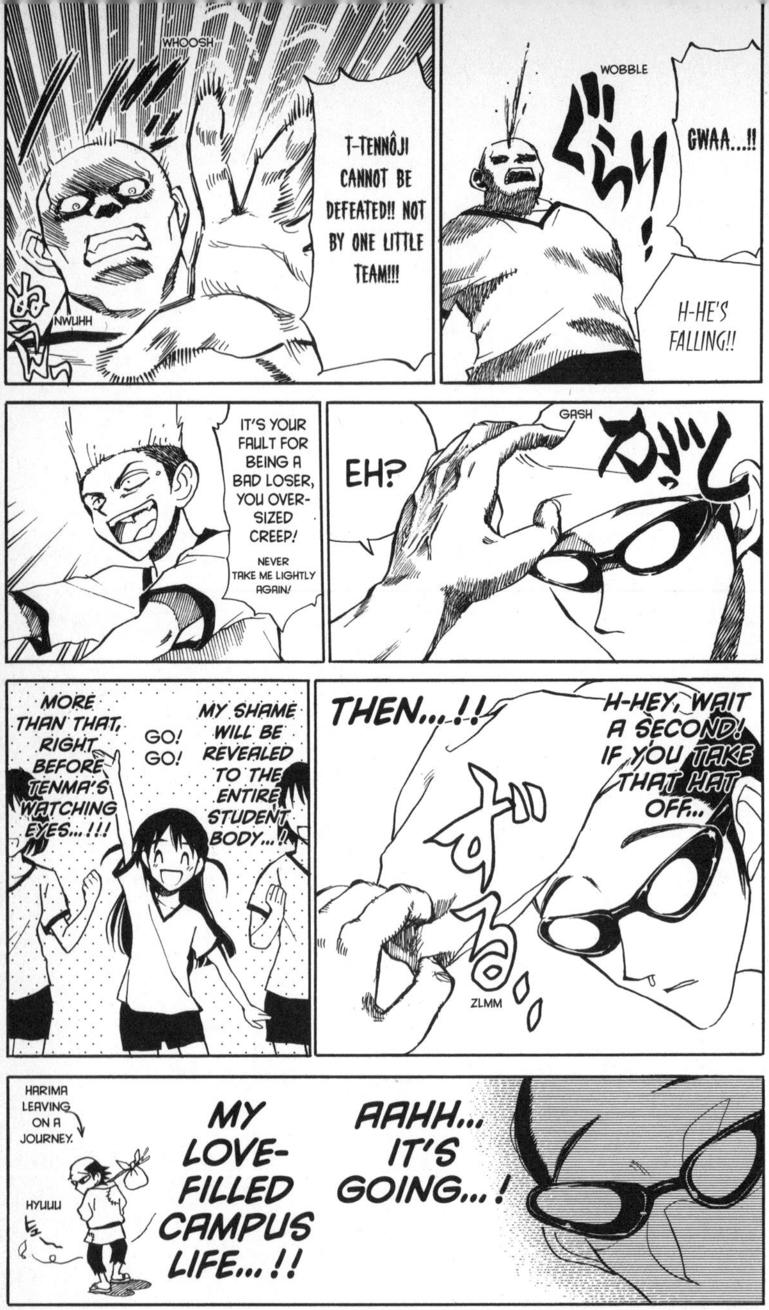
WOBBLE
GWAA...!!
H-HE'S FALLING!!
WHOOSH
T-TENNÔJI CANNOT BE DEFEATED!! NOT BY ONE LITTLE TEAM!!!
NWUHH
GASH
EH?
IT'S YOUR FAULT FOR BEING A BAD LOSER, YOU OVER-SIZED CREEP!
NEVER TAKE ME LIGHTLY AGAIN!
THEN...!!
H-HEY, WAIT A SECOND! IF YOU TAKE THAT HAT OFF...
ZLMM
MY SHAME WILL BE REVEALED TO THE ENTIRE STUDENT BODY...!!
GO! GO!
MORE THAN THAT, RIGHT BEFORE TENMA'S WATCHING EYES...!!!
AAHH... IT'S GOING...!
MY LOVE-FILLED CAMPUS LIFE...!!
HARIMA LEAVING ON A JOURNEY.
HYUUU

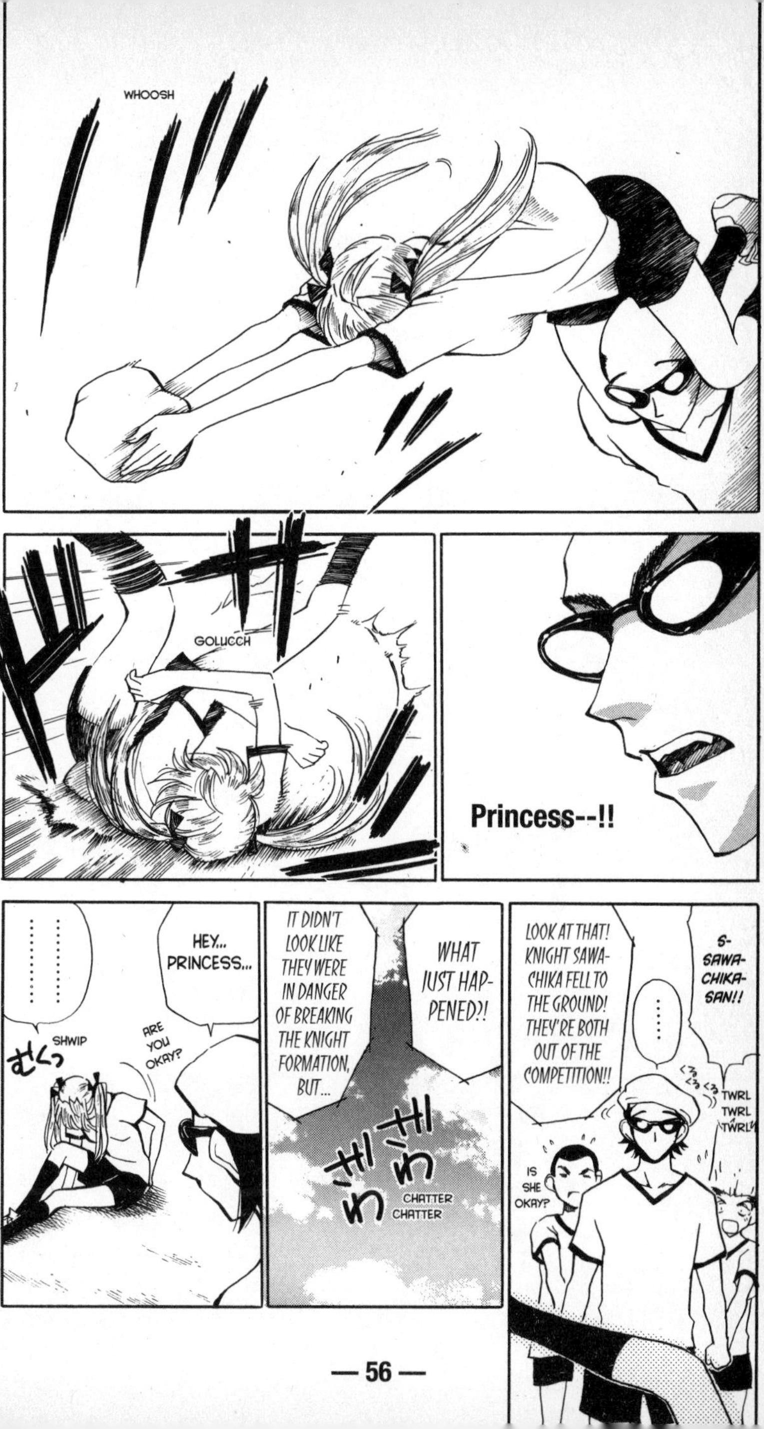
WHOOSH
Princess--!!
GOLUCCH
S-SAWA-CHIKA-SAN!!
......
LOOK AT THAT! KNIGHT SAWA-CHIKA FELL TO THE GROUND! THEY'RE BOTH OUT OF THE COMPETITION!!
くるくるくる
TWRL TWRL TWRL
IS SHE OKAY?
WHAT JUST HAP-PENED?!
IT DIDN'T LOOK LIKE THEY WERE IN DANGER OF BREAKING THE KNIGHT FORMATION, BUT...
ざわざわ
CHATTER CHATTER
HEY... PRINCESS...
......
むくっ
SHWIP
ARE YOU OKAY?

Princess--!!

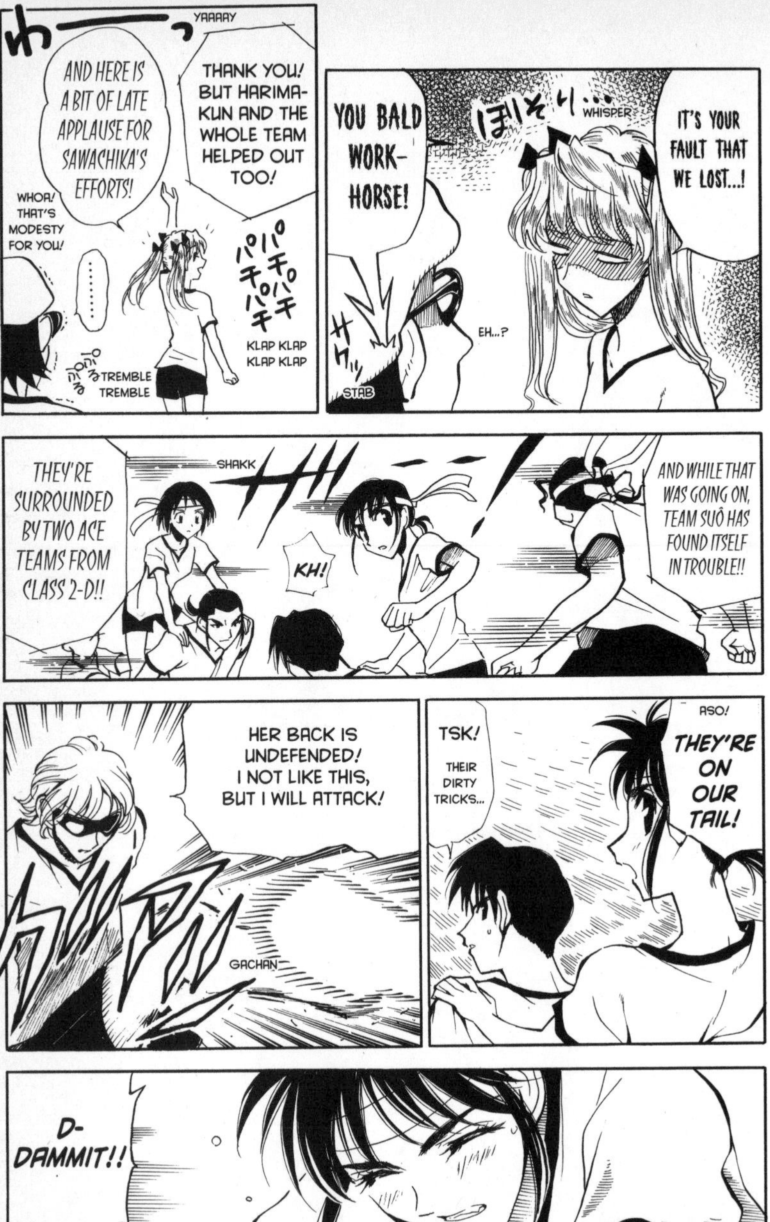
IT'S YOUR FAULT THAT WE LOST...!
ぼそり… WHISPER
YOU BALD WORK-HORSE!
EH...?
サクッ STAB
わーっ YAAAAY
THANK YOU! BUT HARIMA-KUN AND THE WHOLE TEAM HELPED OUT TOO!
AND HERE IS A BIT OF LATE APPLAUSE FOR SAWACHIKA'S EFFORTS!
パチパチパチパチ KLAP KLAP KLAP KLAP
WHOA! THAT'S MODESTY FOR YOU!
......
ぷるぷる TREMBLE TREMBLE
AND WHILE THAT WAS GOING ON, TEAM SUÔ HAS FOUND ITSELF IN TROUBLE!!
KH!
SHAKK
THEY'RE SURROUNDED BY TWO ACE TEAMS FROM CLASS 2-D!!
ASO! THEY'RE ON OUR TAIL!
TSK! THEIR DIRTY TRICKS...
HER BACK IS UNDEFENDED! I NOT LIKE THIS, BUT I WILL ATTACK!
GACHAN
D-DAMMIT!!

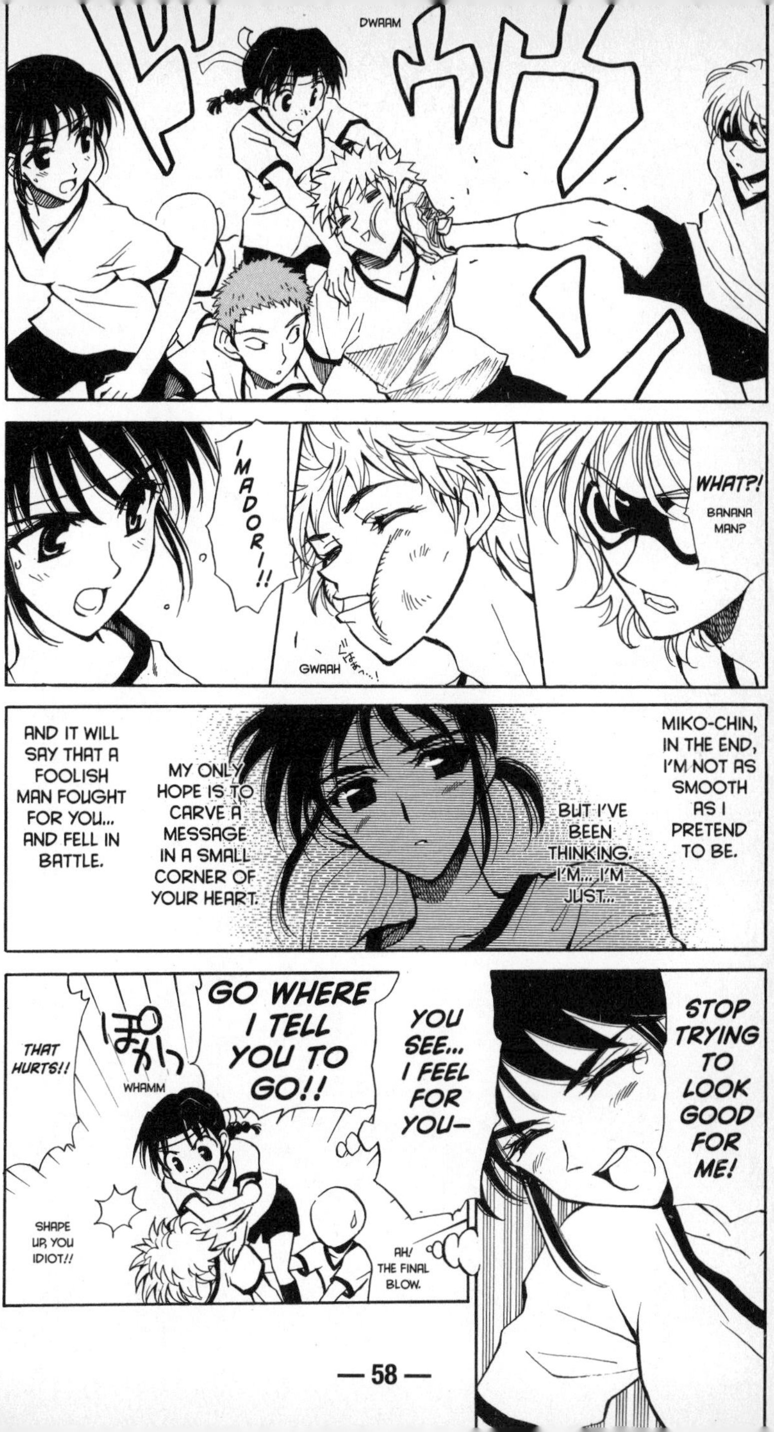
DWAAM
WHAT?!
BANANA MAN?
GWAAH
IMADORI!!
MIKO-CHIN, IN THE END, I'M NOT AS SMOOTH AS I PRETEND TO BE.
BUT I'VE BEEN THINKING. I'M... I'M JUST...
MY ONLY HOPE IS TO CARVE A MESSAGE IN A SMALL CORNER OF YOUR HEART.
AND IT WILL SAY THAT A FOOLISH MAN FOUGHT FOR YOU... AND FELL IN BATTLE.
STOP TRYING TO LOOK GOOD FOR ME!
YOU SEE... I FEEL FOR YOU—
GO WHERE I TELL YOU TO GO!!
ぽかっ
WHAMM
THAT HURTS!!
SHAPE UP, YOU IDIOT!!
AH! THE FINAL BLOW.

Imadori Kyôsuke: Showing His Manly Courage.

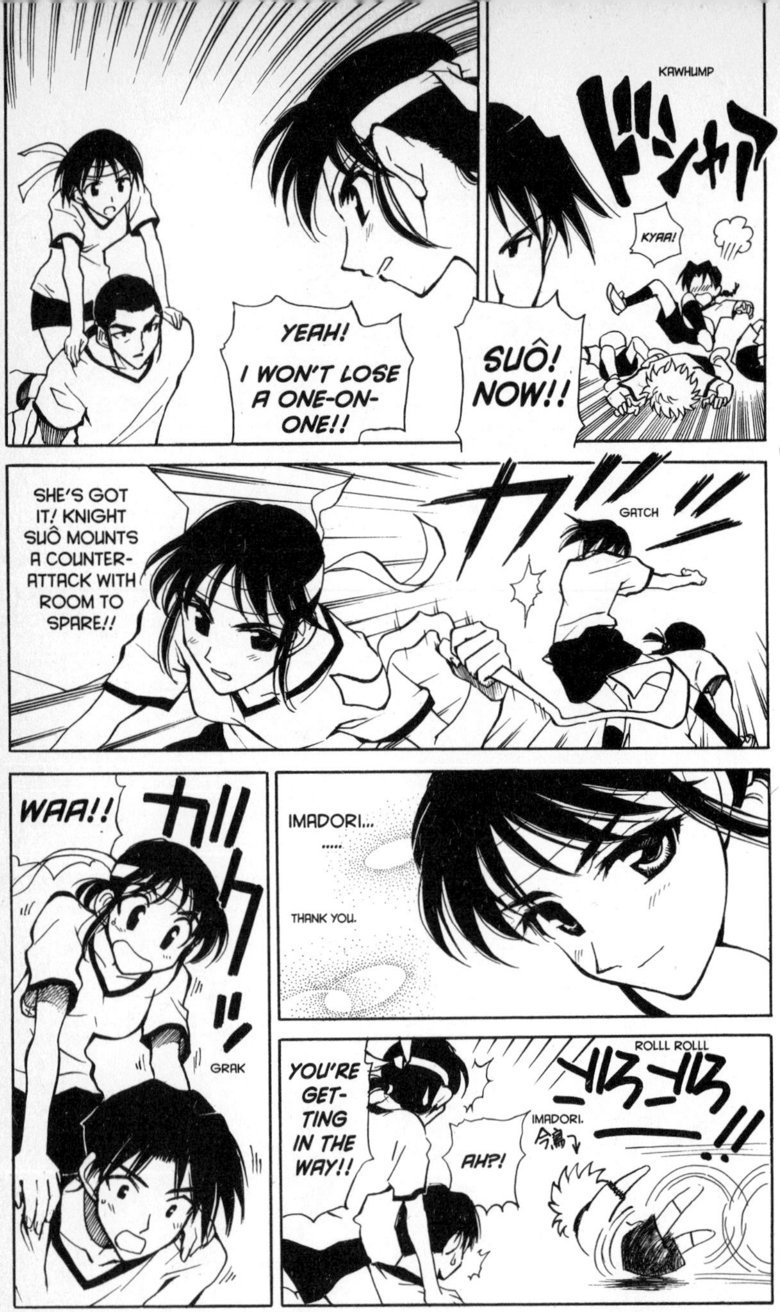
KAWHUMP
KYAA!
SUÔ! NOW!!
YEAH! I WON'T LOSE A ONE-ON-ONE!!
GATCH
SHE'S GOT IT! KNIGHT SUÔ MOUNTS A COUNTER-ATTACK WITH ROOM TO SPARE!!
IMADORI...
.....
THANK YOU.
ROLLL ROLLL
IMADORI.
今鳥
AH?!
YOU'RE GET-TING IN THE WAY!!
WAA!!
GRAK

Or Not.

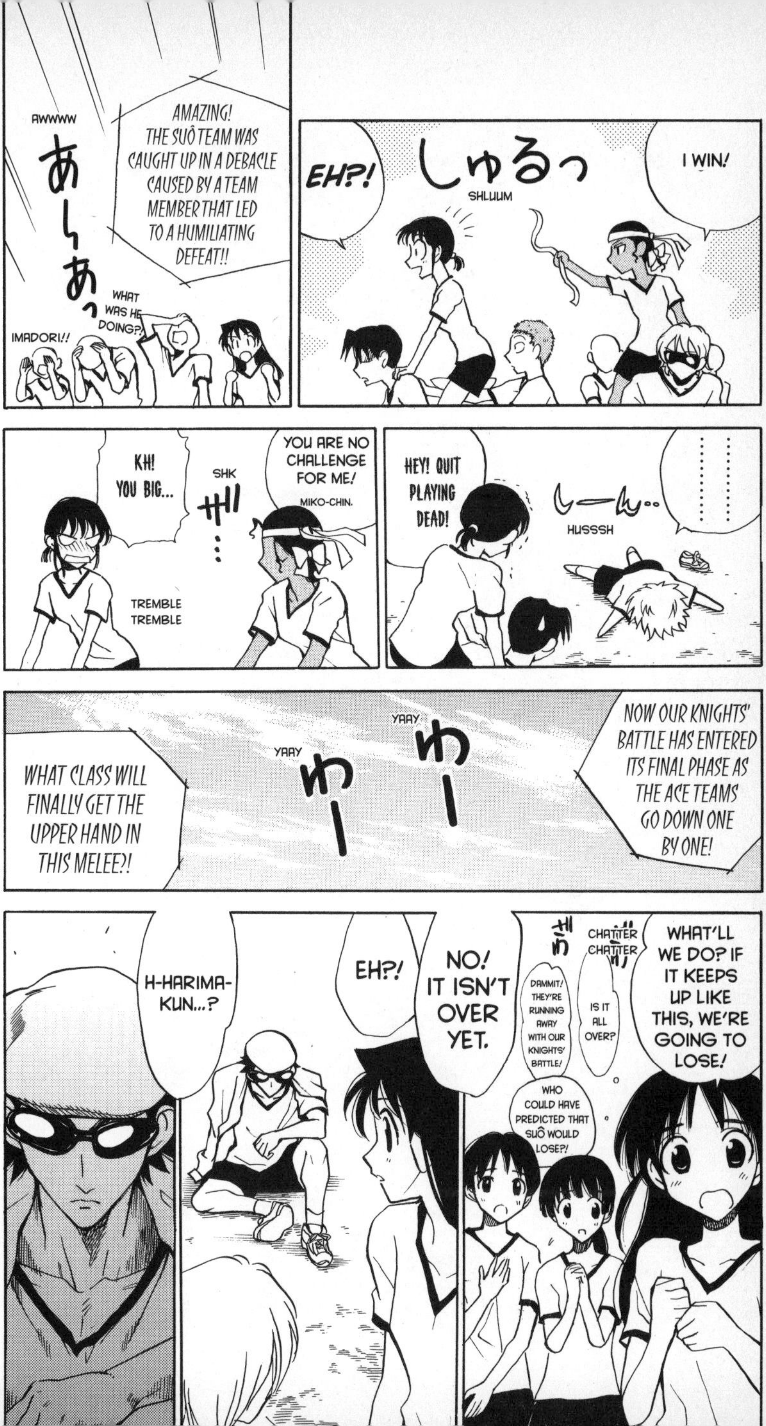
I WIN!
しゅるっ
SHLUUM
EH?!
AMAZING! THE SUÔ TEAM WAS CAUGHT UP IN A DEBACLE CAUSED BY A TEAM MEMBER THAT LED TO A HUMILIATING DEFEAT!!
あ〜あっ
AWWWW
WHAT WAS HE DOING?!
IMADORI!!
......
しーん..
HUSSSH
HEY! QUIT PLAYING DEAD!
YOU ARE NO CHALLENGE FOR ME!
MIKO-CHIN.
ザ
SHK
KH! YOU BIG...
TREMBLE TREMBLE
NOW OUR KNIGHTS' BATTLE HAS ENTERED ITS FINAL PHASE AS THE ACE TEAMS GO DOWN ONE BY ONE!
わー
YAAY
わー
YAAY
WHAT CLASS WILL FINALLY GET THE UPPER HAND IN THIS MELEE?!
WHAT'LL WE DO? IF IT KEEPS UP LIKE THIS, WE'RE GOING TO LOSE!
CHATTER CHATTER
IS IT ALL OVER?
DAMMIT! THEY'RE RUNNING AWAY WITH OUR KNIGHTS' BATTLE!
WHO COULD HAVE PREDICTED THAT SUÔ WOULD LOSE?!
NO! IT ISN'T OVER YET.
EH?!
H-HARIMA-KUN...?

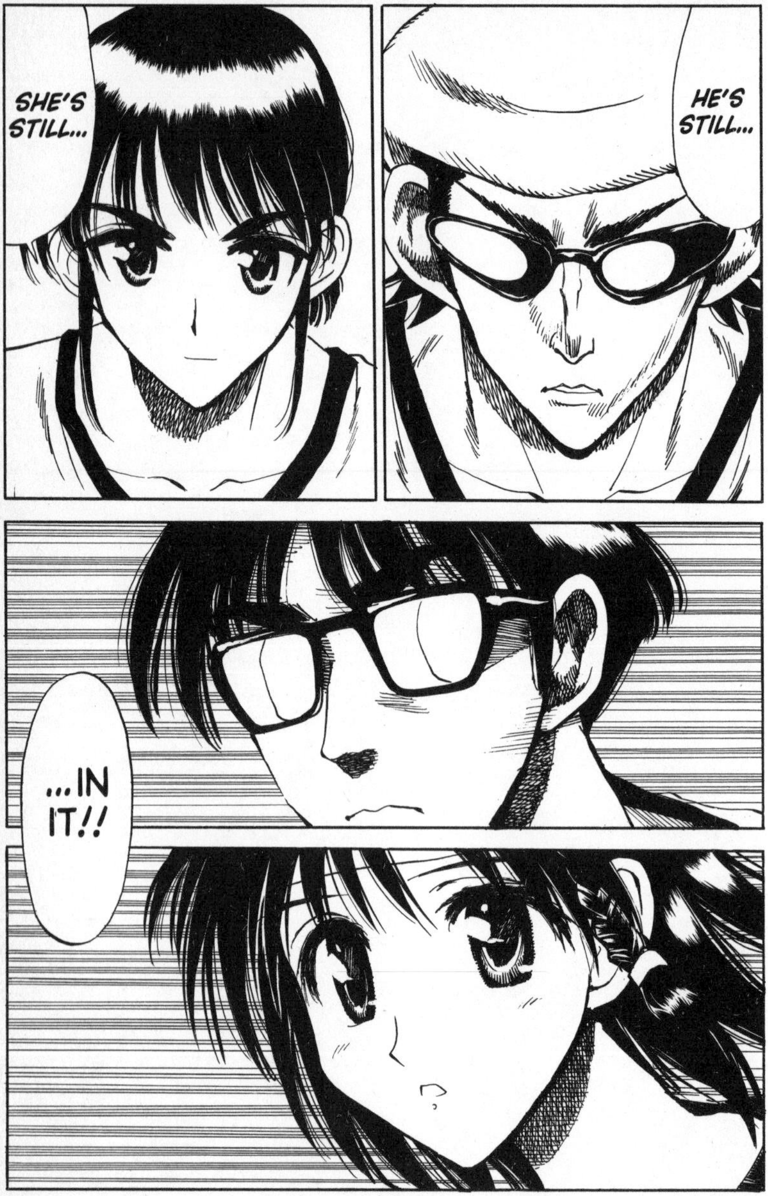
HE'S STILL...
SHE'S STILL...
...IN IT!!

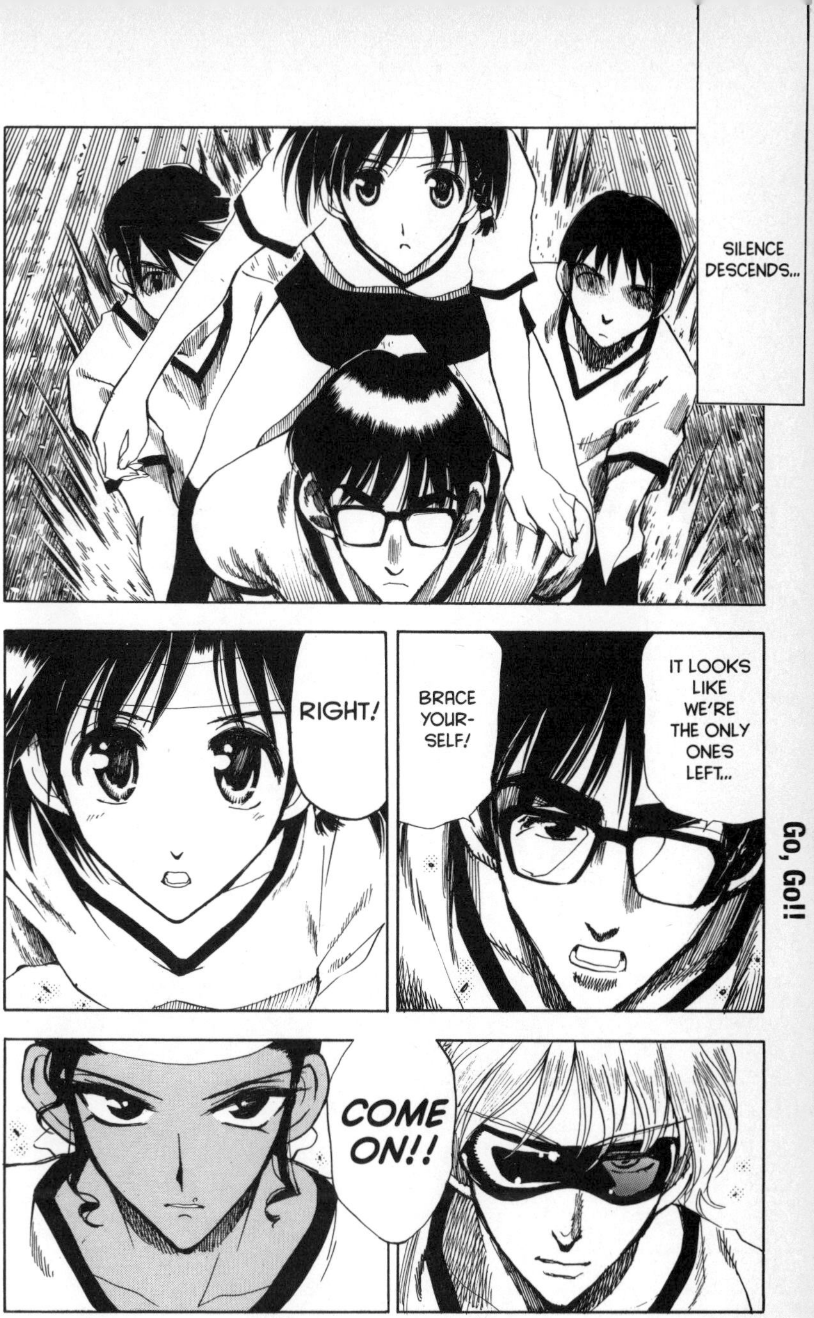
SILENCE DESCENDS...
IT LOOKS LIKE WE'RE THE ONLY ONES LEFT...
BRACE YOUR-SELF!
RIGHT!
COME ON!!

78· · · · · · · · · ·Fin

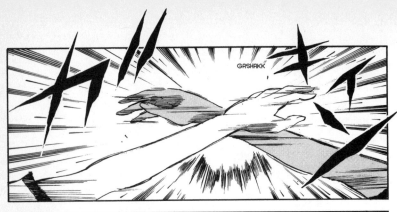

GASHAKK

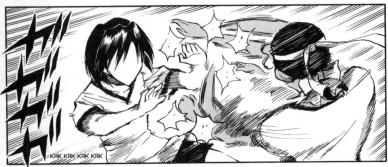

KAK KAK KAK KAK

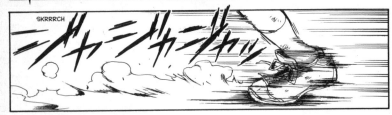

SKRRRCH

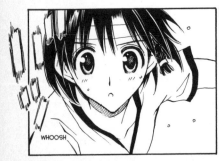

WHOOSH

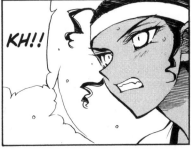

KH!!

#79 SOLDIERS OF INNOCENCE

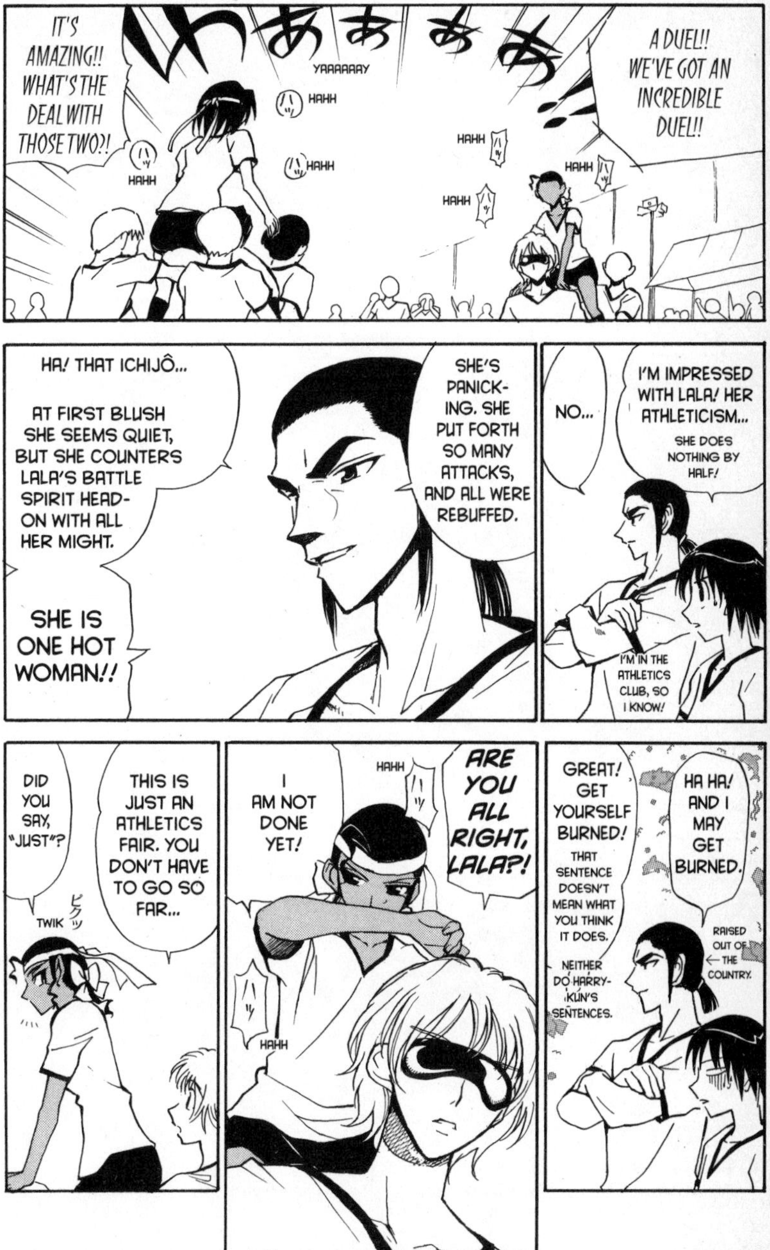
A DUEL!! WE'VE GOT AN INCREDIBLE DUEL!!
わあああああ
YAAAAAAY
ハッ HAHH
ハッ HAHH
ハッ HAHH
ハッ HAHH
ハッ HAHH
ハッ HAHH
IT'S AMAZING!! WHAT'S THE DEAL WITH THOSE TWO?!
I'M IMPRESSED WITH LALA! HER ATHLETICISM...
SHE DOES NOTHING BY HALF!
NO...
I'M IN THE ATHLETICS CLUB, SO I KNOW!
SHE'S PANICKING. SHE PUT FORTH SO MANY ATTACKS, AND ALL WERE REBUFFED.
HA! THAT ICHIJÔ...
AT FIRST BLUSH SHE SEEMS QUIET, BUT SHE COUNTERS LALA'S BATTLE SPIRIT HEAD-ON WITH ALL HER MIGHT.
SHE IS ONE HOT WOMAN!!
HA HA! AND I MAY GET BURNED.
GREAT! GET YOURSELF BURNED!
THAT SENTENCE DOESN'T MEAN WHAT YOU THINK IT DOES.
RAISED OUT OF THE COUNTRY.
NEITHER DO HARRY-KUN'S SENTENCES.
ARE YOU ALL RIGHT, LALA?!
ハッ HAHH
I AM NOT DONE YET!
ハッ HAHH
THIS IS JUST AN ATHLETICS FAIR. YOU DON'T HAVE TO GO SO FAR...
DID YOU SAY, "JUST"?
ピクッ TWIK

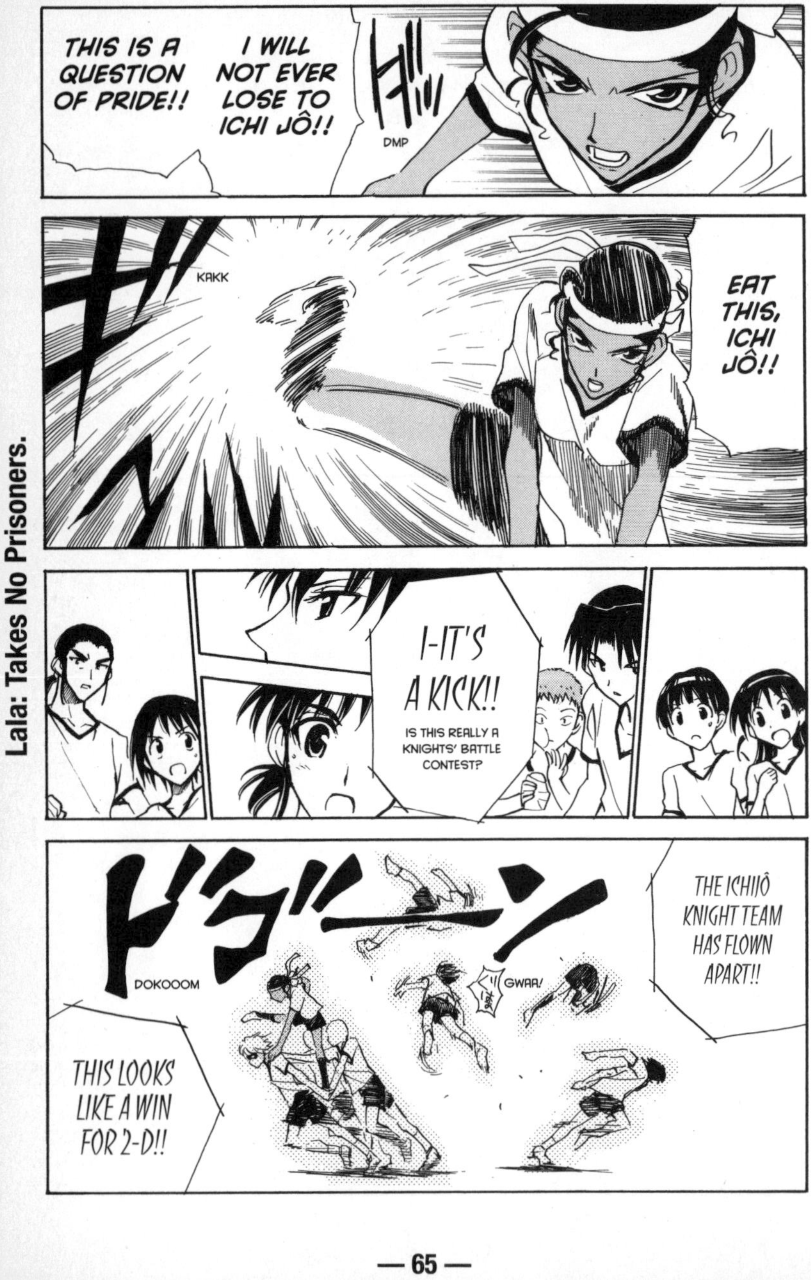
DMP
I WILL NOT EVER LOSE TO ICHI JÔ!!
THIS IS A QUESTION OF PRIDE!!
EAT THIS, ICHI JÔ!!
KAKK
I-IT'S A KICK!!
IS THIS REALLY A KNIGHTS' BATTLE CONTEST?
THE ICHIJÔ KNIGHT TEAM HAS FLOWN APART!!
GWAA!
DOKOOOM
THIS LOOKS LIKE A WIN FOR 2-D!!

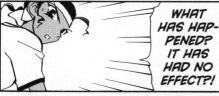

WHAT HAS HAPPENED? IT HAS HAD NO EFFECT?!

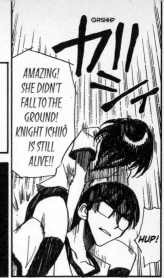

GASHHP

AMAZING! SHE DIDN'T FALL TO THE GROUND! KNIGHT ICHIJÔ IS STILL ALIVE!!

HUP!

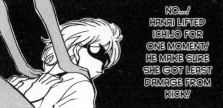

NO...! HANAI LIFTED ICHIJO FOR ONE MOMENT! HE MAKE SURE SHE GOT LEAST DAMAGE FROM KICK!

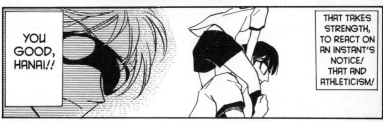

YOU GOOD, HANAI!!

THAT TAKES STRENGTH, TO REACT ON AN INSTANT'S NOTICE! THAT AND ATHLETICISM!

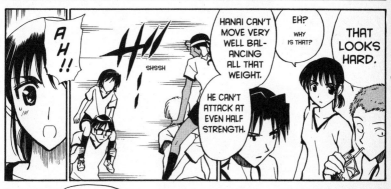

AH!!

HI!

SHSSH

HANAI CAN'T MOVE VERY WELL BALANCING ALL THAT WEIGHT.

HE CAN'T ATTACK AT EVEN HALF STRENGTH.

EH? WHY IS THAT?

THAT LOOKS HARD.

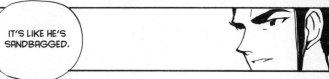

IT'S LIKE HE'S SANDBAGGED.

Riding on Someone's Shoulders Is Okay.

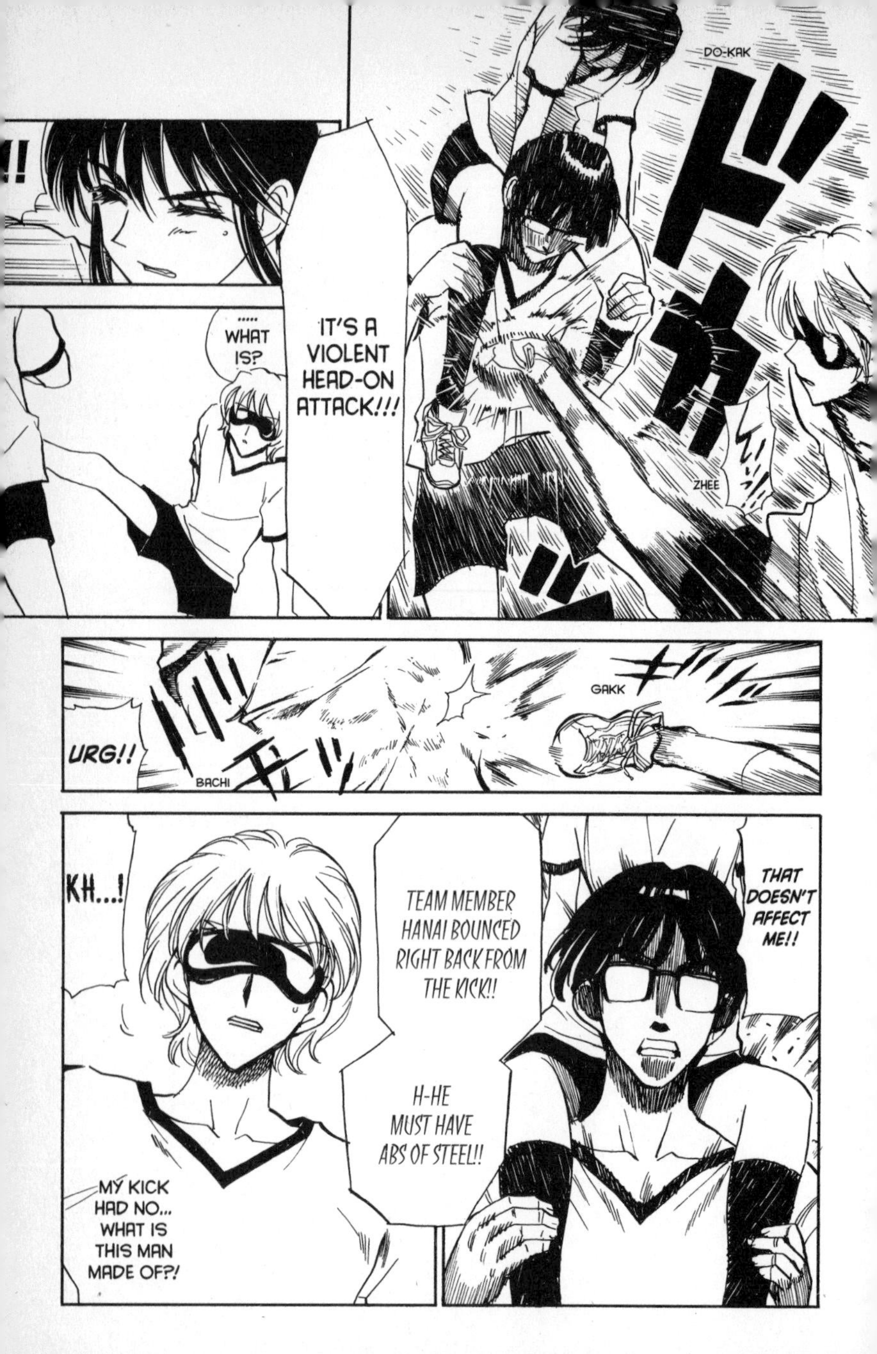
DO-KAK
ZHEE
IT'S A VIOLENT HEAD-ON ATTACK!!!
!!
...... WHAT IS?
GAKK
BACHI
URG!!
THAT DOESN'T AFFECT ME!!
TEAM MEMBER HANAI BOUNCED RIGHT BACK FROM THE KICK!!
H-HE MUST HAVE ABS OF STEEL!!
KH...!
MY KICK HAD NO... WHAT IS THIS MAN MADE OF?!

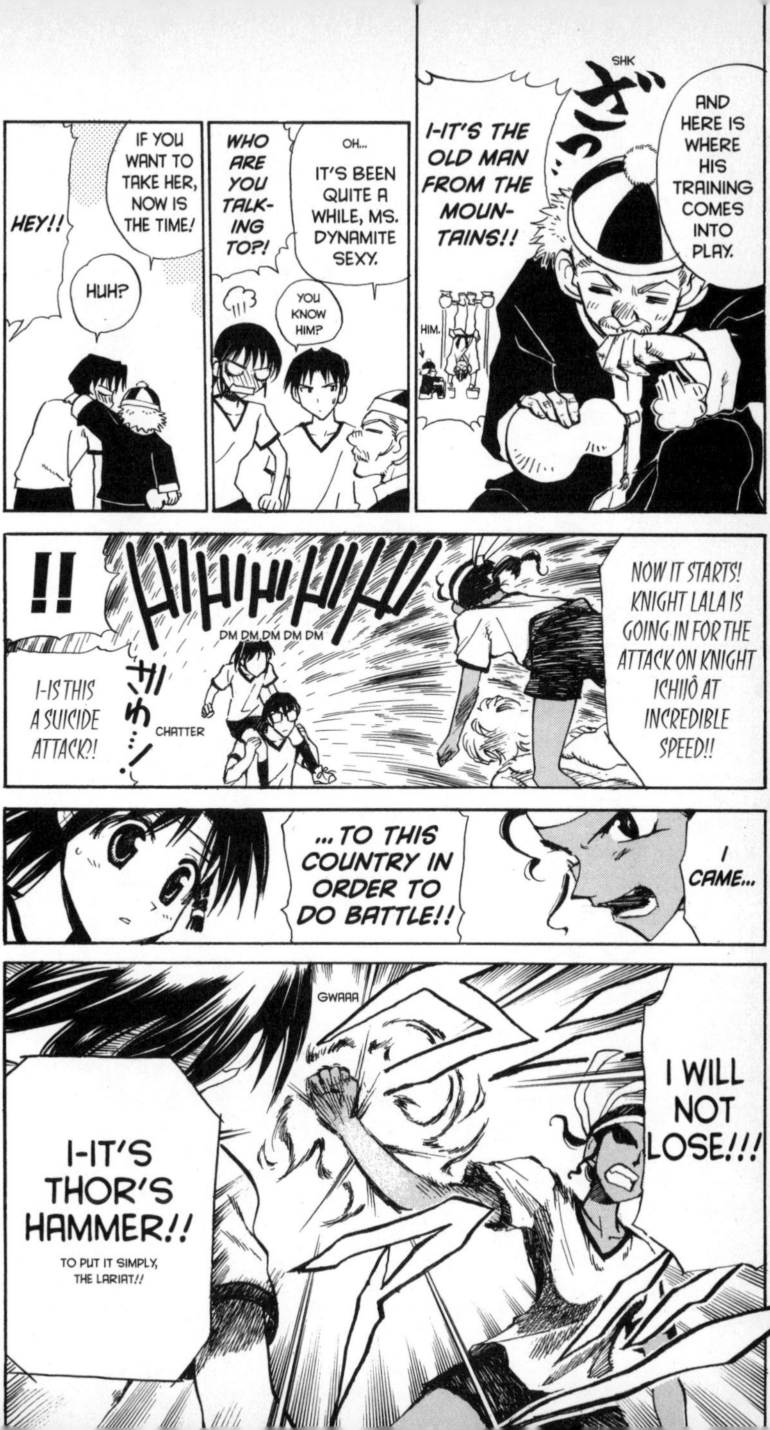
SHK
AND HERE IS WHERE HIS TRAINING COMES INTO PLAY.
I-IT'S THE OLD MAN FROM THE MOUN-TAINS!!
HIM.
OH... IT'S BEEN QUITE A WHILE, MS. DYNAMITE SEXY.
WHO ARE YOU TALK-ING TO?!
YOU KNOW HIM?
IF YOU WANT TO TAKE HER, NOW IS THE TIME!
HEY!!
HUH?
NOW IT STARTS! KNIGHT LALA IS GOING IN FOR THE ATTACK ON KNIGHT ICHIJÔ AT INCREDIBLE SPEED!!
DM DM DM DM DM
CHATTER
I-IS THIS A SUICIDE ATTACK?!
!!
I CAME...
...TO THIS COUNTRY IN ORDER TO DO BATTLE!!
I WILL NOT LOSE!!!
GWAAA
I-IT'S THOR'S HAMMER!!
TO PUT IT SIMPLY, THE LARIAT!!

Old Man: Hanai's Master (Self-Styled).

FFT
D-DID SHE DIS-APPEAR?!
NO!

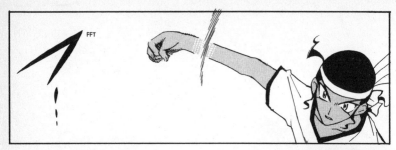

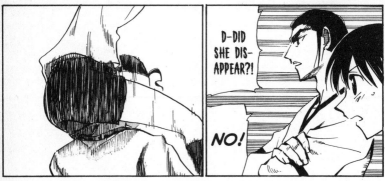

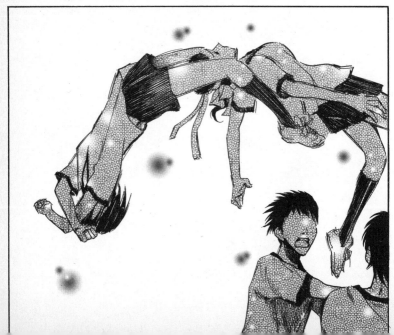

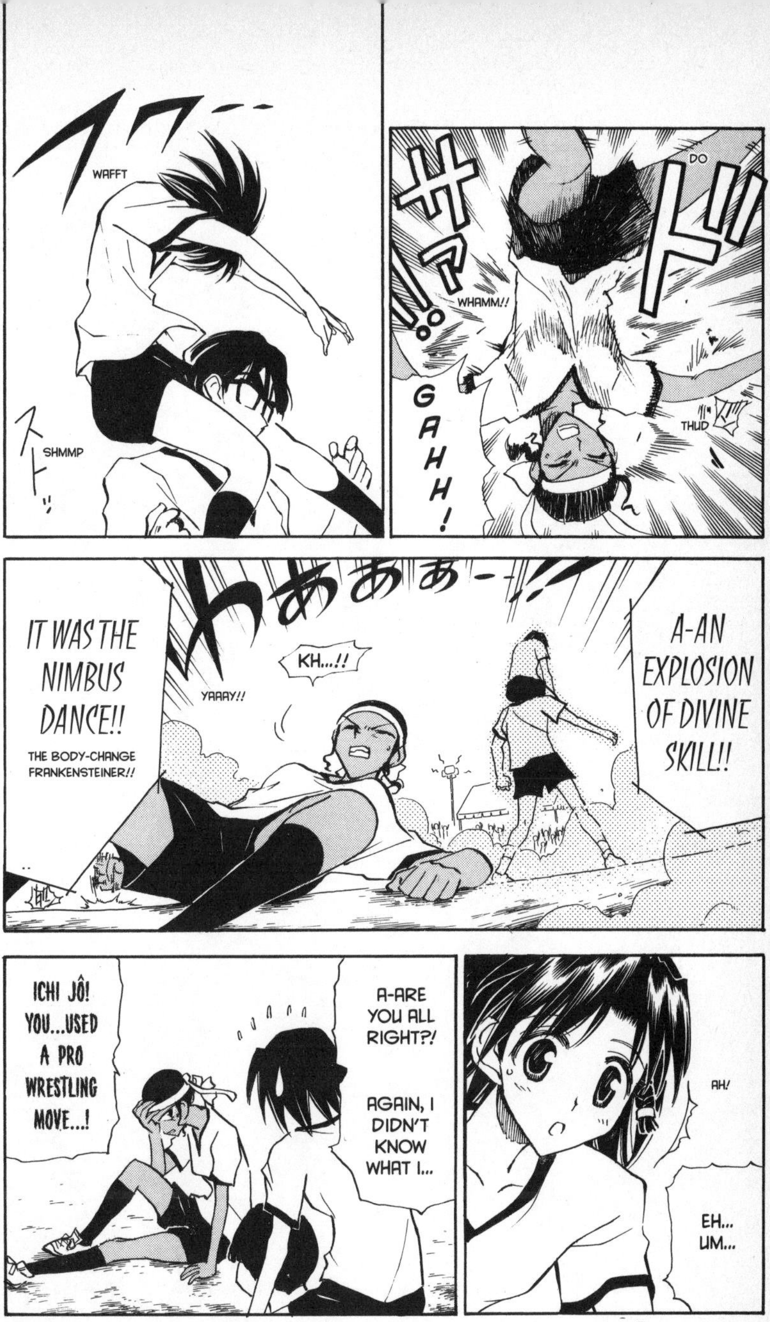
DO
WHAMM!!
GAHHH!
THUD
WAFFT
SHMMP
A-AN EXPLOSION OF DIVINE SKILL!!
KH...!!
YAAAY!!
IT WAS THE NIMBUS DANCE!!
THE BODY-CHANGE FRANKENSTEINER!!
AH!
EH... UM...
A-ARE YOU ALL RIGHT?!
AGAIN, I DIDN'T KNOW WHAT I...
ICHI JÔ! YOU...USED A PRO WRESTLING MOVE...!

Ichi Jô: Second Win.

Hanai Would Lose. Probably.

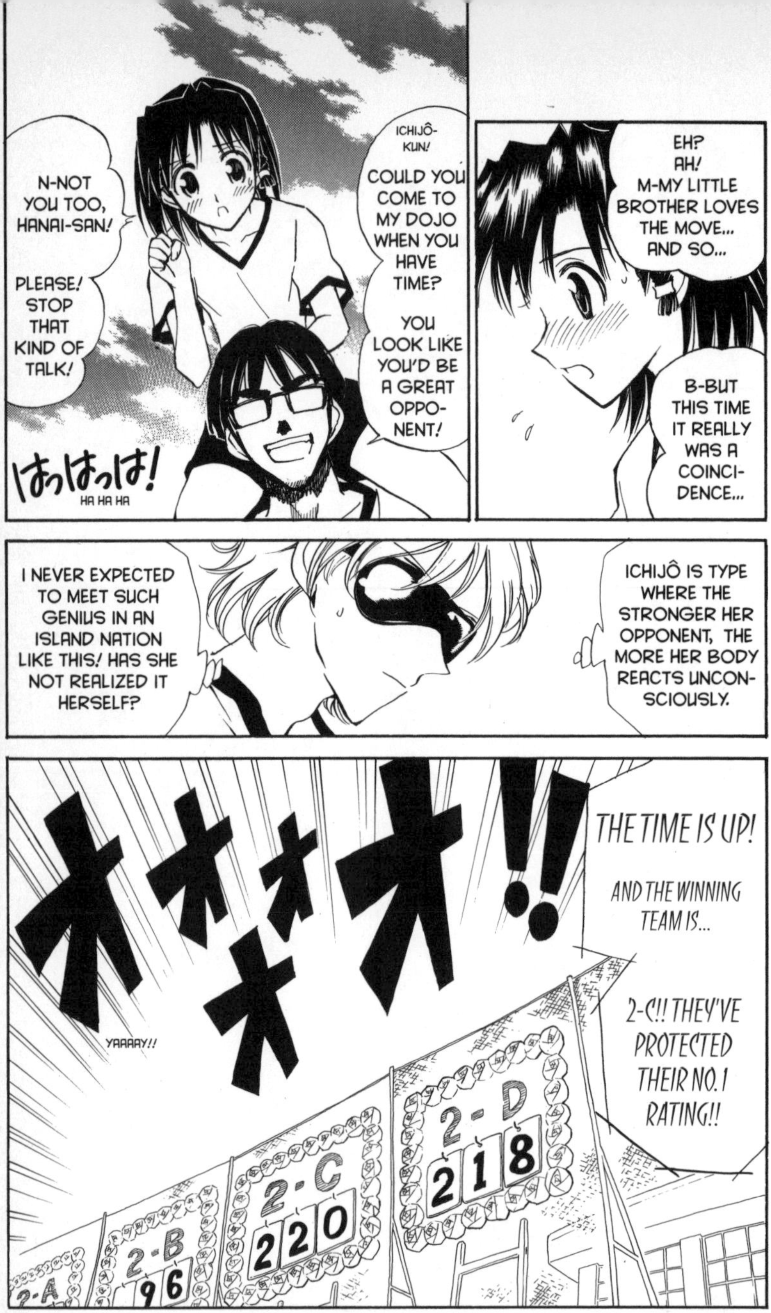

EH? AH! M-MY LITTLE BROTHER LOVES THE MOVE... AND SO...
B-BUT THIS TIME IT REALLY WAS A COINCI-DENCE...
ICHIJÔ-KUN!
COULD YOU COME TO MY DOJO WHEN YOU HAVE TIME?
YOU LOOK LIKE YOU'D BE A GREAT OPPO-NENT!
N-NOT YOU TOO, HANAI-SAN!
PLEASE! STOP THAT KIND OF TALK!
はっはっは!
HA HA HA
ICHIJÔ IS TYPE WHERE THE STRONGER HER OPPONENT, THE MORE HER BODY REACTS UNCON-SCIOUSLY.
I NEVER EXPECTED TO MEET SUCH GENIUS IN AN ISLAND NATION LIKE THIS! HAS SHE NOT REALIZED IT HERSELF?
THE TIME IS UP!
AND THE WINNING TEAM IS...
2-C!! THEY'VE PROTECTED THEIR NO.1 RATING!!
オオォォオ!!
YAAAAY!!
2-D
218
2-C
220
2-B
96
2-A

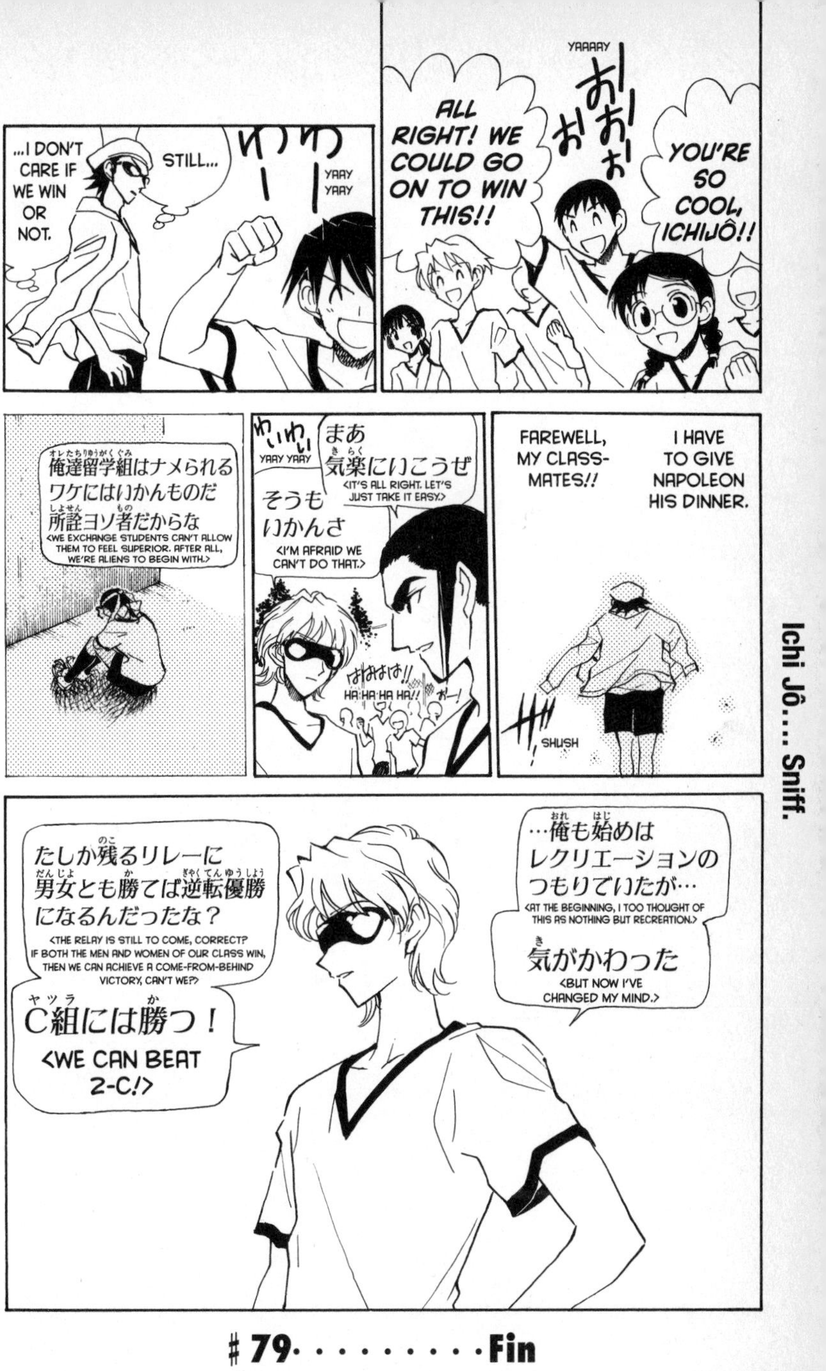
YAAAAY
YOU'RE SO COOL, ICHIJÔ!!
ALL RIGHT! WE COULD GO ON TO WIN THIS!!
YAAY YAAY
STILL...
...I DON'T CARE IF WE WIN OR NOT.
I HAVE TO GIVE NAPOLEON HIS DINNER.
FAREWELL, MY CLASS-MATES!!
SHUSH
わいわい YAAY YAAY
まあ気楽にいこうぜ <IT'S ALL RIGHT. LET'S JUST TAKE IT EASY.>
そうもいかんさ <I'M AFRAID WE CAN'T DO THAT.>
HA HA HA HA!!
俺達留学組はナメられるワケにはいかんものだ所詮ヨソ者だからな <WE EXCHANGE STUDENTS CAN'T ALLOW THEM TO FEEL SUPERIOR. AFTER ALL, WE'RE ALIENS TO BEGIN WITH.>
…俺も始めはレクリエーションのつもりでいたが… <AT THE BEGINNING, I TOO THOUGHT OF THIS AS NOTHING BUT RECREATION.>
気がかわった <BUT NOW I'VE CHANGED MY MIND.>
たしか残るリレーに男女とも勝てば逆転優勝になるんだったな？ <THE RELAY IS STILL TO COME, CORRECT? IF BOTH THE MEN AND WOMEN OF OUR CLASS WIN, THEN WE CAN ACHIEVE A COME-FROM-BEHIND VICTORY, CAN'T WE?>
C組には勝つ！ <WE CAN BEAT 2-C!>

Ichi Jô.... Sniff.

 # 79..........Fin

NAME

HARRY MCKENZIE

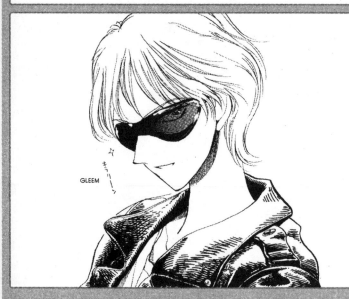

GLEEM

JOB

KNIGHT

POWER(UNIT)

ELITE POWER

SKILL

LADIES FIRST

FINISH BLOW

FENCING

WEAK POINT

SPIDERS

LEVEL

BATTLE POWER
UNDERSTANDING OF JAPAN
POPULARITY AMONG MEN
POPULARITY AMONG WOMEN
ABILITY TO CONTROL LALA

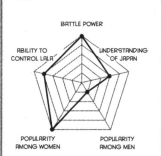

School Rumble

OFFICIAL CHARACTER TRADING CARD

NAME

TÔGÔ MASAKAZU

JOB

GENERAL

POWER(UNIT)

BARKING ORDERS AT EVERYBODY POWER (≥HANAI)

SKILL

ASSURED SPEECH

FINISH BLOW

QUICK STRIKE

WEAK POINT

YOUNGER SISTER

LEVEL

AFFECTED SPEECH
NORMAL CONVERSATION
HAIR IN BACK
GIULIANO GEMMA
PHYSICAL STRENGTH

School Rumble OFFICIAL CHARACTER TRADING CARD

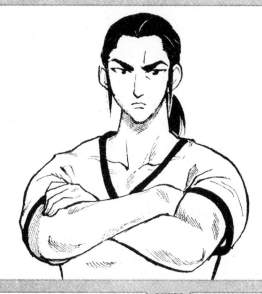

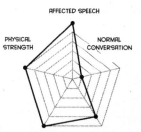

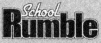

#80 THE PRIDE AND THE PASSION

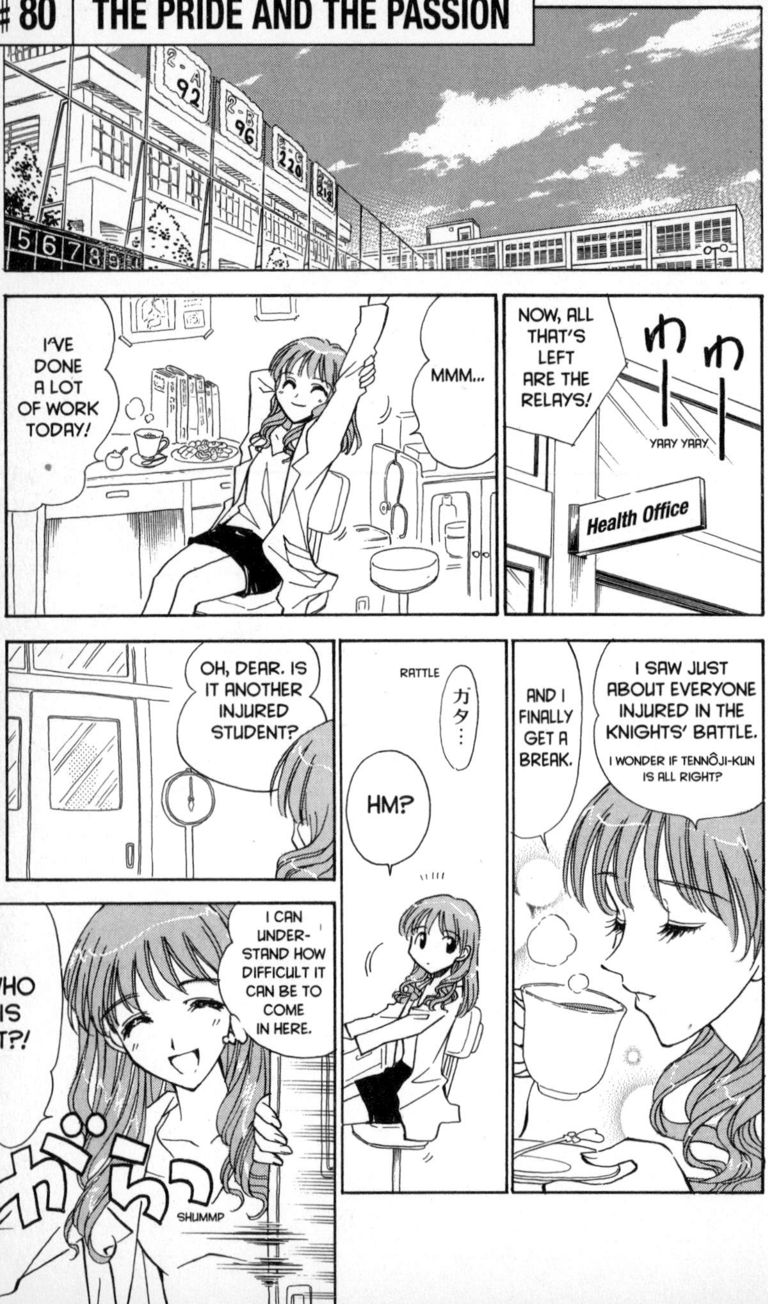

NOW, ALL THAT'S LEFT ARE THE RELAYS!
わーわー
YAAY YAAY
Health Office
MMM...
I'VE DONE A LOT OF WORK TODAY!
I SAW JUST ABOUT EVERYONE INJURED IN THE KNIGHTS' BATTLE.
I WONDER IF TENNÔJI-KUN IS ALL RIGHT?
AND I FINALLY GET A BREAK.
ガタ…
RATTLE
HM?
OH, DEAR. IS IT ANOTHER INJURED STUDENT?
I CAN UNDER-STAND HOW DIFFICULT IT CAN BE TO COME IN HERE.
WHO IS IT?!
がらっ
SHUMMP

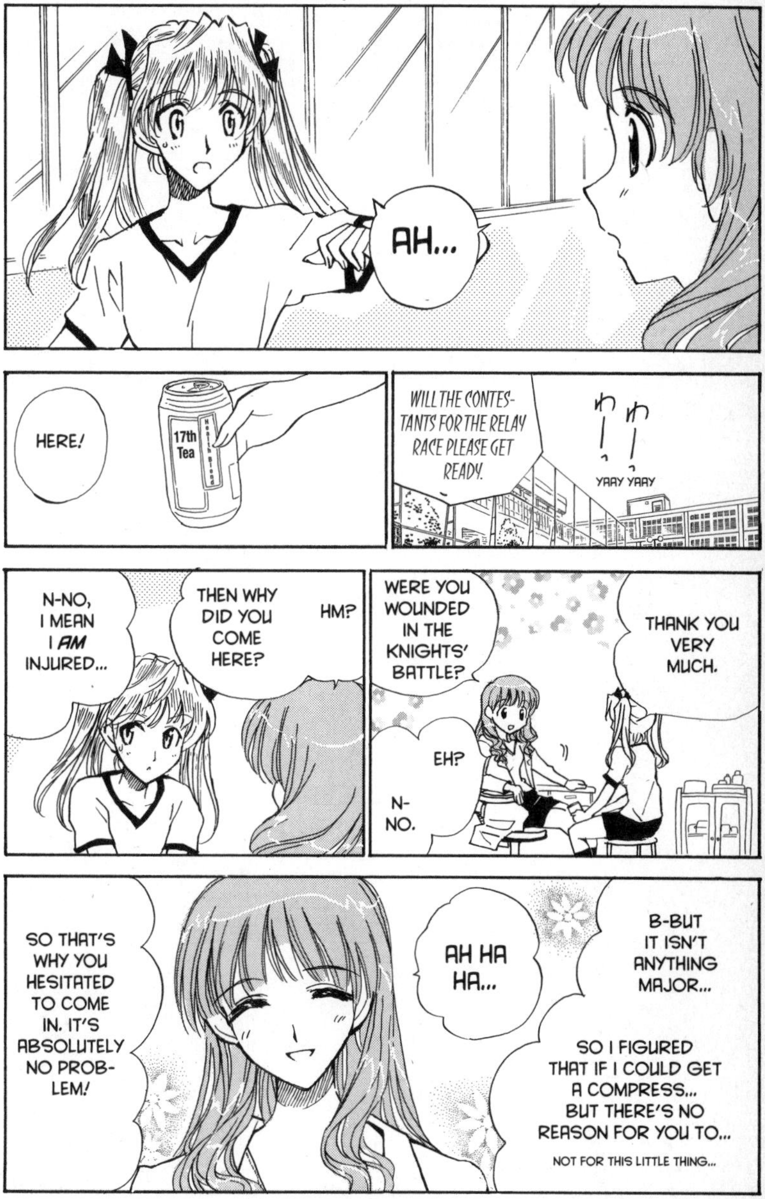
AH...
WILL THE CONTES- TANTS FOR THE RELAY RACE PLEASE GET READY.
わー わー
YAAY YAAY
17th Tea
Health Blend
HERE!
THANK YOU VERY MUCH.
WERE YOU WOUNDED IN THE KNIGHTS' BATTLE?
EH?
N- NO.
HM?
THEN WHY DID YOU COME HERE?
N-NO, I MEAN I *AM* INJURED...
B-BUT IT ISN'T ANYTHING MAJOR...
SO I FIGURED THAT IF I COULD GET A COMPRESS... BUT THERE'S NO REASON FOR YOU TO...
NOT FOR THIS LITTLE THING...
AH HA HA...
SO THAT'S WHY YOU HESITATED TO COME IN. IT'S ABSOLUTELY NO PROB- LEM!

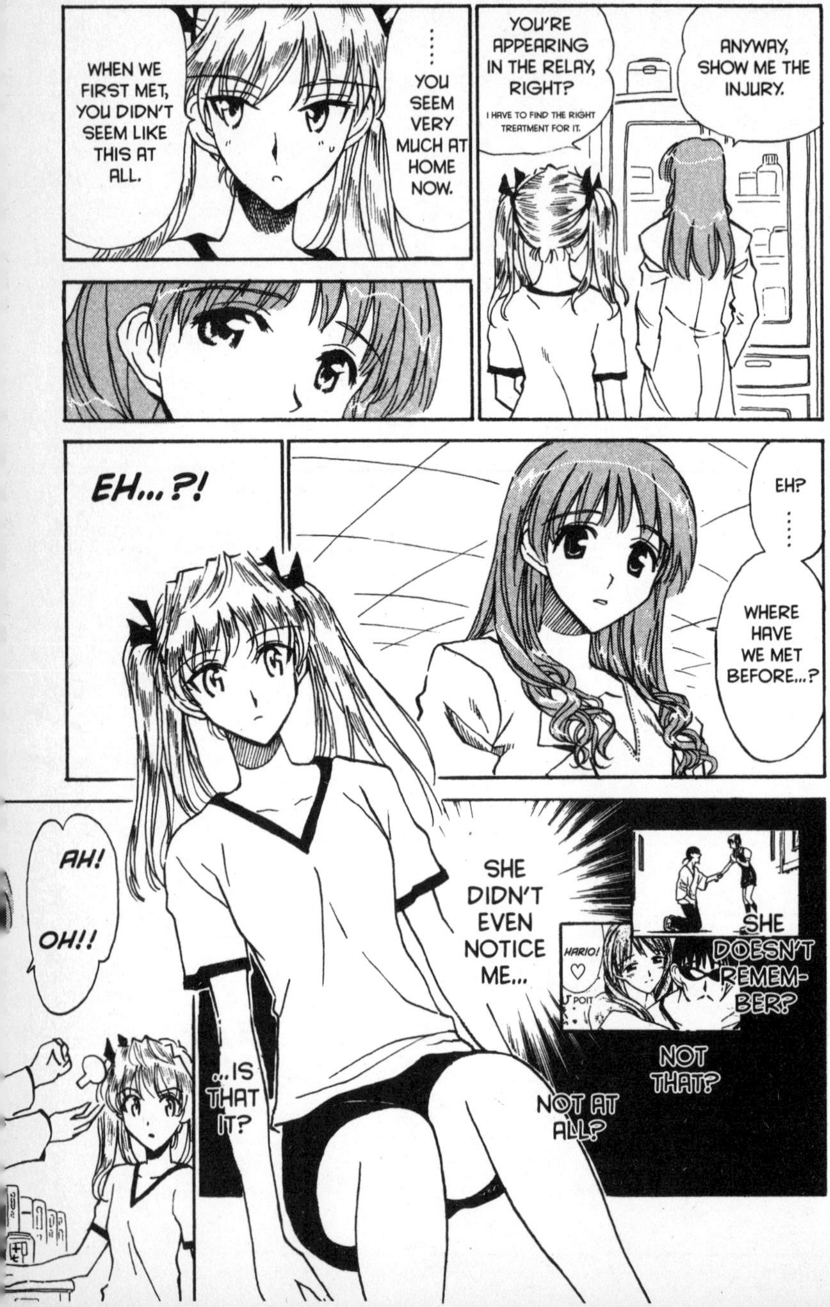
ANYWAY, SHOW ME THE INJURY.
YOU'RE APPEARING IN THE RELAY, RIGHT?
I HAVE TO FIND THE RIGHT TREATMENT FOR IT.
...... YOU SEEM VERY MUCH AT HOME NOW.
WHEN WE FIRST MET, YOU DIDN'T SEEM LIKE THIS AT ALL.
EH?
......
WHERE HAVE WE MET BEFORE...?
EH...?!
SHE DOESN'T REMEMBER?
HARIO! ♡
POIT
NOT THAT?
NOT AT ALL?
SHE DIDN'T EVEN NOTICE ME...
...IS THAT IT?
AH!
OH!!

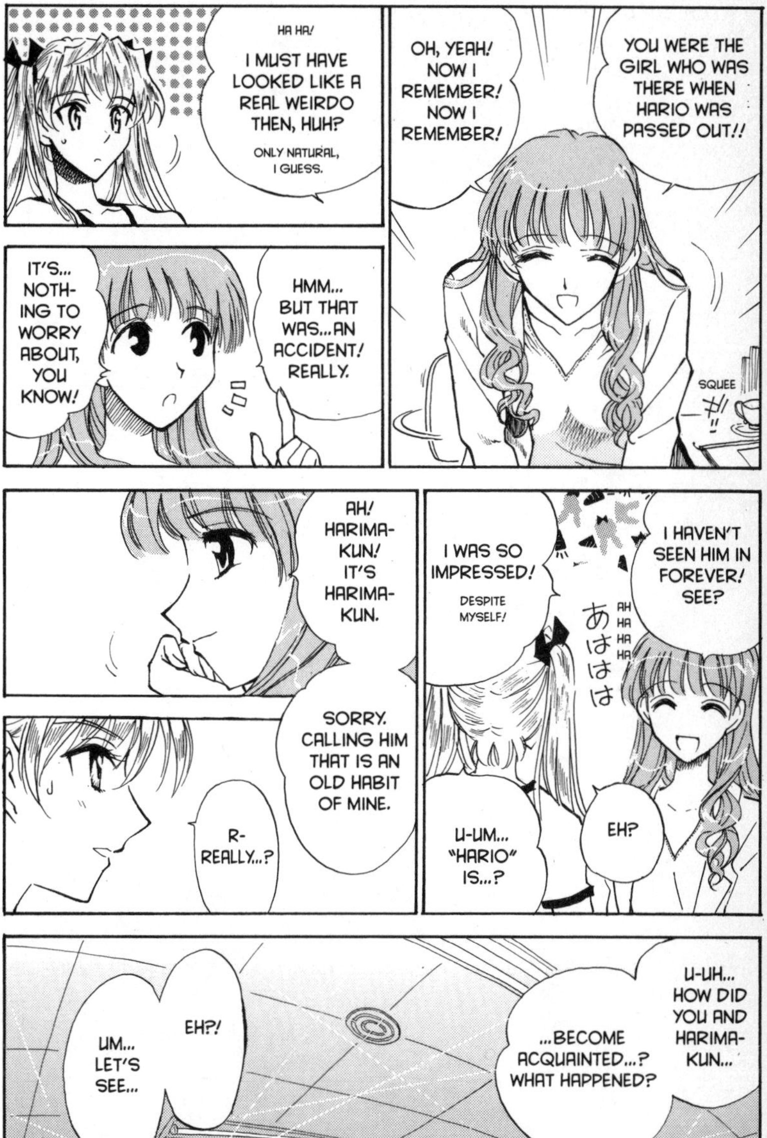
YOU WERE THE GIRL WHO WAS THERE WHEN HARIO WAS PASSED OUT!!
OH, YEAH! NOW I REMEMBER! NOW I REMEMBER!
SQUEE
HA HA!
I MUST HAVE LOOKED LIKE A REAL WEIRDO THEN, HUH?
ONLY NATURAL, I GUESS.
HMM... BUT THAT WAS...AN ACCIDENT! REALLY.
IT'S... NOTHING TO WORRY ABOUT, YOU KNOW!
I HAVEN'T SEEN HIM IN FOREVER! SEE?
I WAS SO IMPRESSED!
DESPITE MYSELF!
AH HA HA HA
あははは
EH?
U-UM... "HARIO" IS...?
AH! HARIMA-KUN! IT'S HARIMA-KUN.
SORRY. CALLING HIM THAT IS AN OLD HABIT OF MINE.
R-REALLY...?
U-UH... HOW DID YOU AND HARIMA-KUN...
...BECOME ACQUAINTED...? WHAT HAPPENED?
EH?!
UM... LET'S SEE...

What Sawachika Is Thinking About Is in Volume 3, Chapter 34.

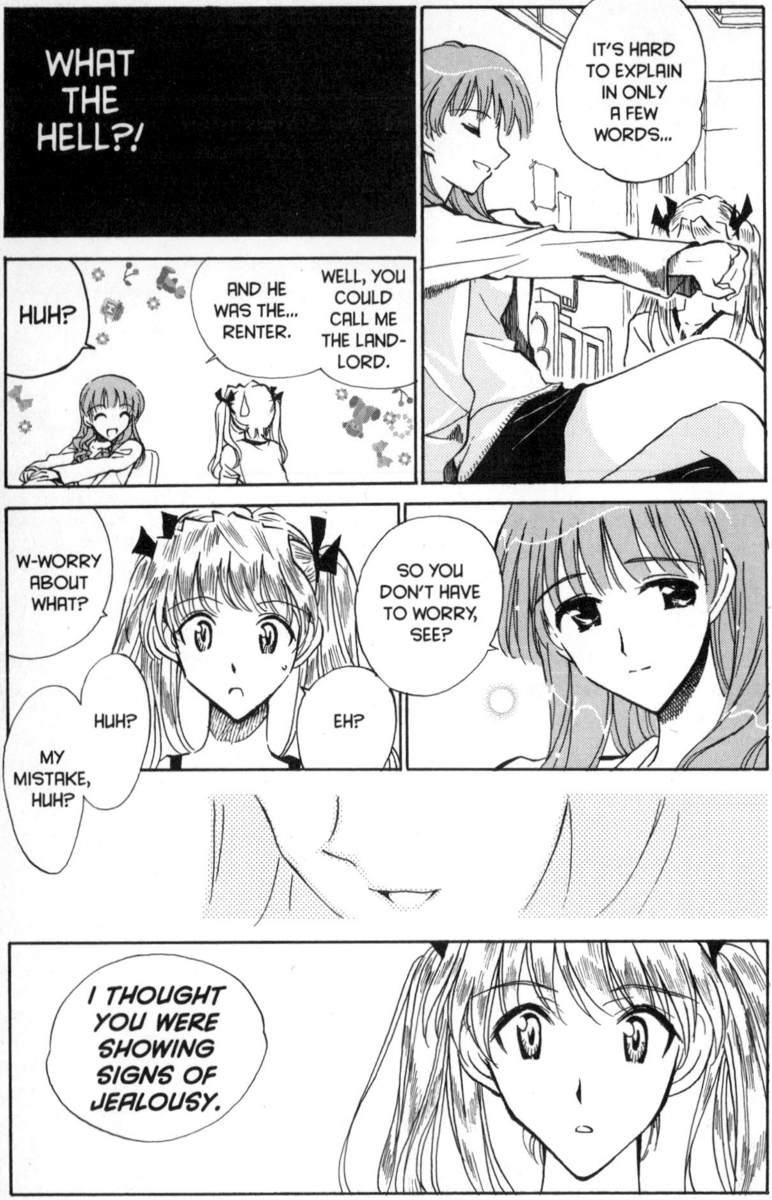
IT'S HARD TO EXPLAIN IN ONLY A FEW WORDS...
WHAT THE HELL?!
WELL, YOU COULD CALL ME THE LAND-LORD.
AND HE WAS THE... RENTER.
HUH?
SO YOU DON'T HAVE TO WORRY, SEE?
W-WORRY ABOUT WHAT?
EH?
HUH?
MY MISTAKE, HUH?
I THOUGHT YOU WERE SHOWING SIGNS OF JEALOUSY.

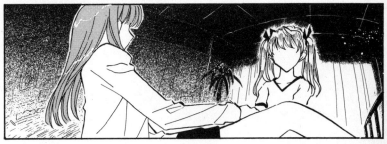

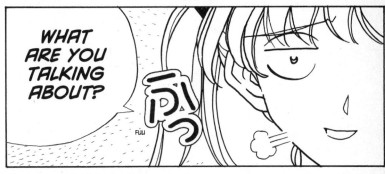

WHAT ARE YOU TALKING ABOUT?
FUU
I HAVE NO FEELINGS FOR HIM WHATSO-EVER!
HE MAY BE IN MY CLASS, BUT HE'S FAMOUS THROUGHOUT THE SCHOOL AS A DELINQUENT.
AND AS THERE'S SOME ARRANGEMENT BETWEEN HIM AND THE NEWLY APPOINTED PRETTY HEALTH OFFICE NURSE...
EVEN SOMEONE COMPLETELY UNRELATED TO THE SITUATION SITS UP AND TAKES NOTICE.
...... AH HA HA HA HA!

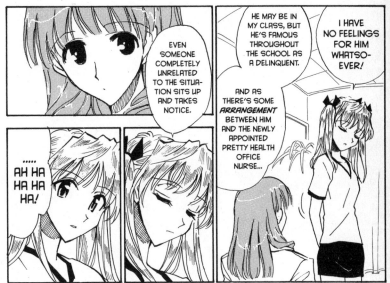

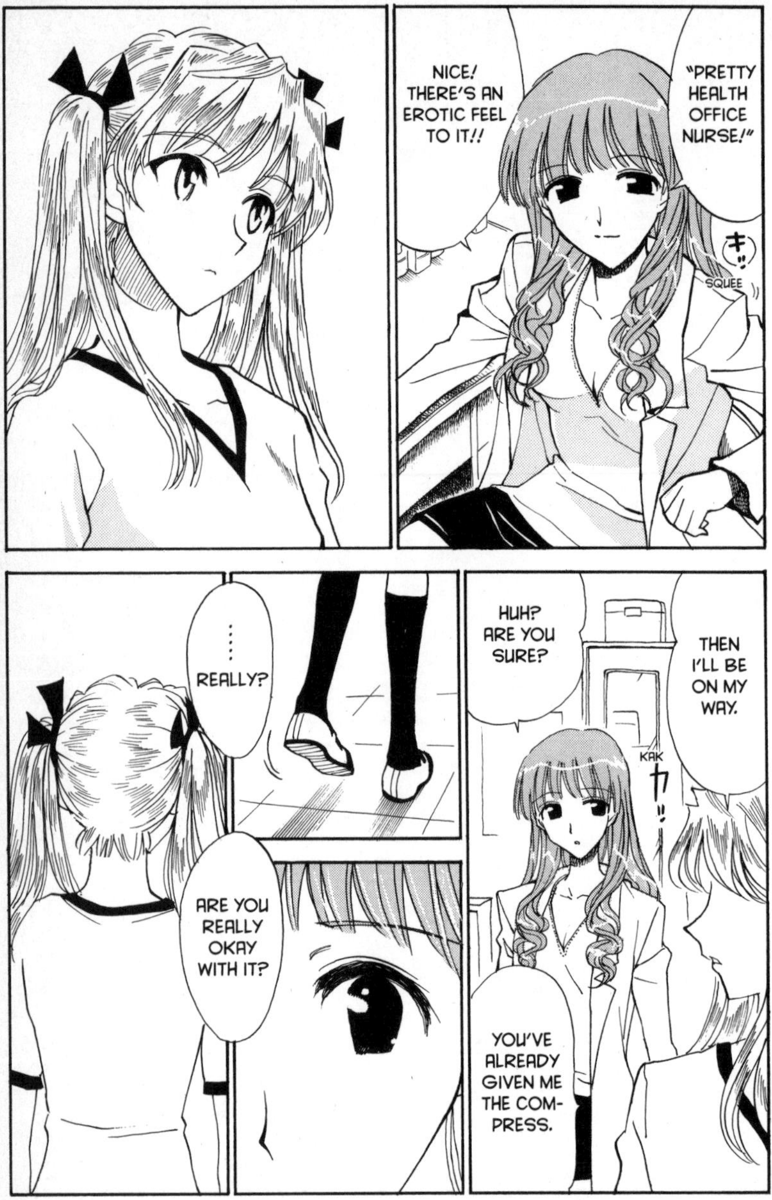
"PRETTY HEALTH OFFICE NURSE!"
NICE! THERE'S AN EROTIC FEEL TO IT!!
キ!!
SQUEE
THEN I'LL BE ON MY WAY.
HUH? ARE YOU SURE?
KAK
カ!!
YOU'VE ALREADY GIVEN ME THE COMPRESS.
...... REALLY?
ARE YOU REALLY OKAY WITH IT?

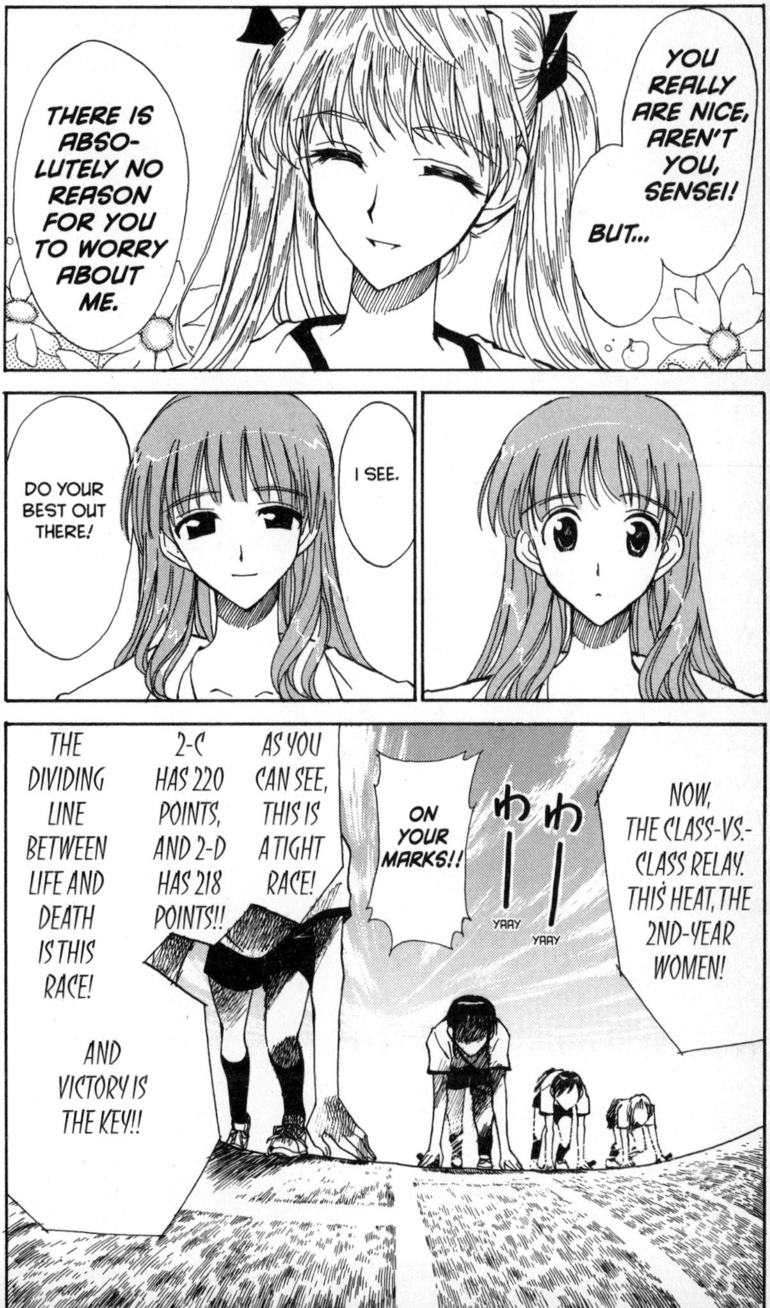
YOU REALLY ARE NICE, AREN'T YOU, SENSEI!
BUT...
THERE IS ABSO-LUTELY NO REASON FOR YOU TO WORRY ABOUT ME.
I SEE.
DO YOUR BEST OUT THERE!
NOW, THE CLASS-VS.-CLASS RELAY. THIS HEAT, THE 2ND-YEAR WOMEN!
わー
YAAY
わー
YAAY
ON YOUR MARKS!!
AS YOU CAN SEE, THIS IS A TIGHT RACE!
2-C HAS 220 POINTS, AND 2-D HAS 218 POINTS!!
THE DIVIDING LINE BETWEEN LIFE AND DEATH IS THIS RACE!
AND VICTORY IS THE KEY!!

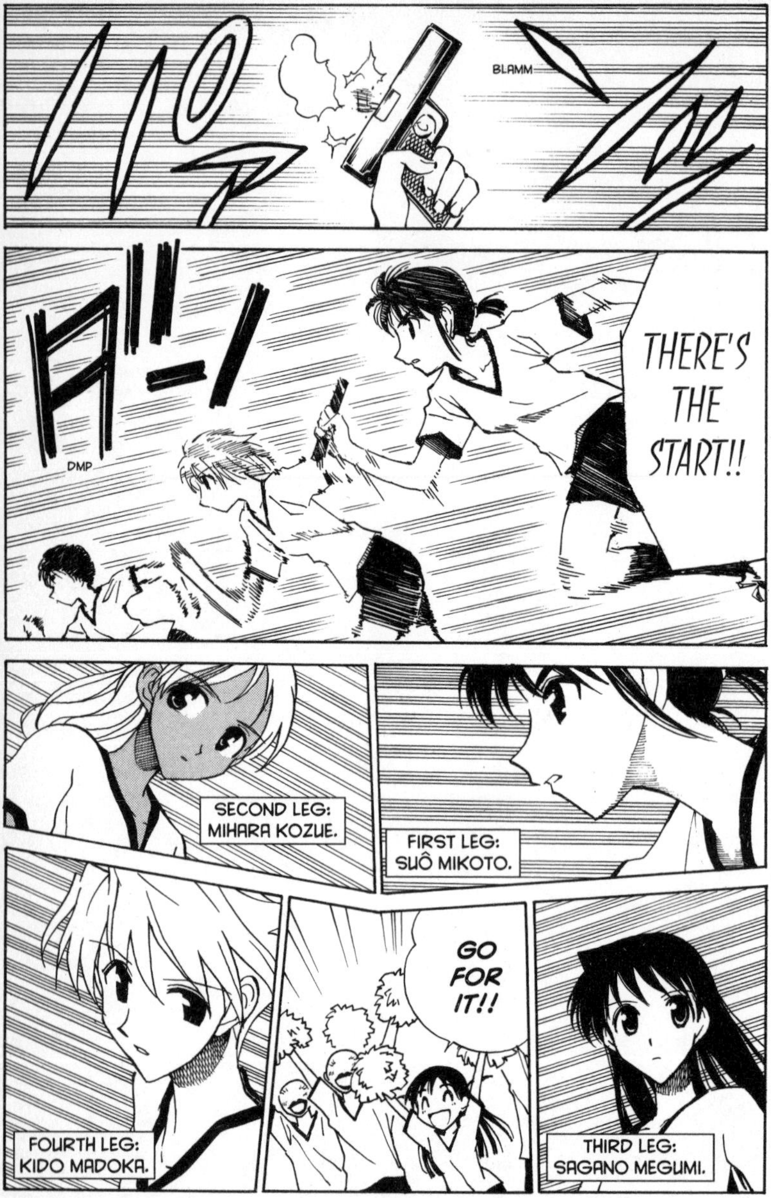
BLAMM
THERE'S THE START!!
DMP
FIRST LEG: SUÔ MIKOTO.
SECOND LEG: MIHARA KOZUE.
THIRD LEG: SAGANO MEGUMI.
GO FOR IT!!
FOURTH LEG: KIDO MADOKA.

Mihara Kozue: Actually She's Appeared Once.

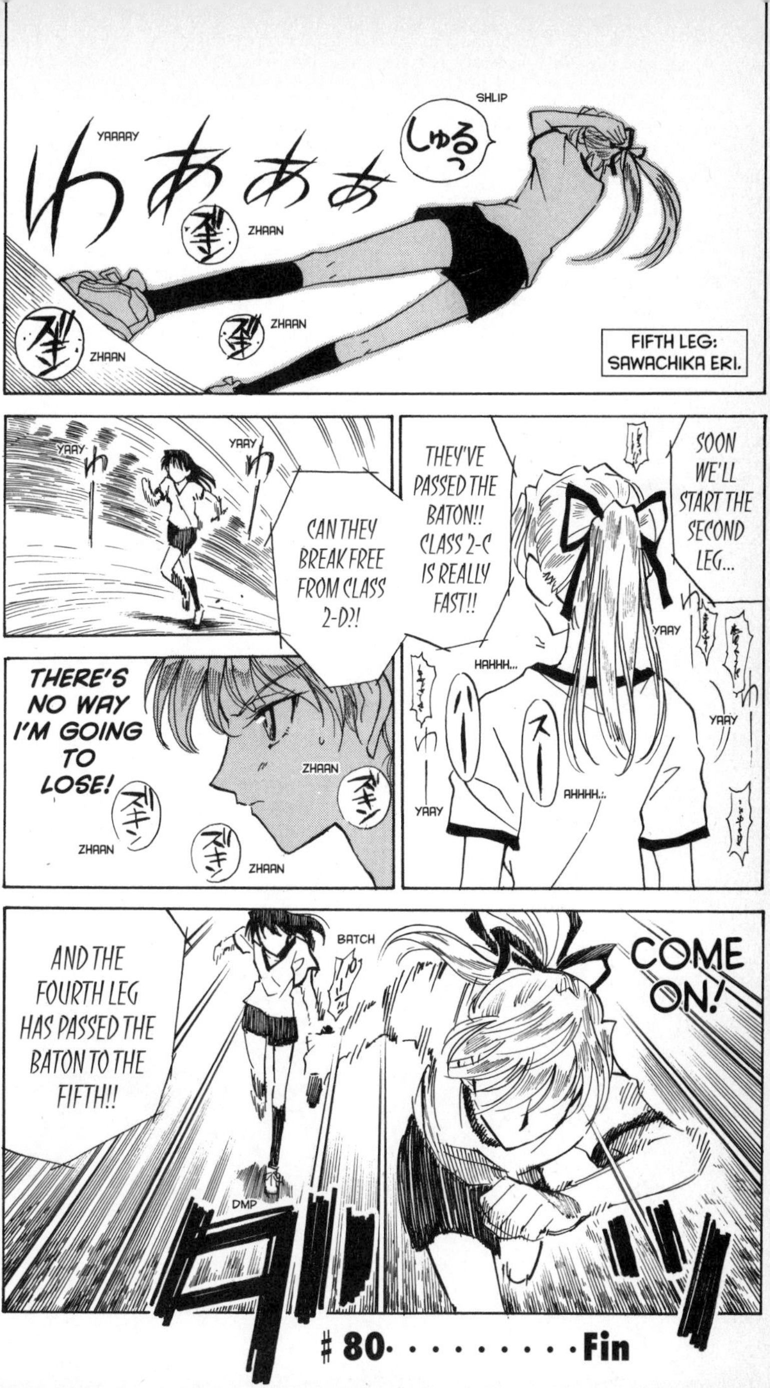
SHLIP
しゅるっ
YAAAAY
わあああぁ
ZHAAN
ZHAAN
ZHAAN
FIFTH LEG: SAWACHIKA ERI.
SOON WE'LL START THE SECOND LEG...
THEY'VE PASSED THE BATON!! CLASS 2-C IS REALLY FAST!!
YAAY
YAAY
HAHHH...
AHHHH...
YAAY
CAN THEY BREAK FREE FROM CLASS 2-D?!
YAAY
YAAY
ZHAAN
THERE'S NO WAY I'M GOING TO LOSE!
ZHAAN
ZHAAN
COME ON!
BATCH
AND THE FOURTH LEG HAS PASSED THE BATON TO THE FIFTH!!
DMP

Pride.

\# 80. . . . . Fin

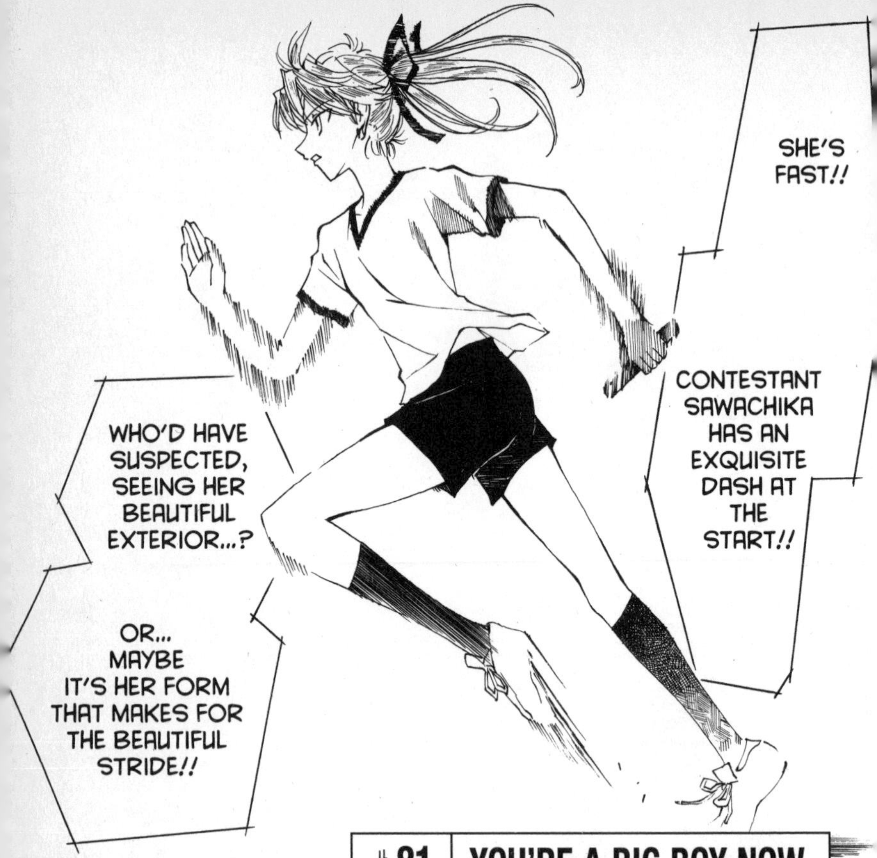
SHE'S FAST!!
CONTESTANT SAWACHIKA HAS AN EXQUISITE DASH AT THE START!!
WHO'D HAVE SUSPECTED, SEEING HER BEAUTIFUL EXTERIOR...?
OR... MAYBE IT'S HER FORM THAT MAKES FOR THE BEAUTIFUL STRIDE!!

81 YOU'RE A BIG BOY NOW

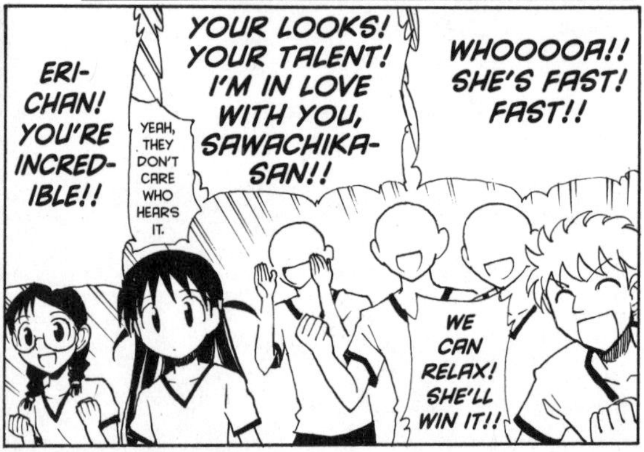
WHOOOOA!! SHE'S FAST! FAST!!
YOUR LOOKS! YOUR TALENT! I'M IN LOVE WITH YOU, SAWACHIKA-SAN!!
YEAH, THEY DON'T CARE WHO HEARS IT.
ERI-CHAN! YOU'RE INCRED-IBLE!!
WE CAN RELAX! SHE'LL WIN IT!!

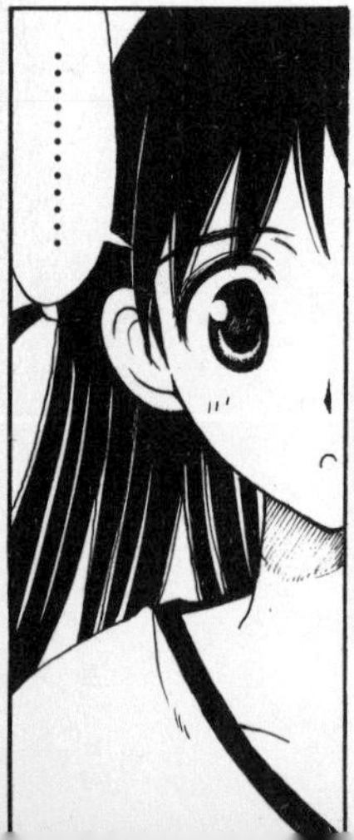
....

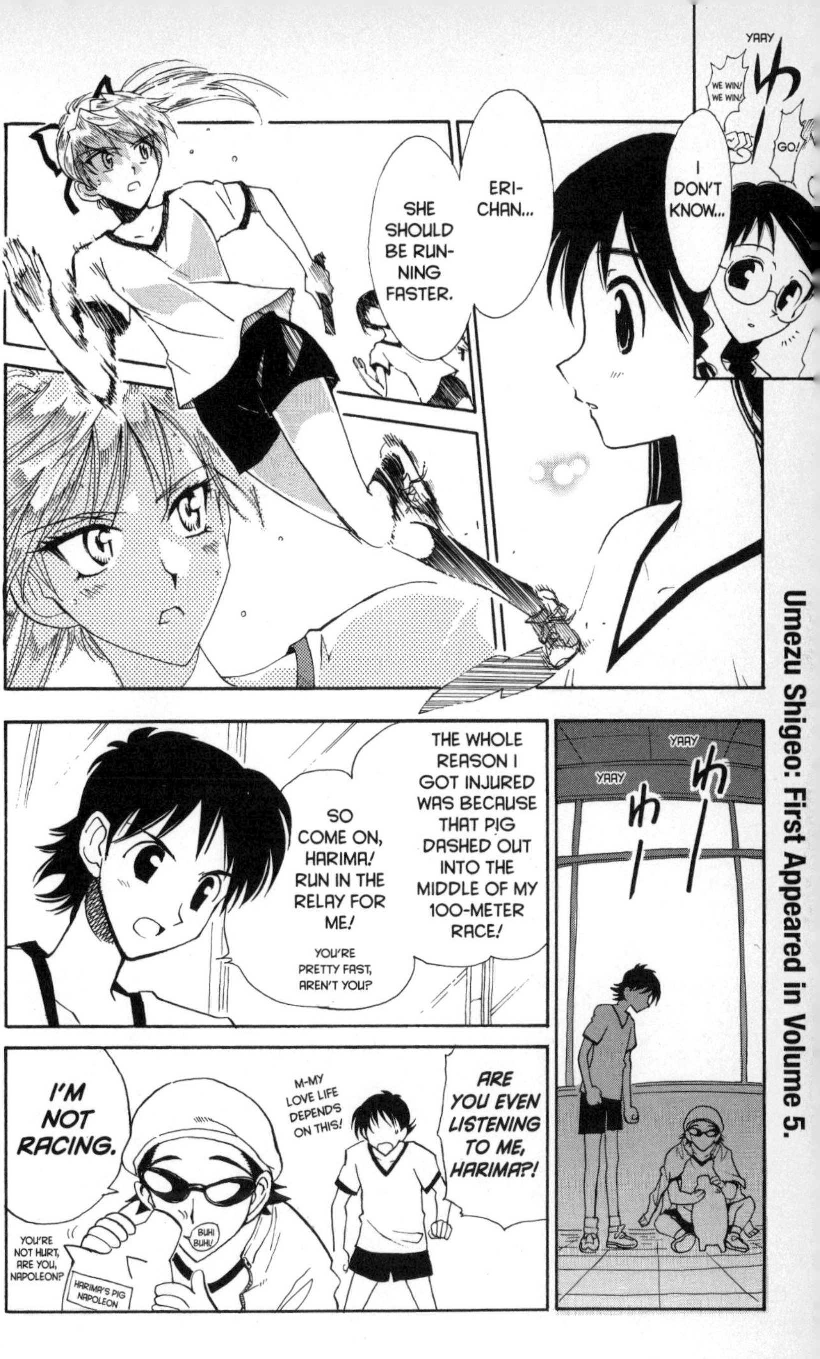
YAAY
WE WIN! WE WIN!
GO!
I DON'T KNOW...
ERI-CHAN...
SHE SHOULD BE RUN-NING FASTER.
YAAY
YAAY
THE WHOLE REASON I GOT INJURED WAS BECAUSE THAT PIG DASHED OUT INTO THE MIDDLE OF MY 100-METER RACE!
SO COME ON, HARIMA! RUN IN THE RELAY FOR ME!
YOU'RE PRETTY FAST, AREN'T YOU?
ARE YOU EVEN LISTENING TO ME, HARIMA?!
M-MY LOVE LIFE DEPENDS ON THIS!
I'M NOT RACING.
BUHI BUHI!
YOU'RE NOT HURT, ARE YOU, NAPOLEON?
HARIMA'S PIG NAPOLEON

Umezu Shigeo: First Appeared in Volume 5.

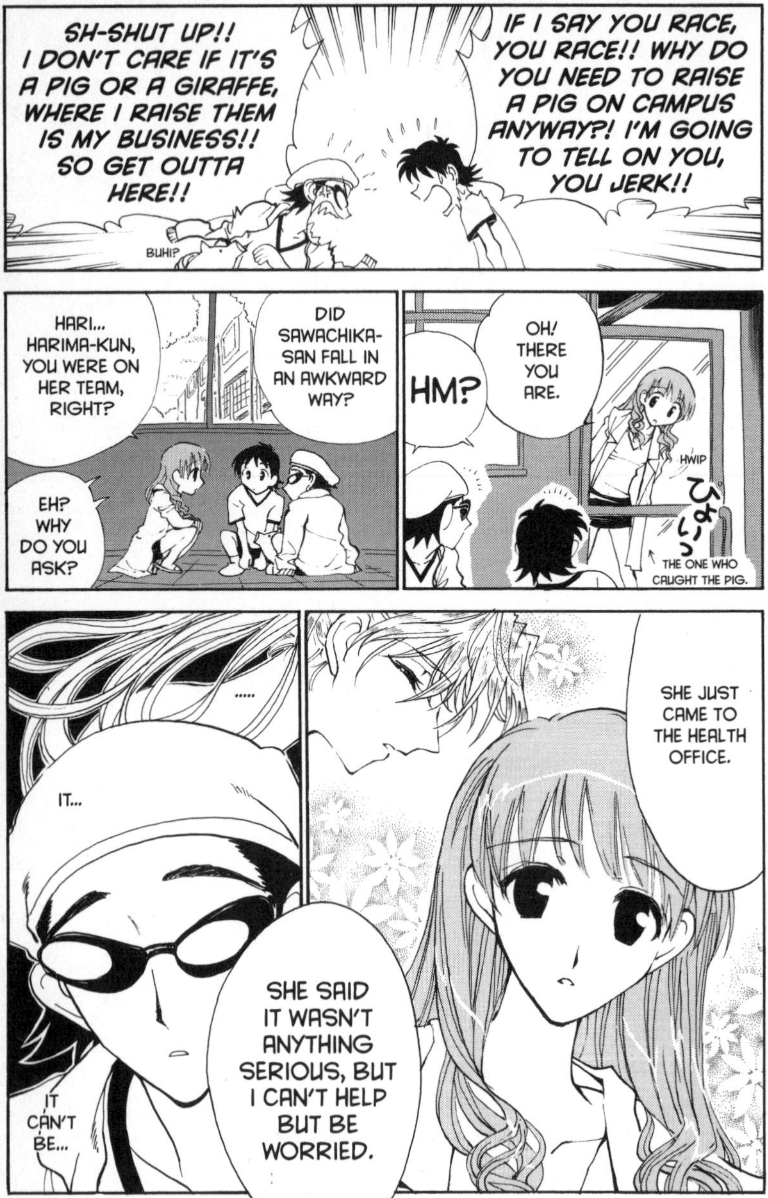
IF I SAY YOU RACE, YOU RACE!! WHY DO YOU NEED TO RAISE A PIG ON CAMPUS ANYWAY?! I'M GOING TO TELL ON YOU, YOU JERK!!
SH-SHUT UP!! I DON'T CARE IF IT'S A PIG OR A GIRAFFE, WHERE I RAISE THEM IS MY BUSINESS!! SO GET OUTTA HERE!!
BUHI?
OH! THERE YOU ARE.
HM?
HWIP
ひょいっ
THE ONE WHO CAUGHT THE PIG.
DID SAWACHIKA-SAN FALL IN AN AWKWARD WAY?
HARI... HARIMA-KUN, YOU WERE ON HER TEAM, RIGHT?
EH? WHY DO YOU ASK?
SHE JUST CAME TO THE HEALTH OFFICE.
SHE SAID IT WASN'T ANYTHING SERIOUS, BUT I CAN'T HELP BUT BE WORRIED.
.....
IT...
IT CAN'T BE...

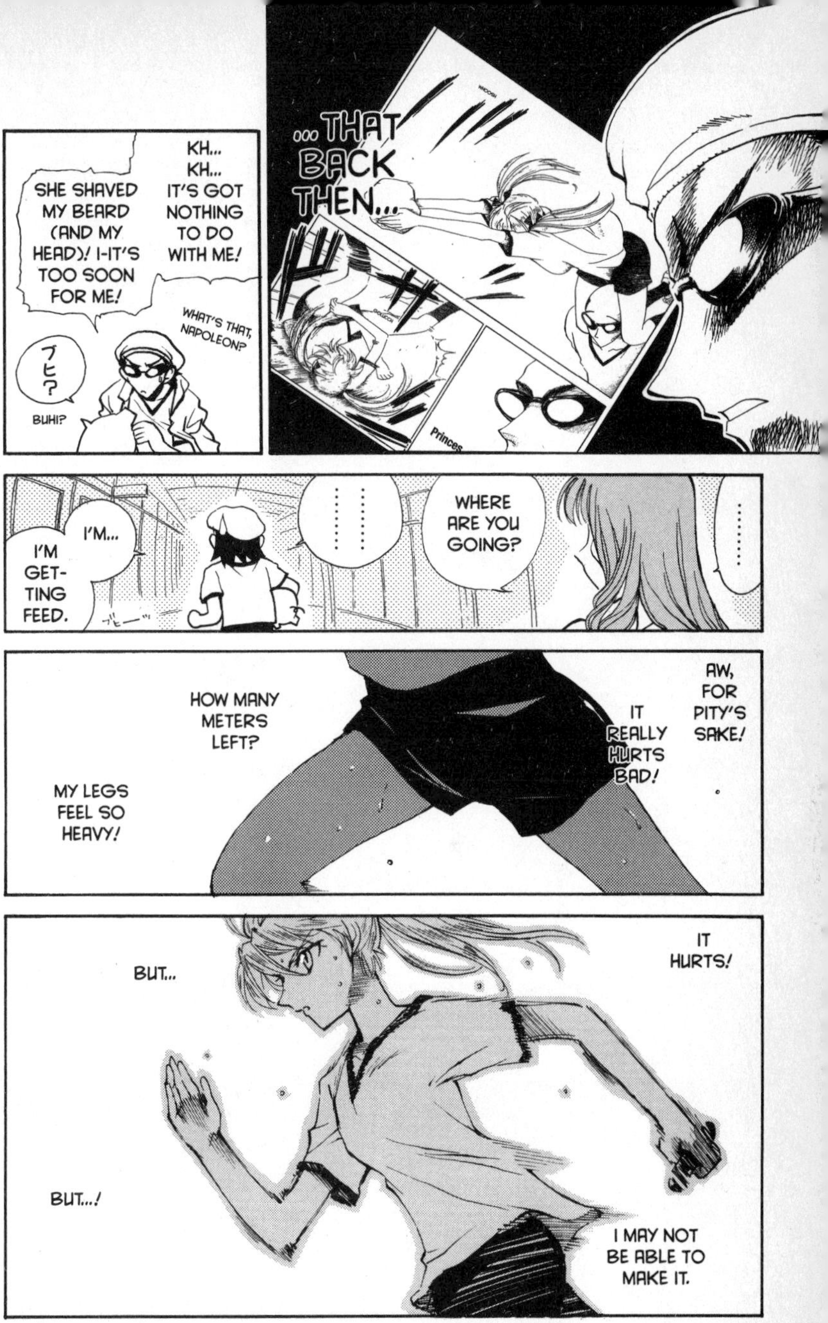
...THAT BACK THEN...
KH... KH... IT'S GOT NOTHING TO DO WITH ME!
SHE SHAVED MY BEARD (AND MY HEAD)! I-IT'S TOO SOON FOR ME!
WHAT'S THAT, NAPOLEON?
ブヒ?
BUHI?
......
WHERE ARE YOU GOING?
......
I'M...
I'M GET-TING FEED.
ブヒーッ
AW, FOR PITY'S SAKE!
IT REALLY HURTS BAD!
HOW MANY METERS LEFT?
MY LEGS FEEL SO HEAVY!
IT HURTS!
BUT...
I MAY NOT BE ABLE TO MAKE IT.
BUT...!

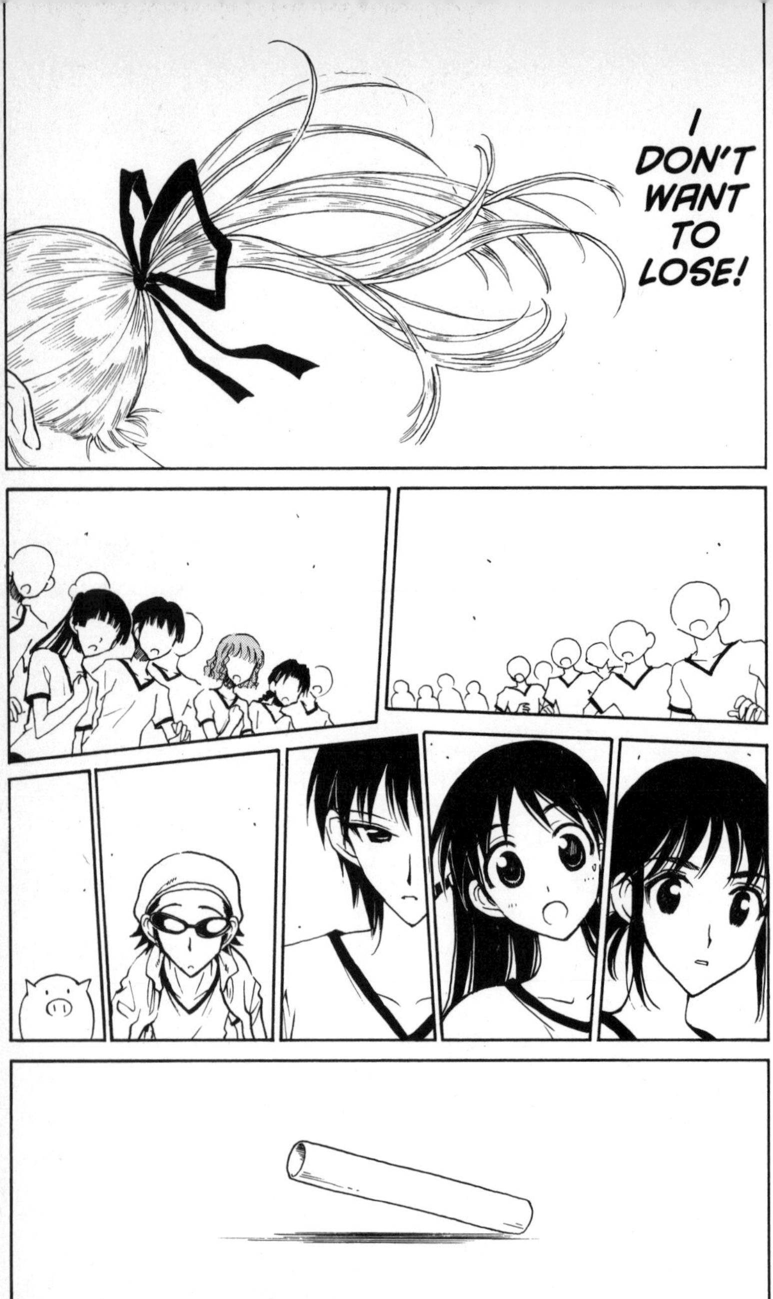
I DON'T WANT TO LOSE!

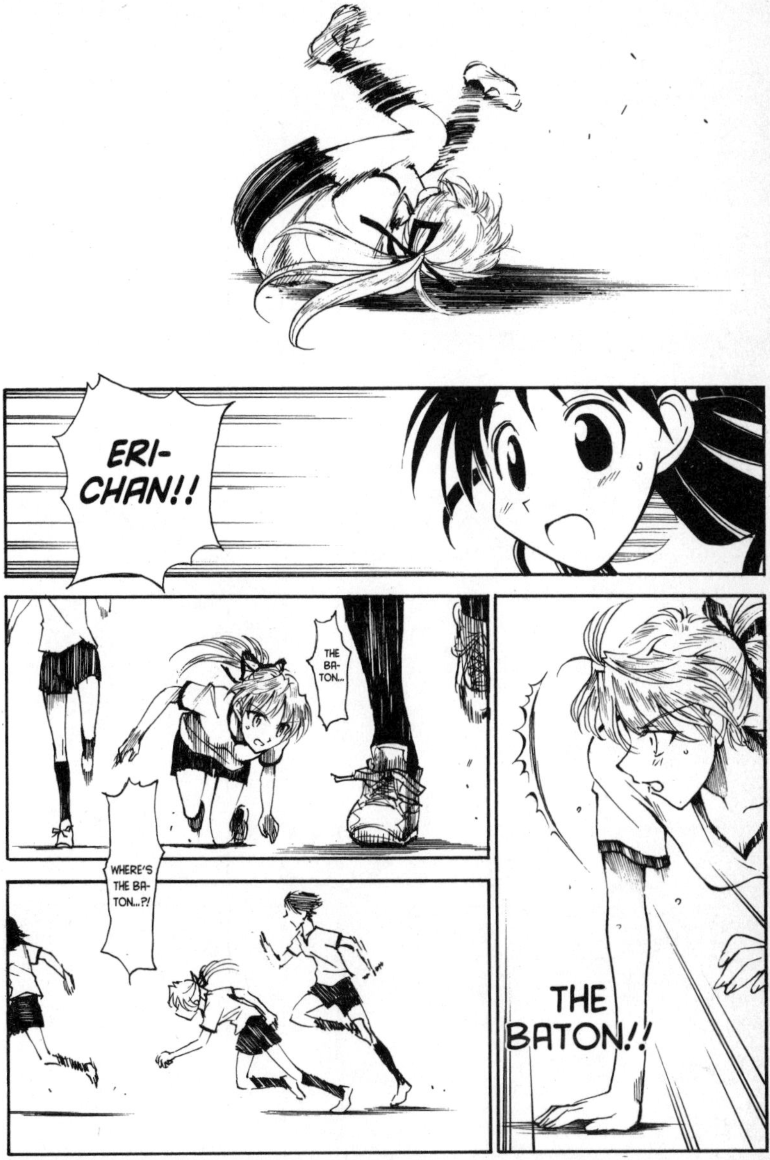
ERI-CHAN!!
THE BATON!!
THE BA-TON...
WHERE'S THE BA-TON...?!

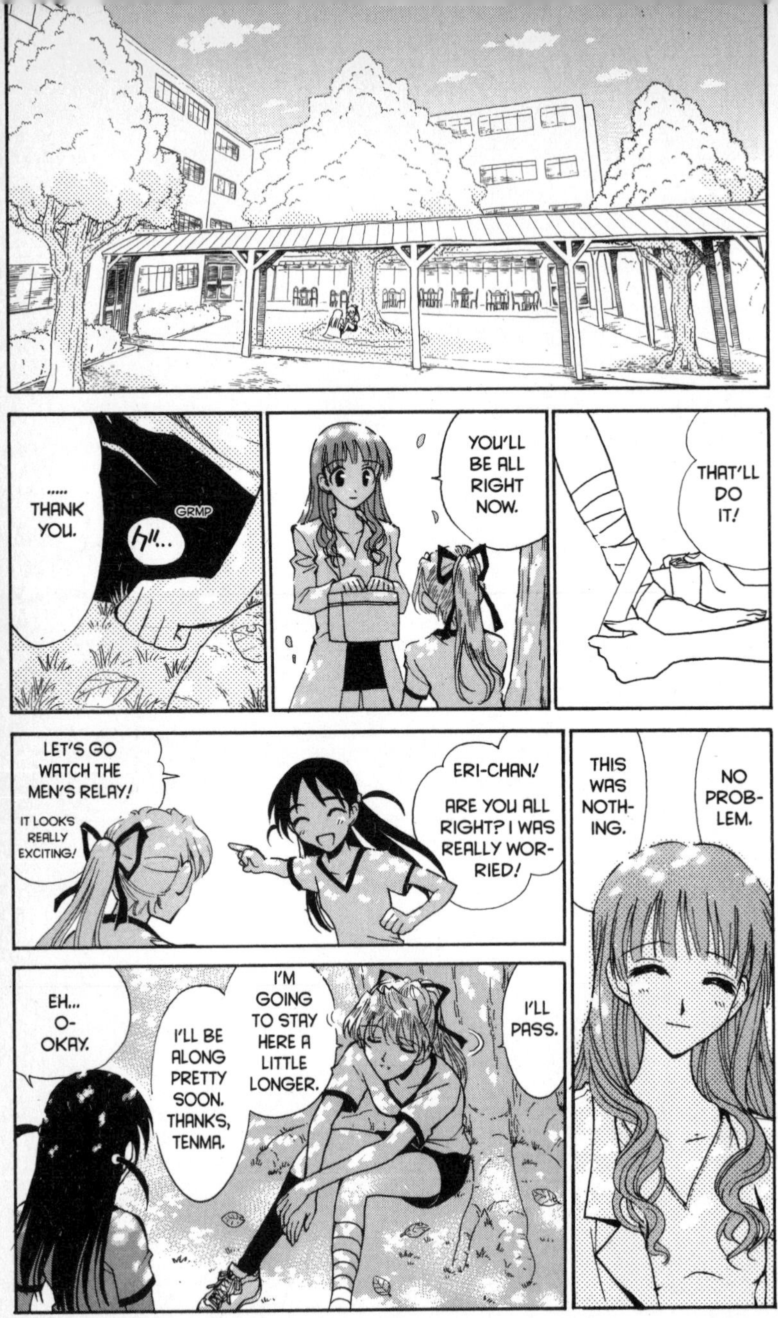
THAT'LL DO IT!
YOU'LL BE ALL RIGHT NOW.
..... THANK YOU.
GRMP
NO PROBLEM.
THIS WAS NOTHING.
ERI-CHAN! ARE YOU ALL RIGHT? I WAS REALLY WORRIED!
LET'S GO WATCH THE MEN'S RELAY!
IT LOOKS REALLY EXCITING!
I'LL PASS.
I'M GOING TO STAY HERE A LITTLE LONGER.
I'LL BE ALONG PRETTY SOON. THANKS, TENMA.
EH... O-OKAY.

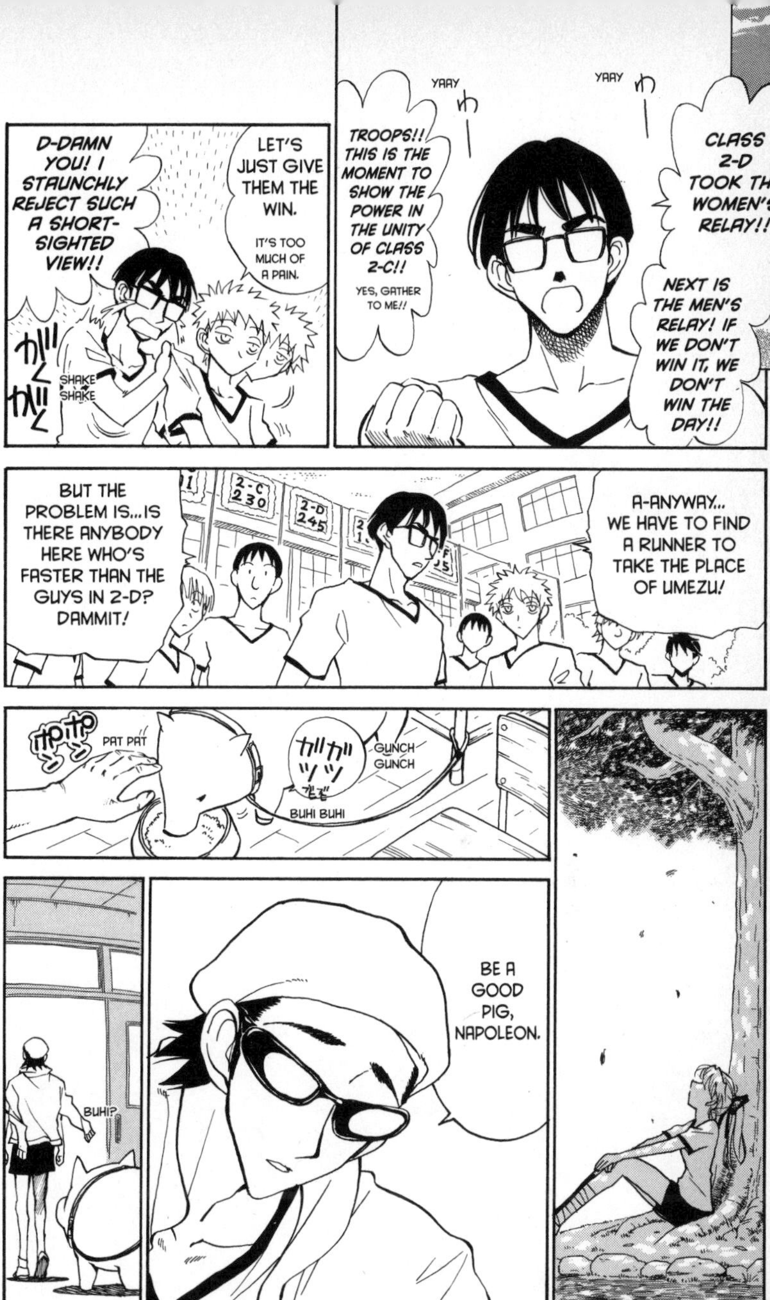
YAAY
YAAY
CLASS 2-D TOOK THE WOMEN'S RELAY!!
NEXT IS THE MEN'S RELAY! IF WE DON'T WIN IT, WE DON'T WIN THE DAY!!
TROOPS!! THIS IS THE MOMENT TO SHOW THE POWER IN THE UNITY OF CLASS 2-C!!
YES, GATHER TO ME!!
LET'S JUST GIVE THEM THE WIN.
IT'S TOO MUCH OF A PAIN.
D-DAMN YOU! I STAUNCHLY REJECT SUCH A SHORT-SIGHTED VIEW!!
SHAKE SHAKE
A-ANYWAY... WE HAVE TO FIND A RUNNER TO TAKE THE PLACE OF UMEZU!
2-C 230
2-D 245
BUT THE PROBLEM IS...IS THERE ANYBODY HERE WHO'S FASTER THAN THE GUYS IN 2-D? DAMMIT!
GUNCH GUNCH
BUHI BUHI
PAT PAT
BE A GOOD PIG, NAPOLEON.
BUHI?

Centripetal Force: Zero.

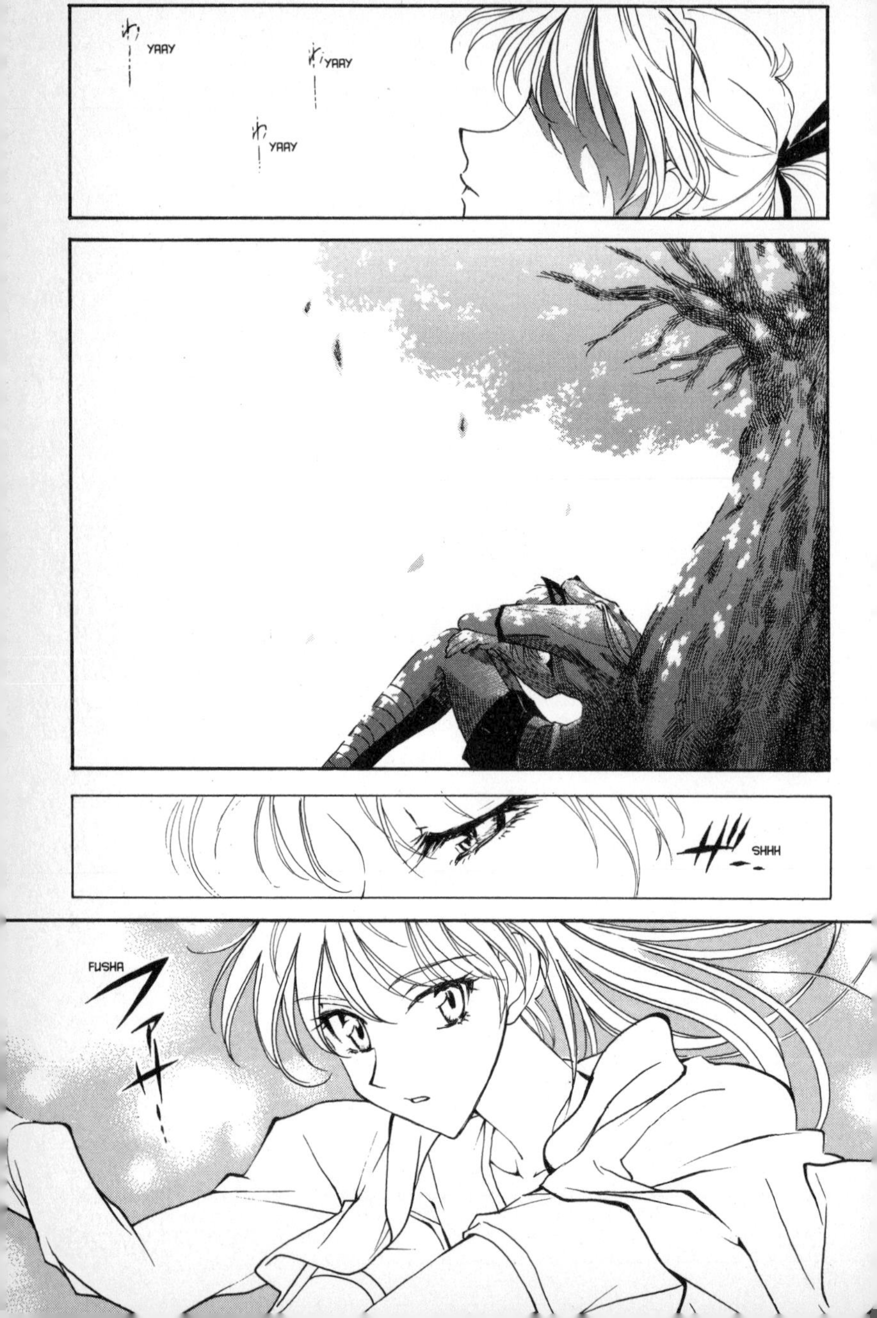
YAAY
YAAY
YAAY
SHHH
FUSHA

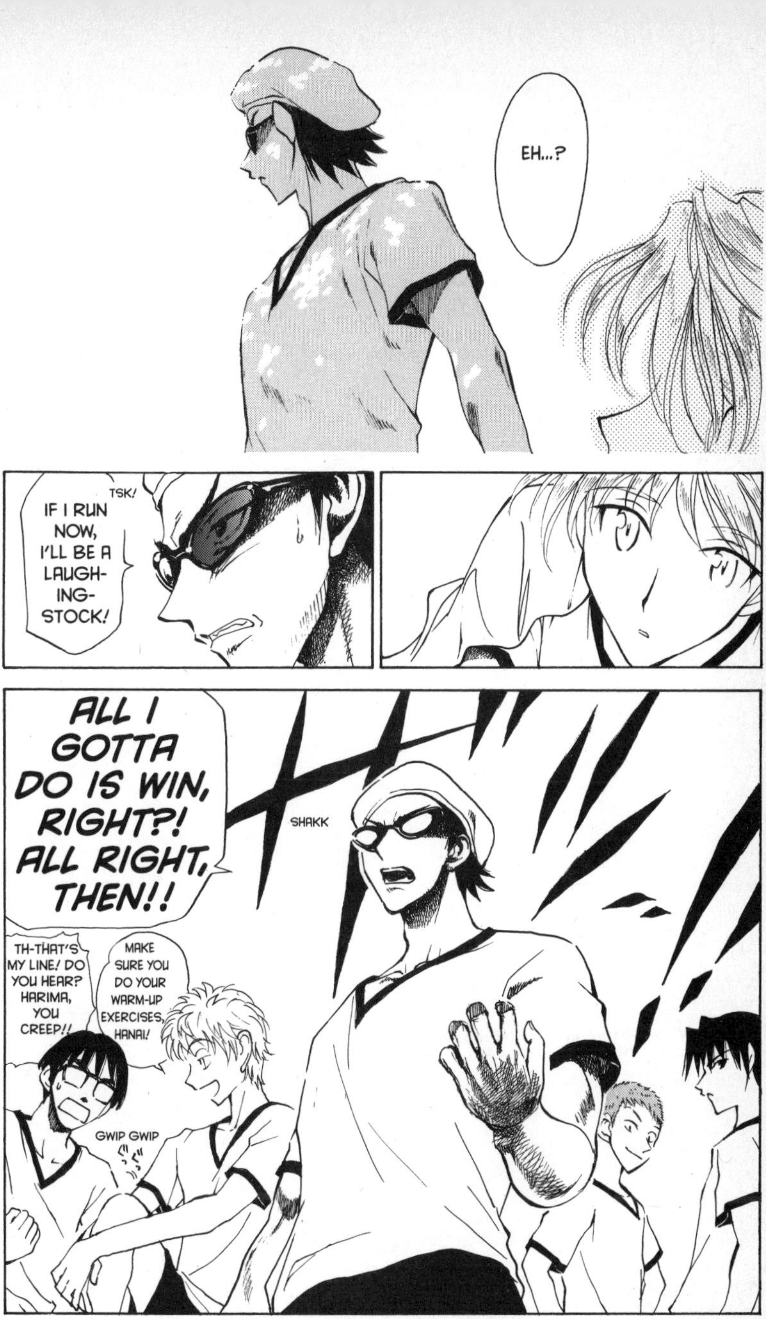
EH...?
TSK!
IF I RUN NOW, I'LL BE A LAUGHING-STOCK!
ALL I GOTTA DO IS WIN, RIGHT?! ALL RIGHT, THEN!!
SHAKK
MAKE SURE YOU DO YOUR WARM-UP EXERCISES, HANAI!
TH-THAT'S MY LINE! DO YOU HEAR? HARIMA, YOU CREEP!!
GWIP GWIP

Even Shaved, He Stands!!

 # 81 · · · · · · · · · Fin

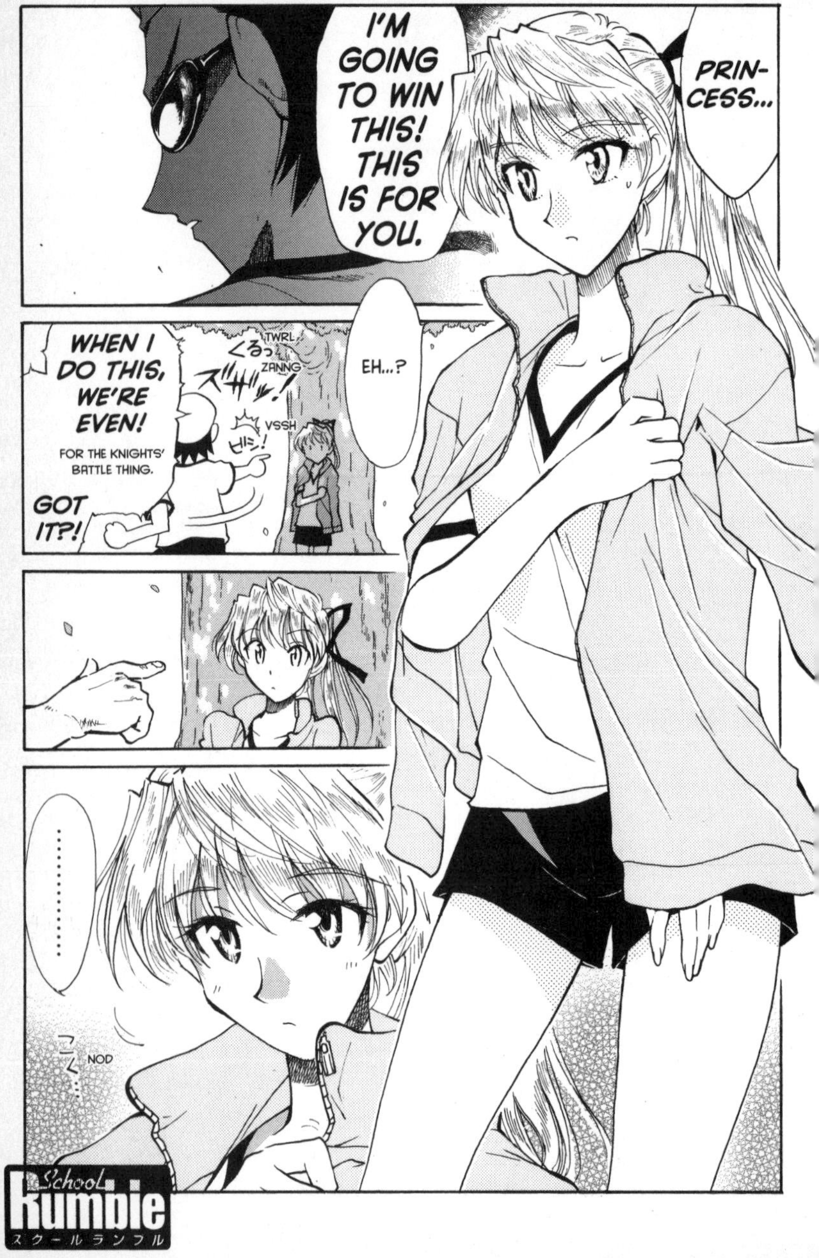
PRIN-CESS...
I'M GOING TO WIN THIS! THIS IS FOR YOU.
EH...?
WHEN I DO THIS, WE'RE EVEN!
FOR THE KNIGHTS' BATTLE THING.
GOT IT?!
くるっ TWRL
ズザッ ZANNG
ビシ VSSH
......
こく... NOD

School Rumble
スクールランブル

82 SOME CAME RUNNING

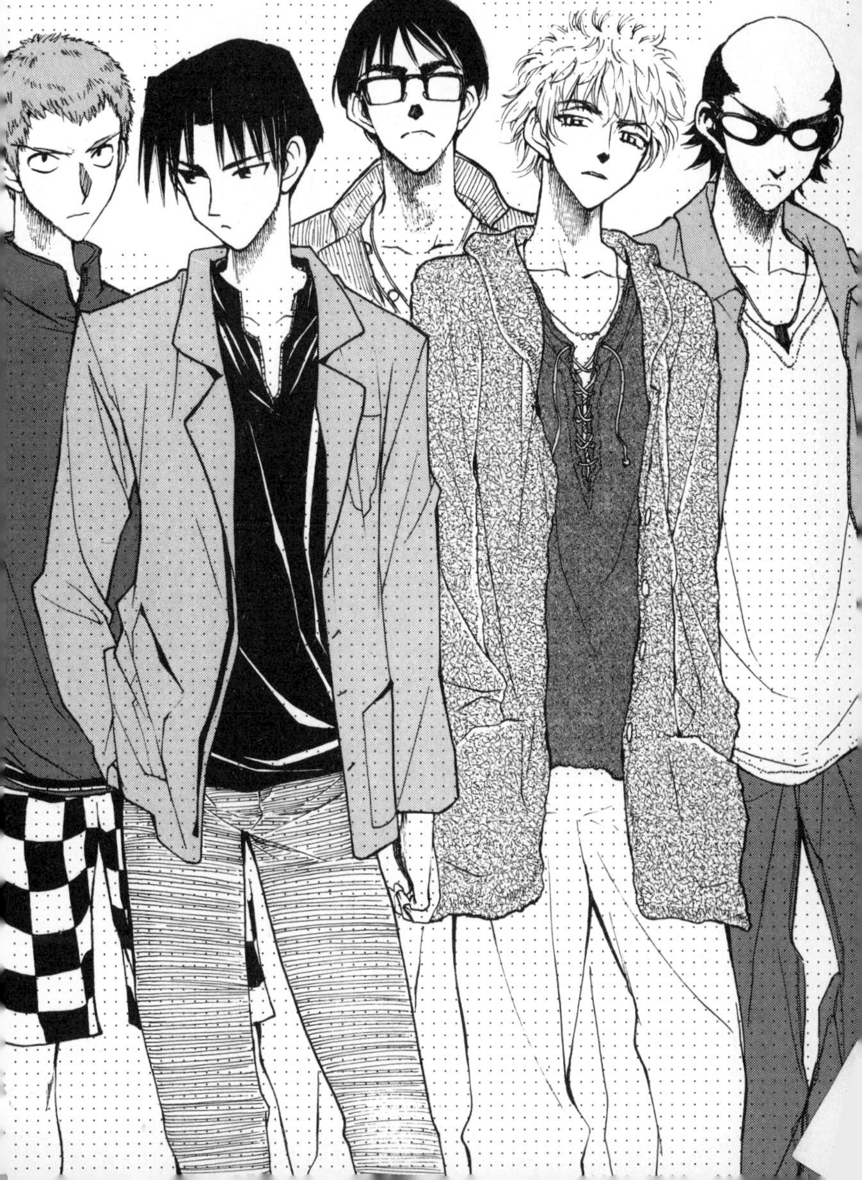

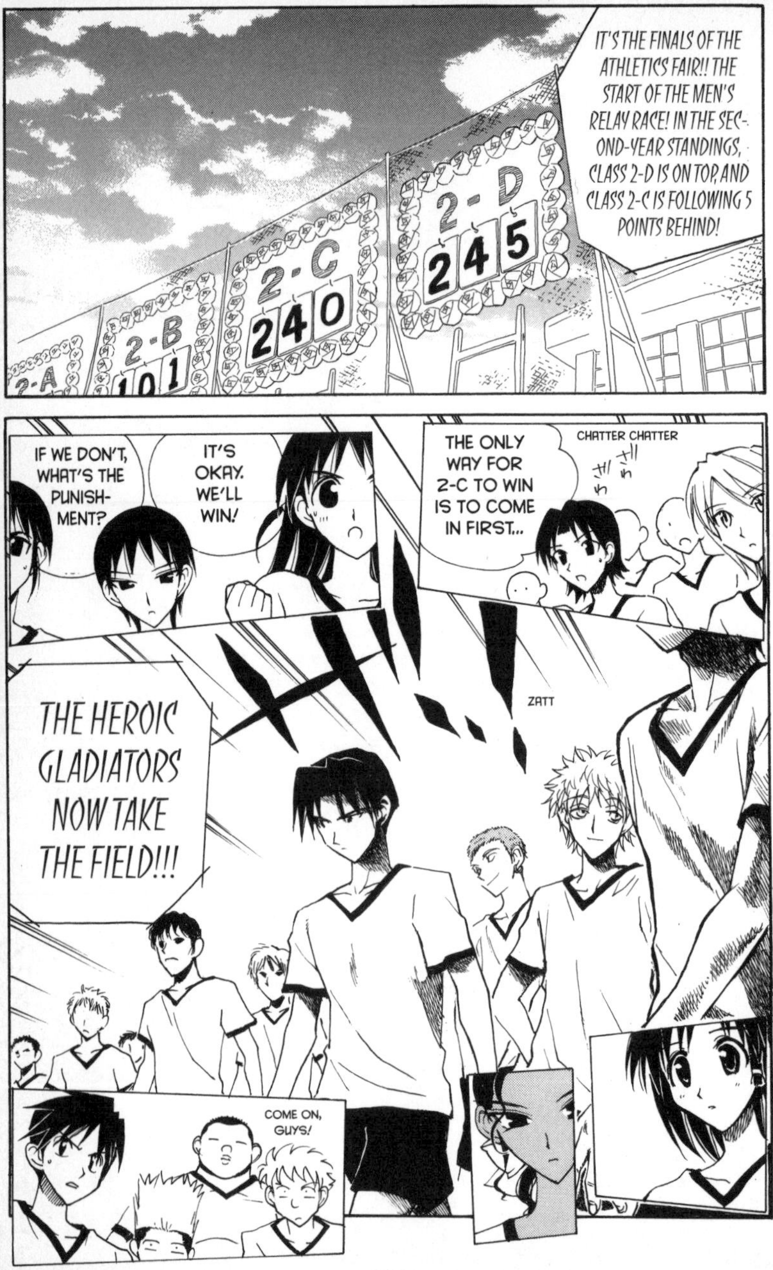
IT'S THE FINALS OF THE ATHLETICS FAIR!! THE START OF THE MEN'S RELAY RACE! IN THE SEC-OND-YEAR STANDINGS, CLASS 2-D IS ON TOP, AND CLASS 2-C IS FOLLOWING 5 POINTS BEHIND!
2-D 245
2-C 240
2-B 101
2-A
THE ONLY WAY FOR 2-C TO WIN IS TO COME IN FIRST...
CHATTER CHATTER
IT'S OKAY. WE'LL WIN!
IF WE DON'T, WHAT'S THE PUNISH-MENT?
ZATT
THE HEROIC GLADIATORS NOW TAKE THE FIELD!!!
COME ON, GUYS!

Takano Akira: Always Cool.

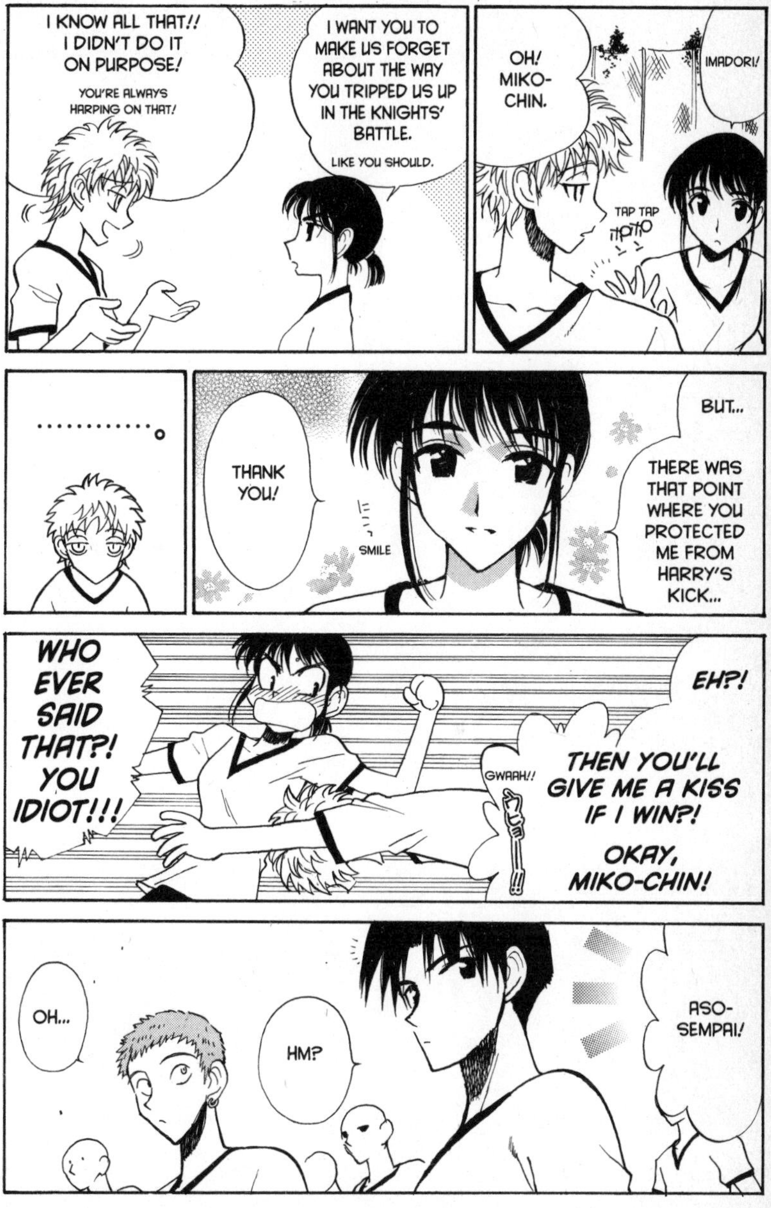
IMADORI!
OH! MIKO-CHIN.
TAP TAP
I WANT YOU TO MAKE US FORGET ABOUT THE WAY YOU TRIPPED US UP IN THE KNIGHTS' BATTLE.
LIKE YOU SHOULD.
I KNOW ALL THAT!! I DIDN'T DO IT ON PURPOSE!
YOU'RE ALWAYS HARPING ON THAT!
BUT...
THERE WAS THAT POINT WHERE YOU PROTECTED ME FROM HARRY'S KICK...
THANK YOU!
SMILE
............。
EH?!
THEN YOU'LL GIVE ME A KISS IF I WIN?!
OKAY, MIKO-CHIN!
GWAAH!!
WHO EVER SAID THAT?! YOU IDIOT!!!
ASO-SEMPAI!
HM?
OH...

Suô Mikoto: She Supports Her People. Even Imadori.

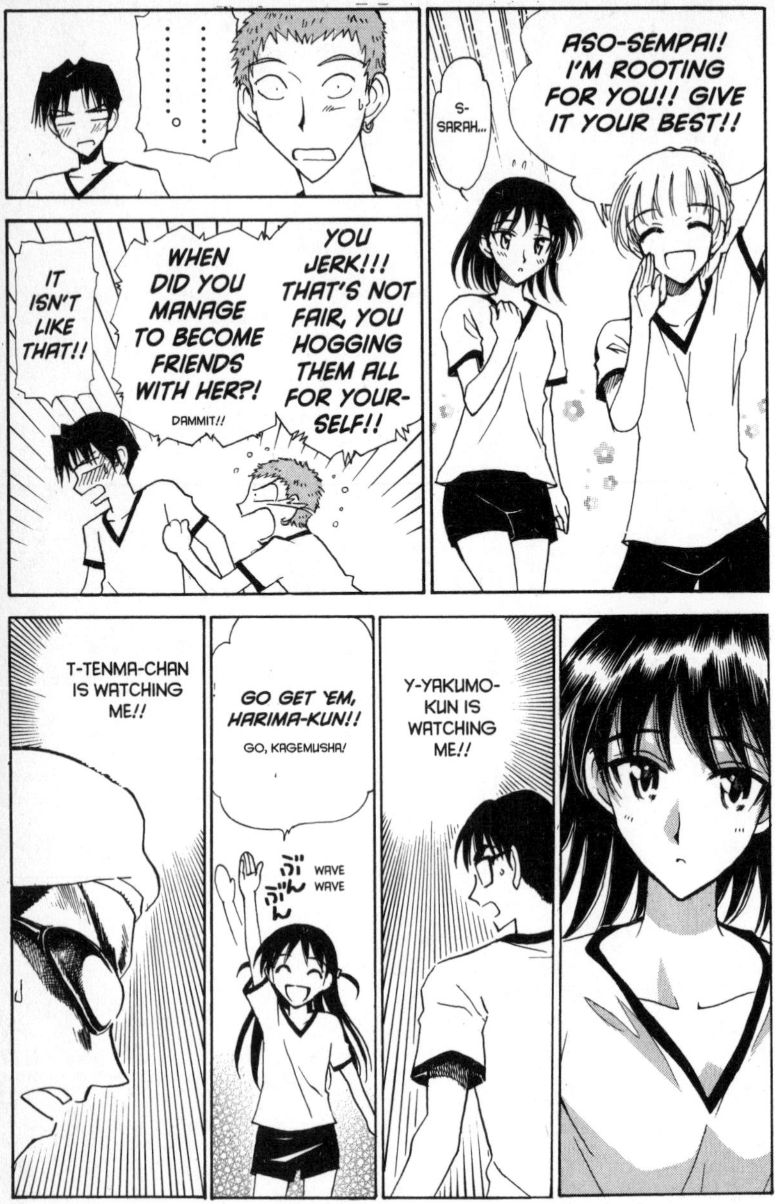
ASO-SEMPAI! I'M ROOTING FOR YOU!! GIVE IT YOUR BEST!!
S-SARAH...
......
......。
YOU JERK!!! THAT'S NOT FAIR, YOU HOGGING THEM ALL FOR YOURSELF!!
WHEN DID YOU MANAGE TO BECOME FRIENDS WITH HER?!
DAMMIT!!
IT ISN'T LIKE THAT!!
Y-YAKUMO-KUN IS WATCHING ME!!
GO GET 'EM, HARIMA-KUN!!
GO, KAGEMUSHA!
ぶん ぶん
WAVE WAVE
T-TENMA-CHAN IS WATCHING ME!!

They're Losers. Probably.

にへら——
HEH-HEHN
HEY, LOOK AT THEM! THEY'VE GOT COMPLETELY DISTRACTED LOOKS ON THEIR FACES!
THEY DON'T EVEN LOOK INTER-ESTED IN WINNING!!
HEY! ARE YOU GUYS REALLY ALL RIGHT?
DON'T TELL ME YOU'RE THROWING THE RACE!
ははははは!!!
HA HA HA HA!!!
YOU CAN'T GET NERVOUS!!
HOW ABOUT WE RACE IN YOUR PLACE!
OH, COME ON!!
JUST SHAPE UP, WILL YOU?!
YEAH.
ABOUT WHAT I EXPECTED.
WHAT'S GOING ON WITH CLASS 2-C?
IT'S LIKE THEY'RE GATH-ERING TO TALK THEMSELVES OUT OF THE CONTEST!
HA HA HA HA HA HA!!
はははははは!!
HEH HEHN
MIKO-CHIN!
INTRODUCE ME TO AT LEAST ONE!
LET GO OF ME!
THEY VERY FRAGILE.
HA! WOMEN ARE AS EFFECTIVE AS LIQUOR!

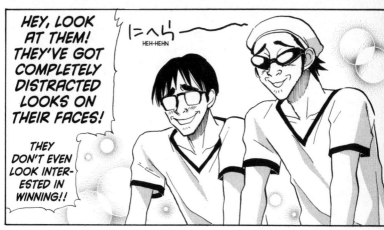

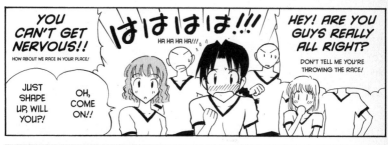

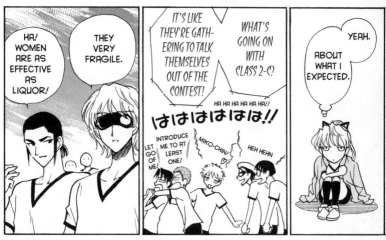

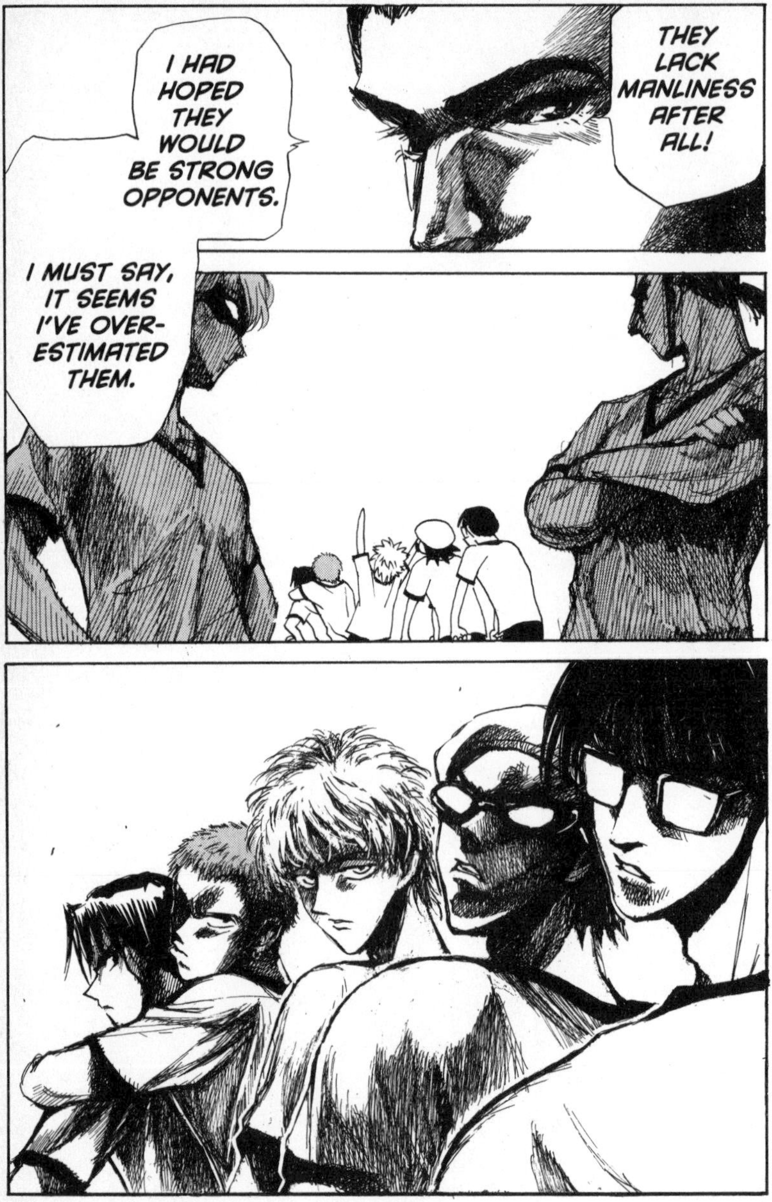
THEY LACK MANLINESS AFTER ALL!
I HAD HOPED THEY WOULD BE STRONG OPPONENTS.
I MUST SAY, IT SEEMS I'VE OVER-ESTIMATED THEM.

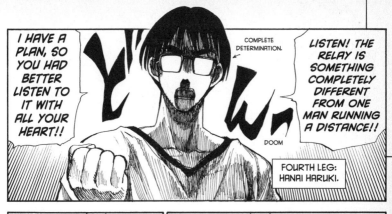

LISTEN! THE RELAY IS SOMETHING COMPLETELY DIFFERENT FROM ONE MAN RUNNING A DISTANCE!!
COMPLETE DETERMINATION.
I HAVE A PLAN, SO YOU HAD BETTER LISTEN TO IT WITH ALL YOUR HEART!!
DOOM
FOURTH LEG: HANAI HARUKI.
LISTEN! EVERYTHING IN A RELAY DEPENDS ON PASSING THE BATON! YOU HAVE TO CALCULATE THE TIMING OF THE PASS BEFORE YOU START RUNNING...
TH-THAT'S WHAT I WAS GOING TO SAY!!
REALLY ...?
YOU'RE PRETTY WELL INFORMED ABOUT THIS.
I NEVER EXPECTED THAT.
HA! THIS RELAY WILL WIN ME BACK THE GOOD NAME I LOST IN THE KNIGHTS' BATTLE.
JUST WATCH ME.
THEN YOU... ME TOO...
CHATTER CHATTER
MUMBLE
MUMBLE
ANYWAY...
I CAN GET SERIOUS ABOUT SOMETHING EVERY NOW AND THEN.
OTHERWISE PEOPLE WILL THINK I'M A FOOL.
SHHH
THIRD LEG: IMADORI KYÔSUKE.

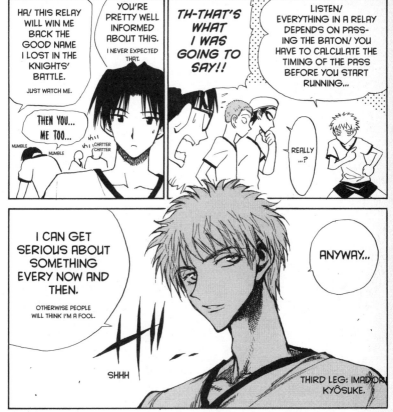

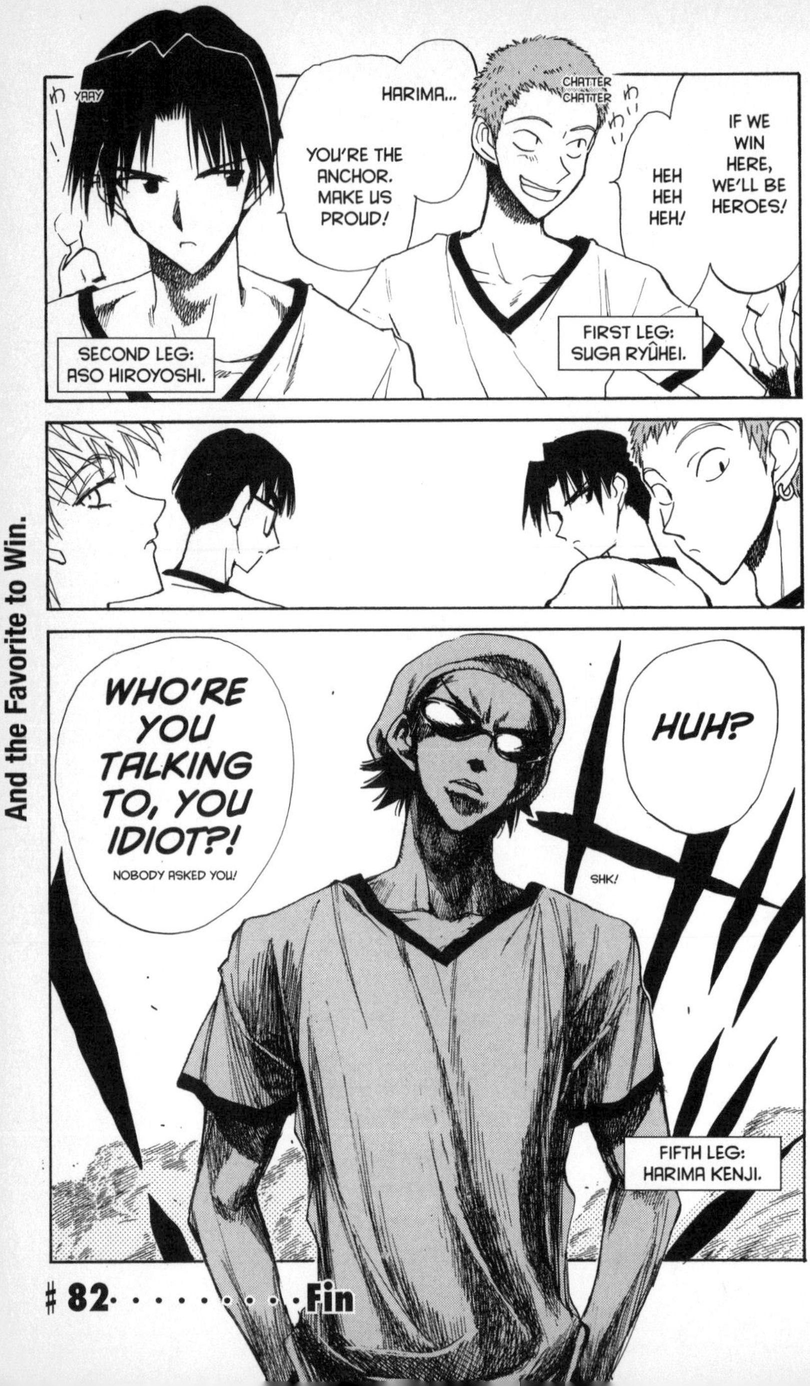
IF WE WIN HERE, WE'LL BE HEROES!
HEH HEH HEH!
CHATTER CHATTER
HARIMA...
YOU'RE THE ANCHOR. MAKE US PROUD!
FIRST LEG: SUGA RYÛHEI.
YAAY
SECOND LEG: ASO HIROYOSHI.
HUH?
SHK!
WHO'RE YOU TALKING TO, YOU IDIOT?!
NOBODY ASKED YOU!
FIFTH LEG: HARIMA KENJI.

82 .... Fin

#83 TRUE BLOOD

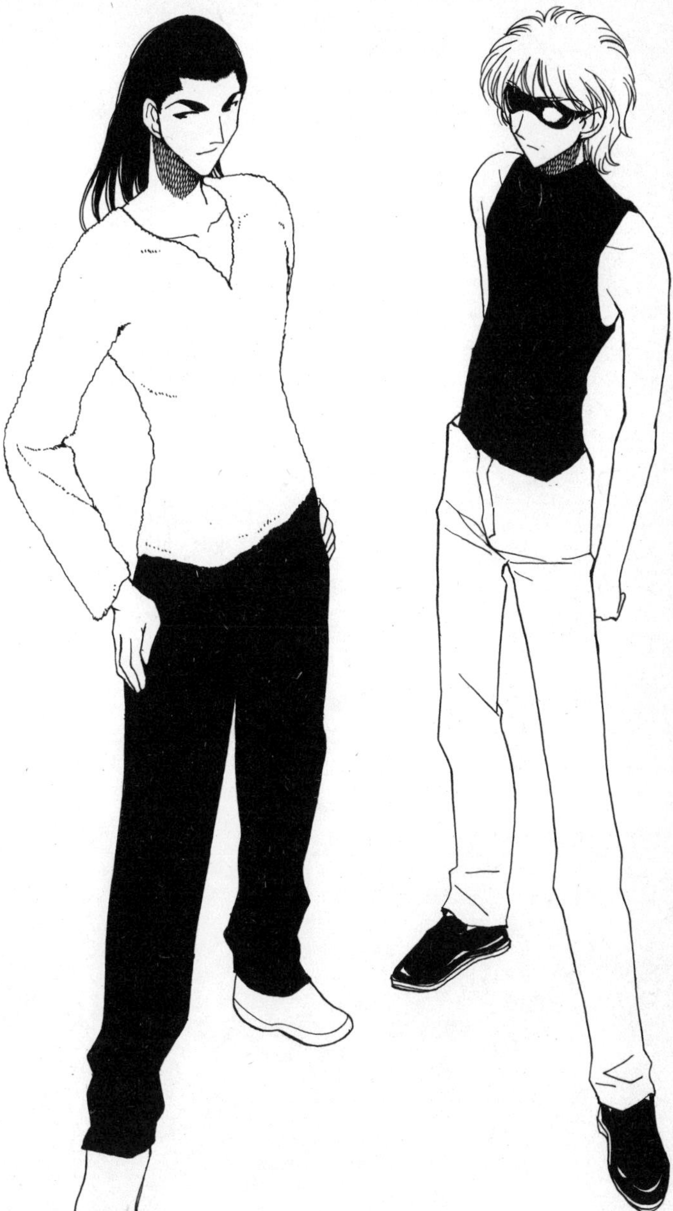

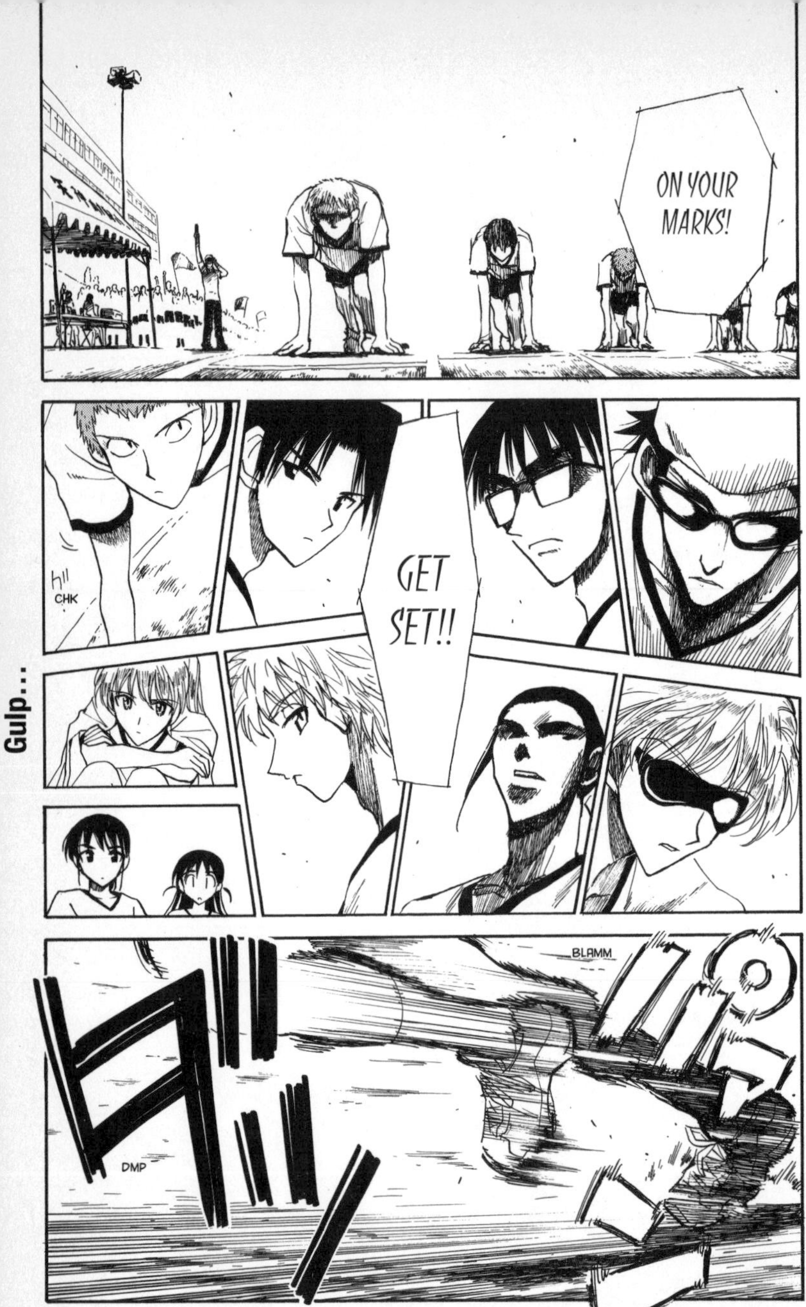
ON YOUR MARKS!
GET SET!!
CHK
Gulp...
BLAMM
DMP

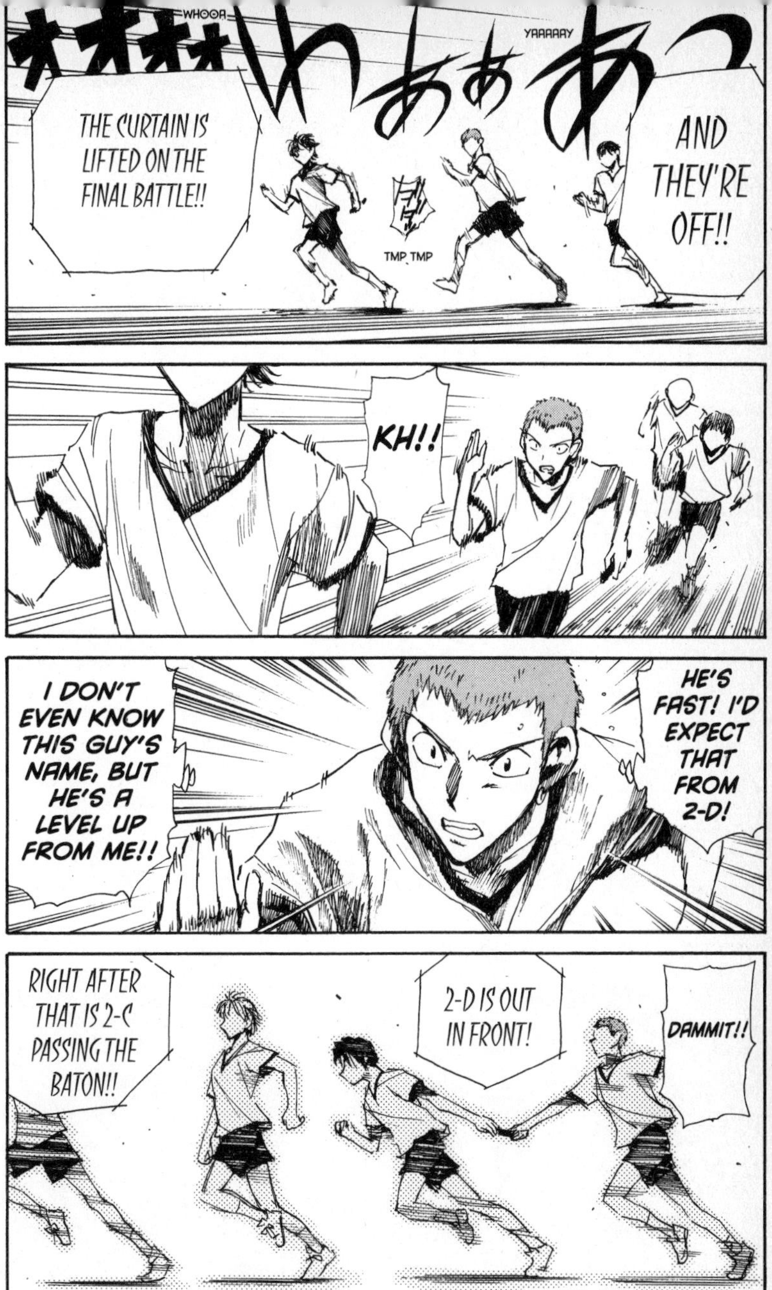
YAAAAAY
WHOOA
AND THEY'RE OFF!!
THE CURTAIN IS LIFTED ON THE FINAL BATTLE!!
TMP TMP
KH!!
HE'S FAST! I'D EXPECT THAT FROM 2-D!
I DON'T EVEN KNOW THIS GUY'S NAME, BUT HE'S A LEVEL UP FROM ME!!
DAMMIT!!
2-D IS OUT IN FRONT!
RIGHT AFTER THAT IS 2-C PASSING THE BATON!!

Suga Ryûhei: Loves Ramen. You Didn't Need to Know That but...

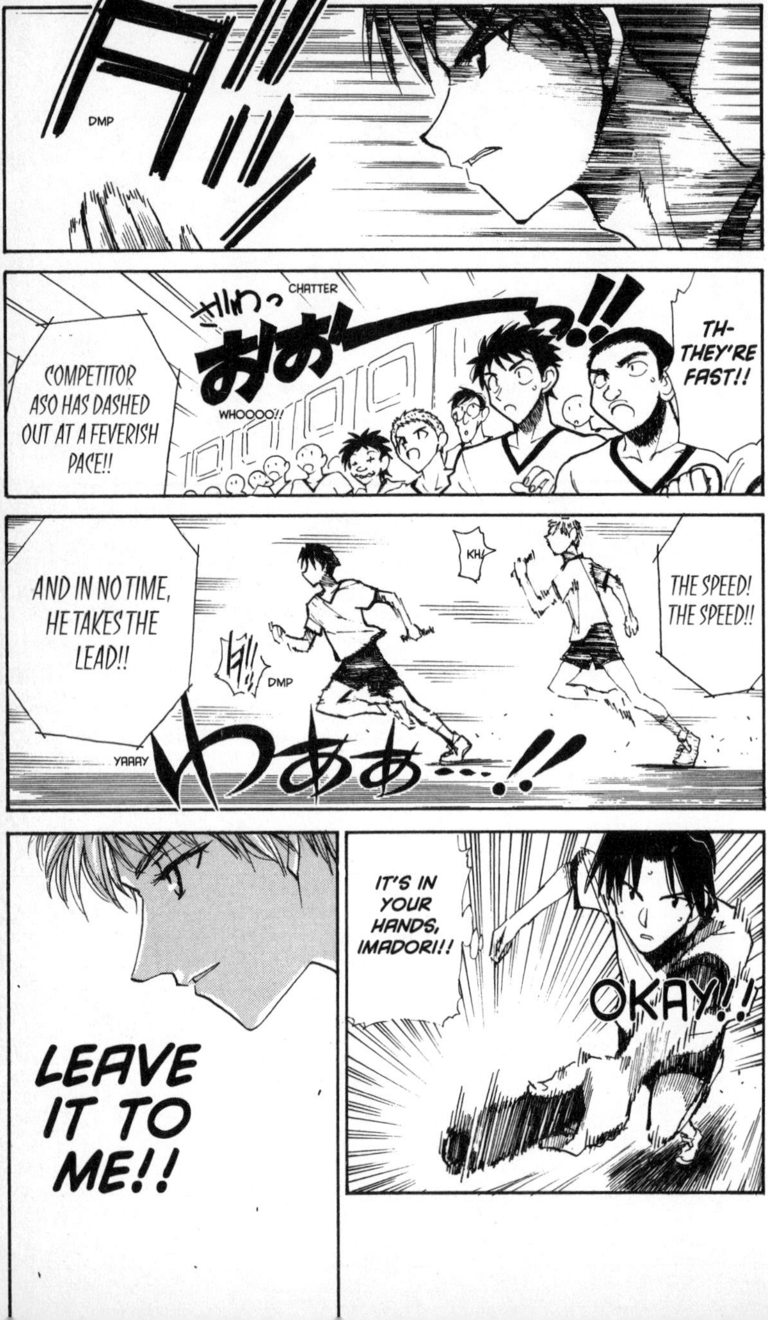
DMP
TH- THEY'RE FAST!!
CHATTER
WHOOOO!!
COMPETITOR ASO HAS DASHED OUT AT A FEVERISH PACE!!
THE SPEED! THE SPEED!!
KH!
DMP
AND IN NO TIME, HE TAKES THE LEAD!!
YAAAY
IT'S IN YOUR HANDS, IMADORI!!
OKAY!!!
LEAVE IT TO ME!!

Aso Hiroyoshi: You Knew He'd Be an All-Around Athlete.

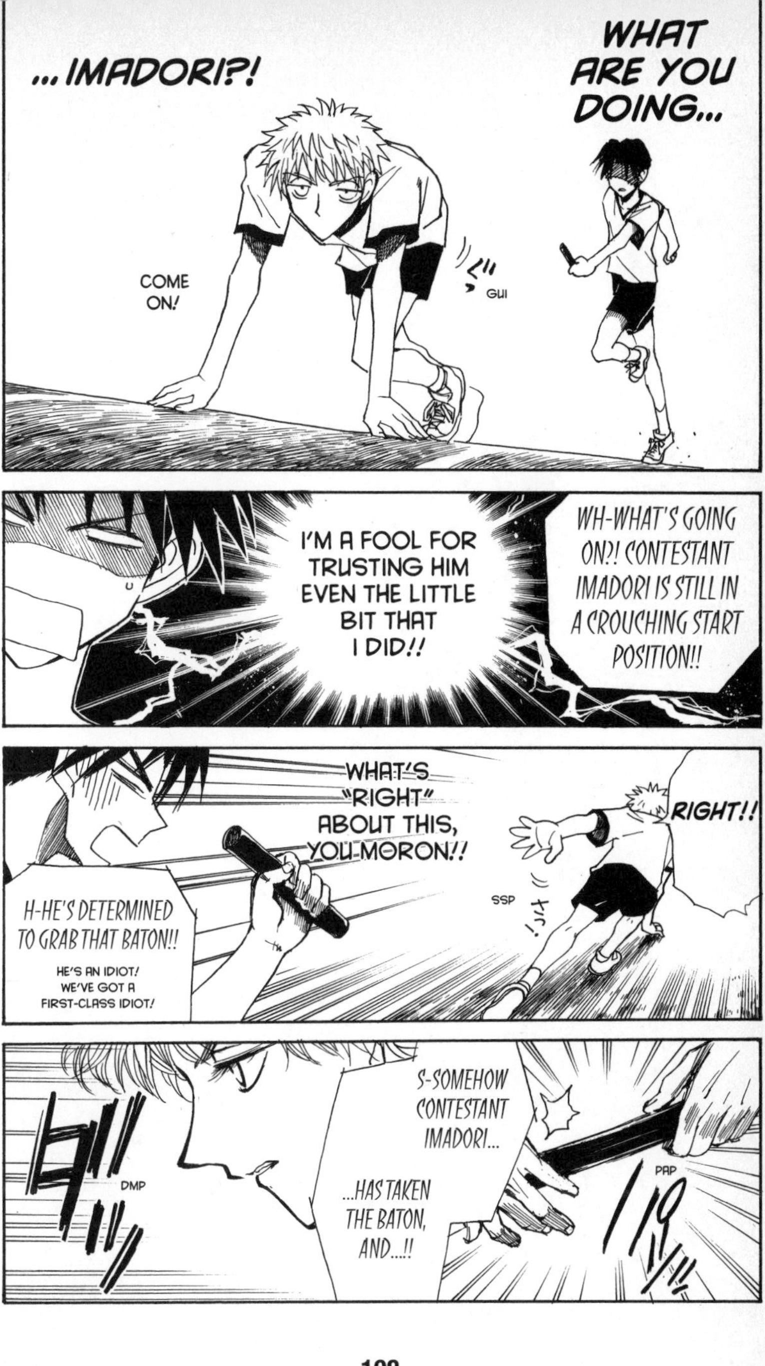
WHAT ARE YOU DOING...
GUI
...IMADORI?!
COME ON!
WH-WHAT'S GOING ON?! CONTESTANT IMADORI IS STILL IN A CROUCHING START POSITION!!
I'M A FOOL FOR TRUSTING HIM EVEN THE LITTLE BIT THAT I DID!!
RIGHT!!
SSP
WHAT'S "RIGHT" ABOUT THIS, YOU MORON!!
H-HE'S DETERMINED TO GRAB THAT BATON!!
HE'S AN IDIOT! WE'VE GOT A FIRST-CLASS IDIOT!
PAP
S-SOMEHOW CONTESTANT IMADORI...
...HAS TAKEN THE BATON, AND...!!
DMP

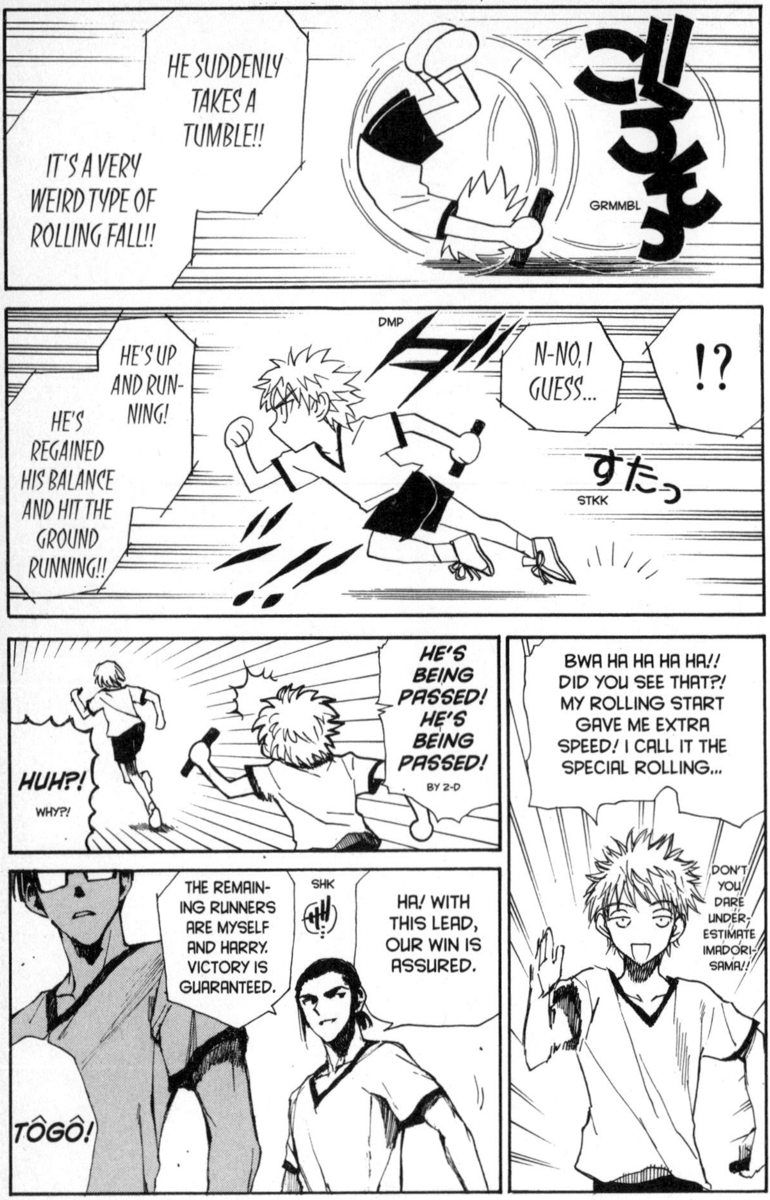
GRMMBL
HE SUDDENLY TAKES A TUMBLE!!
IT'S A VERY WEIRD TYPE OF ROLLING FALL!!
!?
N-NO, I GUESS...
DMP
すたっ
STKK
HE'S UP AND RUN-NING!
HE'S REGAINED HIS BALANCE AND HIT THE GROUND RUNNING!!
BWA HA HA HA HA!! DID YOU SEE THAT?! MY ROLLING START GAVE ME EXTRA SPEED! I CALL IT THE SPECIAL ROLLING...
DON'T YOU DARE UNDER-ESTIMATE IMADORI-SAMA!!
HE'S BEING PASSED! HE'S BEING PASSED!
BY 2-D
HUH?!
WHY?!
HA! WITH THIS LEAD, OUR WIN IS ASSURED.
SHK
THE REMAIN-ING RUNNERS ARE MYSELF AND HARRY. VICTORY IS GUARANTEED.
TÔGÔ!

100 meters in 12 seconds: Unverified.

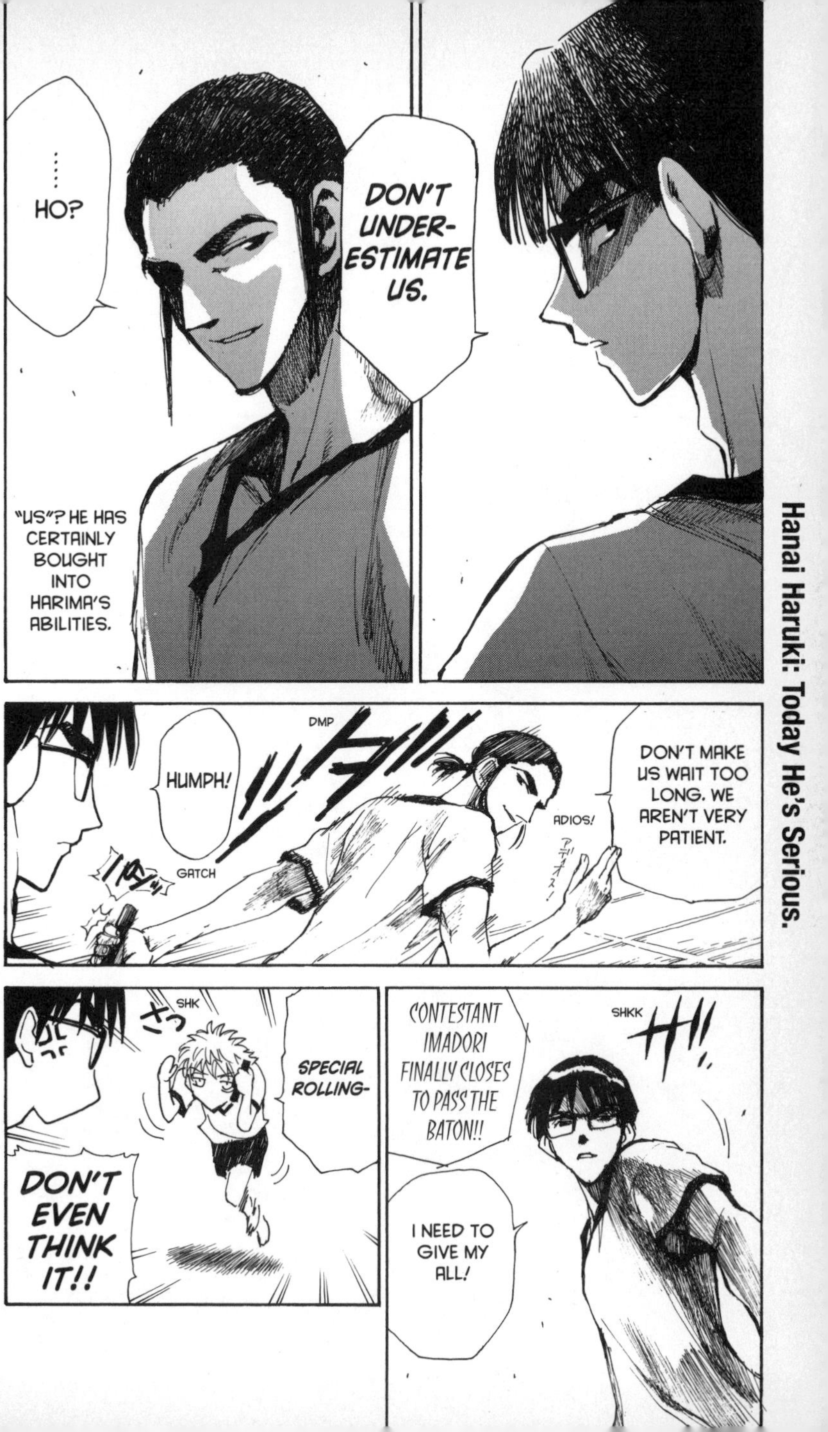
DON'T UNDER-ESTIMATE US.
…… HO?
"US"? HE HAS CERTAINLY BOUGHT INTO HARIMA'S ABILITIES.
DON'T MAKE US WAIT TOO LONG. WE AREN'T VERY PATIENT.
ADIOS!
アディオス!
DMP
HUMPH!
GATCH
SHKK
CONTESTANT IMADORI FINALLY CLOSES TO PASS THE BATON!!
I NEED TO GIVE MY ALL!
SHK
さっ
SPECIAL ROLLING-
DON'T EVEN THINK IT!!

Hanai Haruki: Almost a Different Person.

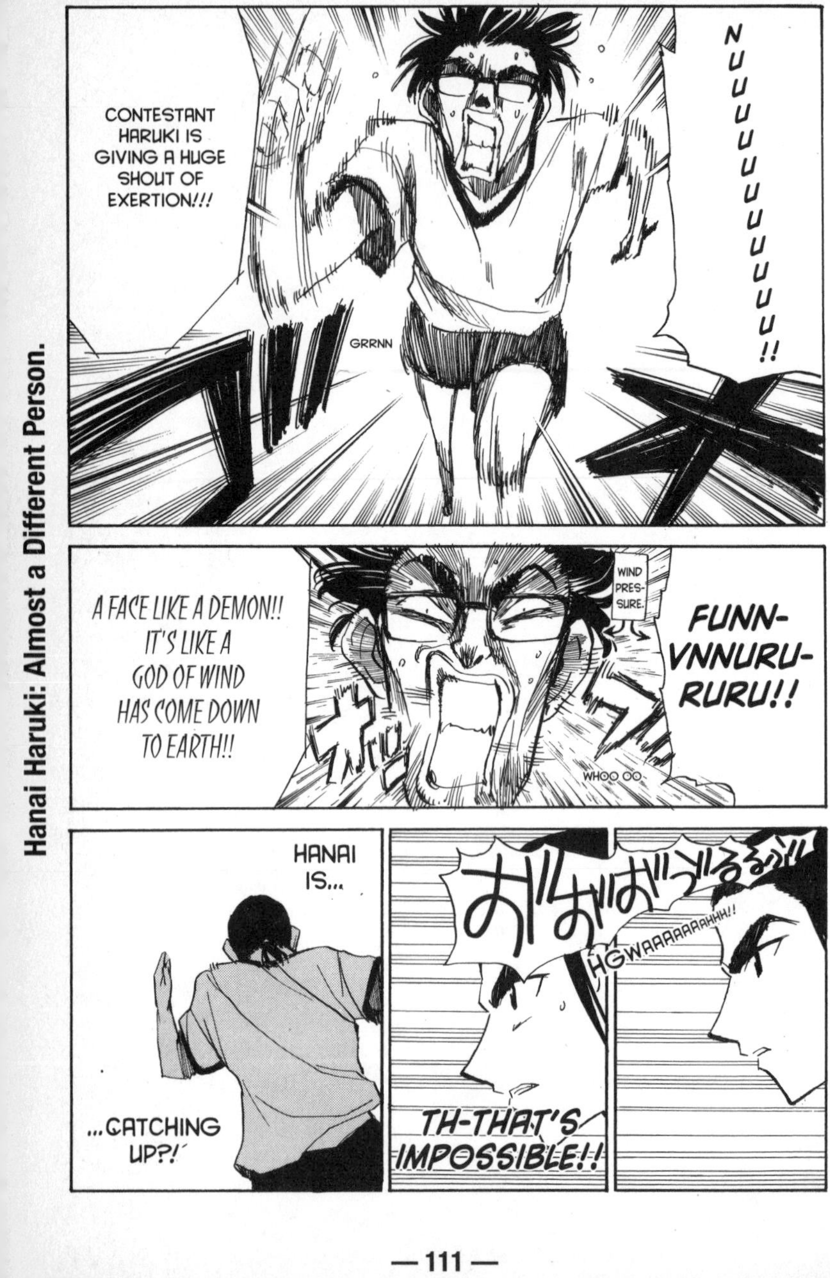
NUUUUUUUUUUU!!
CONTESTANT HARUKI IS GIVING A HUGE SHOUT OF EXERTION!!!
GRRNN
FUNN-VNNURU-RURU!!
WIND PRES-SURE.
A FACE LIKE A DEMON!! IT'S LIKE A GOD OF WIND HAS COME DOWN TO EARTH!!
WHOO OO
HGWAAAAAAAHHH!!
TH-THAT'S IMPOSSIBLE!!
HANAI IS...
...CATCHING UP?!

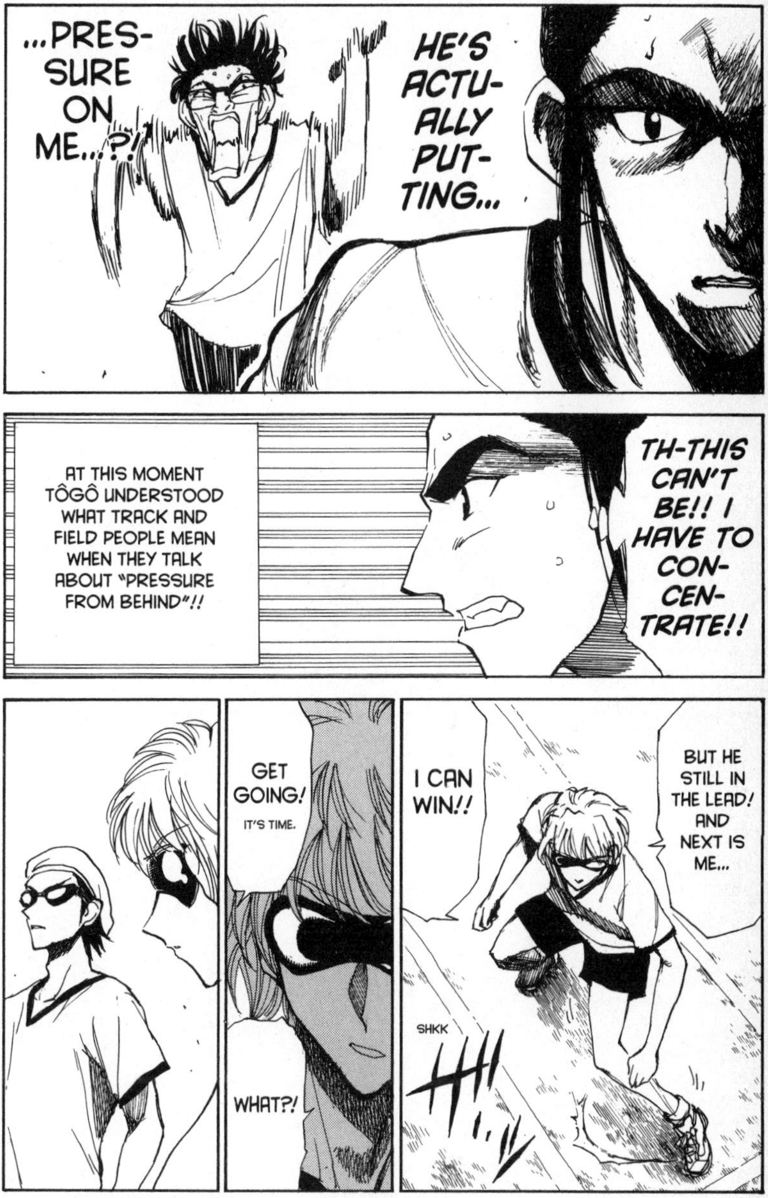
HE'S ACTU-
ALLY
PUT-
TING...
...PRES-
SURE
ON
ME...?!
TH-THIS CAN'T BE!! I HAVE TO CON-CEN-TRATE!!
AT THIS MOMENT TÔGÔ UNDERSTOOD WHAT TRACK AND FIELD PEOPLE MEAN WHEN THEY TALK ABOUT "PRESSURE FROM BEHIND"!!
BUT HE STILL IN THE LEAD! AND NEXT IS ME...
I CAN WIN!!
SHKK
GET GOING!
IT'S TIME.
WHAT?!

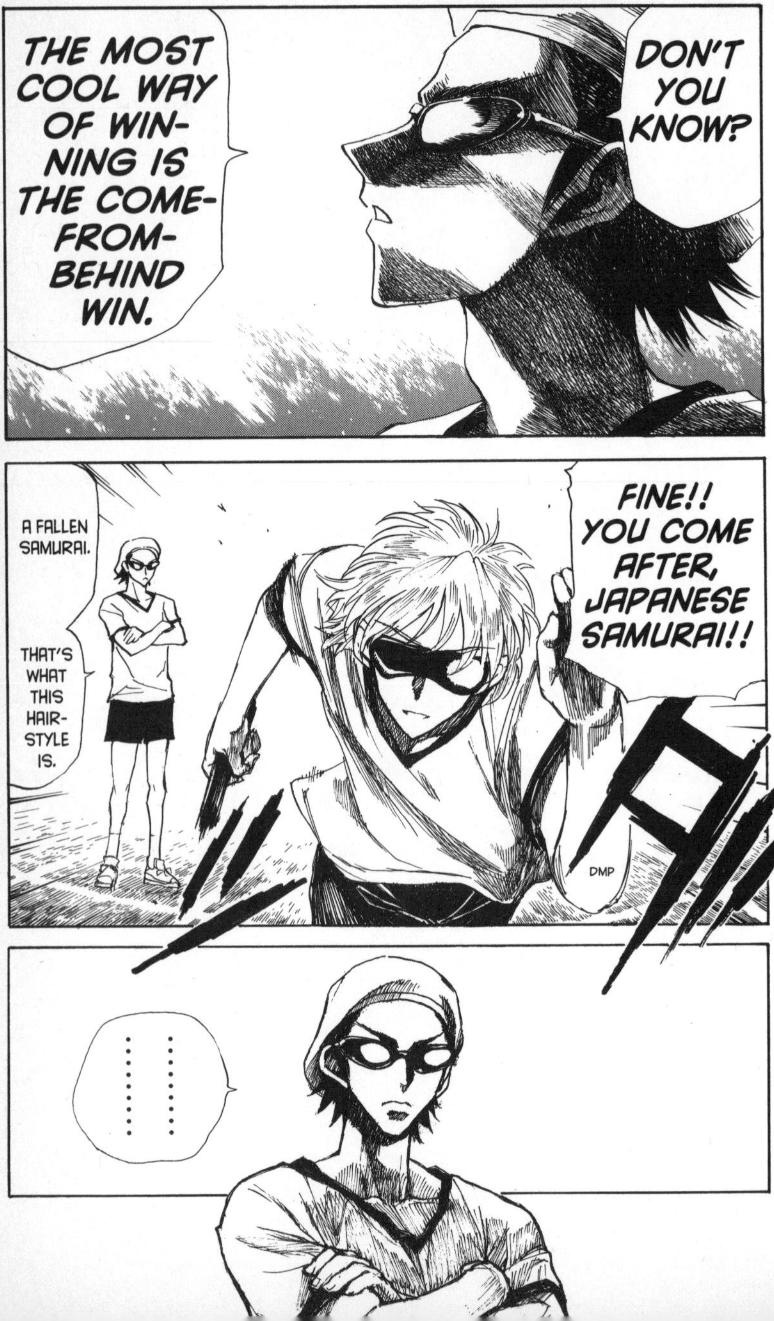
DON'T YOU KNOW?
THE MOST COOL WAY OF WIN-NING IS THE COME-FROM-BEHIND WIN.
FINE!! YOU COME AFTER, JAPANESE SAMURAI!!
DMP
A FALLEN SAMURAI.
THAT'S WHAT THIS HAIR-STYLE IS.
......

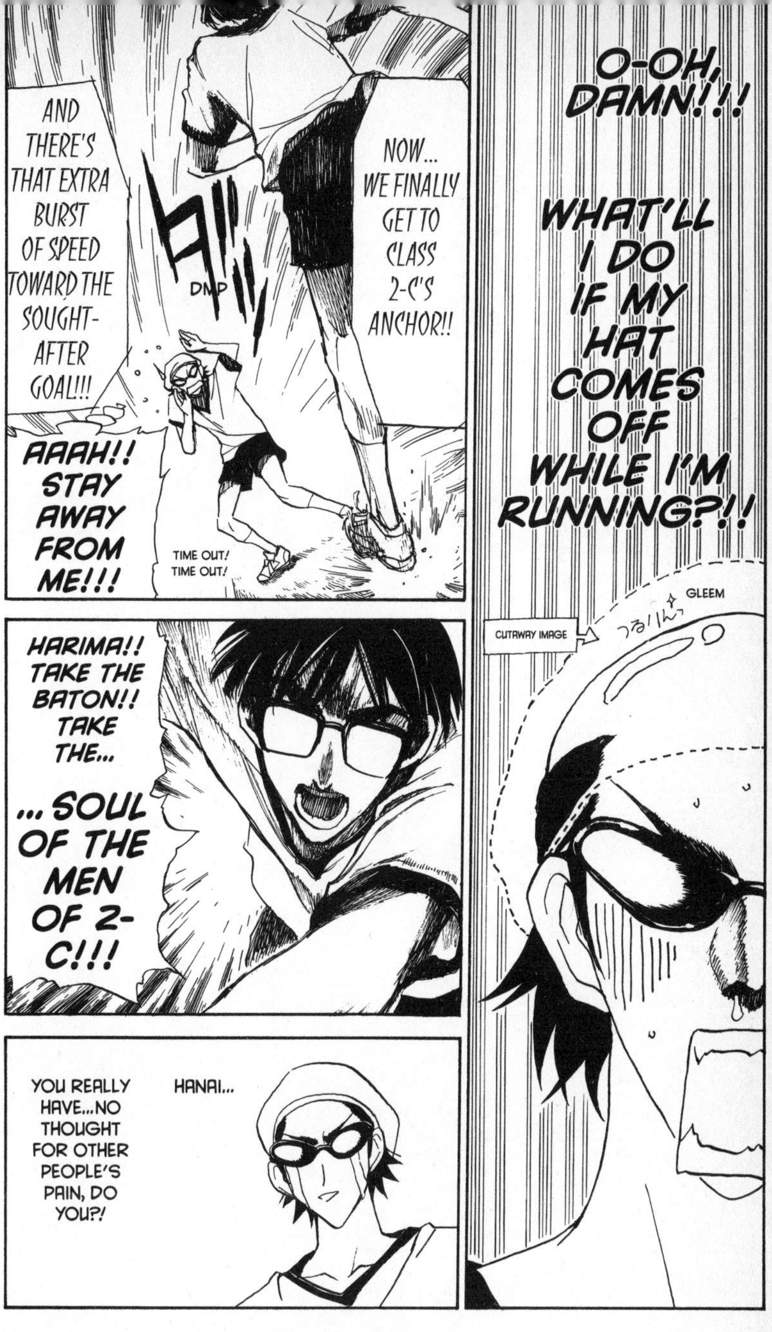
O-OH, DAMN!!!
WHAT'LL I DO IF MY HAT COMES OFF WHILE I'M RUNNING?!!
GLEEM
CUTAWAY IMAGE
つるりんっ
NOW... WE FINALLY GET TO CLASS 2-C'S ANCHOR!!
AND THERE'S THAT EXTRA BURST OF SPEED TOWARD THE SOUGHT-AFTER GOAL!!!
DMP
TIME OUT! TIME OUT!
AAAH!! STAY AWAY FROM ME!!!
HARIMA!! TAKE THE BATON!! TAKE THE...
...SOUL OF THE MEN OF 2-C!!!
HANAI...
YOU REALLY HAVE...NO THOUGHT FOR OTHER PEOPLE'S PAIN, DO YOU?!

For the First Time They Are All Praising Him.

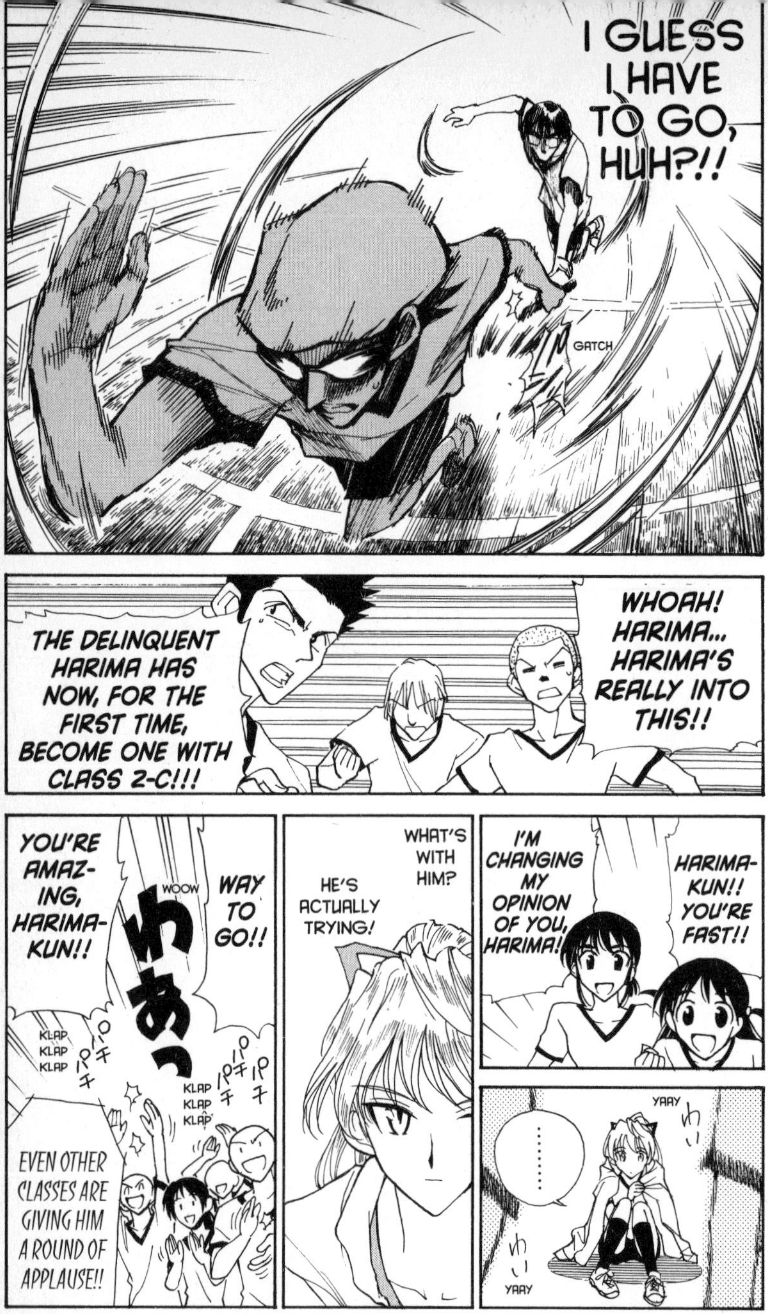

I GUESS I HAVE TO GO, HUH?!!
GATCH
WHOAH! HARIMA... HARIMA'S REALLY INTO THIS!!
THE DELINQUENT HARIMA HAS NOW, FOR THE FIRST TIME, BECOME ONE WITH CLASS 2-C!!!
HARIMA-KUN!! YOU'RE FAST!!
I'M CHANGING MY OPINION OF YOU, HARIMA!
YAAY
......
YAAY
WHAT'S WITH HIM?
HE'S ACTUALLY TRYING!
WAY TO GO!!
わあっ
WOOW
YOU'RE AMAZ-ING, HARIMA-KUN!!
パチパチ
KLAP KLAP KLAP
パチパチ
KLAP KLAP KLAP
EVEN OTHER CLASSES ARE GIVING HIM A ROUND OF APPLAUSE!!

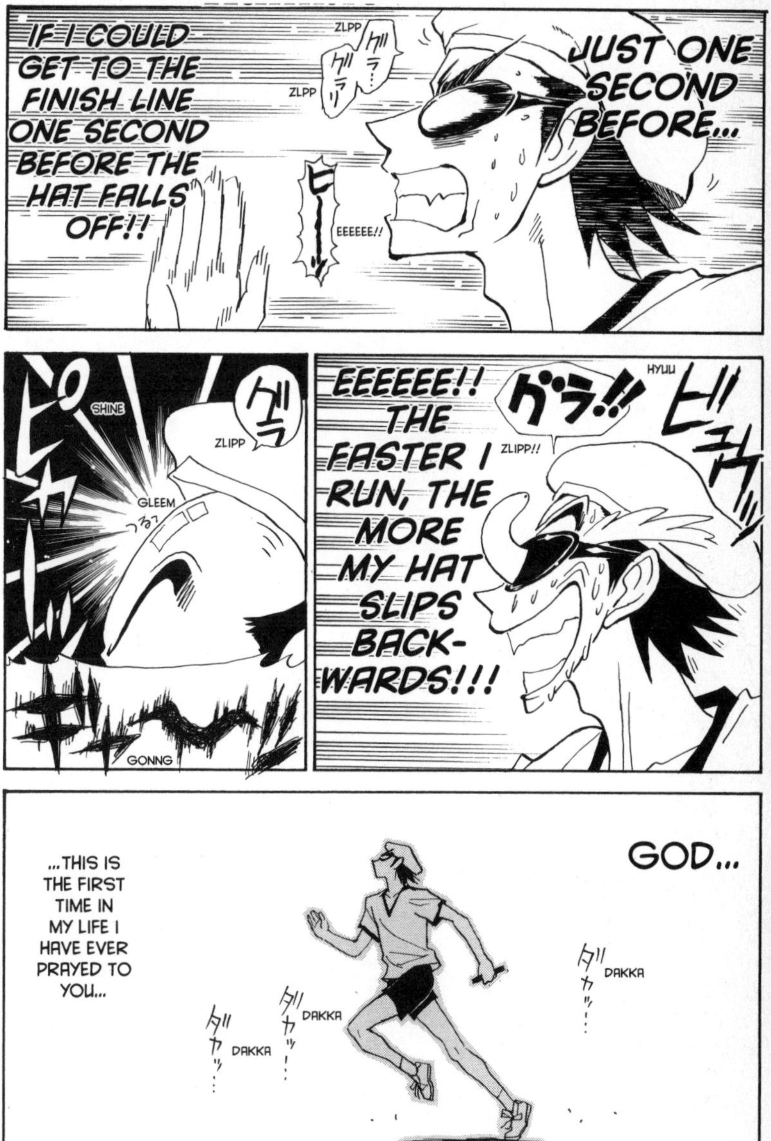
JUST ONE SECOND BEFORE...
ZLPP
ZLPP
EEEEEE!!
IF I COULD GET TO THE FINISH LINE ONE SECOND BEFORE THE HAT FALLS OFF!!
HYUU
ZLIPP!!
EEEEEE!! THE FASTER I RUN, THE MORE MY HAT SLIPS BACKWARDS!!!
ZLIPP
SHINE
GLEEM
GONNG
GOD...
DAKKA
DAKKA
DAKKA
...THIS IS THE FIRST TIME IN MY LIFE I HAVE EVER PRAYED TO YOU...

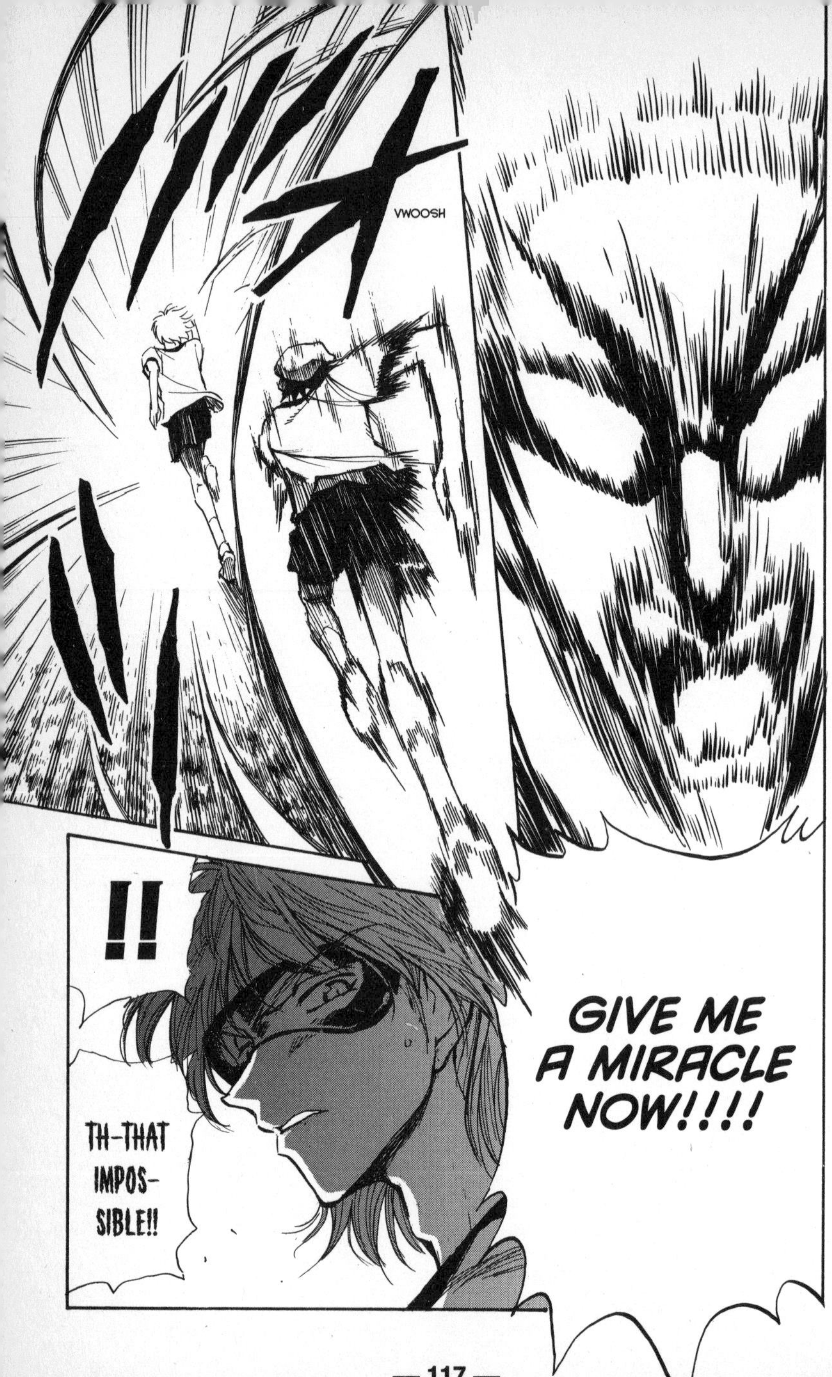
VWOOSH
GIVE ME A MIRACLE NOW!!!!
!!
TH-THAT IMPOS-SIBLE!!

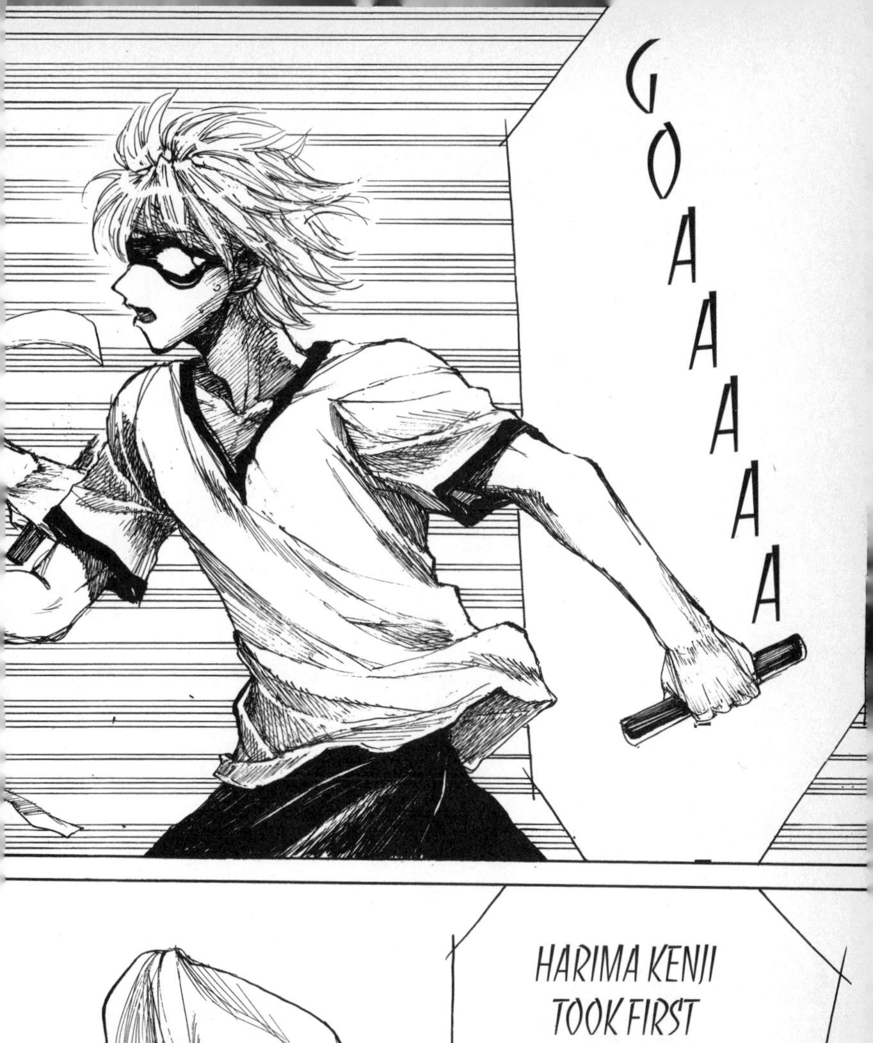
GOAAAAAA

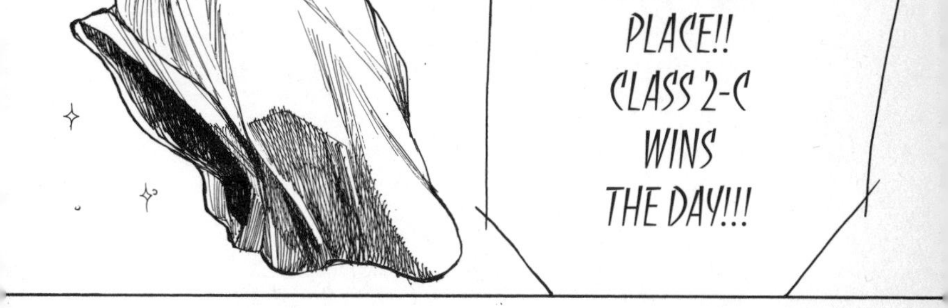
HARIMA KENJI TOOK FIRST PLACE!! CLASS 2-C WINS THE DAY!!!

KH... EVEN MY EYES ARE SWEATING... (HARIMA)

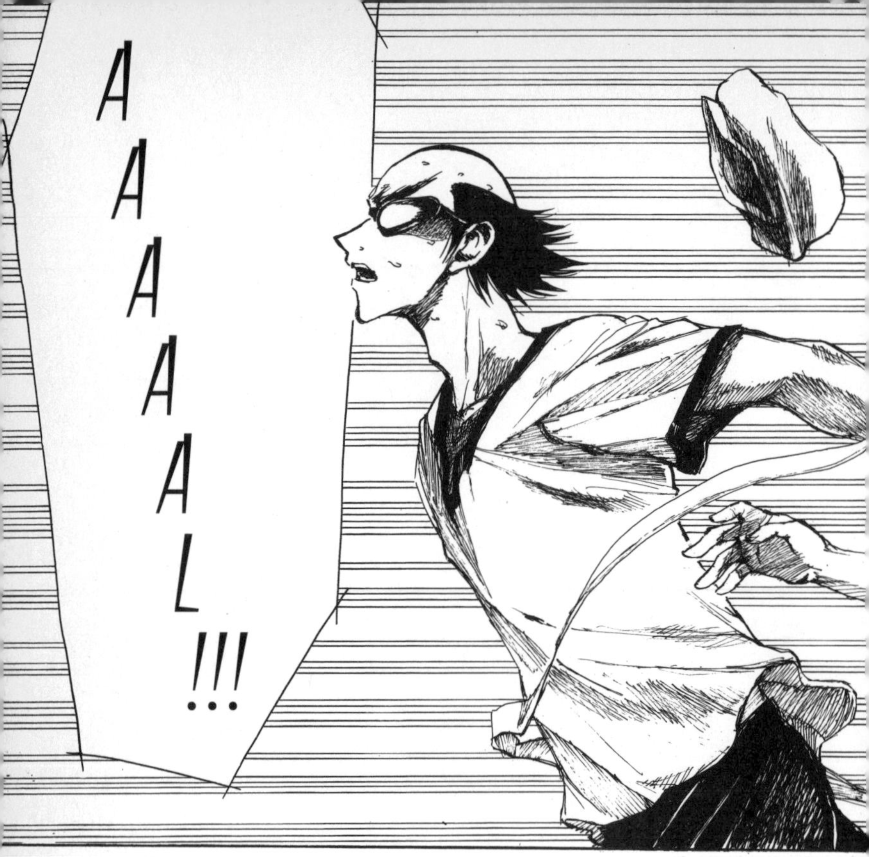
AAAAAL!!!

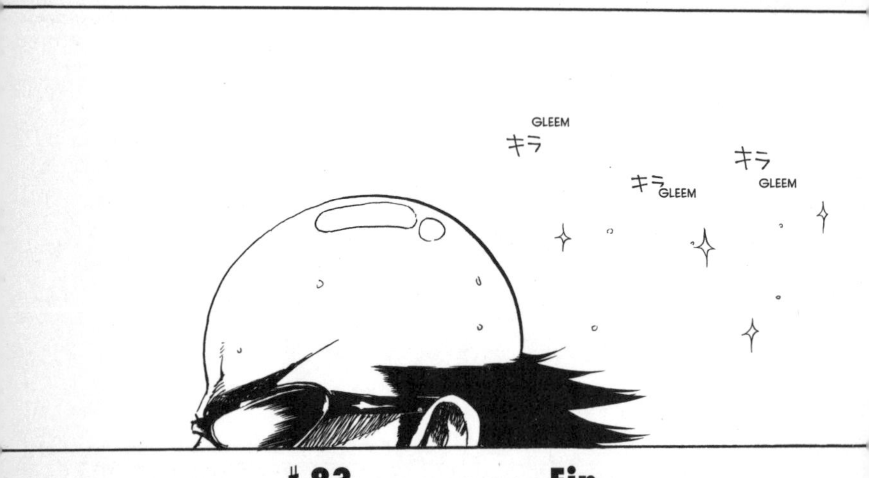
キラ GLEEM
キラ GLEEM
キラ GLEEM

 # 83 .... Fin

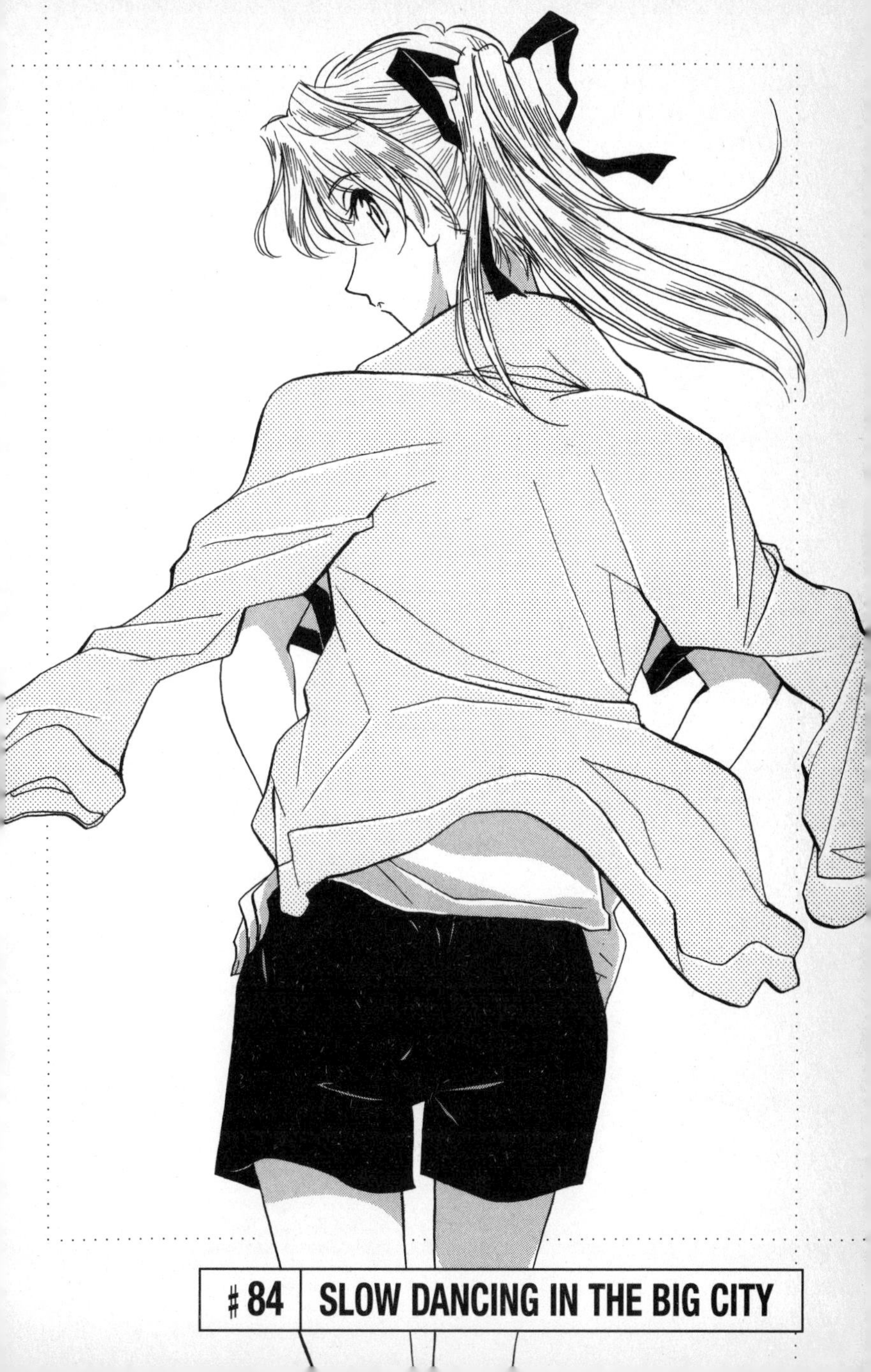

84 SLOW DANCING IN THE BIG CITY

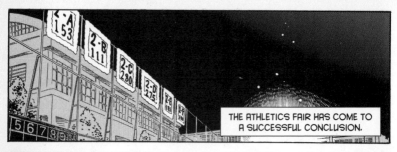

THE ATHLETICS FAIR HAS COME TO A SUCCESSFUL CONCLUSION.

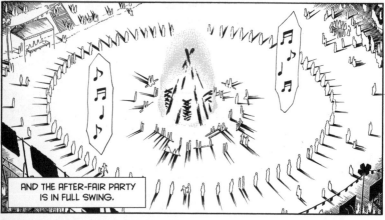

AND THE AFTER-FAIR PARTY IS IN FULL SWING.

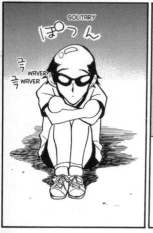

SOLITARY

WAVER
WAVER

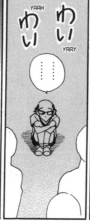

YAAH

YAAY

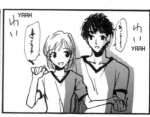

YAAH

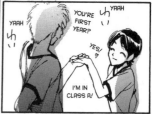

YOU'RE FIRST YEAR?

YAAH

YES!

I'M IN CLASS A!

And Somewhere Deep Down Is: Gentility.

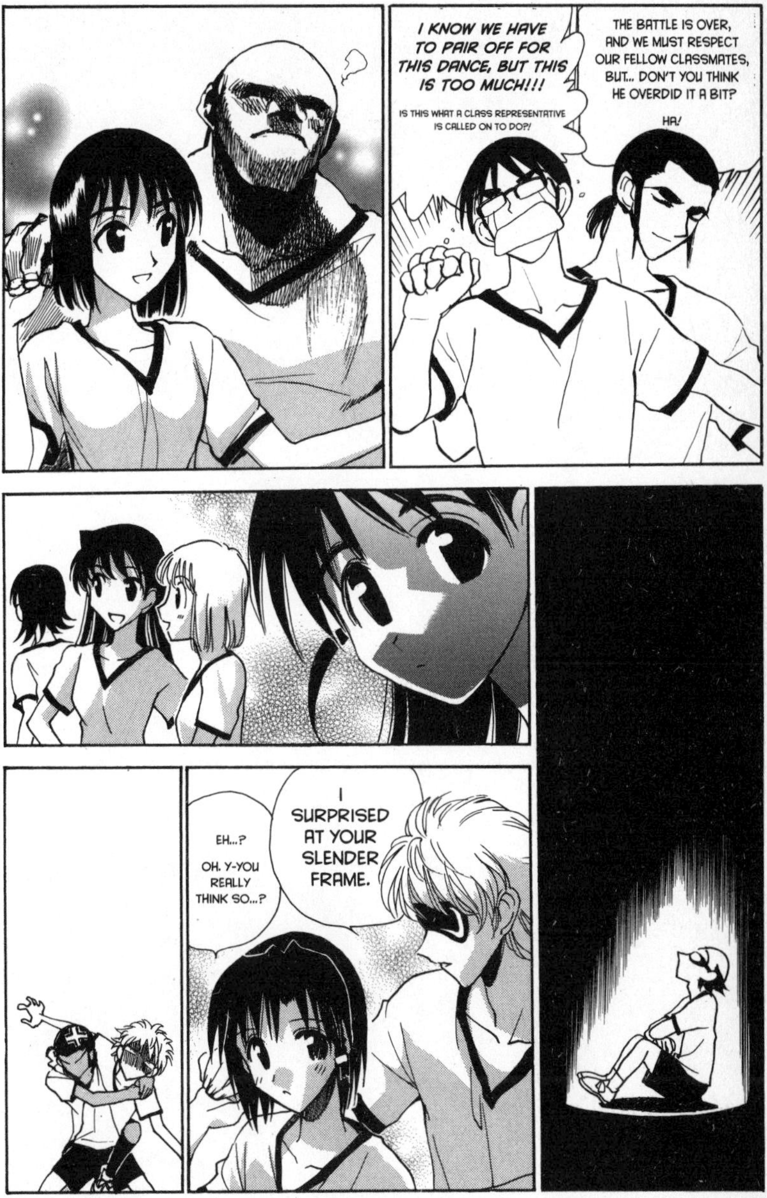
THE BATTLE IS OVER, AND WE MUST RESPECT OUR FELLOW CLASSMATES, BUT... DON'T YOU THINK HE OVERDID IT A BIT?
HA!
I KNOW WE HAVE TO PAIR OFF FOR THIS DANCE, BUT THIS IS TOO MUCH!!!
IS THIS WHAT A CLASS REPRESENTATIVE IS CALLED ON TO DO?!
I SURPRISED AT YOUR SLENDER FRAME.
EH...?
OH. Y-YOU REALLY THINK SO...?

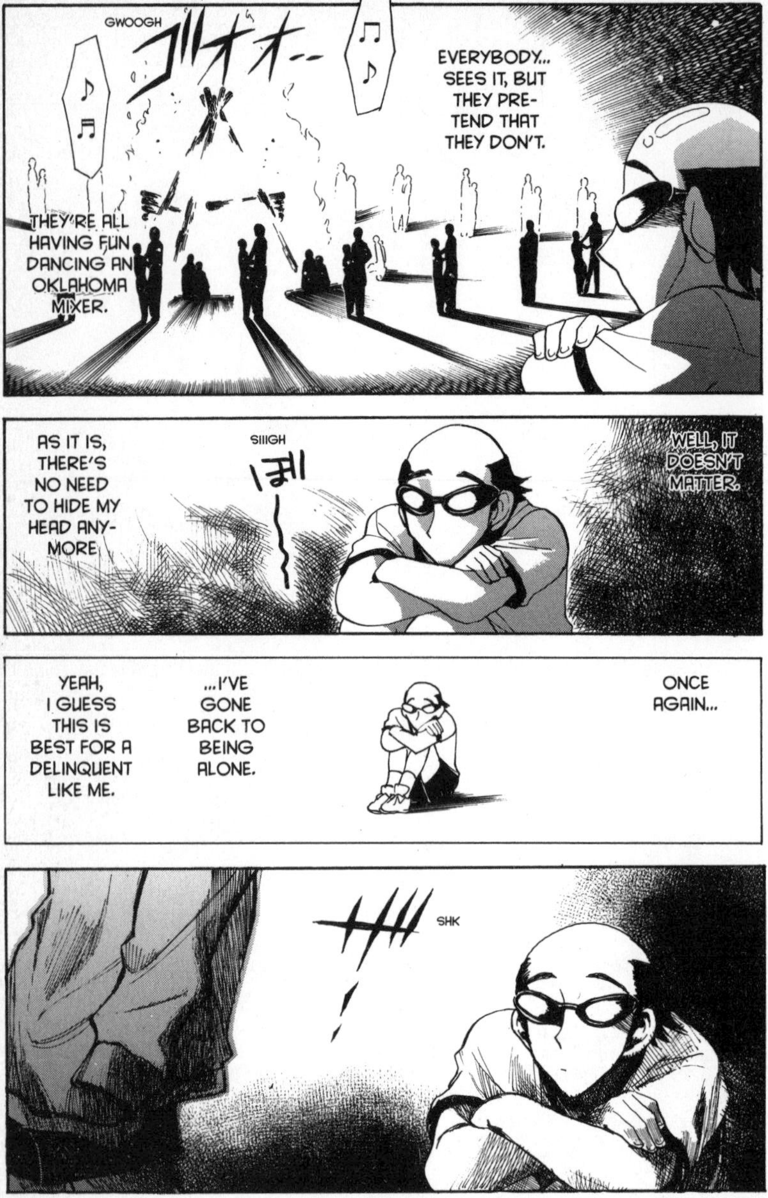
EVERYBODY... SEES IT, BUT THEY PRE-TEND THAT THEY DON'T.
GWOOGH
THEY'RE ALL HAVING FUN DANCING AN OKLAHOMA MIXER.
WELL, IT DOESN'T MATTER.
SIIIGH
AS IT IS, THERE'S NO NEED TO HIDE MY HEAD ANY-MORE
ONCE AGAIN...
...I'VE GONE BACK TO BEING ALONE.
YEAH, I GUESS THIS IS BEST FOR A DELINQUENT LIKE ME.
SHK

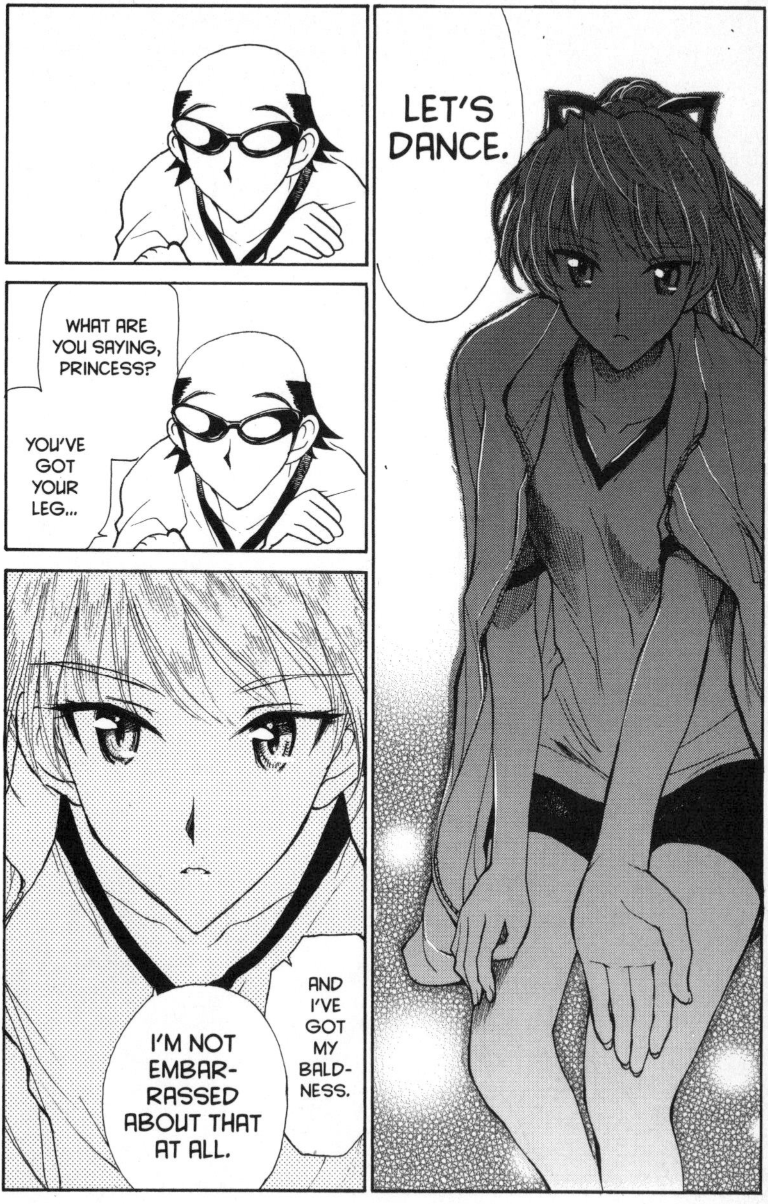
LET'S DANCE.
WHAT ARE YOU SAYING, PRINCESS?
YOU'VE GOT YOUR LEG...
AND I'VE GOT MY BALD-NESS.
I'M NOT EMBAR-RASSED ABOUT THAT AT ALL.

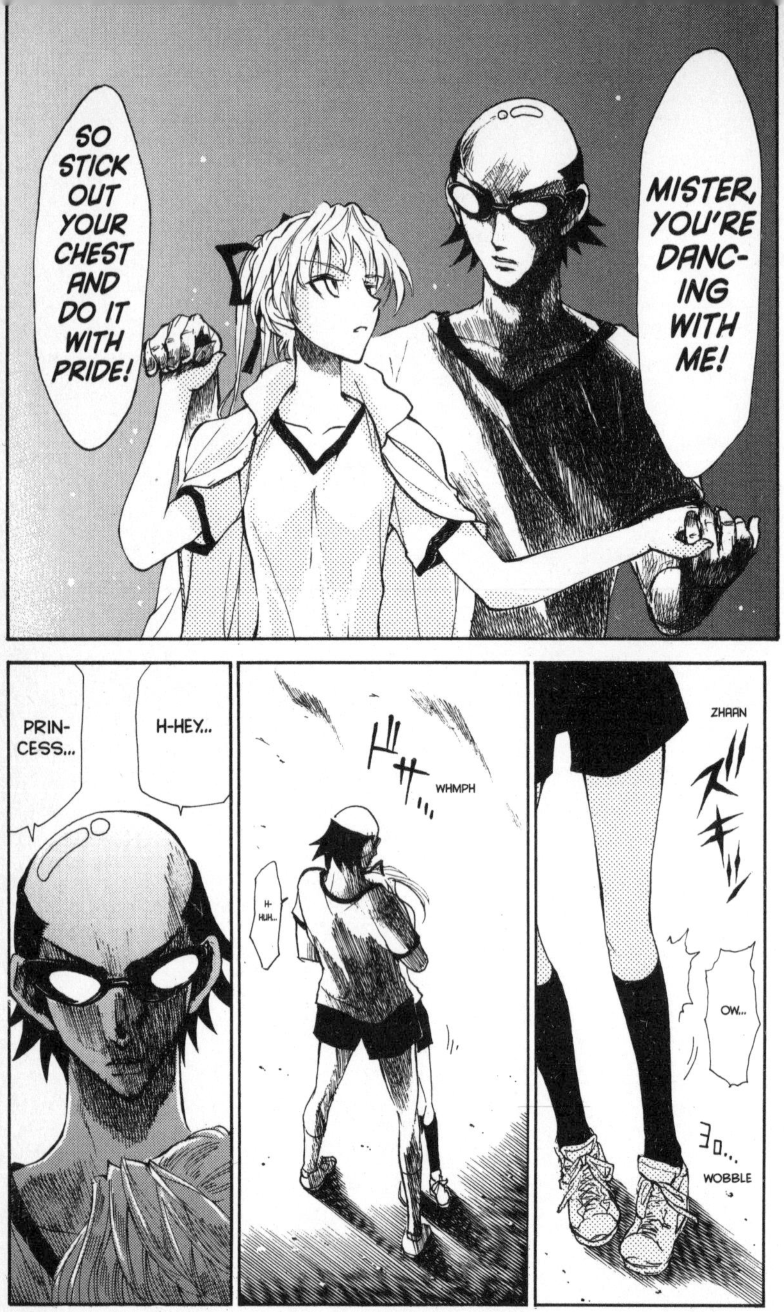
MISTER, YOU'RE DANC-ING WITH ME!
SO STICK OUT YOUR CHEST AND DO IT WITH PRIDE!
ZHAAN
ズキッ
OW...
ヨロ...
WOBBLE
ドサ...
WHMPH
H-HUH...
H-HEY...
PRIN-CESS...

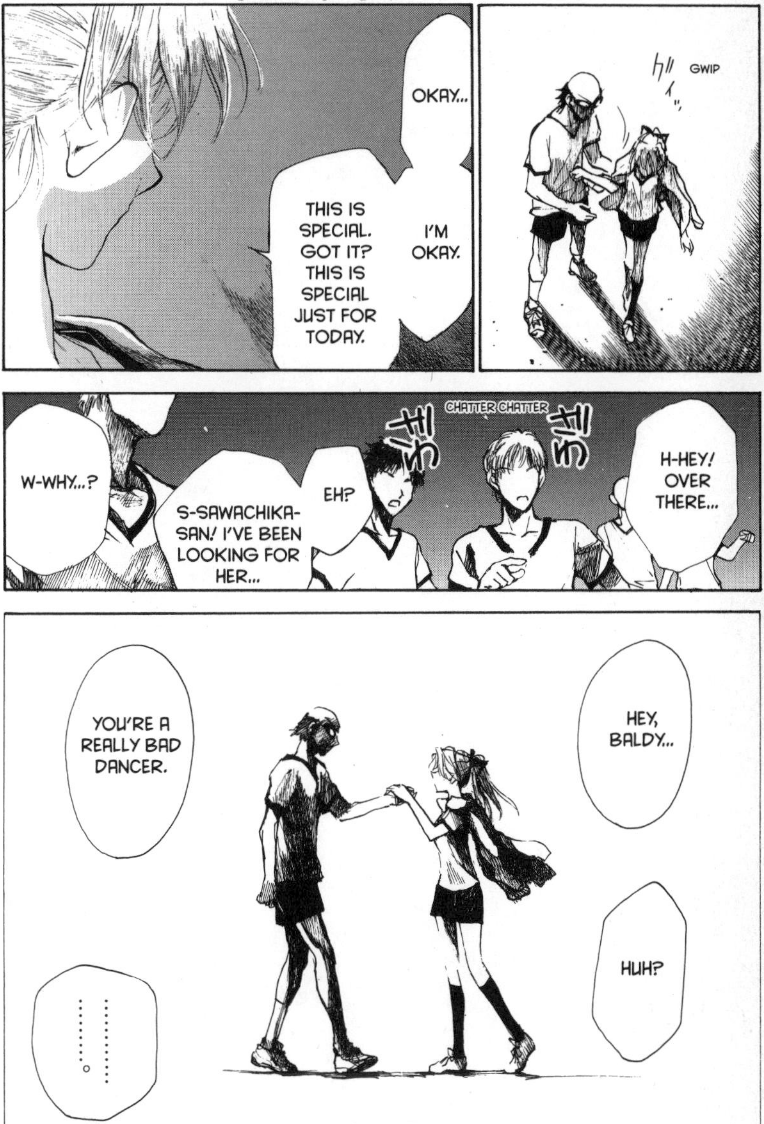
GWIP
OKAY...
I'M OKAY.
THIS IS SPECIAL. GOT IT? THIS IS SPECIAL JUST FOR TODAY.
H-HEY! OVER THERE...
CHATTER CHATTER
EH?
S-SAWACHIKA-SAN! I'VE BEEN LOOKING FOR HER...
W-WHY...?
HEY, BALDY...
HUH?
YOU'RE A REALLY BAD DANCER.
......。

The End. (That's a Lie.)

 # 84· · · · · · · · ·Fin

NAME

MIHARA KOZUE

JOB

MERMAID

POWER(UNIT)

GAL POWER

SKILL

PICKING UP GUYS

FINISH BLOW

DOUBLE HEADER DATE

WEAK POINT

KARAOKE

LEVEL

POPULARITY WITH GUYS
FASHION LEVEL
ASKING GUYS ON DATES
BODY BOARDING
FOOT SPEED

School Rumble OFFICIAL CHARACTER TRADING CARD

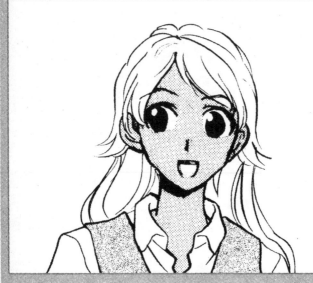

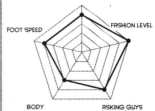

SAGANO MEGUMI

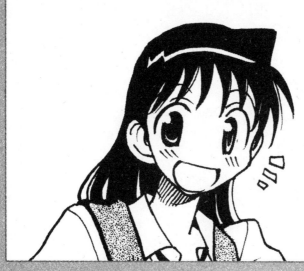

JOB

TOWN GIRL

POWER(UNIT)

MAKING BENTÔ POWER

SKILL

MYSTERY STORIES MANIAC

FINISH BLOW

ONI-ZUMO MAHJONG HAND

WEAK POINT

LIQUOR

LEVEL

TIMES SHE'S APPEARED

WISDOM

LOVE OF GOSSIP

SPIKY HAIR

BENTÔ SCENE LEVEL

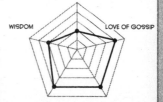

School **Rumble**

OFFICIAL
CHARACTER
TRADING
CARD

♭17 EYE OF THE CAT

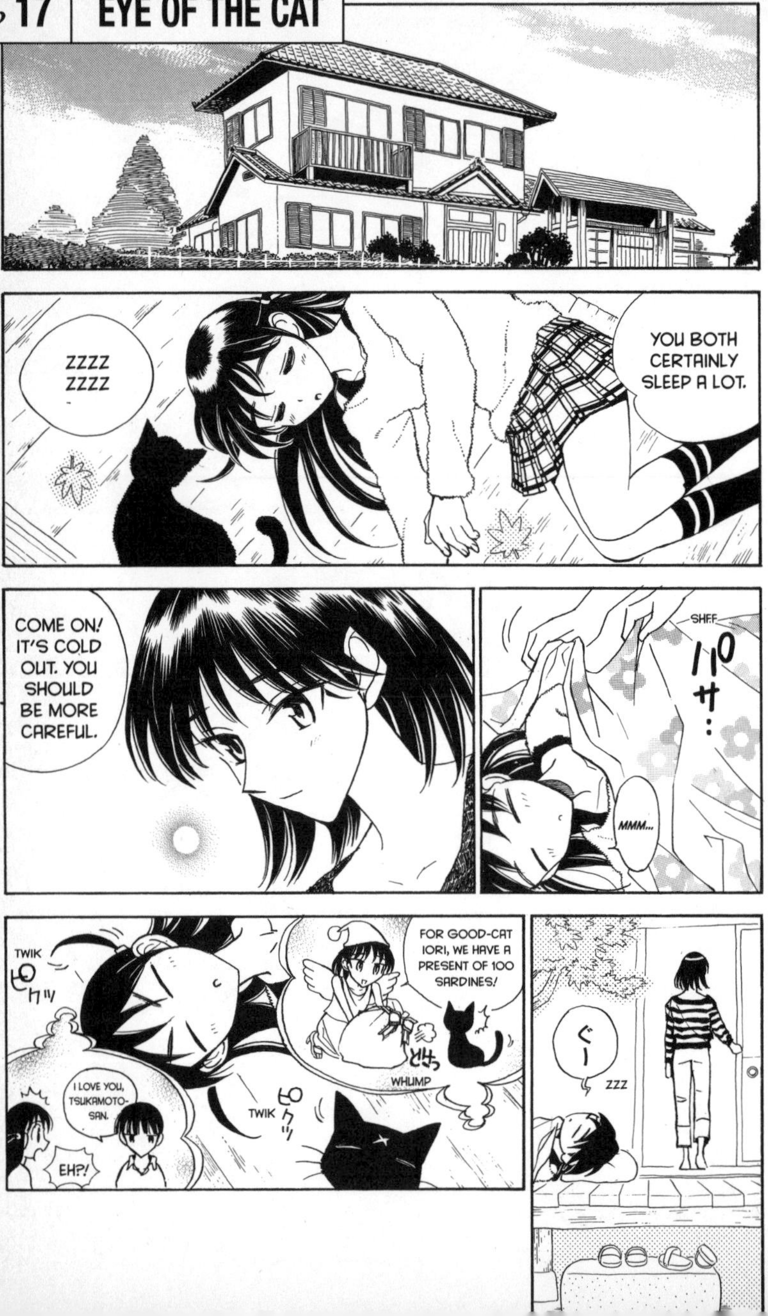

YOU BOTH CERTAINLY SLEEP A LOT.
ZZZZ ZZZZ
SHFF
ハサ…
MMM...
COME ON! IT'S COLD OUT. YOU SHOULD BE MORE CAREFUL.
ぐー
ZZZ
FOR GOOD-CAT IORI, WE HAVE A PRESENT OF 100 SARDINES!
TWIK
ピクッ
どさっ
WHUMP
TWIK
ピクッ
I LOVE YOU, TSUKAMOTO-SAN.
EH?!

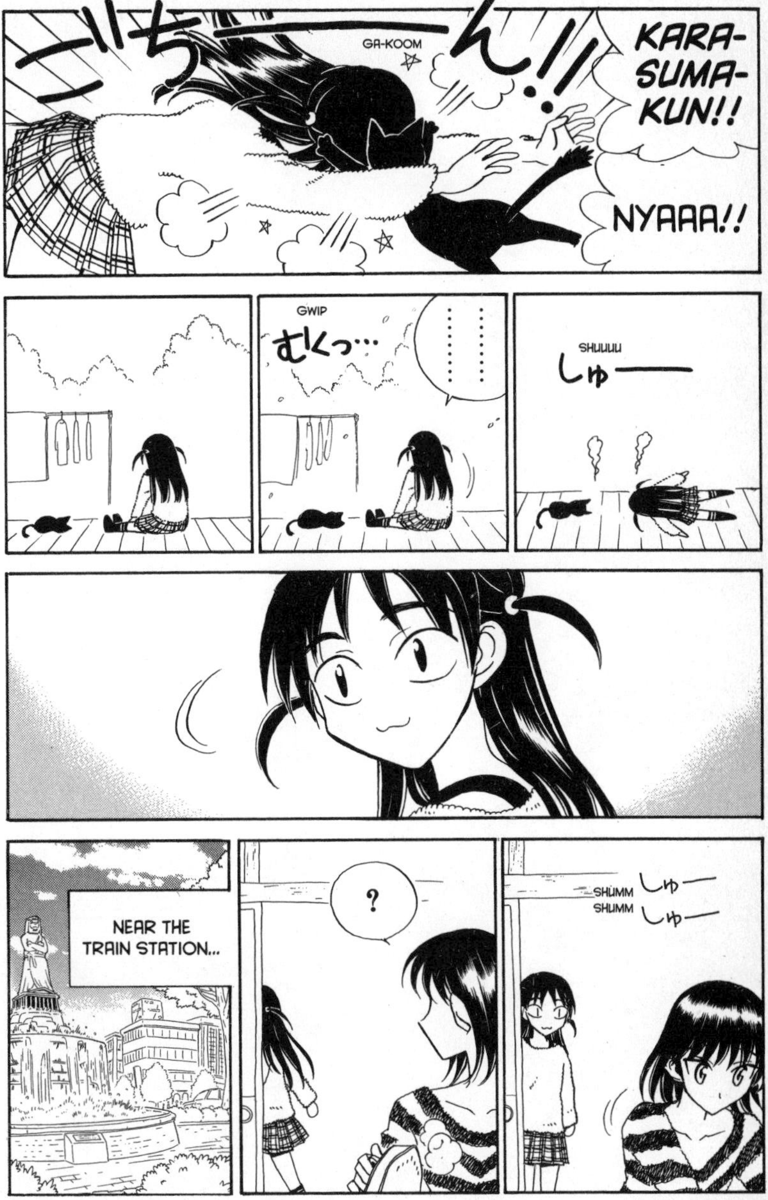
KARA-SUMA-KUN!!
NYAAA!!
ごちーーん!!
GA-KOOM
しゅーー
SHUUUU
......
むくっ…
GWIP
しゅー
SHUMM
しゅー
SHUMM
?
NEAR THE TRAIN STATION...

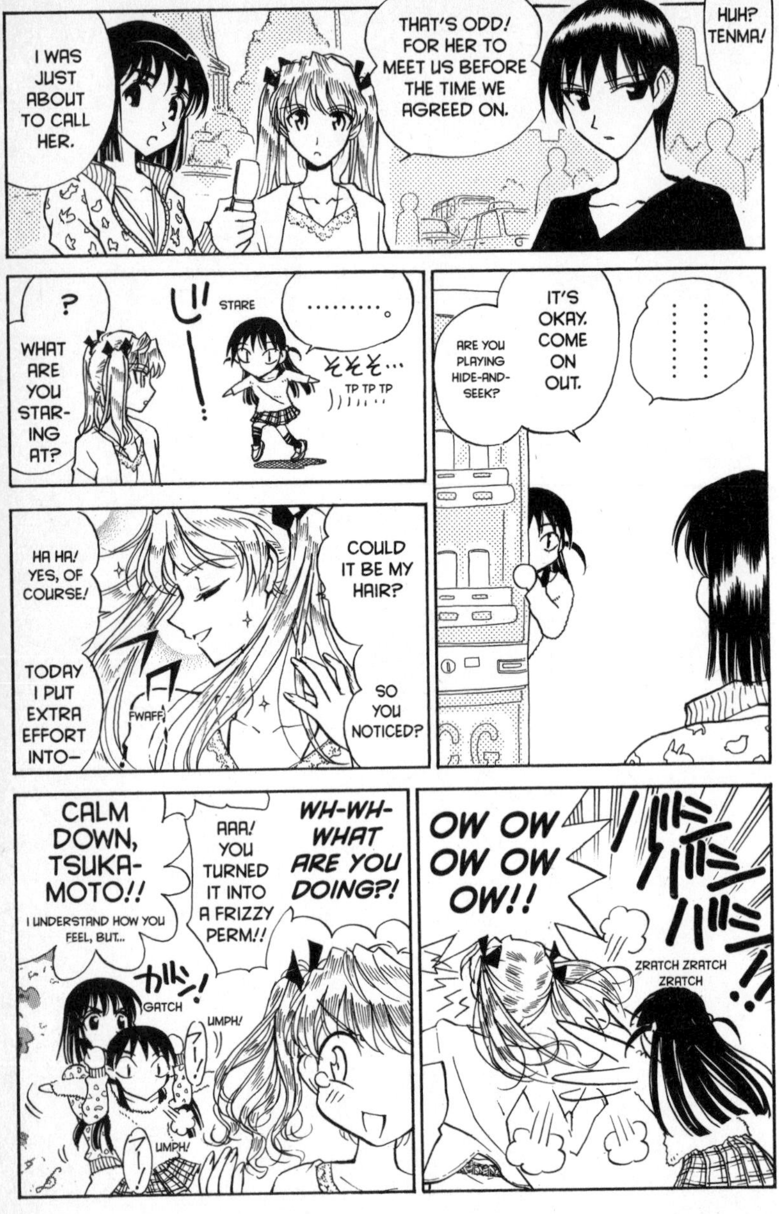
HUH? TENMA!
THAT'S ODD! FOR HER TO MEET US BEFORE THE TIME WE AGREED ON.
I WAS JUST ABOUT TO CALL HER.
......
IT'S OKAY. COME ON OUT.
ARE YOU PLAYING HIDE-AND-SEEK?
..........。
そそそ…
TP TP TP
STARE
?
WHAT ARE YOU STAR-ING AT?
COULD IT BE MY HAIR?
SO YOU NOTICED?
HA HA! YES, OF COURSE!
TODAY I PUT EXTRA EFFORT INTO—
FWAFF
ZRATCH ZRATCH ZRATCH
OW OW OW OW OW!!
WH-WH-WHAT ARE YOU DOING?!
AAA! YOU TURNED IT INTO A FRIZZY PERM!!
CALM DOWN, TSUKA-MOTO!!
I UNDERSTAND HOW YOU FEEL, BUT...
GATCH
UMPH!
UMPH!

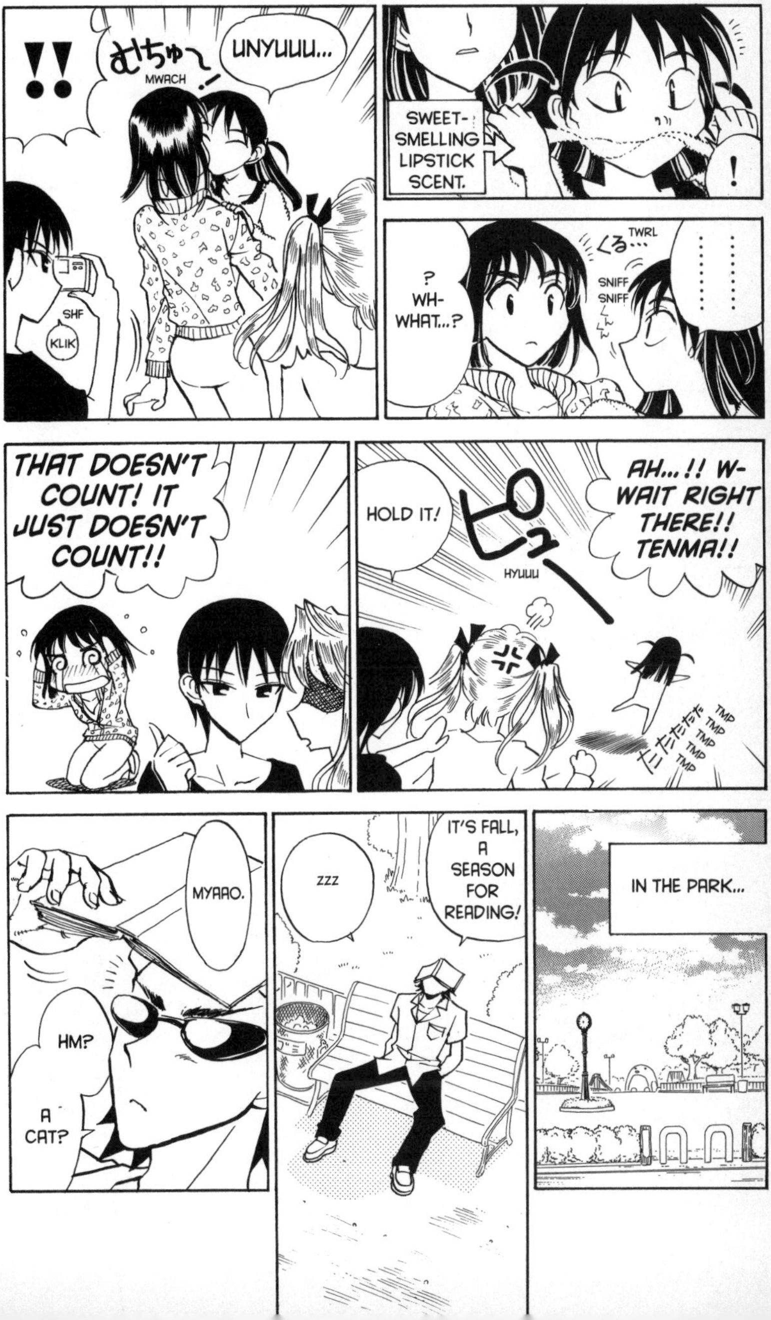
SWEET-SMELLING LIPSTICK SCENT.
!
......
くる…
TWRL
SNIFF SNIFF
? WH-WHAT...?
!!
むちゅ〜
MWACH
UNYUUU...
SHF
KLIK
AH...!! W-WAIT RIGHT THERE!! TENMA!!
HOLD IT!
HYUUU
TMP TMP TMP TMP TMP
THAT DOESN'T COUNT! IT JUST DOESN'T COUNT!!
IN THE PARK...
IT'S FALL, A SEASON FOR READING!
ZZZ
MYAAO.
HM?
A CAT?

He's Popular Among the Animals.

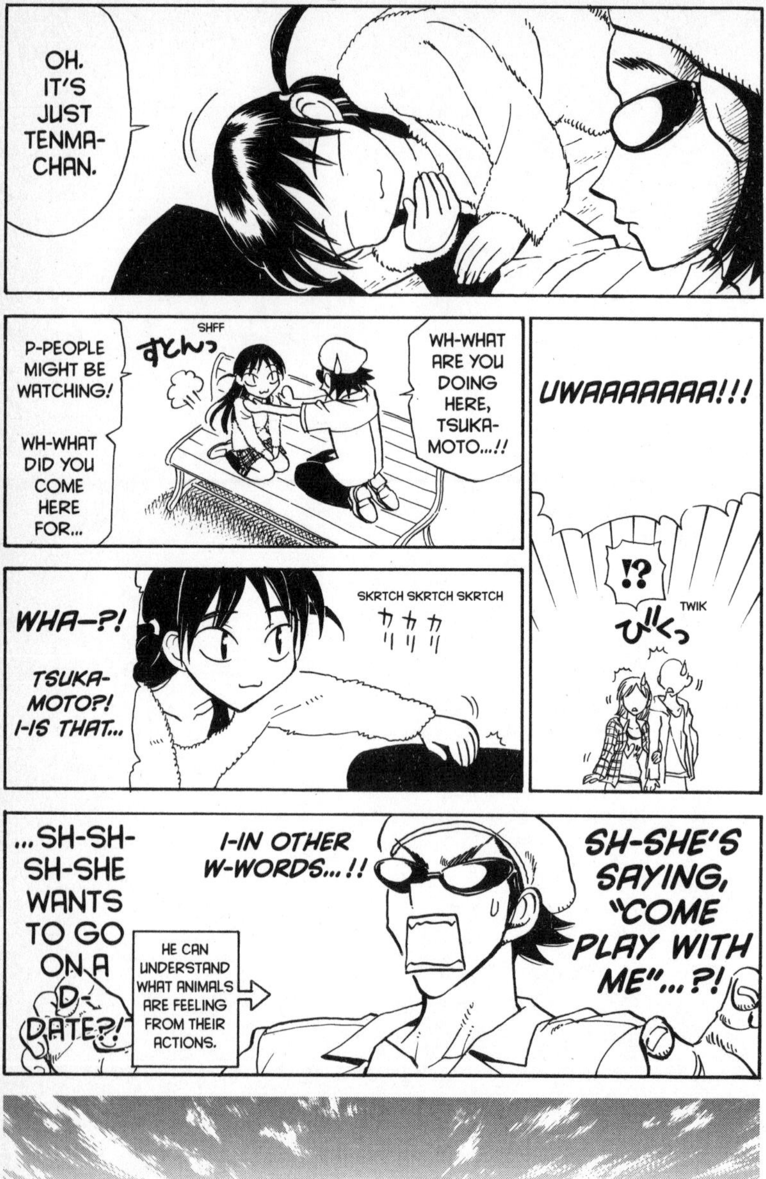

OH. IT'S JUST TENMA-CHAN.
UWAAAAAAAA!!!
!?
びくっ
TWIK
WH-WHAT ARE YOU DOING HERE, TSUKA-MOTO...!!
すとんっ
SHFF
P-PEOPLE MIGHT BE WATCHING!
WH-WHAT DID YOU COME HERE FOR...
SKRTCH SKRTCH SKRTCH
カカカ
WHA-?!
TSUKA-MOTO?! I-IS THAT...
SH-SHE'S SAYING, "COME PLAY WITH ME"...?!
I-IN OTHER W-WORDS...!!
HE CAN UNDERSTAND WHAT ANIMALS ARE FEELING FROM THEIR ACTIONS.
...SH-SH-SH-SHE WANTS TO GO ON A D-DATE?!

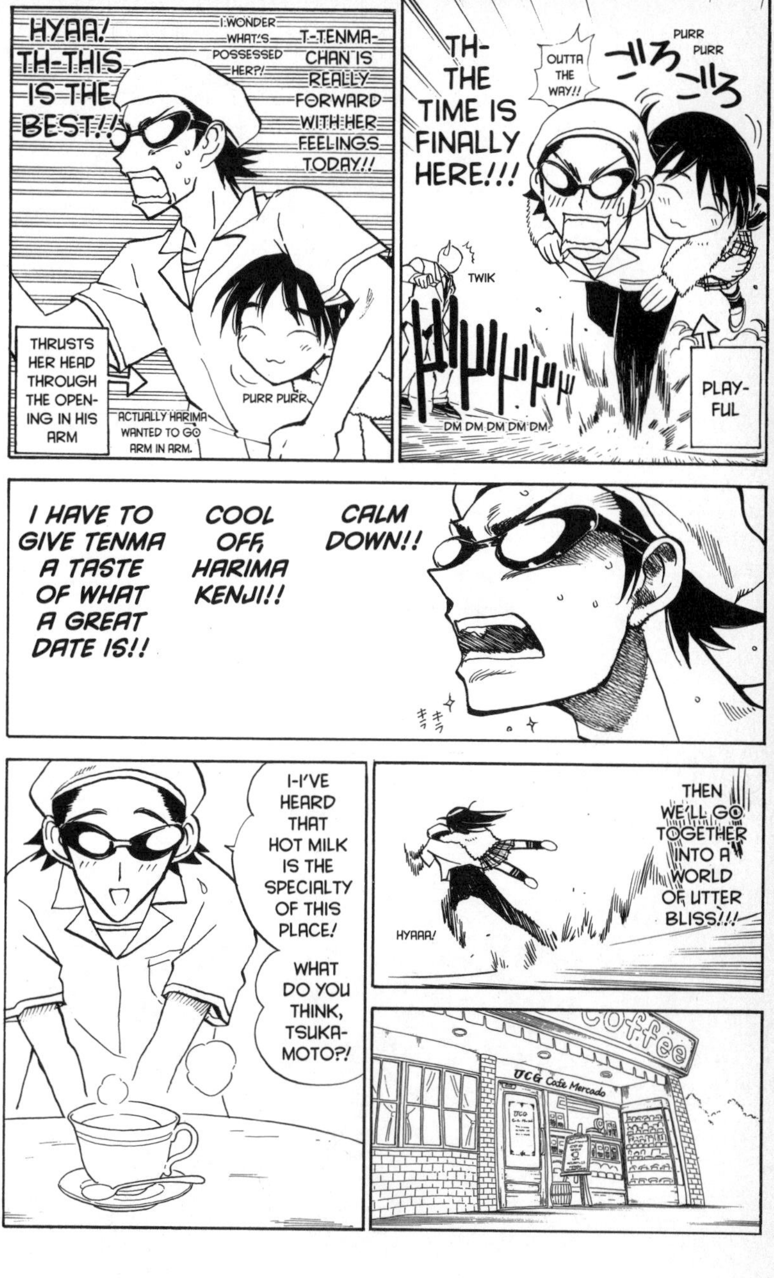
TH-THE TIME IS FINALLY HERE!!!
OUTTA THE WAY!!
ごろごろ
PURR PURR
TWIK
PLAY-FUL
DM DM DM DM DM
T-TENMA-CHAN IS REALLY FORWARD WITH HER FEELINGS TODAY!!
I WONDER WHAT'S POSSESSED HER?!
HYAA! TH-THIS IS THE BEST!!
THRUSTS HER HEAD THROUGH THE OPEN-ING IN HIS ARM
PURR PURR
ACTUALLY HARIMA WANTED TO GO ARM IN ARM.
CALM DOWN!!
COOL OFF, HARIMA KENJI!!
I HAVE TO GIVE TENMA A TASTE OF WHAT A GREAT DATE IS!!
THEN WE'LL GO TOGETHER INTO A WORLD OF UTTER BLISS!!!
HYAAA!
Coffee
UCG Cafe Mercado
I-I'VE HEARD THAT HOT MILK IS THE SPECIALTY OF THIS PLACE!
WHAT DO YOU THINK, TSUKAMOTO?!

Harima: Carried the Entire Conversation Himself.

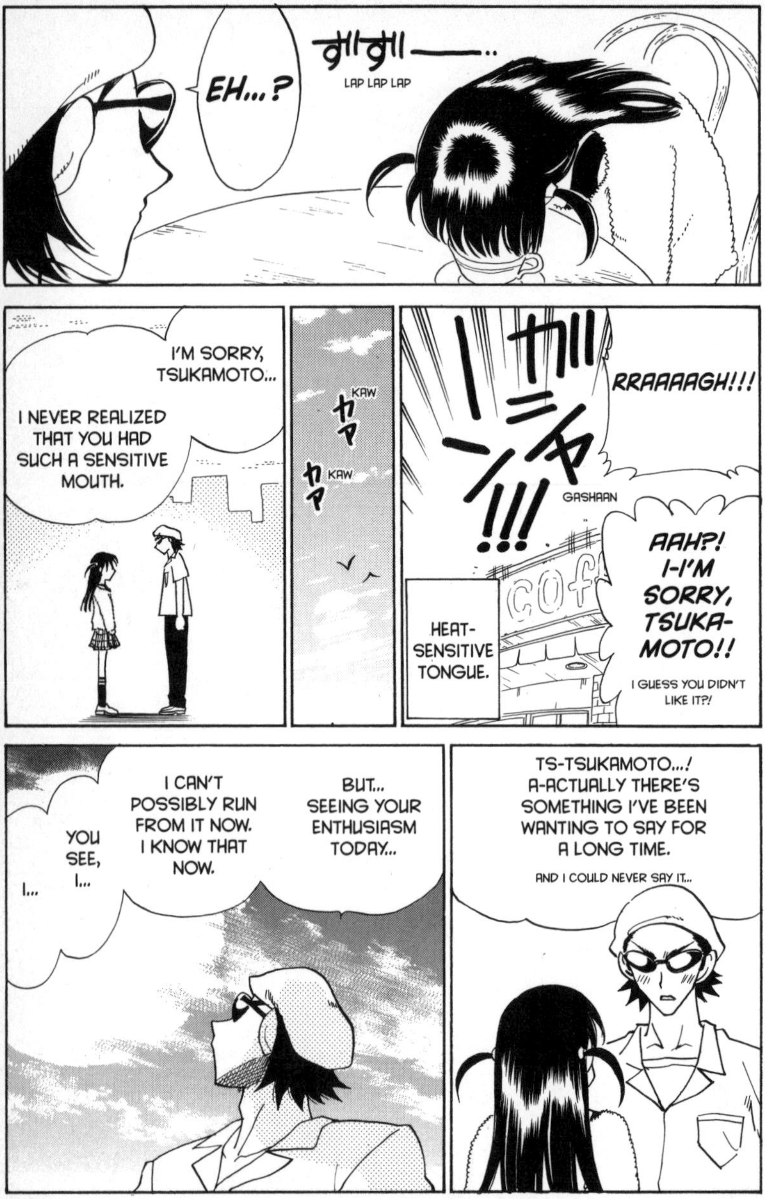

すりすり——..
LAP LAP LAP
EH...?
RRAAAAGH!!!
ガシャーン!!!
GASHAAN
AAH?! I-I'M SORRY, TSUKA-MOTO!!
I GUESS YOU DIDN'T LIKE IT?!
HEAT-SENSITIVE TONGUE.
cof
カァ KAW
カァ KAW
I'M SORRY, TSUKAMOTO...
I NEVER REALIZED THAT YOU HAD SUCH A SENSITIVE MOUTH.
TS-TSUKAMOTO...! A-ACTUALLY THERE'S SOMETHING I'VE BEEN WANTING TO SAY FOR A LONG TIME.
AND I COULD NEVER SAY IT...
BUT... SEEING YOUR ENTHUSIASM TODAY...
I CAN'T POSSIBLY RUN FROM IT NOW. I KNOW THAT NOW.
YOU SEE, I...
I...

WHOOSH
DO YOU MIND IF I ASK YOU OUT AGAIN?!
NYAA!
......
WH-WHAT DID THAT MEAN?!
"NYAA"...?
S-SOME KIND OF GREETING?
I-IS THAT IT? IT MUST BE! THAT MUST BE THE MOST POPULAR WAY OF SAYING "HI" AND "BYE" BETWEEN TENMA-CHAN AND HER FRIENDS!!
TH-THAT'S IT! SHE WAS SO EMBARRASSED, SHE EVADED THE QUESTION! HA! THAT'S SO CUTE, TENMA!
WANT TO GO HOME?
NYAA.
AH! ONEE-SAN, WELCOME HOME.
YOU'RE QUIET TODAY, HUH?
......
SLEPT THROUGH THE WHOLE THING.
ZZZ ZZZ
THE NEXT DAY...
NYAA!
HUH?
ZWIP ZWIP

♭17··········Fin

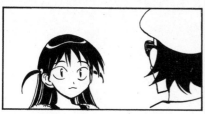

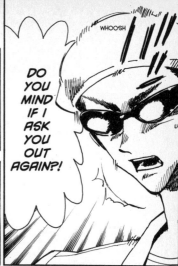

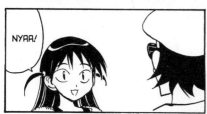

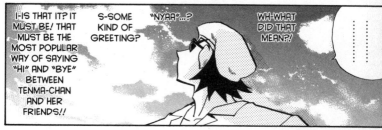

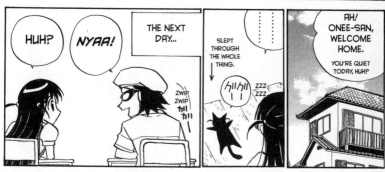

NAME

KIDO MADOKA

JOB

SPRINTER

POWER(UNIT)

12.6 SEC/100 METERS

SKILL

ACTUALLY THAT WASN'T HER FIRST KISS.

FINISH BLOW

THE SUDDEN KISS

WEAK POINT

VIDEO GAMES

LEVEL

SPEED
FORWARD ATTITUDE
INTEREST IN GUYS
SHIGEO LOVE
WISDOM

School Rumble OFFICIAL CHARACTER TRADING CARD

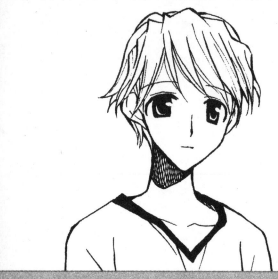

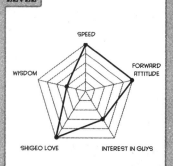

NAME

UMEZU SHIGEO

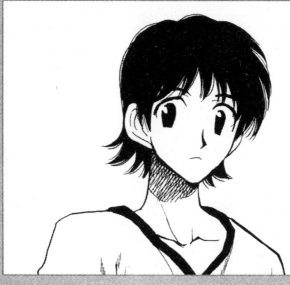

JOB

RUNNER

POWER(UNIT)

DESIRE TO KISS POWER

SKILL

CIRCULATING THROUGH DATE SPOTS

FINISH BLOW

NAPOLEON ATTACK

WEAK POINT

PIG

LEVEL

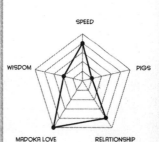

SPEED
PIGS
RELATIONSHIP ADVANCEMENT LEVEL
MADOKA LOVE
WISDOM

School Rumble OFFICIAL CHARACTER TRADING CARD

♭ 18 JUMP INTO HELL

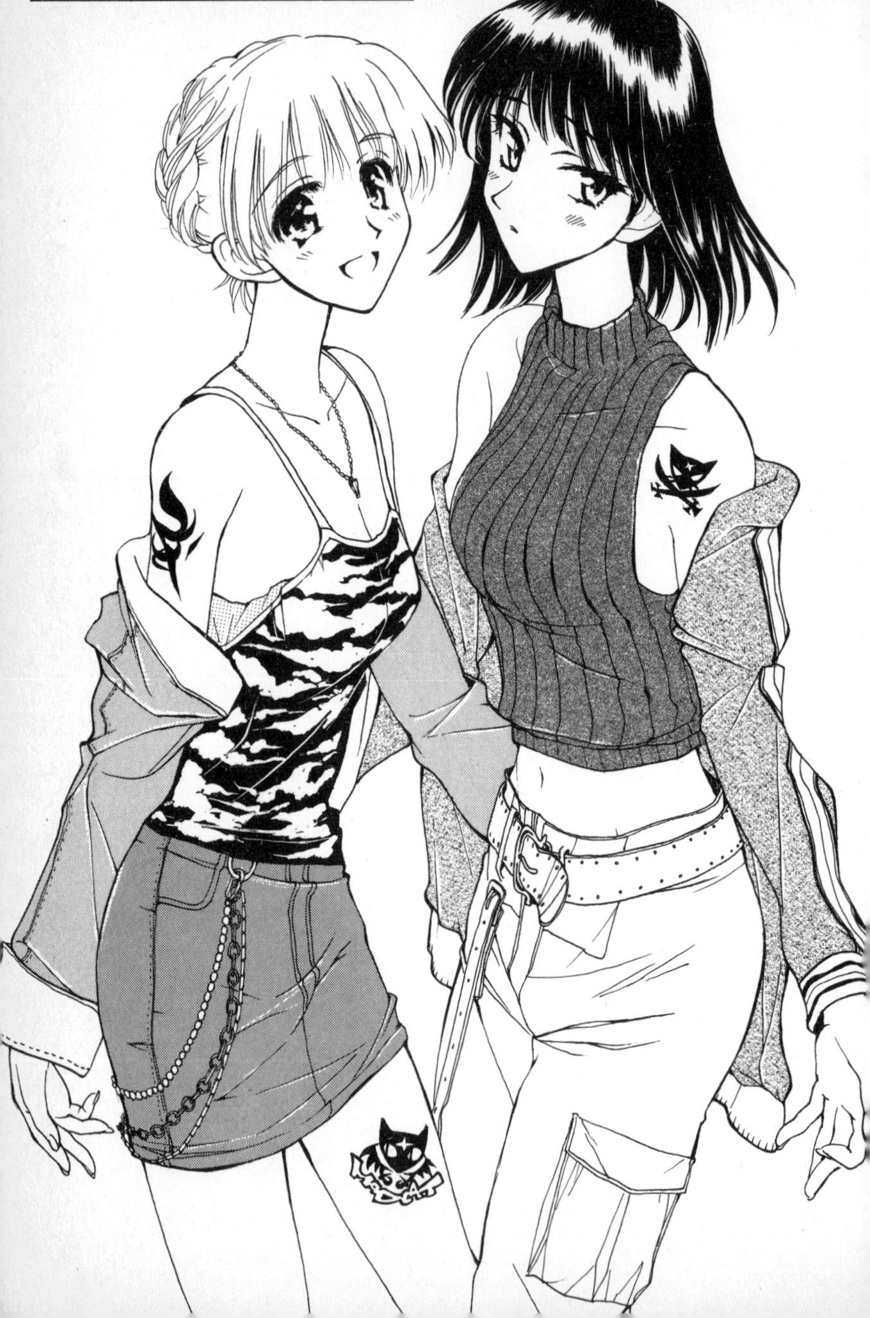

Now It Can Be Revealed: Everything About This Man.

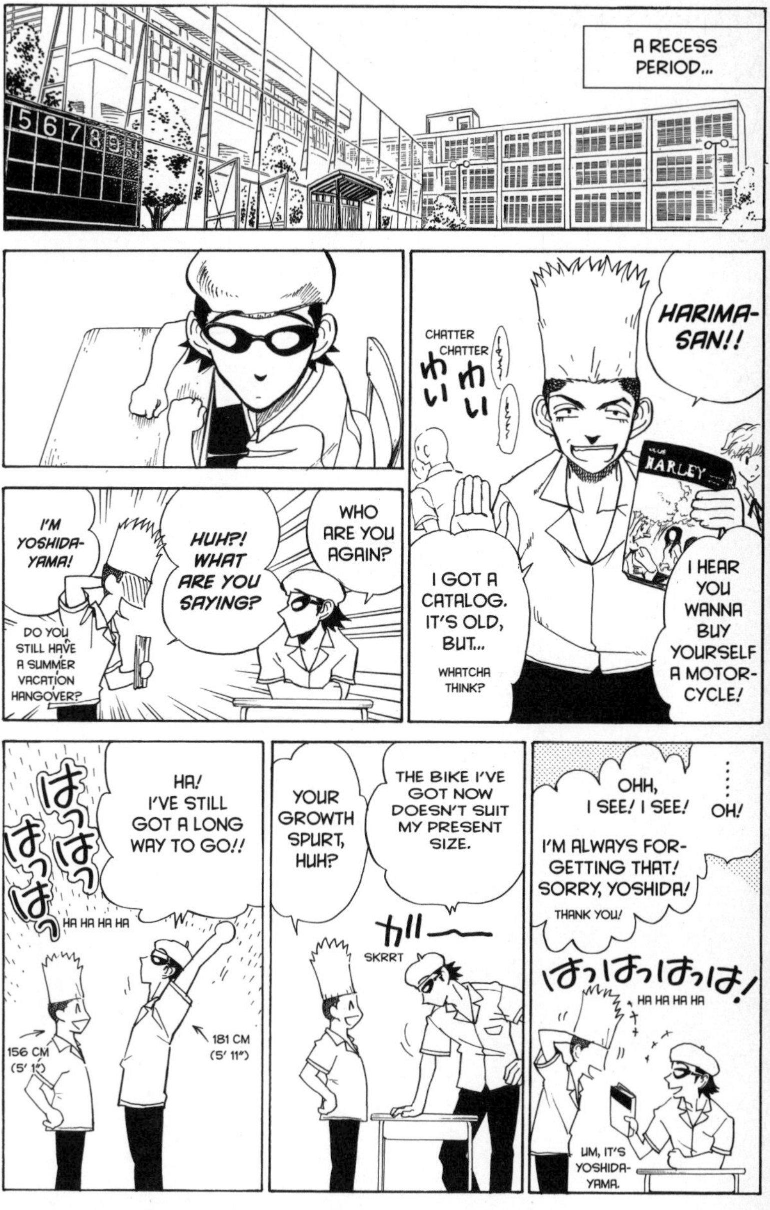
A RECESS PERIOD...
HARIMA-SAN!!
わいわい
CHATTER CHATTER
I HEAR YOU WANNA BUY YOURSELF A MOTORCYCLE!
HARLEY
I GOT A CATALOG. IT'S OLD, BUT...
WHATCHA THINK?
WHO ARE YOU AGAIN?
HUH?! WHAT ARE YOU SAYING?
I'M YOSHIDA-YAMA!
DO YOU STILL HAVE A SUMMER VACATION HANGOVER?
.....OH!
OHH, I SEE! I SEE!
I'M ALWAYS FOR-GETTING THAT! SORRY, YOSHIDA!
THANK YOU!
はっはっはっは!
HA HA HA HA
UM, IT'S YOSHIDA-YAMA.
THE BIKE I'VE GOT NOW DOESN'T SUIT MY PRESENT SIZE.
YOUR GROWTH SPURT, HUH?
ガー
SKRRT
HA! I'VE STILL GOT A LONG WAY TO GO!!
はっはっはっはっ
HA HA HA HA
181 CM (5' 11")
156 CM (5' 1")

Yoshidayama: His Head Length Beats Out Harima's.

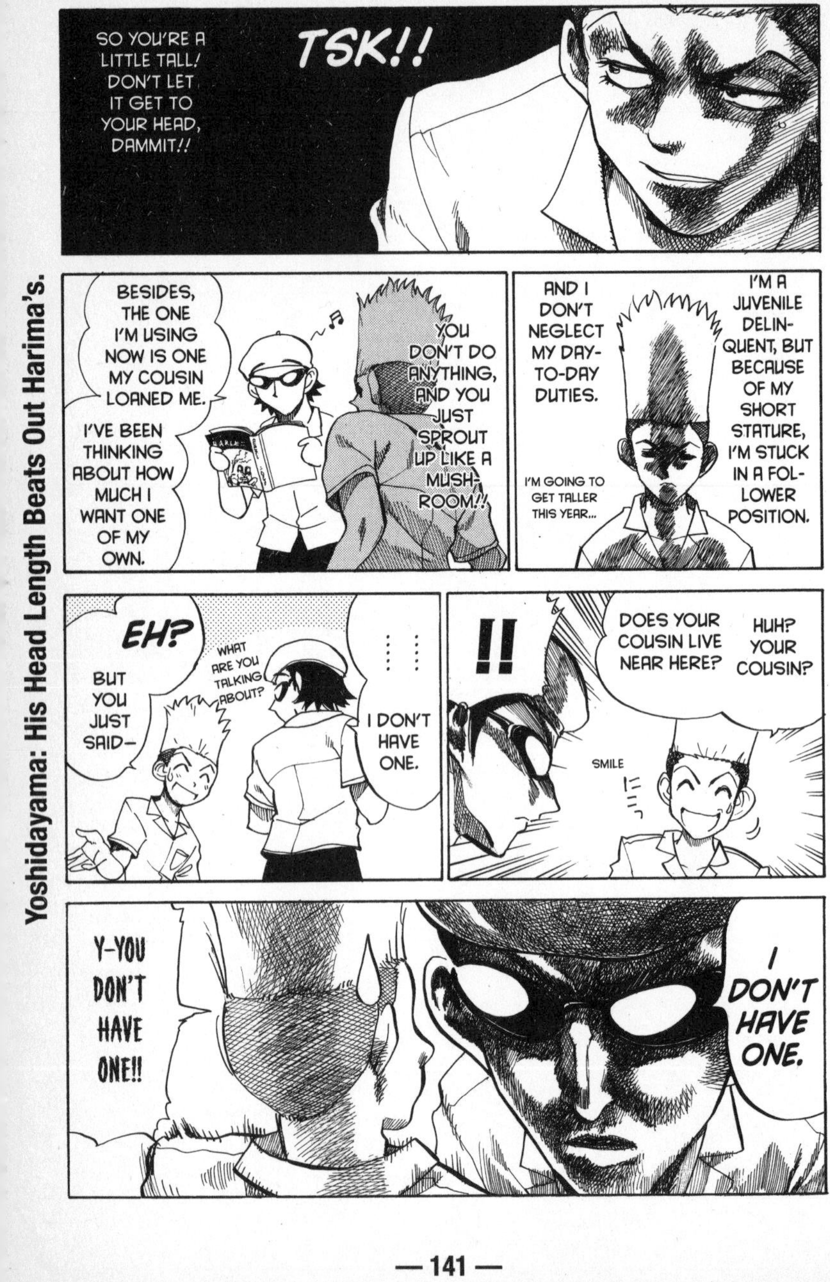

TSK!!
SO YOU'RE A LITTLE TALL! DON'T LET IT GET TO YOUR HEAD, DAMMIT!!
I'M A JUVENILE DELIN-QUENT, BUT BECAUSE OF MY SHORT STATURE, I'M STUCK IN A FOL-LOWER POSITION.
AND I DON'T NEGLECT MY DAY-TO-DAY DUTIES.
I'M GOING TO GET TALLER THIS YEAR...
YOU DON'T DO ANYTHING, AND YOU JUST SPROUT UP LIKE A MUSH-ROOM!!
BESIDES, THE ONE I'M USING NOW IS ONE MY COUSIN LOANED ME.
I'VE BEEN THINKING ABOUT HOW MUCH I WANT ONE OF MY OWN.
HUH? YOUR COUSIN?
DOES YOUR COUSIN LIVE NEAR HERE?
!!
SMILE
......
I DON'T HAVE ONE.
WHAT ARE YOU TALKING ABOUT?
EH?
BUT YOU JUST SAID—
I DON'T HAVE ONE.
Y-YOU DON'T HAVE ONE!!

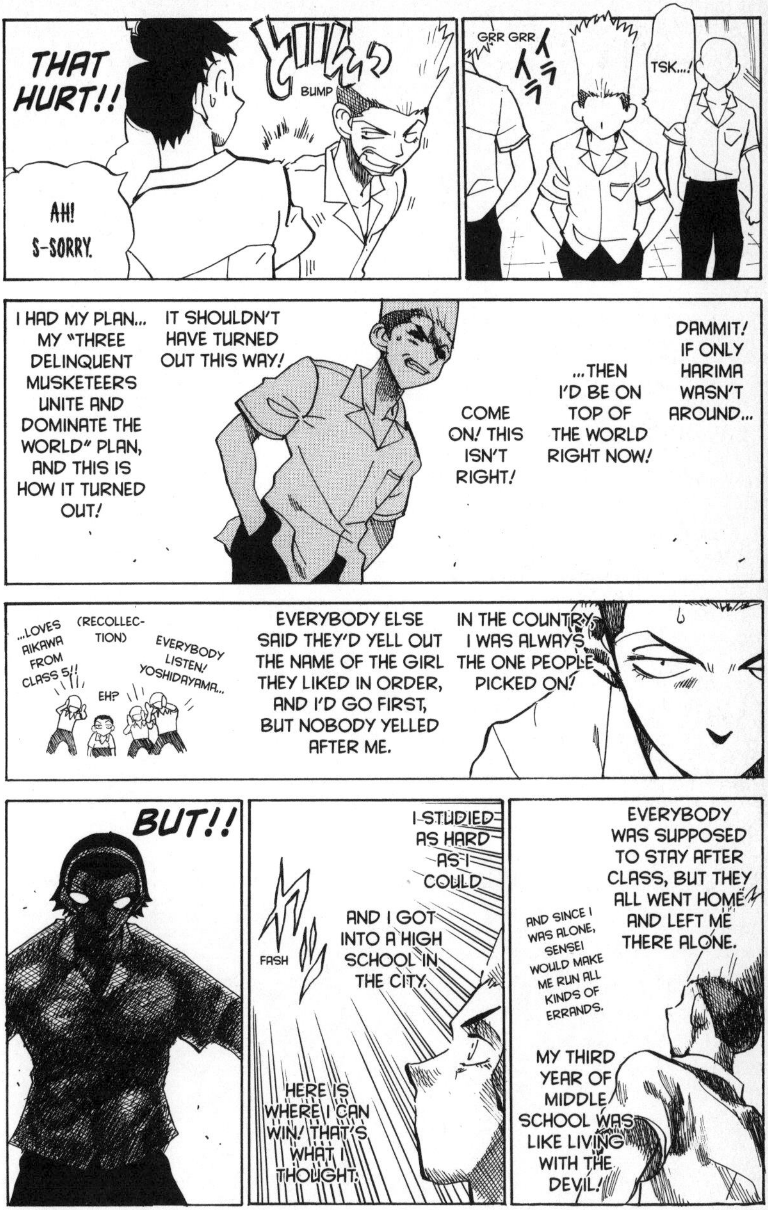
GRR GRR
TSK...!
THAT HURT!!
BUMP
AH! S-SORRY.
DAMMIT! IF ONLY HARIMA WASN'T AROUND...
...THEN I'D BE ON TOP OF THE WORLD RIGHT NOW!
COME ON! THIS ISN'T RIGHT!
IT SHOULDN'T HAVE TURNED OUT THIS WAY!
I HAD MY PLAN... MY "THREE DELINQUENT MUSKETEERS UNITE AND DOMINATE THE WORLD" PLAN, AND THIS IS HOW IT TURNED OUT!
IN THE COUNTRY, I WAS ALWAYS THE ONE PEOPLE PICKED ON!
EVERYBODY ELSE SAID THEY'D YELL OUT THE NAME OF THE GIRL THEY LIKED IN ORDER, AND I'D GO FIRST, BUT NOBODY YELLED AFTER ME.
(RECOLLECTION)
EVERYBODY LISTEN! YOSHIDAYAMA...
EH?
...LOVES AIKAWA FROM CLASS 5!!
EVERYBODY WAS SUPPOSED TO STAY AFTER CLASS, BUT THEY ALL WENT HOME AND LEFT ME THERE ALONE.
AND SINCE I WAS ALONE, SENSEI WOULD MAKE ME RUN ALL KINDS OF ERRANDS.
MY THIRD YEAR OF MIDDLE SCHOOL WAS LIKE LIVING WITH THE DEVIL!
I STUDIED AS HARD AS I COULD
AND I GOT INTO A HIGH SCHOOL IN THE CITY.
FASH
HERE IS WHERE I CAN WIN! THAT'S WHAT I THOUGHT.
BUT!!

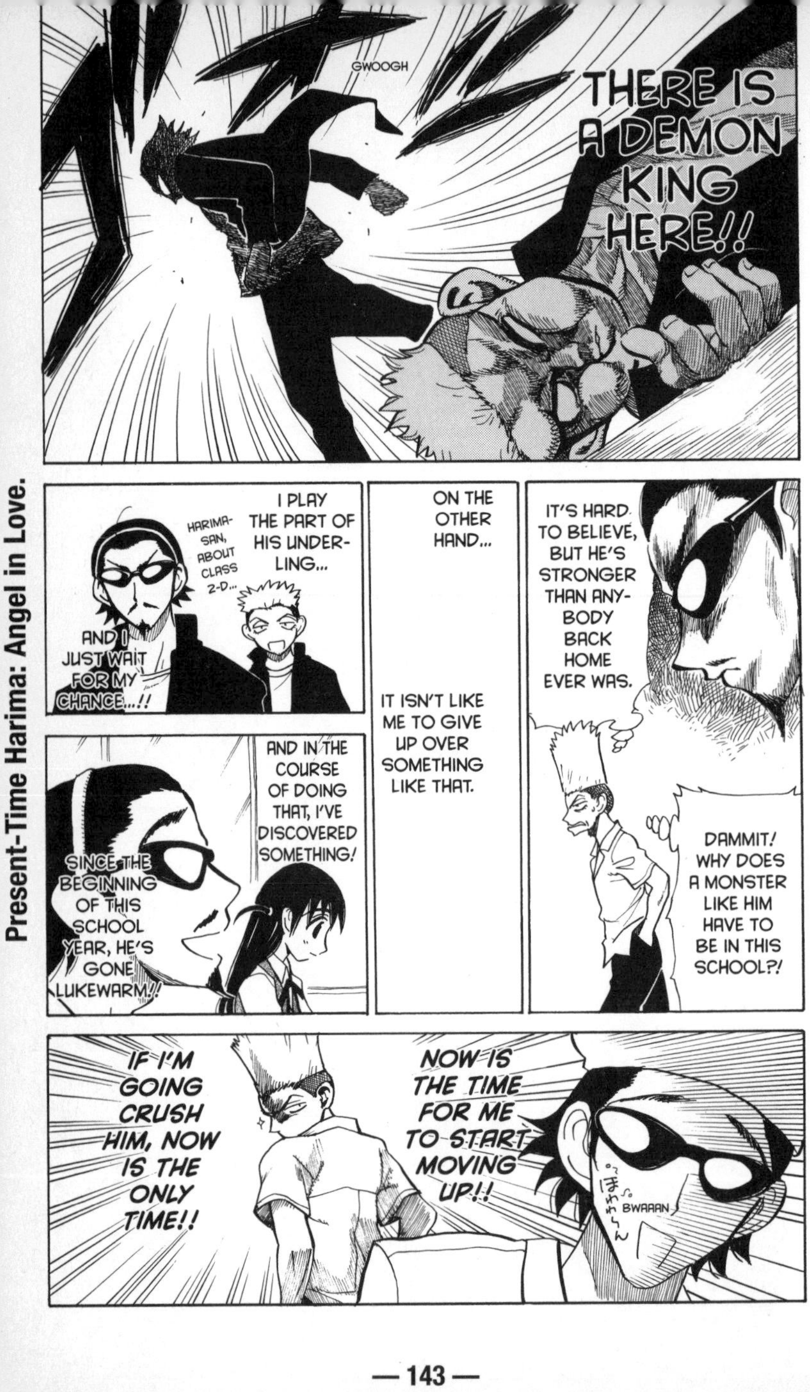
THERE IS A DEMON KING HERE!!
GWOOGH
IT'S HARD TO BELIEVE, BUT HE'S STRONGER THAN ANYBODY BACK HOME EVER WAS.
DAMMIT! WHY DOES A MONSTER LIKE HIM HAVE TO BE IN THIS SCHOOL?!
ON THE OTHER HAND...
IT ISN'T LIKE ME TO GIVE UP OVER SOMETHING LIKE THAT.
I PLAY THE PART OF HIS UNDERLING...
HARIMA-SAN, ABOUT CLASS 2-D...
AND I JUST WAIT FOR MY CHANCE...!!
AND IN THE COURSE OF DOING THAT, I'VE DISCOVERED SOMETHING!
SINCE THE BEGINNING OF THIS SCHOOL YEAR, HE'S GONE LUKEWARM!!
NOW IS THE TIME FOR ME TO START MOVING UP!!
ほわ〜ん
BWAAAN
IF I'M GOING CRUSH HIM, NOW IS THE ONLY TIME!!

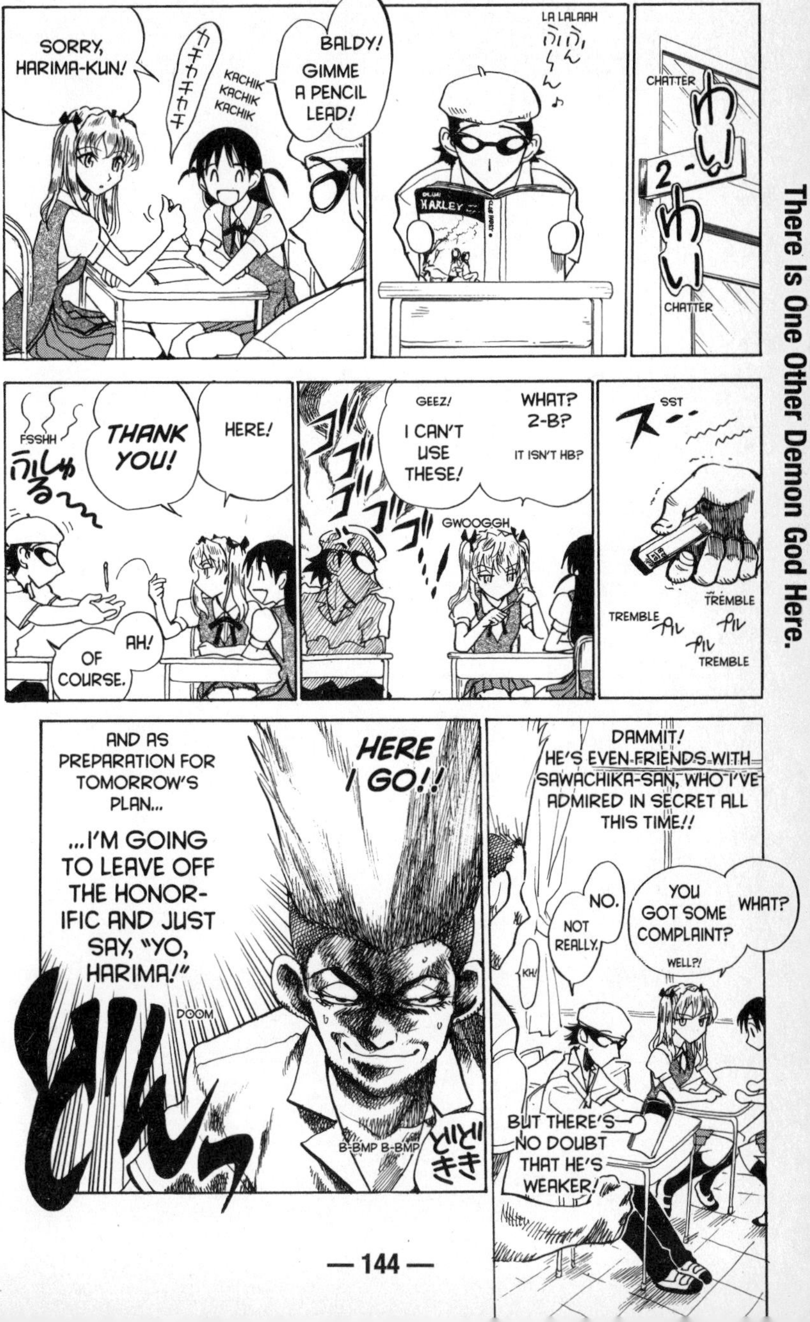

CHATTER
CHATTER
2-
LA LALAAH
BALDY!
GIMME A PENCIL LEAD!
KACHIK KACHIK KACHIK
カチカチカチ
SORRY, HARIMA-KUN!
SST
TREMBLE
TREMBLE
TREMBLE
WHAT? 2-B?
IT ISN'T HB?
GEEZ!
I CAN'T USE THESE!
GWOOGGH
HERE!
THANK YOU!
FSSHH
AH!
OF COURSE.
DAMMIT! HE'S EVEN FRIENDS WITH SAWACHIKA-SAN, WHO I'VE ADMIRED IN SECRET ALL THIS TIME!!
WHAT?
YOU GOT SOME COMPLAINT?
WELL?!
NO.
NOT REALLY.
KH!
BUT THERE'S NO DOUBT THAT HE'S WEAKER!
HERE I GO!!
AND AS PREPARATION FOR TOMORROW'S PLAN...
...I'M GOING TO LEAVE OFF THE HONOR-IFIC AND JUST SAY, "YO, HARIMA!"
DOOM
B-BMP B-BMP

He's Taken a Step Toward Looking Pitiful.

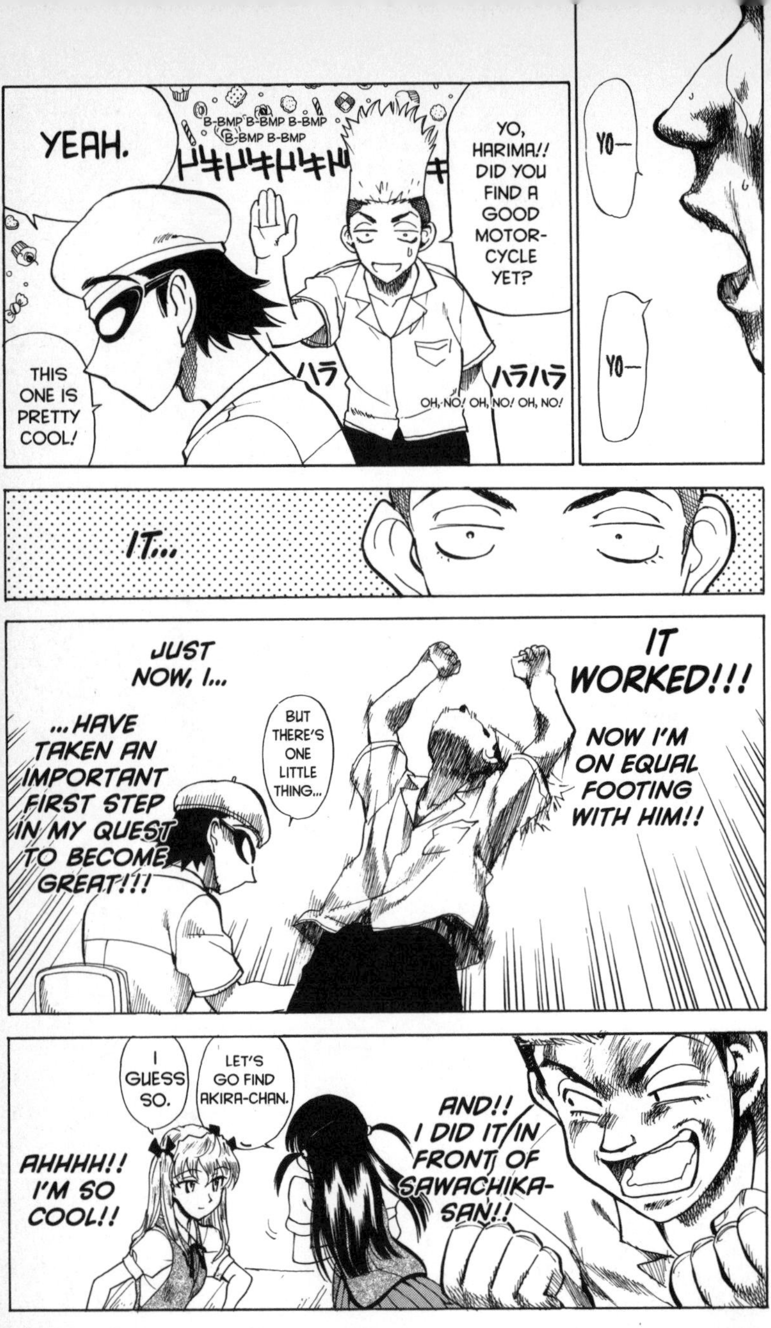
YO—
YO—
YO, HARIMA!! DID YOU FIND A GOOD MOTORCYCLE YET?
ドキドキドキドキ
B-BMP B-BMP B-BMP B-BMP B-BMP
YEAH.
ハラハラ
OH, NO! OH, NO! OH, NO!
ハラ
THIS ONE IS PRETTY COOL!
IT...
IT WORKED!!!
NOW I'M ON EQUAL FOOTING WITH HIM!!
JUST NOW, I...
BUT THERE'S ONE LITTLE THING...
...HAVE TAKEN AN IMPORTANT FIRST STEP IN MY QUEST TO BECOME GREAT!!!
AND!! I DID IT IN FRONT OF SAWACHIKA-SAN!!
LET'S GO FIND AKIRA-CHAN.
I GUESS SO.
AHHHH!! I'M SO COOL!!

Social Climbing Mission: Not Accomplished.

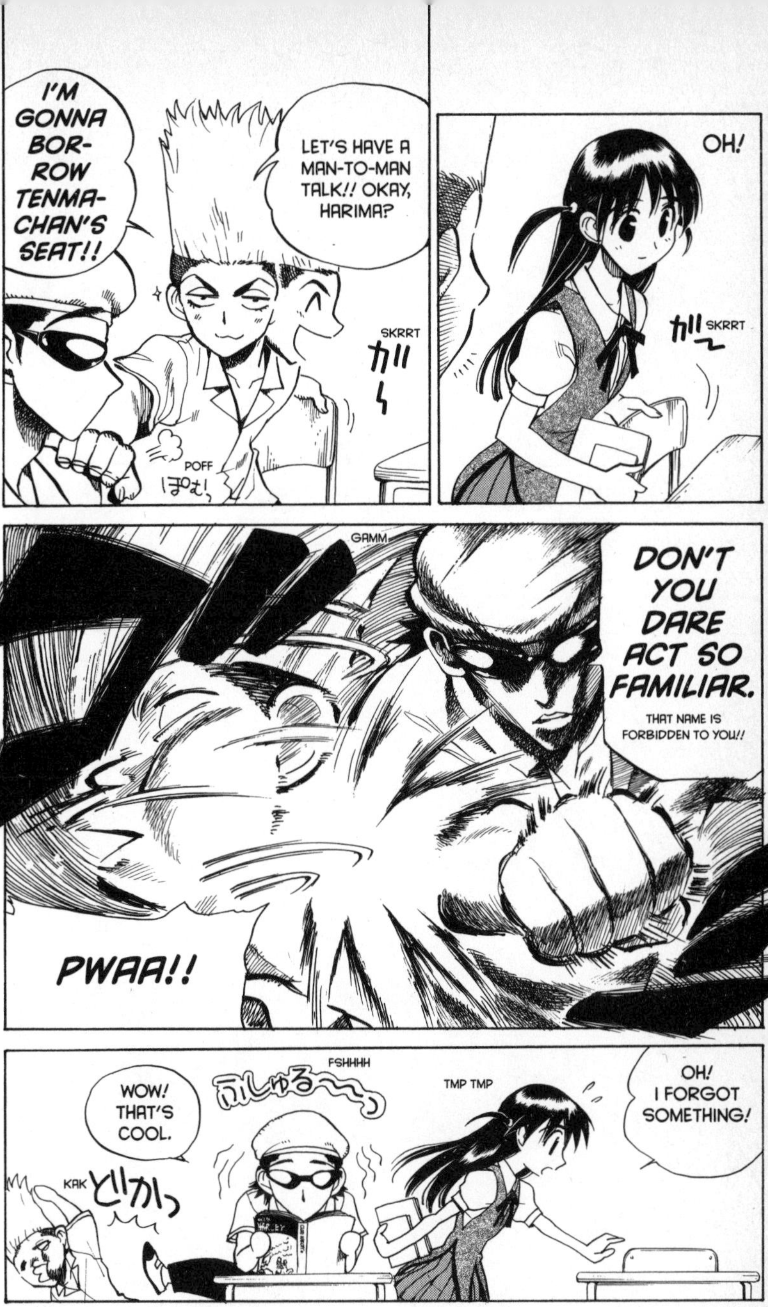
OH!
カリ~ SKRRT
LET'S HAVE A MAN-TO-MAN TALK!! OKAY, HARIMA?
I'M GONNA BOR-ROW TENMA-CHAN'S SEAT!!
SKRRT カリ
POFF ぽむっ
DON'T YOU DARE ACT SO FAMILIAR.
THAT NAME IS FORBIDDEN TO YOU!!
GAMM
PWAA!!
OH! I FORGOT SOMETHING!
TMP TMP
FSHHHH ふしゅる~っ
WOW! THAT'S COOL.
KAK とりかっ

♭18·........·Fin

NAME

YOSHIDAYAMA JIRÔ

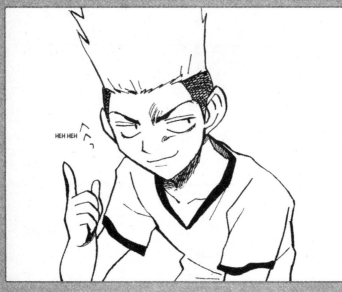

HEH HEH

JOB

MINION

POWER(UNIT)

UPSTART POWER

SKILL

BEING PEOPLE'S GOFER

FINISH BLOW

TREASON

WEAK POINT

HARIMA

LEVEL

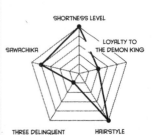

SHORTNESS LEVEL
LOYALTY TO THE DEMON KING
HAIRSTYLE
THREE DELINQUENT MUSKETEERS UNITE AND DOMINATE THE WORLD PLAN
SAWACHIKA

School Rumble OFFICIAL CHARACTER TRADING CARD

NAME

ÔTSUKA MAI

JOB

DEMON SERGEANT

POWER(UNIT)

CLASS REP POWER

SKILL

SCHOOL COUNCIL MAJORITY DECISION

FINISH BLOW

MAI-CHAN PUNCH

WEAK POINT

HANAI

LEVEL

TELLS OTHERS WHAT TO DO
WISDOM
IMADORI
ANGRY PARTNER
PHYSICAL STRENGTH

School Rumble

OFFICIAL CHARACTER TRADING CARD

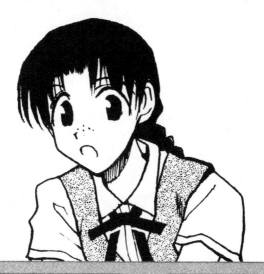

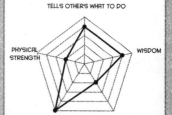

♭19 BEST FRIENDS

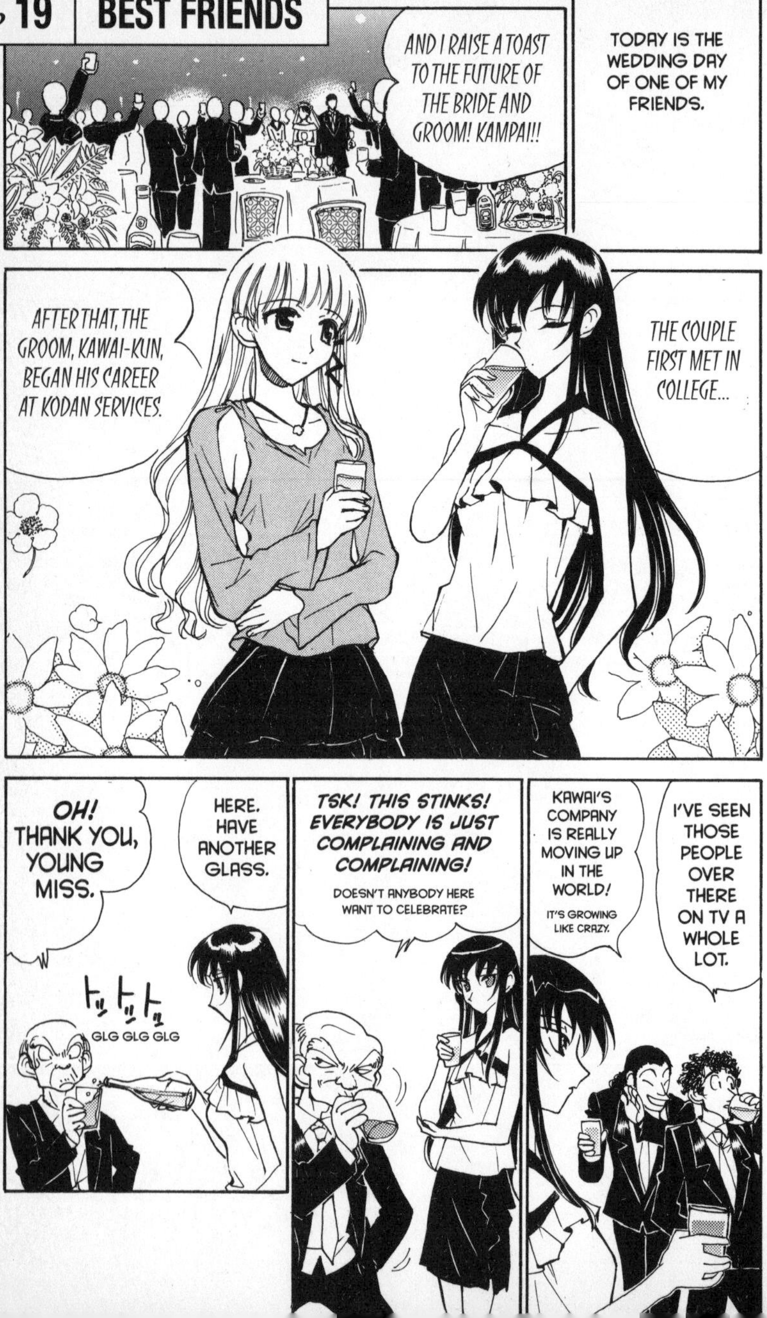
TODAY IS THE WEDDING DAY OF ONE OF MY FRIENDS.
AND I RAISE A TOAST TO THE FUTURE OF THE BRIDE AND GROOM! KAMPAI!!
THE COUPLE FIRST MET IN COLLEGE...
AFTER THAT, THE GROOM, KAWAI-KUN, BEGAN HIS CAREER AT KODAN SERVICES.
I'VE SEEN THOSE PEOPLE OVER THERE ON TV A WHOLE LOT.
KAWAI'S COMPANY IS REALLY MOVING UP IN THE WORLD!
IT'S GROWING LIKE CRAZY.
TSK! THIS STINKS! EVERYBODY IS JUST COMPLAINING AND COMPLAINING!
DOESN'T ANYBODY HERE WANT TO CELEBRATE?
HERE. HAVE ANOTHER GLASS.
OH! THANK YOU, YOUNG MISS.
トットットッ
GLG GLG GLG

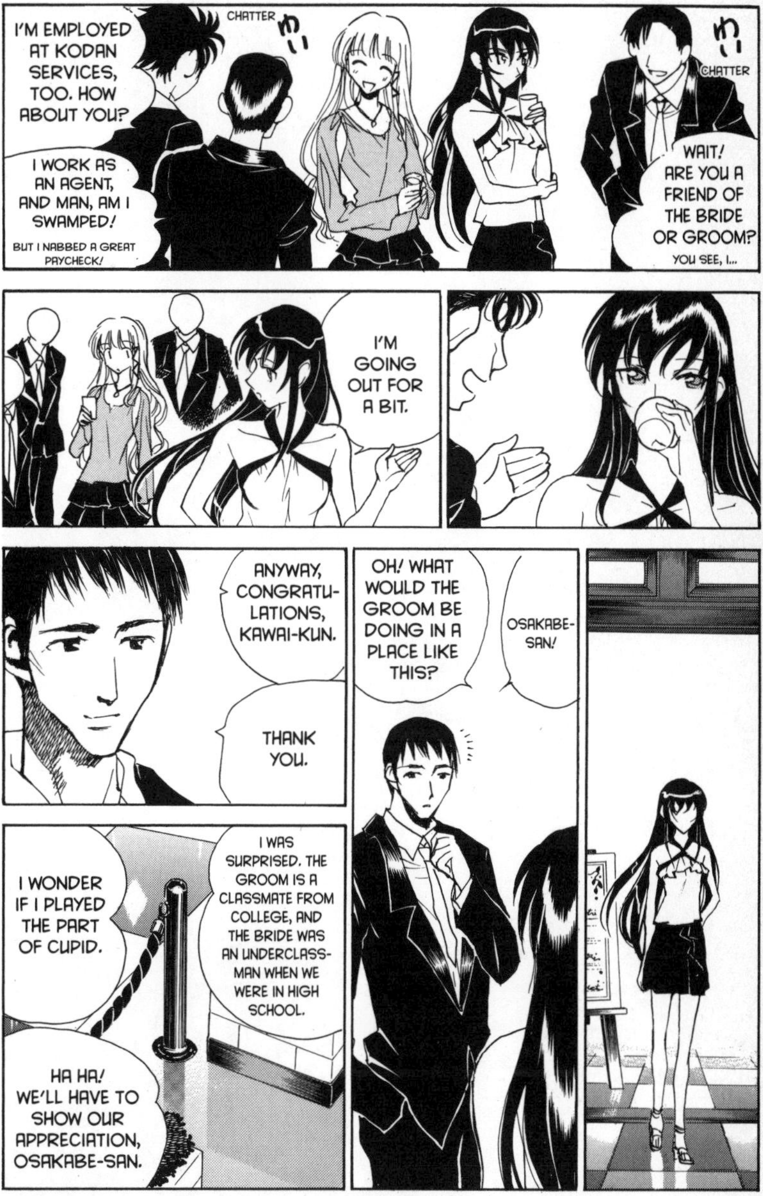
わい
CHATTER
WAIT! ARE YOU A FRIEND OF THE BRIDE OR GROOM?
YOU SEE, I...
CHATTER
わい
I'M EMPLOYED AT KODAN SERVICES, TOO. HOW ABOUT YOU?
I WORK AS AN AGENT, AND MAN, AM I SWAMPED!
BUT I NABBED A GREAT PAYCHECK!
I'M GOING OUT FOR A BIT.
OSAKABE-SAN!
OH! WHAT WOULD THE GROOM BE DOING IN A PLACE LIKE THIS?
ANYWAY, CONGRATULATIONS, KAWAI-KUN.
THANK YOU.
I WAS SURPRISED. THE GROOM IS A CLASSMATE FROM COLLEGE, AND THE BRIDE WAS AN UNDERCLASSMAN WHEN WE WERE IN HIGH SCHOOL.
I WONDER IF I PLAYED THE PART OF CUPID.
HA HA! WE'LL HAVE TO SHOW OUR APPRECIATION, OSAKABE-SAN.

Standard Scenes from a Wedding: No. 1.

Itoko and Yôko: Graduated from the Same High School.

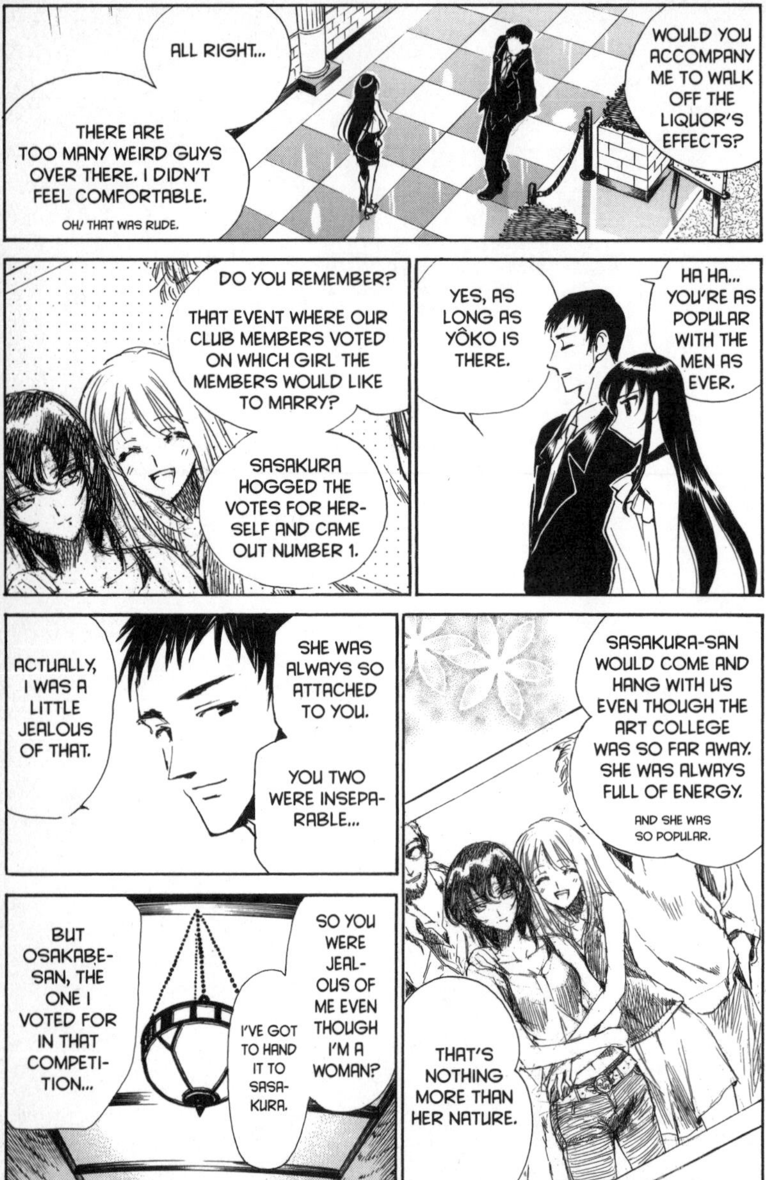
WOULD YOU ACCOMPANY ME TO WALK OFF THE LIQUOR'S EFFECTS?
ALL RIGHT...
THERE ARE TOO MANY WEIRD GUYS OVER THERE. I DIDN'T FEEL COMFORTABLE.
OH! THAT WAS RUDE.
HA HA... YOU'RE AS POPULAR WITH THE MEN AS EVER.
YES, AS LONG AS YÔKO IS THERE.
DO YOU REMEMBER?
THAT EVENT WHERE OUR CLUB MEMBERS VOTED ON WHICH GIRL THE MEMBERS WOULD LIKE TO MARRY?
SASAKURA HOGGED THE VOTES FOR HER-SELF AND CAME OUT NUMBER 1.
SASAKURA-SAN WOULD COME AND HANG WITH US EVEN THOUGH THE ART COLLEGE WAS SO FAR AWAY. SHE WAS ALWAYS FULL OF ENERGY.
AND SHE WAS SO POPULAR.
THAT'S NOTHING MORE THAN HER NATURE.
SHE WAS ALWAYS SO ATTACHED TO YOU.
YOU TWO WERE INSEPA-RABLE...
ACTUALLY, I WAS A LITTLE JEALOUS OF THAT.
SO YOU WERE JEAL-OUS OF ME EVEN THOUGH I'M A WOMAN?
I'VE GOT TO HAND IT TO SASA-KURA.
BUT OSAKABE-SAN, THE ONE I VOTED FOR IN THAT COMPETI-TION...

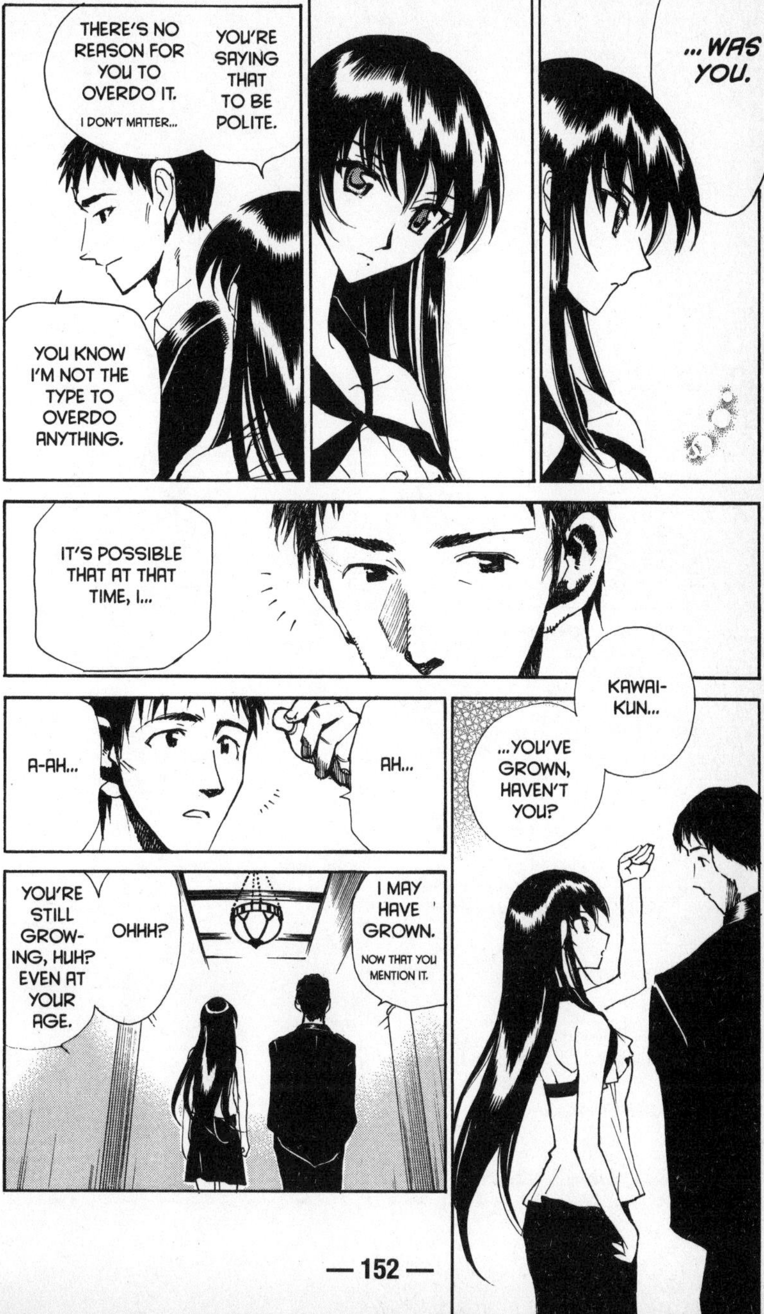
...WAS YOU.
YOU'RE SAYING THAT TO BE POLITE.
THERE'S NO REASON FOR YOU TO OVERDO IT.
I DON'T MATTER...
YOU KNOW I'M NOT THE TYPE TO OVERDO ANYTHING.
IT'S POSSIBLE THAT AT THAT TIME, I...
KAWAI-KUN...
...YOU'VE GROWN, HAVEN'T YOU?
AH...
A-AH...
I MAY HAVE GROWN.
NOW THAT YOU MENTION IT.
OHHH?
YOU'RE STILL GROWING, HUH? EVEN AT YOUR AGE.

Standard Scene from a Wedding: No. 2.

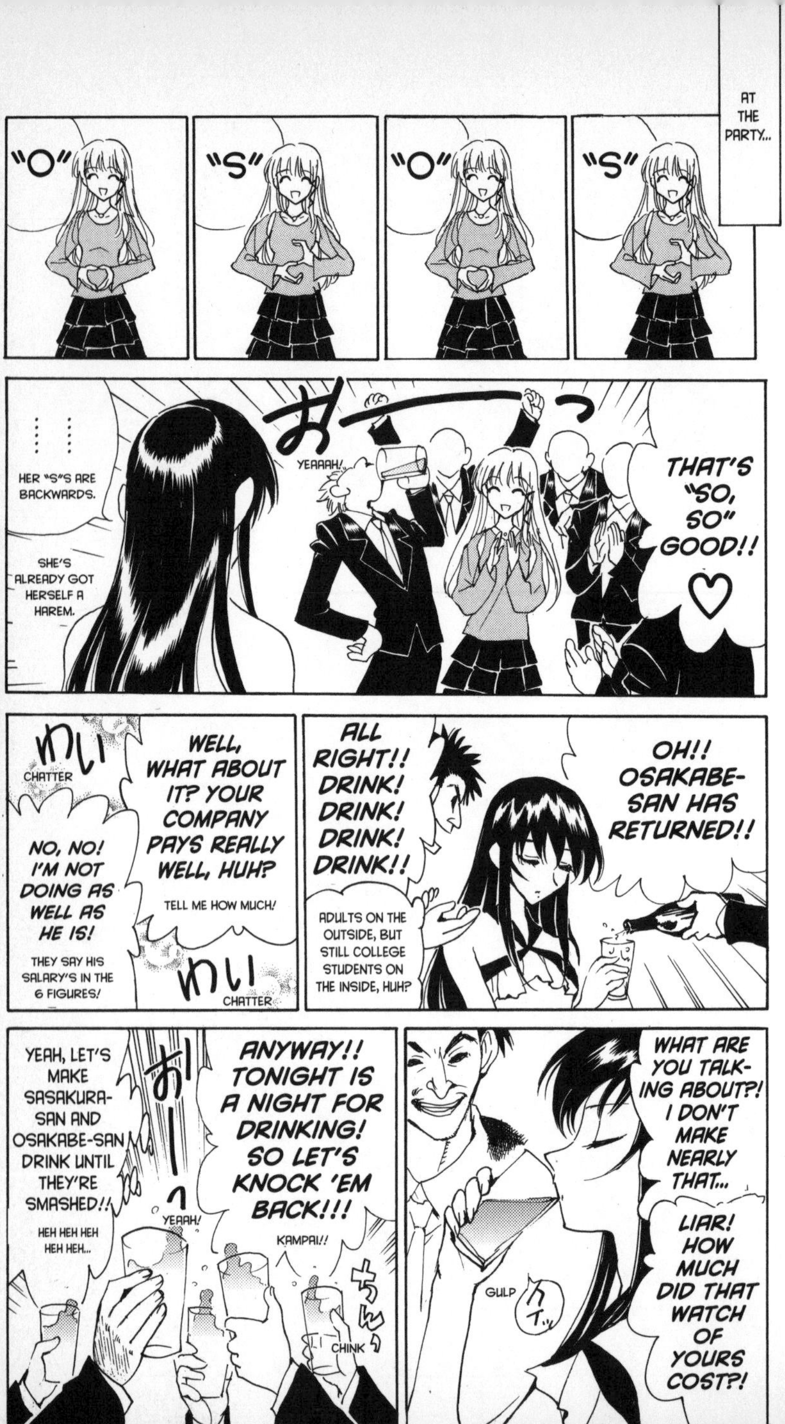
AT THE PARTY...
"S"
"O"
"S"
"O"
THAT'S "SO, SO" GOOD!! ♡
おーーっ
YEAAAH!
......
HER "S"S ARE BACKWARDS.
SHE'S ALREADY GOT HERSELF A HAREM.
OH!! OSAKABE-SAN HAS RETURNED!!
ALL RIGHT!! DRINK! DRINK! DRINK! DRINK!!
ADULTS ON THE OUTSIDE, BUT STILL COLLEGE STUDENTS ON THE INSIDE, HUH?
WELL, WHAT ABOUT IT? YOUR COMPANY PAYS REALLY WELL, HUH?
TELL ME HOW MUCH!
わい
CHATTER
NO, NO! I'M NOT DOING AS WELL AS HE IS!
THEY SAY HIS SALARY'S IN THE 6 FIGURES!
わい
CHATTER
WHAT ARE YOU TALKING ABOUT?! I DON'T MAKE NEARLY THAT...
LIAR! HOW MUCH DID THAT WATCH OF YOURS COST?!
クイッ
GULP
ANYWAY!! TONIGHT IS A NIGHT FOR DRINKING! SO LET'S KNOCK 'EM BACK!!!
おーーっ
YEAAH!
KAMPAI!!
ちーん
CHINK
YEAH, LET'S MAKE SASAKURA-SAN AND OSAKABE-SAN DRINK UNTIL THEY'RE SMASHED!!
HEH HEH HEH HEH HEH...

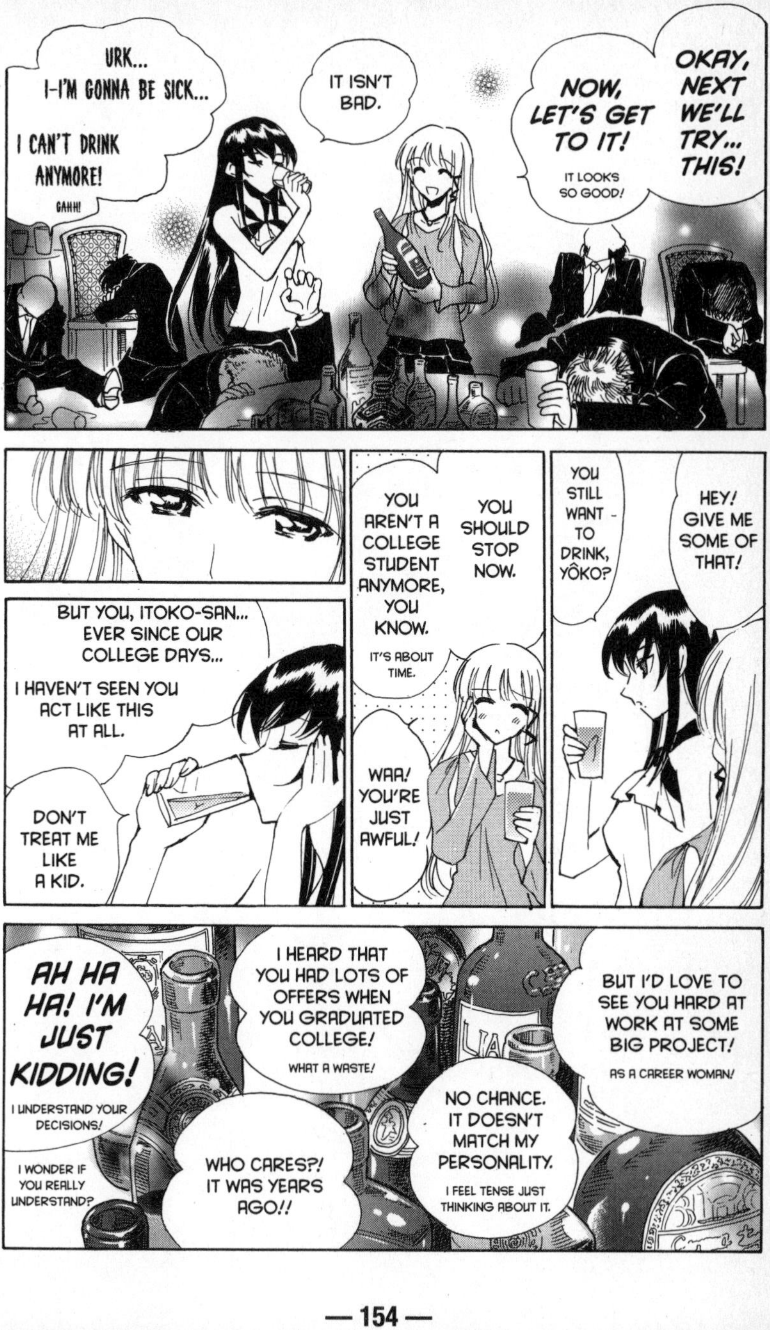
OKAY, NEXT WE'LL TRY... THIS!
NOW, LET'S GET TO IT!
IT LOOKS SO GOOD!
IT ISN'T BAD.
URK... I-I'M GONNA BE SICK...
I CAN'T DRINK ANYMORE!
GAHH!
HEY! GIVE ME SOME OF THAT!
YOU STILL WANT TO DRINK, YÔKO?
YOU SHOULD STOP NOW.
YOU AREN'T A COLLEGE STUDENT ANYMORE, YOU KNOW.
IT'S ABOUT TIME.
WAA! YOU'RE JUST AWFUL!
BUT YOU, ITOKO-SAN... EVER SINCE OUR COLLEGE DAYS...
I HAVEN'T SEEN YOU ACT LIKE THIS AT ALL.
DON'T TREAT ME LIKE A KID.
BUT I'D LOVE TO SEE YOU HARD AT WORK AT SOME BIG PROJECT!
AS A CAREER WOMAN!
NO CHANCE. IT DOESN'T MATCH MY PERSONALITY.
I FEEL TENSE JUST THINKING ABOUT IT.
I HEARD THAT YOU HAD LOTS OF OFFERS WHEN YOU GRADUATED COLLEGE!
WHAT A WASTE!
WHO CARES?! IT WAS YEARS AGO!!
AH HA HA! I'M JUST KIDDING!
I UNDERSTAND YOUR DECISIONS!
I WONDER IF YOU REALLY UNDERSTAND?

An Adult Conversation.

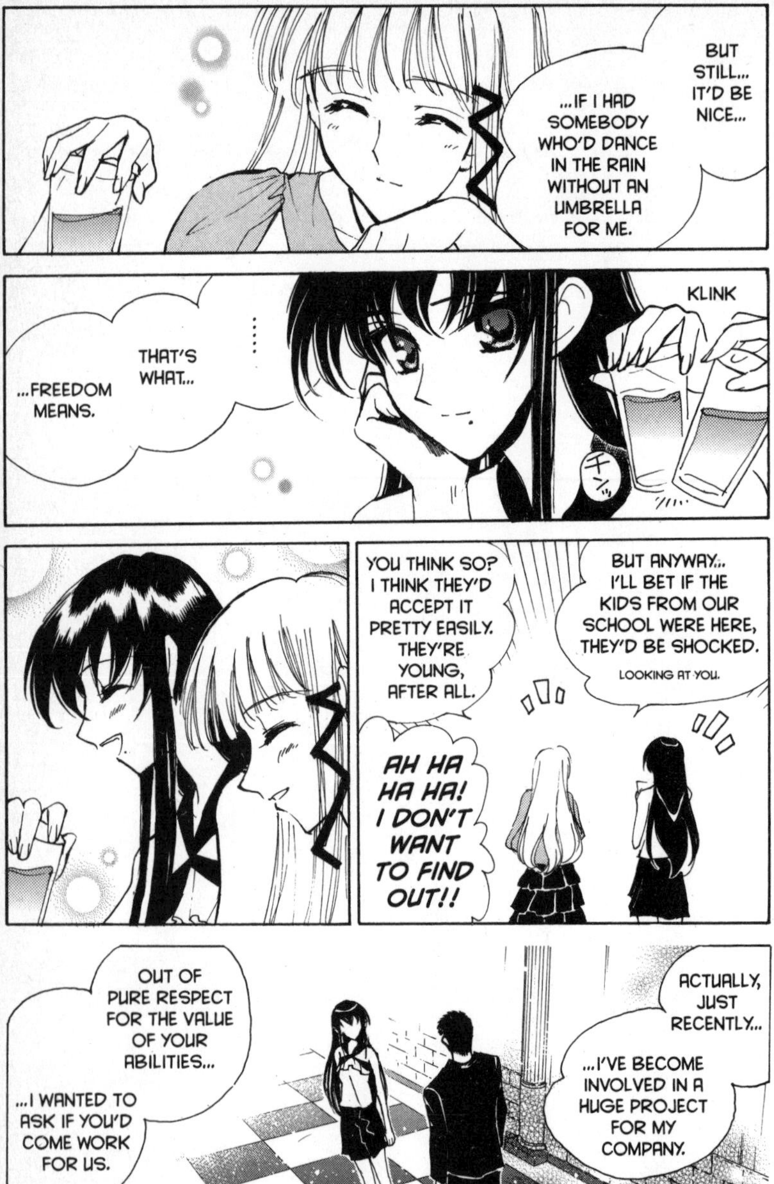

BUT STILL... IT'D BE NICE...
...IF I HAD SOMEBODY WHO'D DANCE IN THE RAIN WITHOUT AN UMBRELLA FOR ME.
KLINK
......
THAT'S WHAT...
...FREEDOM MEANS.
BUT ANYWAY... I'LL BET IF THE KIDS FROM OUR SCHOOL WERE HERE, THEY'D BE SHOCKED.
LOOKING AT YOU.
YOU THINK SO? I THINK THEY'D ACCEPT IT PRETTY EASILY. THEY'RE YOUNG, AFTER ALL.
AH HA HA HA! I DON'T WANT TO FIND OUT!!
ACTUALLY, JUST RECENTLY...
...I'VE BECOME INVOLVED IN A HUGE PROJECT FOR MY COMPANY.
OUT OF PURE RESPECT FOR THE VALUE OF YOUR ABILITIES...
...I WANTED TO ASK IF YOU'D COME WORK FOR US.

A World That Harima Wouldn't Understand.

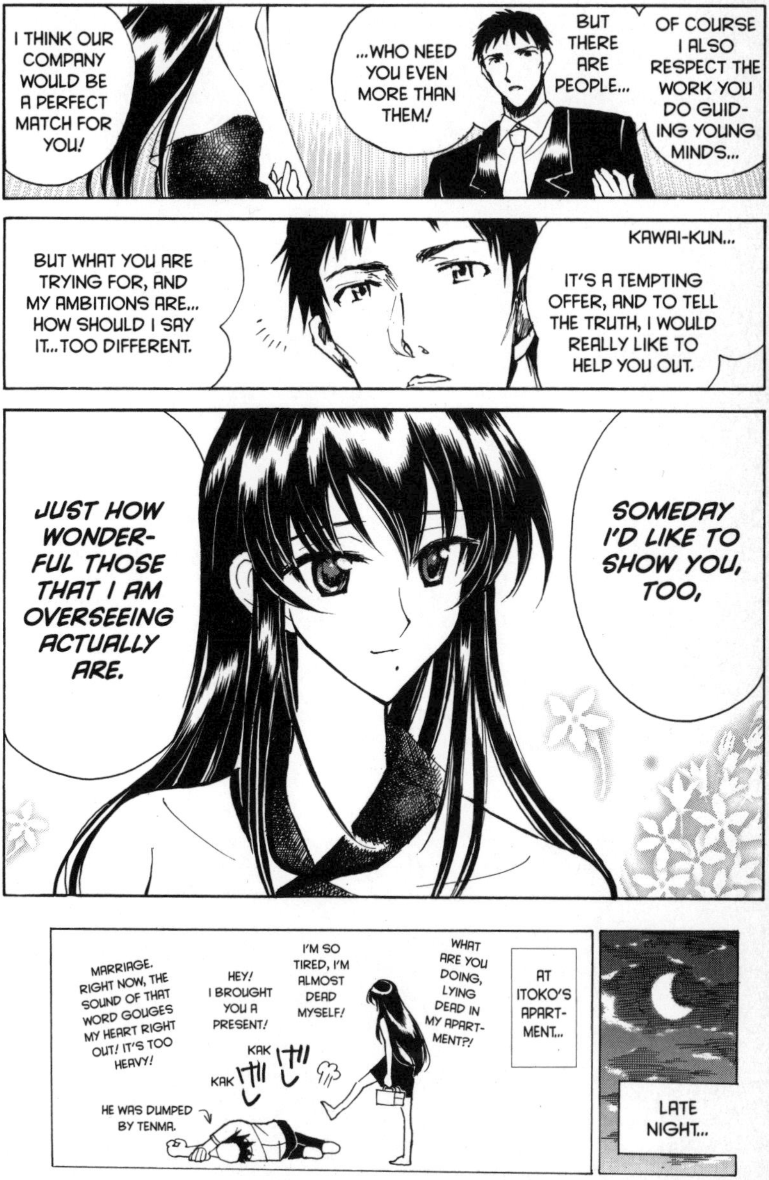
OF COURSE I ALSO RESPECT THE WORK YOU DO GUID-ING YOUNG MINDS...
BUT THERE ARE PEOPLE...
...WHO NEED YOU EVEN MORE THAN THEM!
I THINK OUR COMPANY WOULD BE A PERFECT MATCH FOR YOU!
KAWAI-KUN...
IT'S A TEMPTING OFFER, AND TO TELL THE TRUTH, I WOULD REALLY LIKE TO HELP YOU OUT.
BUT WHAT YOU ARE TRYING FOR, AND MY AMBITIONS ARE... HOW SHOULD I SAY IT...TOO DIFFERENT.
SOMEDAY I'D LIKE TO SHOW YOU, TOO,
JUST HOW WONDER-FUL THOSE THAT I AM OVERSEEING ACTUALLY ARE.
LATE NIGHT...
AT ITOKO'S APART-MENT...
WHAT ARE YOU DOING, LYING DEAD IN MY APART-MENT?!
I'M SO TIRED, I'M ALMOST DEAD MYSELF!
HEY! I BROUGHT YOU A PRESENT!
KAK
KAK
MARRIAGE. RIGHT NOW, THE SOUND OF THAT WORD GOUGES MY HEART RIGHT OUT! IT'S TOO HEAVY!
HE WAS DUMPED BY TENMA.

CONTINUED IN VOLUME 7

♭ 19 .... FIN

NAME

ANEGASAKI TAE

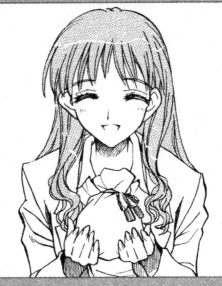

JOB

PRIEST

POWER(UNIT)

PRETTY HEALTH OFFICE NURSE POWER

SKILL

ENHANCING THE WILL TO FIGHT ♡

FINISH BLOW

HARIO

WEAK POINT

EARLY RISING

LEVEL

HARIO
CARETAKING
WINSOMENESS
THE MAN IN FRONT OF HER
BOLDNESS

School Rumble

OFFICIAL CHARACTER TRADING CARD

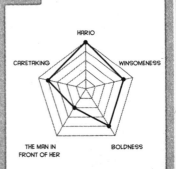

NAME

TANI-SENSEI

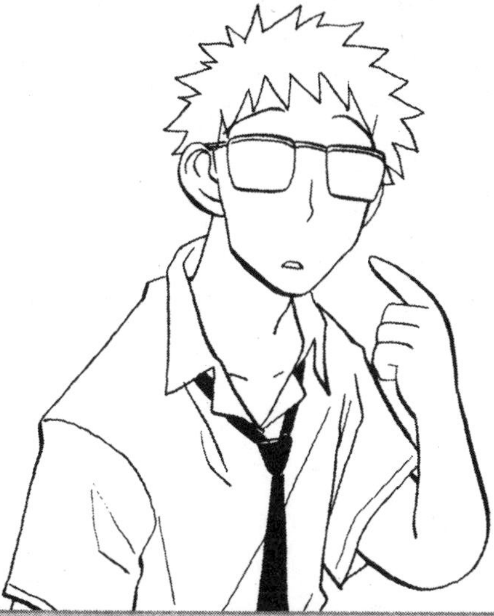

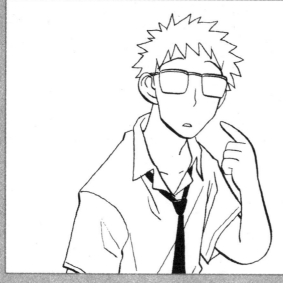

JOB

TEACHER

POWER(UNIT)

DINOSAUR POWER

SKILL

MASS PURCHASES

FINISH BLOW

HOMEWORK

WEAK POINT

KATÔ-SENSEI

LEVEL

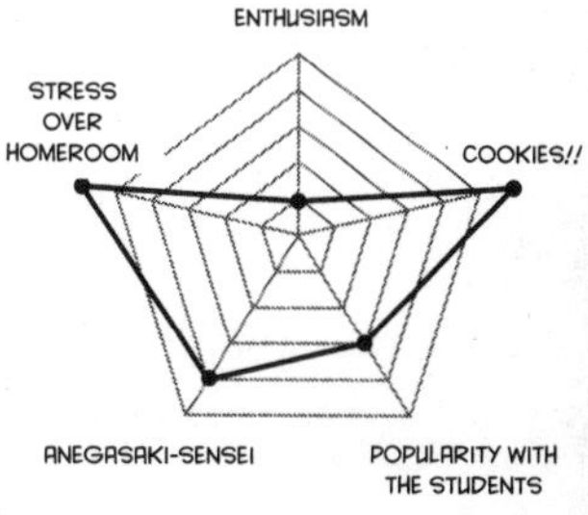
ENTHUSIASM
COOKIES!!
POPULARITY WITH THE STUDENTS
ANEGASAKI-SENSEI
STRESS OVER HOMEROOM

School Rumble OFFICIAL CHARACTER TRADING CARD

Incredibly Rare Card

NAME

YURIPPE

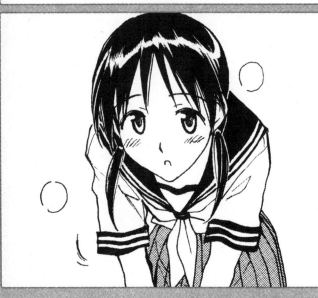

JOB

CHILDHOOD FRIEND

POWER(UNIT)

15X BEAUTIFICATION THROUGH FAULTY MEMORY

SKILL

FALSE MEMORIES

FINISH BLOW

ACORN COOKIES

WEAK POINT

THE PHENOMENON CALLED TIME

LEVEL

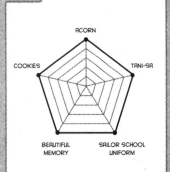

ACORN
TANI-SA
SAILOR SCHOOL UNIFORM
BEAUTIFUL MEMORY
COOKIES

School Rumble OFFICIAL CHARACTER TRADING CARD

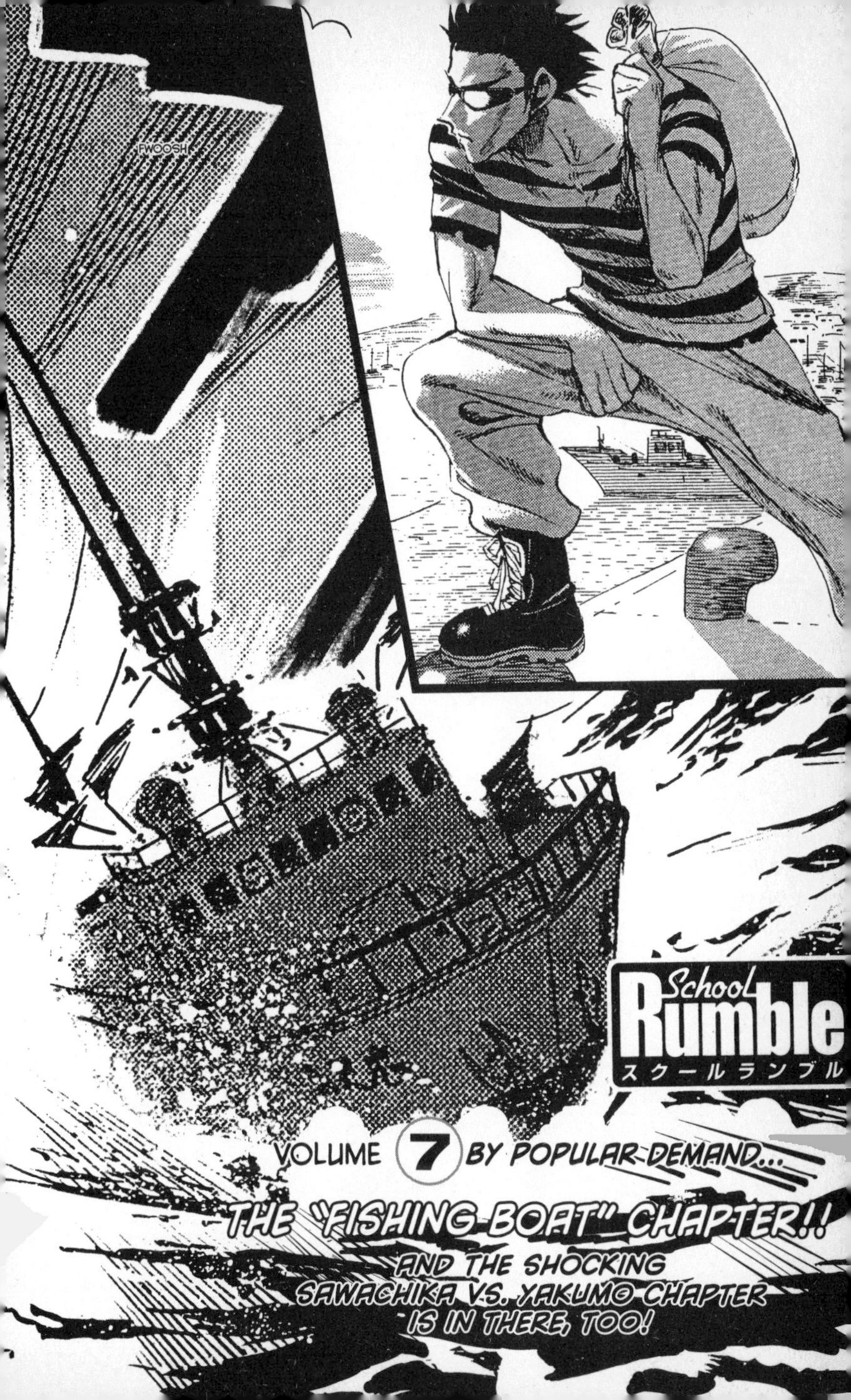

FWOOSH
School Rumble
スクールランブル
VOLUME 7 BY POPULAR DEMAND...
THE "FISHING BOAT" CHAPTER!!
AND THE SHOCKING
SAWACHIKA VS. YAKUMO CHAPTER
IS IN THERE, TOO!

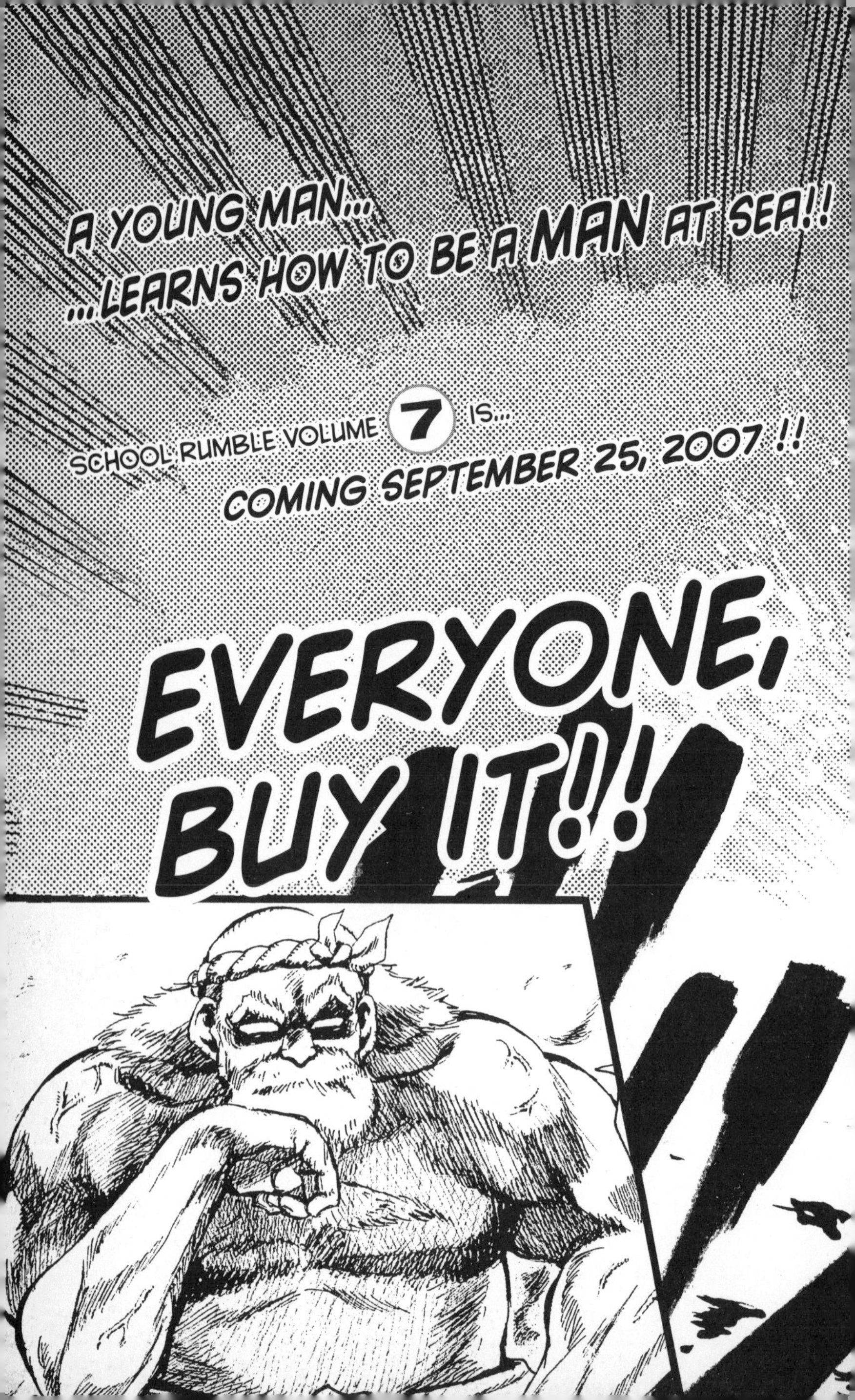
A YOUNG MAN...
...LEARNS HOW TO BE A MAN AT SEA!!
SCHOOL RUMBLE VOLUME 7 IS...
COMING SEPTEMBER 25, 2007 !!
EVERYONE, BUY IT!!

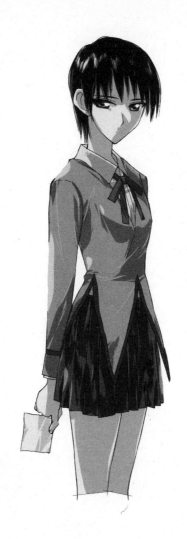

About the Creator

Jin Kobayashi was born in Tokyo. *School Rumble* is his first manga series. He has answered these questions from his fans:

What is your hobby?
Basketball

Which manga inspired you to become a creator?
Dragon Ball

Which character in your manga do you like best?
Kenji Harima

What type of manga do you want to create in the future?
Action

Name one book, piece of music, or movie you like.
The Indiana Jones series

Translation Notes

Japanese is a tricky language for most Westerners, and translation is often more art than science. For your edification and reading pleasure, here are notes on some of the places where we could have gone in a different direction in our translation of the work, or where a Japanese cultural reference is used.

Family or Personal Names

Most students in a Japanese classroom are identified by their family names, for example, Karasuma-kun. Even a close friend may use the last name, such as when Mikoto addresses Tenma, but you'll find that most people with a friendly relationship will call their friends by their personal names.

Hollywood, page 9

Yes, Tani-sensei did say Hollywood. Nearly every Hollywood movie is distributed in Japan, so even an underpaid high school teacher would get to see some of them.

Balls-in-the-Basket (*Tamaire*), page 15

Balls-in-the-Basket isn't an official name of the Japanese grade-school game, but it's a pretty close description of the game and translation of the Japanese. The Japanese name, *Tamaire,* means "balls inside." In the game, about two hundred balls of two colors are scattered on the ground. There are two teams, each is assigned a color, and the team to get the most of their colored balls into their own basket is the winner. Using the balls for a "dodgeball" battle is a novel twist on the game.

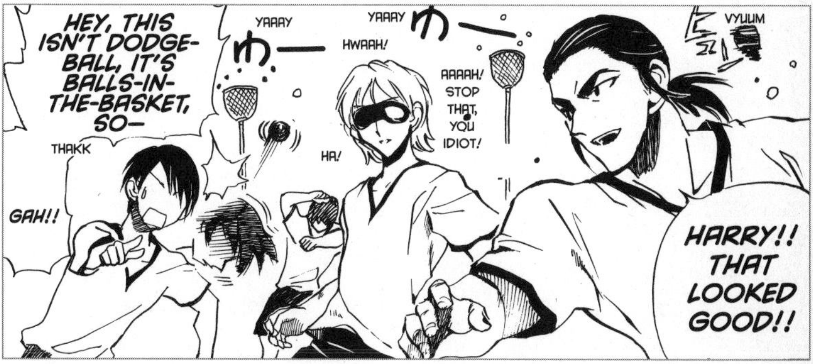
VYUUM
HARRY!! THAT LOOKED GOOD!!
YAAAY
わー
AAAAH! STOP THAT, YOU IDIOT!
HWAAH!
HA!
YAAAY
わー
HEY, THIS ISN'T DODGE-BALL, IT'S BALLS-IN-THE-BASKET, SO—
THAKK
GAH!!

Knight's Battle, page 22

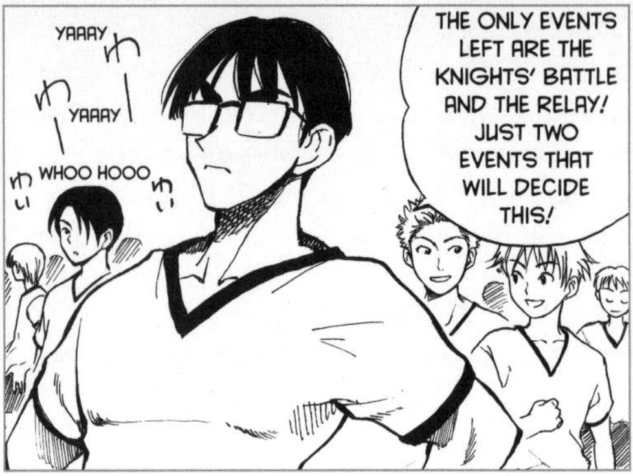
THE ONLY EVENTS LEFT ARE THE KNIGHTS' BATTLE AND THE RELAY! JUST TWO EVENTS THAT WILL DECIDE THIS!
YAAAY
YAAAY
WHOO HOOO

The Japanese name for it, *kibasen,* can mean either horsemen's battle, knights' battle, or cavalry games. Three guys are the "horse." The front guy joins hands with each of the guys behind, left-to-left and right-to-right—and that's where the "rider" places her feet. The guys behind place their other arms on the front guy's shoulders creating a "saddle" for the rider. When the rider's headband is taken, the team of horse and rider is out of the game. The team left standing in the end is the winner. It is played in many Japanese schools from elementary school through high school, and usually the teams are single gender.

Seiza, page 28

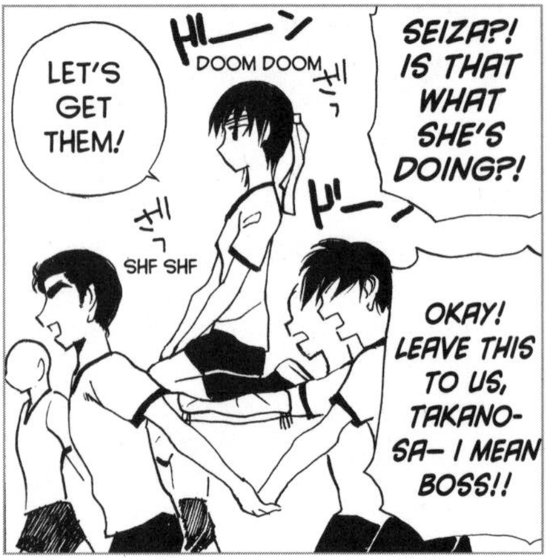
SEIZA?! IS THAT WHAT SHE'S DOING?!
DOOM DOOM
LET'S GET THEM!
OKAY! LEAVE THIS TO US, TAKANO-SA— I MEAN BOSS!!
SHF SHF

Seiza is the traditional style of sitting on the floor with calves and feet tucked under the thighs and rear end. Even modern Japanese young people have trouble sitting *seiza* for any length of time. Those who can are usually involved in the Japanese arts, from very traditional Japanese families, or a part of the *yakuza* (criminal organization).

Boss, page 28

Because Takano Akira is sitting *seiza* (see note on previous page) and barking out orders, her horse section is treating her as if she were someone higher up in the *yakuza*. Such people are called older brother (or in Takano's case, older sister) in the *yakuza*, but it is the equivalent of American mob people calling their leaders "boss."

Glutton Triplets, page 37

This is almost a direct translation. The Japanese use the words *oogui sankyôdai*, which literally means eat-a-lot triplets.

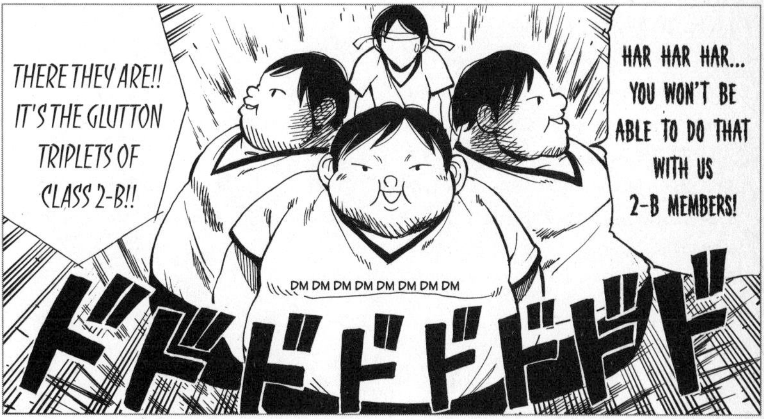
HAR HAR HAR... YOU WON'T BE ABLE TO DO THAT WITH US 2-B MEMBERS!
THERE THEY ARE!! IT'S THE GLUTTON TRIPLETS OF CLASS 2-B!!
DM DM DM DM DM DM DM DM
ドドドドドドドドド

Statue of Ashura, page 37

Ashura (or Asura) represents a demigod that is often compared to the Greek Titans. A famous 8th-century statue of Ashura in the Kofukuji Temple in Nara represents Ashura as having three heads, one looking forward and the other two looking left and right, and six arms, but otherwise being one relatively thin being.

Daruma, page 37

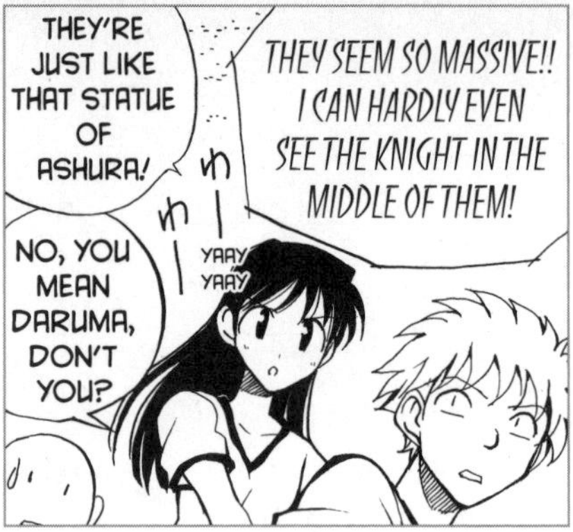
THEY SEEM SO MASSIVE!! I CAN HARDLY EVEN SEE THE KNIGHT IN THE MIDDLE OF THEM!
THEY'RE JUST LIKE THAT STATUE OF ASHURA!
YAAY YAAY
NO, YOU MEAN DARUMA, DON'T YOU?

Although Bodhidharma (Daruma in Japanese), an Indian sage who lived in the 5th or 6th century, is the undisputed founder of Zen Buddhism, he is associated in Japanese minds not with Buddhism but with roundness. Snowmen are called *yuki*-Daruma (snow Daruma), and pot-bellied stoves are called Daruma *sutoobu*, or Daruma stoves. It is said that while he meditated, his arms and legs withered away, making his roundness even more pronounced.

One-Knight Stand, page 45

The pun was a little different. The dialogue uses a word for horseman or knight in the phrase *ikkitôsen* (meaning, great warrior), so the translator decided to go for a relatively similar pun.

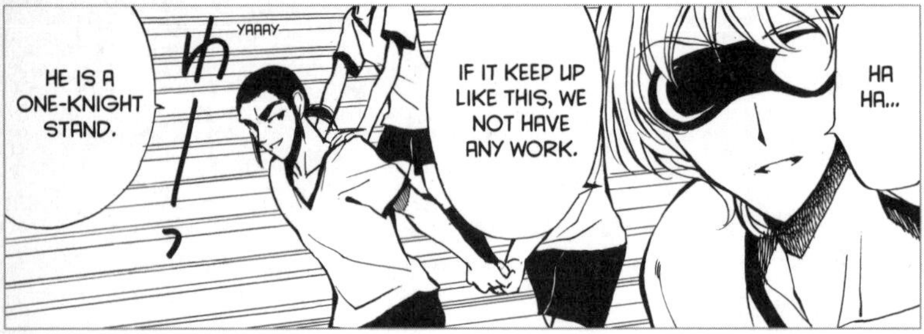
HA HA...
IF IT KEEP UP LIKE THIS, WE NOT HAVE ANY WORK.
-YAAAY-
HE IS A ONE-KNIGHT STAND.

Abs of Steel, page 67

That was a literal translation.

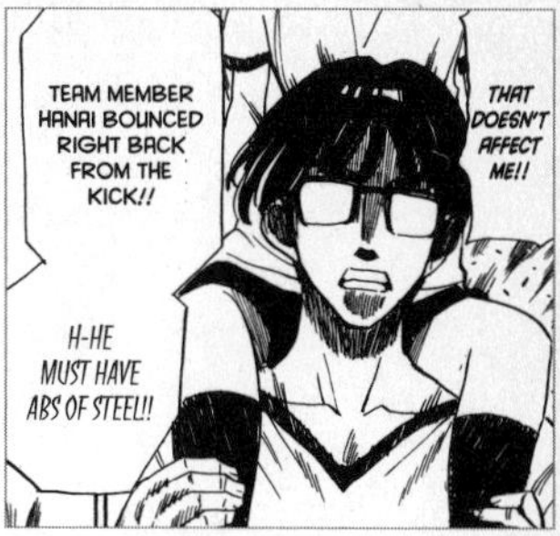
THAT DOESN'T AFFECT ME!!
TEAM MEMBER HANAI BOUNCED RIGHT BACK FROM THE KICK!!
H-HE MUST HAVE ABS OF STEEL!!

Move Names, page, 68 and 70

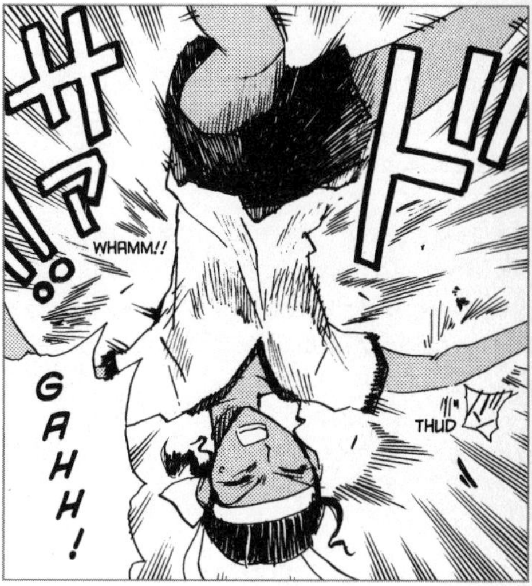
THUD
WHAMM!!
GAHH!

The *kanji* for Thor's Hammer was *Raijin no Tsuchi,* which translates as Thunder God's Hammer, but it had a pronunciation guide of Thor's Hammer. The Lariat used the English word. Similar to Thor's Hammer, Nimbus Dance used the *kanji Yosei no Mai,* which means Fairy Dance, but the pronunciation guide said Nimbus Dance in English. Frankensteiner was a direct transliteration. Are these the names of real pro wrestling moves? I doubt it...

Buhi, page 86

The Japanese sound for *oink* is *buhi*, and that's what was written in the Japanese.

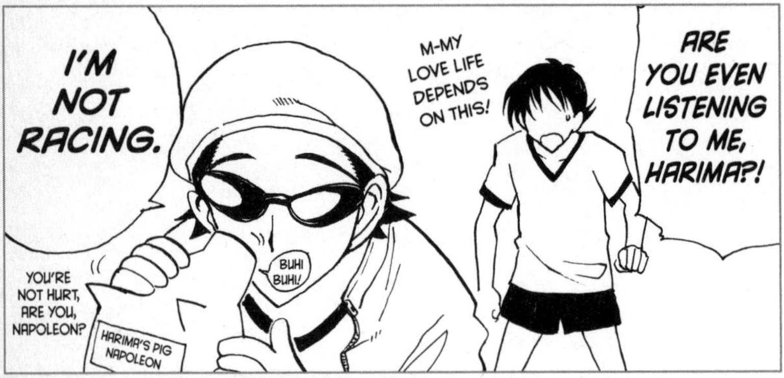
ARE YOU EVEN LISTENING TO ME, HARIMA?!
M-MY LOVE LIFE DEPENDS ON THIS!
I'M NOT RACING.
BUHI BUHI!
YOU'RE NOT HURT, ARE YOU, NAPOLEON?
HARIMA'S PIG NAPOLEON

Kagemusha, page 99

Fans of Akira Kurosawa movies may know that *kagemusha* means a man's double used to attract assassins away from the real person, but it can also mean the person behind the scenes who is pulling the strings.

Imadori-sama, page 109

It's unusual, but sometimes people (especially in manga) who are full of themselves name themselves using the honorific *-sama*.

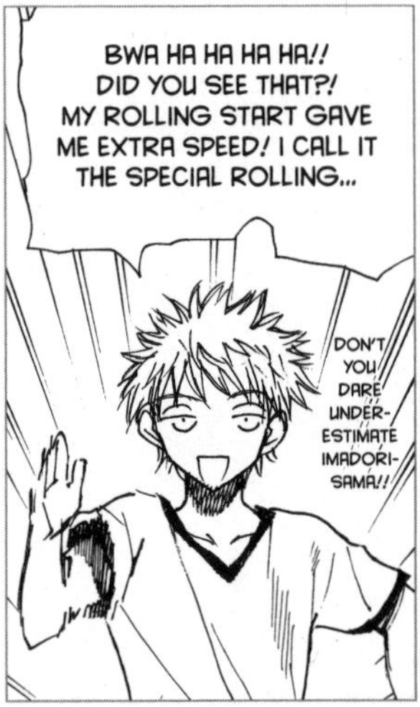
BWA HA HA HA HA!! DID YOU SEE THAT?! MY ROLLING START GAVE ME EXTRA SPEED! I CALL IT THE SPECIAL ROLLING...
DON'T YOU DARE UNDER-ESTIMATE IMADORI-SAMA!!

Oklahoma Mixer, page 123

It's likely that Japanese school children know this folk dance better than young people from Oklahoma, because it is danced in Japanese grade schools and middle schools. Traditionally performed to tunes like "Turkey in the Straw," it usually features two circles of couples (mostly male-female couples despite the Hanai-Tôgô couple) dancing to the prescribed steps of the folk dance.

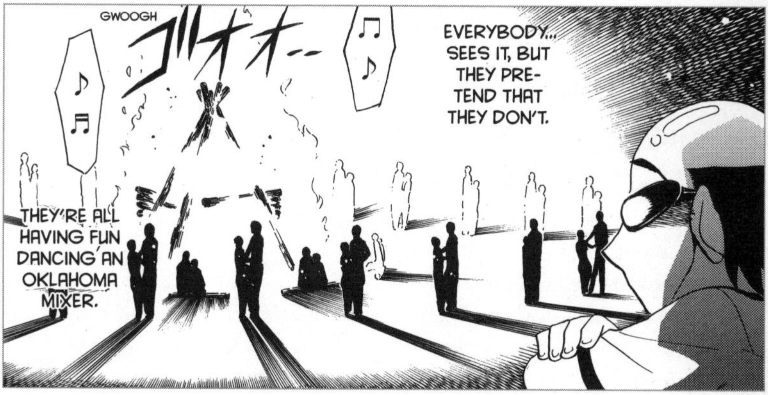
EVERYBODY... SEES IT, BUT THEY PRETEND THAT THEY DON'T.
GWOOGH
THEY'RE ALL HAVING FUN DANCING AN OKLAHOMA MIXER.

Near the Train Station, page 130

Because of the narrow streets, it is easier, more time-efficient, and more cost-effective to take the train than to drive in Japan. That has made train stations very important in almost every Japanese town. Nearly everything is measured by the distance from the nearest station, and if friends meet, it is most likely to be at or near the station. "Near the station" can be considered the most busy district of any town.

Hide-and-Seek, page 131

The Japanese game *kakurenbo* is basically Hide-and-Seek, so the translation uses the English name for the game.

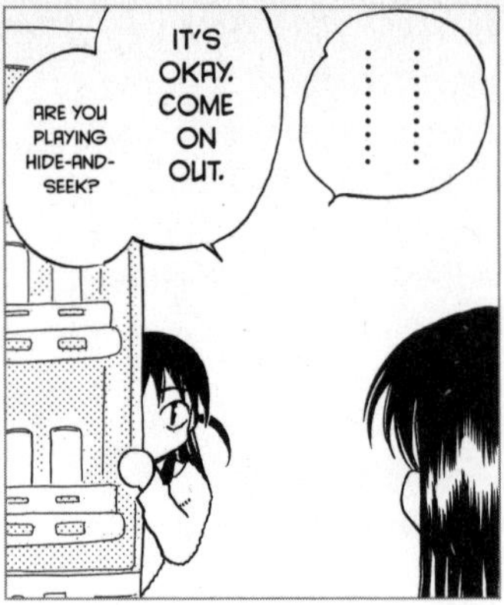
......
IT'S OKAY. COME ON OUT.
ARE YOU PLAYING HIDE-AND-SEEK?

That Doesn't Count, page 132

Are you still wondering what it doesn't count as? First kisses are very important in manga land, so Mikoto is afraid that her first kiss was with Tenma. Is it as important to real-life Japanese girls? As with nearly everything, it depends on the girl.

Sensitive Tongue, page 135

This is a pun that got away. A tongue that is sensitive to heat is called in Japanese *nekoshita* or a "cat's tongue." So it would make sense that Iori in Tenma's body would have a too-sensitive tongue.

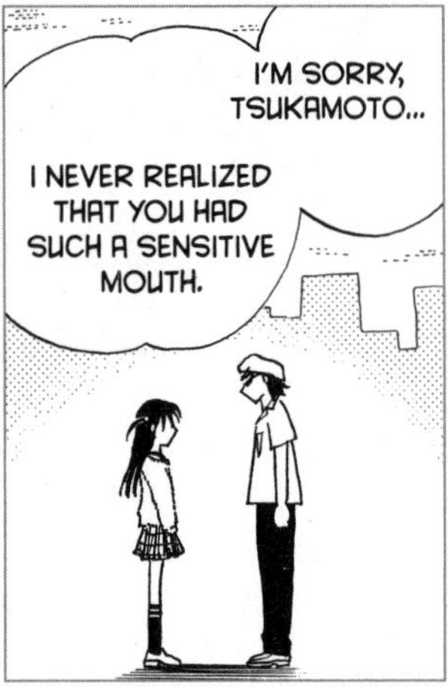
I'M SORRY, TSUKAMOTO...
I NEVER REALIZED THAT YOU HAD SUCH A SENSITIVE MOUTH.

Third Year of Middle School, page 142

Just as a reminder, in Japan, elementary school means years 1-6. Years 7-9 are referred to as middle school, first year through third year. Years 10-12 are counted as high school, first year through third year.

Angry Partner, page 148

TELLS OTHERS WHAT TO DO
WISDOM
IMADORI
ANGRY PARTNER
PHYSICAL STRENGTH

This is another reference to the classic comedy duos called *Manzai*. Like Laurel and Hardy, they have one dumb partner and one angry partner.

***Kampai*, page 149**

Every culture has its way of making a toast with a drink, and the standard word in Japanese is *kampai!* (alternatively spelled *kanpai* and pronounced "kahm-pie"). *Kampai* is used in every situation in which English speakers would use "Cheers," and means simply "empty glass."

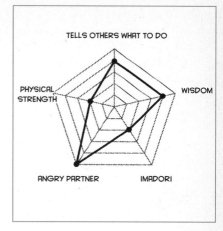

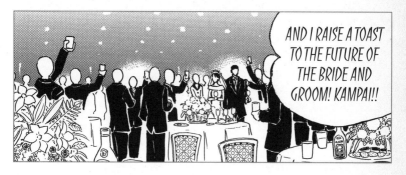

AND I RAISE A TOAST TO THE FUTURE OF THE BRIDE AND GROOM! KAMPAI!!

So so, page 153

Sasakura-sensei's odd SOS that became So-so was the Japanese phrase that means "yes, that's right," but in this case it means "that's the spirit," as people drink. The English had to use "so so," and therefore I did my best to come up with something appropriate.

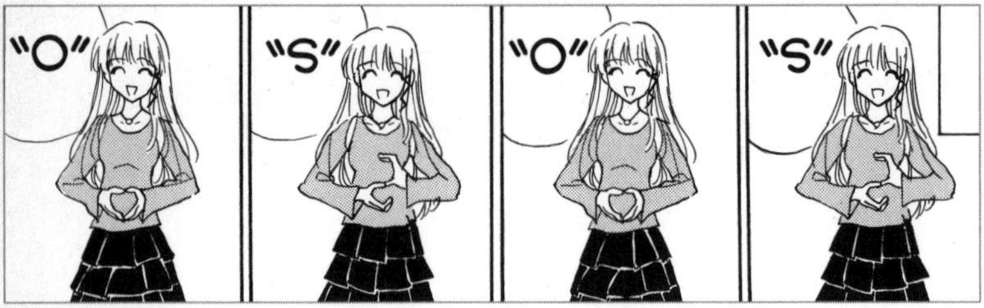
"S"
"O"
"S"
"O"

Six Figures, page 153

The Japanese said four figures, but that is four figures above *man-en* (10,000 yen). So a four-figure salary would be 10,000,000 yen, which roughly corresponds to $100,000, or six figures in terms of US dollars. To save on explanation, this version just used the more familiar "6 figures" in the translation.

Preview

We're pleased to present you a preview of *School Rumble* volume 7. This volume will be available in English September 25, 2007, but for now you'll have to make do with Japanese!

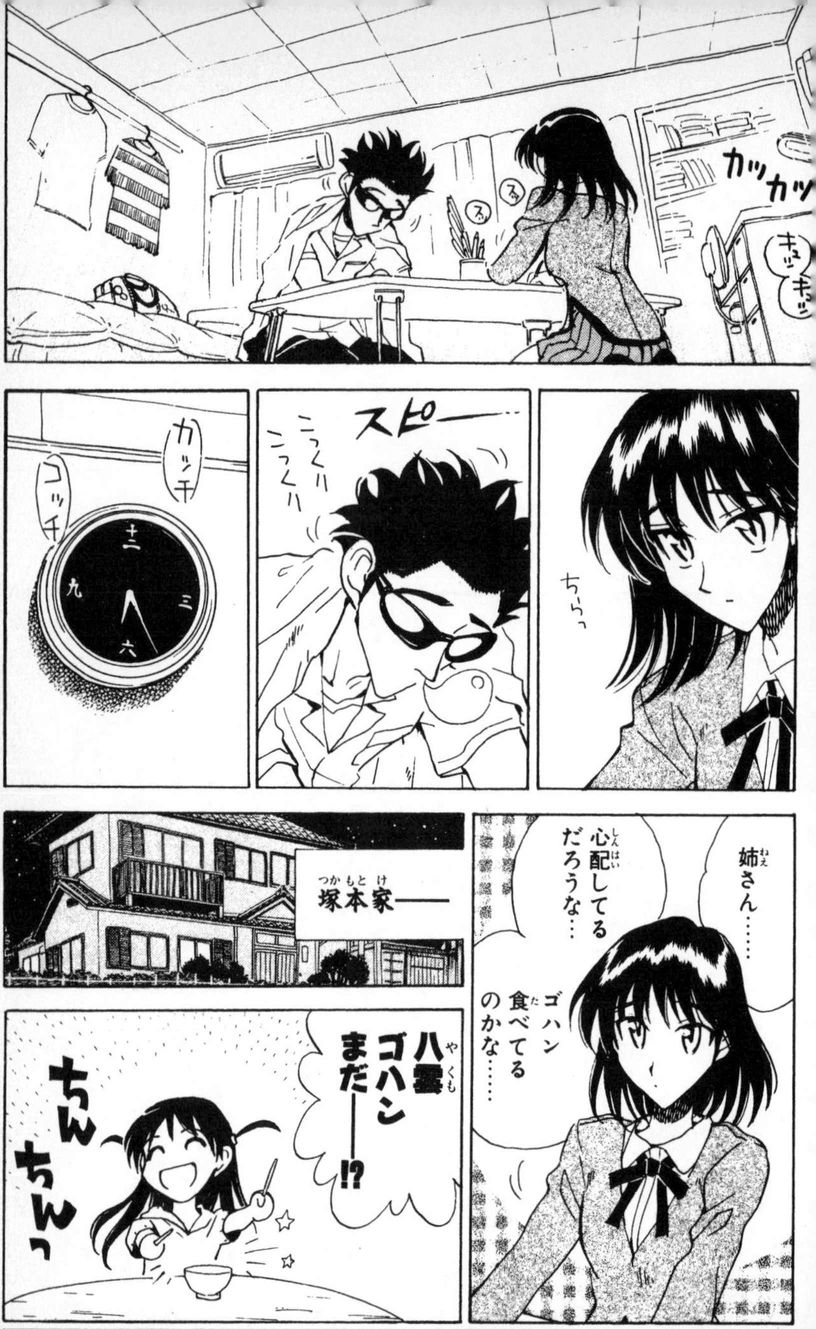
カッカッ
キュッキュッ
ズッ
ズッ
ちらっ
スピー……
カッチ
コッチ
姉さん……
心配してるだろうな…
ゴハン食べてるのかな……
塚本家——
八雲ゴハンまだ——!?
ちんちんっ

#94 THREE BEWILDERED PEOPLE IN THE NIGHT

塚本八雲、要領良し。

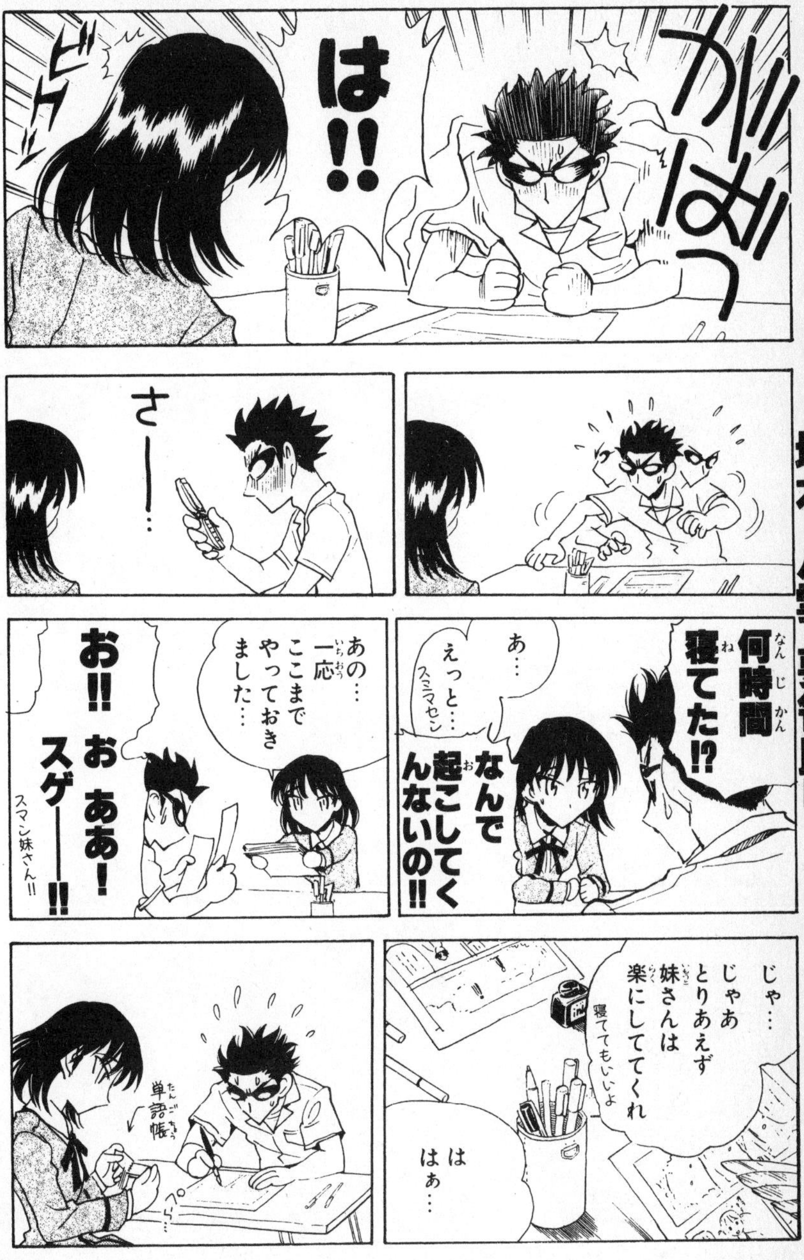
がばっ
は!!
ビクッ!!
さー…
何時間寝てた!?
あ…
えっと…
スミマセン
なんで起こしてくんないの!!
あの… 一応ここまでやっておきました…
お!! お ああ! スゲー!!
スマン妹さん!!
じゃ… じゃあとりあえず妹さんは楽にしててくれ
寝ててもいいよ
は はぁ…
単語帳
ペラ…

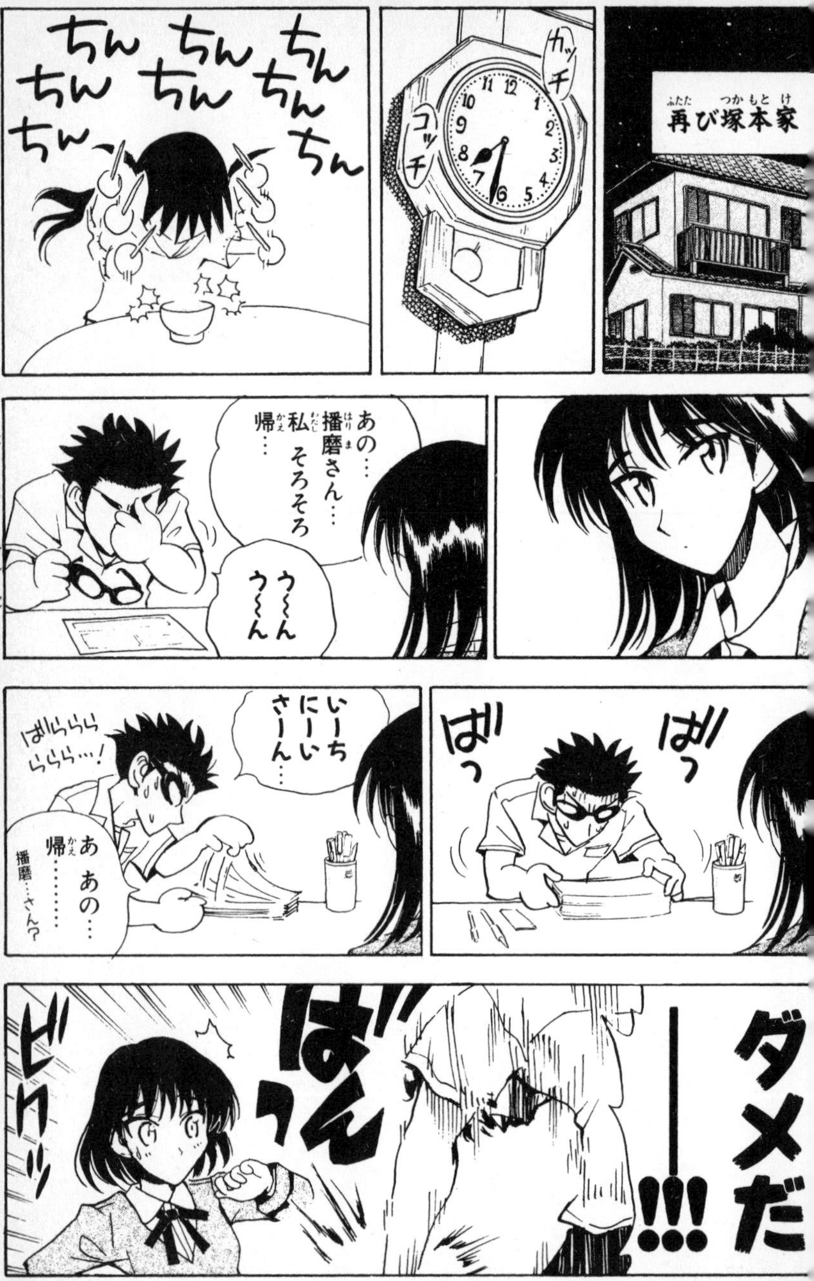
再び塚本家
カッチ
コッチ
ちんちんちんちんちんちんちんちんちん〜
あの…播磨さん…私 そろそろ帰…
う〜ん う〜ん
ぱっ
ぱっ
いーち にーい さーん…
ぱららららららら…!
あ あの… 帰……… 播磨…さん?
ダメだーーー!!!
ばん
ビクッ

播磨拳児、ムダばかり。

天満に思いを伝えるため、漫画描いてる。

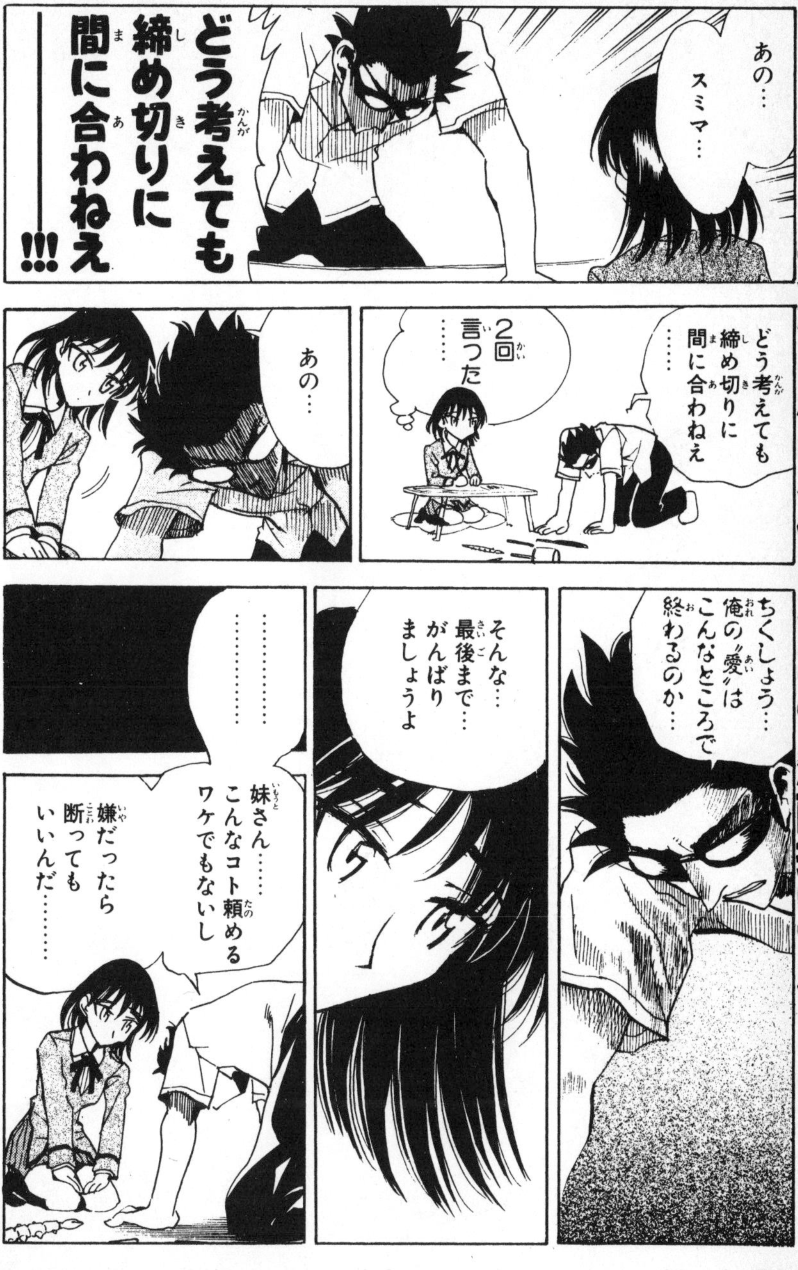
あの…
スミマ…
どう考えても締め切りに間に合わねえ——!!!
どう考えても締め切りに間に合わねえ……
2回言った……
あの…
ちくしょう…俺の〃愛〃はこんなところで終わるのか…
そんな…最後まで…がんばりましょうよ
………………
妹さん……こんなコト頼めるワケでもないし
嫌だったら断ってもいいんだ………

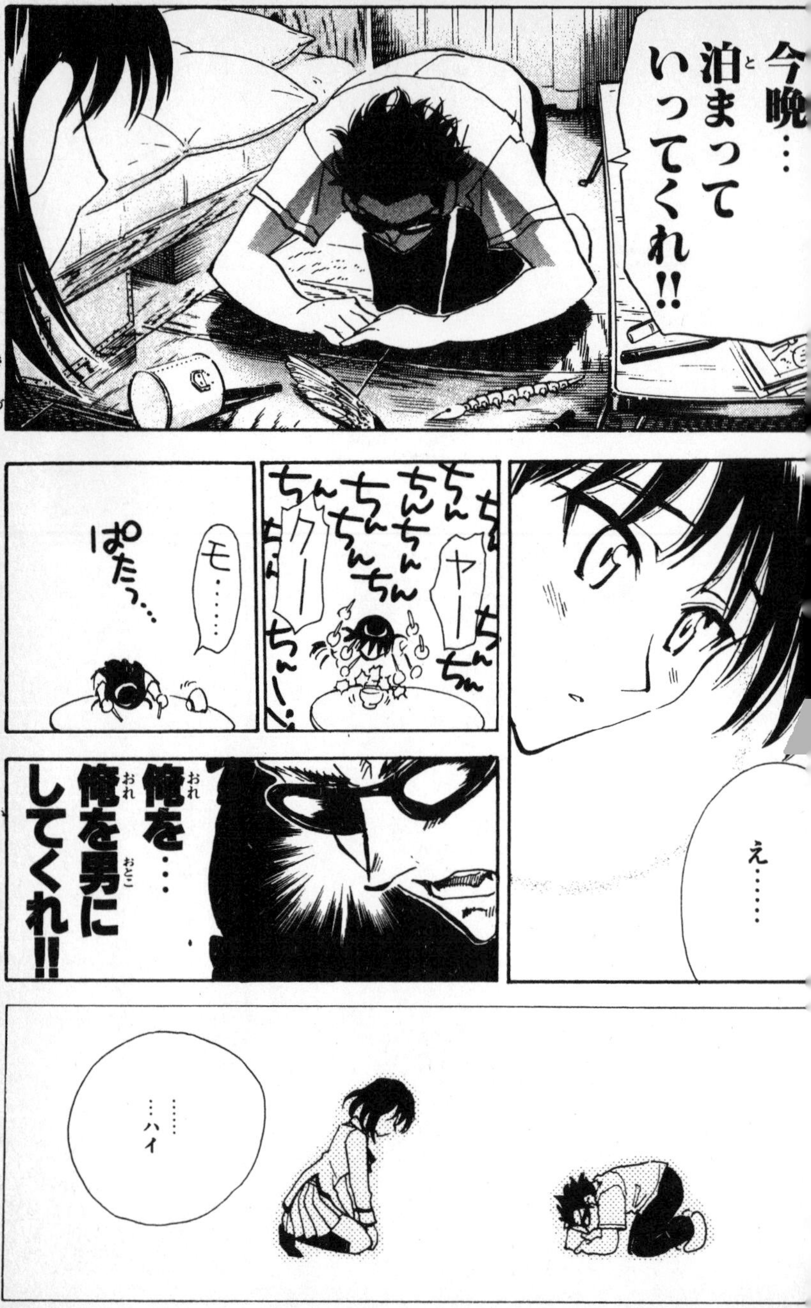
今晩…泊まっていってくれ!!
え……
ちんちんちんちんちんちんちんちん
ヤー
クー
モ……
ぱたっ…
俺を…俺を男にしてくれ!!
……ハイ

気付かずにスゴイこと言ってる。

おやつ持って来たわよ、とか言う場面。

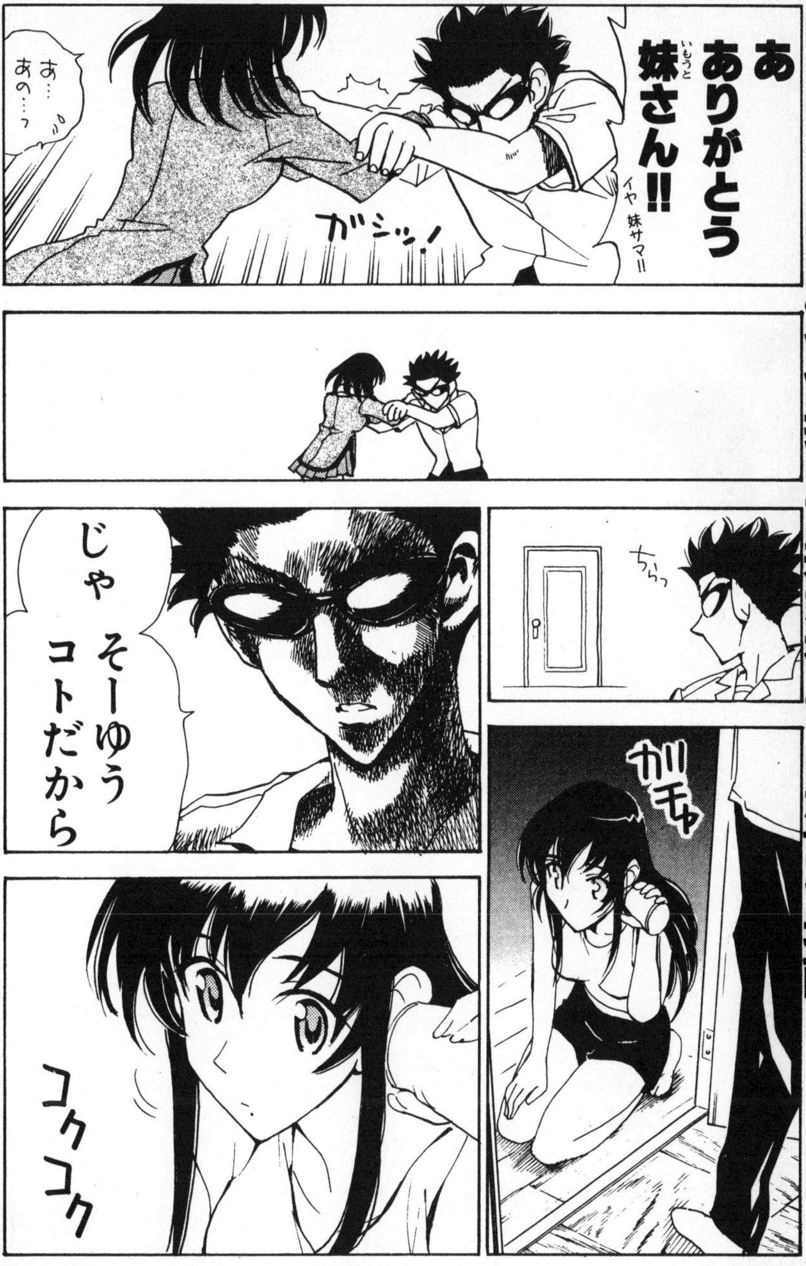
あ ありがとう 妹さん!!
イヤ 妹サマ!!
ガシッ!
あ… あの…っ
ちらっ
カチャ
じゃ そーゆう コトだから
コクコク

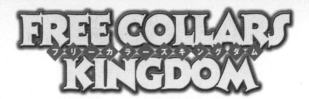

FREE COLLARS KINGDOM

フリーカラーズキングダム

TAKUYA FUJIMI

THOSE FEISTY FELINES!

It's hard to resist Cyan: he's an adorable catboy, whose cute ears and tail have made him a beloved pet. But then his family abandons him, leaving the innocent Cyan to fend for himself.

Just when Cyan thinks he's all alone in the world, he meets the Free Collars, a cool gang of stray cats who believe that no feline should allow a human to imprison

his Wild Spirit. They invite Cyan to join them, and the reluctant housecat has to decide fast, because a rival gang of cats is threatening the Free Collars' territory! Can Cyan learn to free his Wild Spirit—and help his new friends save their home?

1
FREE COLLARS
KINGDOM
TAKUYA FUJIMA

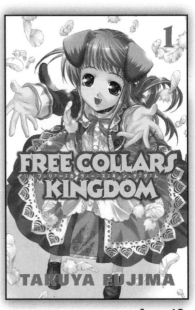

Ages 16+

Special extras in each volume! Read them all!

tanoshimi

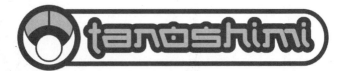

Guru Guru Pon-Chan

RUFF RUFF LIFE

Ponta is a Labrador retriever puppy, the Koizumi family's pet. She's full of energy and usually up to some kind of mischief. But when Grandpa Koizumi, an amateur inventor, creates the Guru Guru Bone, Ponta's curiosity causes trouble. She nibbles the bone—and turns into a human girl!

Surprised but undaunted, Ponta ventures out of the house and meets Mirai Iwaki, the most popular boy at school. When Mirai saves her from a speeding car, Ponta changes back into her puppy self. Yet much has changed for Ponta during her short adventure as a human. Her heart races and her face flushes when she thinks of Mirai now. She's in love! Using the power of the Guru Guru Bone, Ponta switches back and forth from dog to girl—but can she win Mirai's affections?

1
Guru Guru Pon-Chan
SATOMI IKEZAWA Creator of Othello!

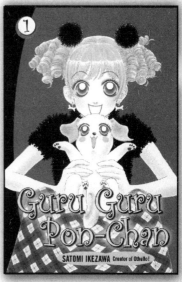

Ages: 13+

Winner of the Kodansha Manga of the Year Award!

Includes special extras after the story!

tanoshimi

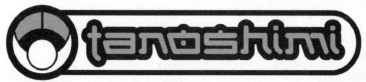

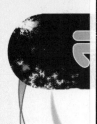

STOP!!

YOU'RE GOING THE WRONG WAY!

MANGA IS A COMPLETELY DIFFERENT TYPE OF READING EXPERIENCE.

TO START AT THE BEGINNING, GO TO THE END!

THAT'S RIGHT! AUTHENTIC MANGA IS READ THE TRADITIONAL JAPANESE WAY—FROM RIGHT TO LEFT. EXACTLY THE OPPOSITE OF HOW ENGLISH BOOKS ARE READ. IT'S EASY TO FOLLOW: JUST GO TO THE OTHER END OF THE BOOK, AND READ EACH PAGE—AND EACH PANEL—FROM THE RIGHT SIDE TO THE LEFT SIDE, STARTING AT THE TOP RIGHT. NOW YOU'RE EXPERIENCING MANGA AS IT WAS MEANT TO BE.

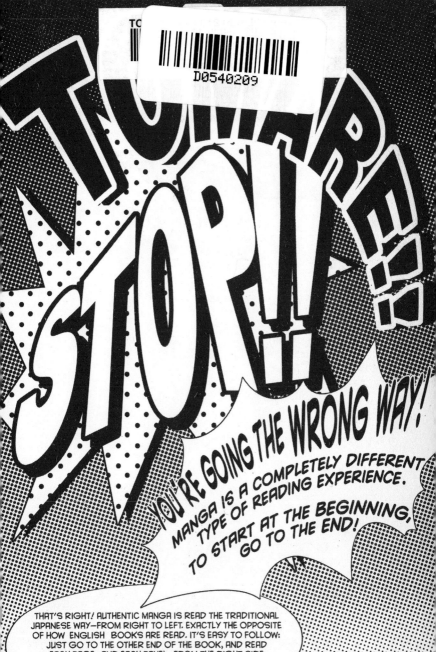